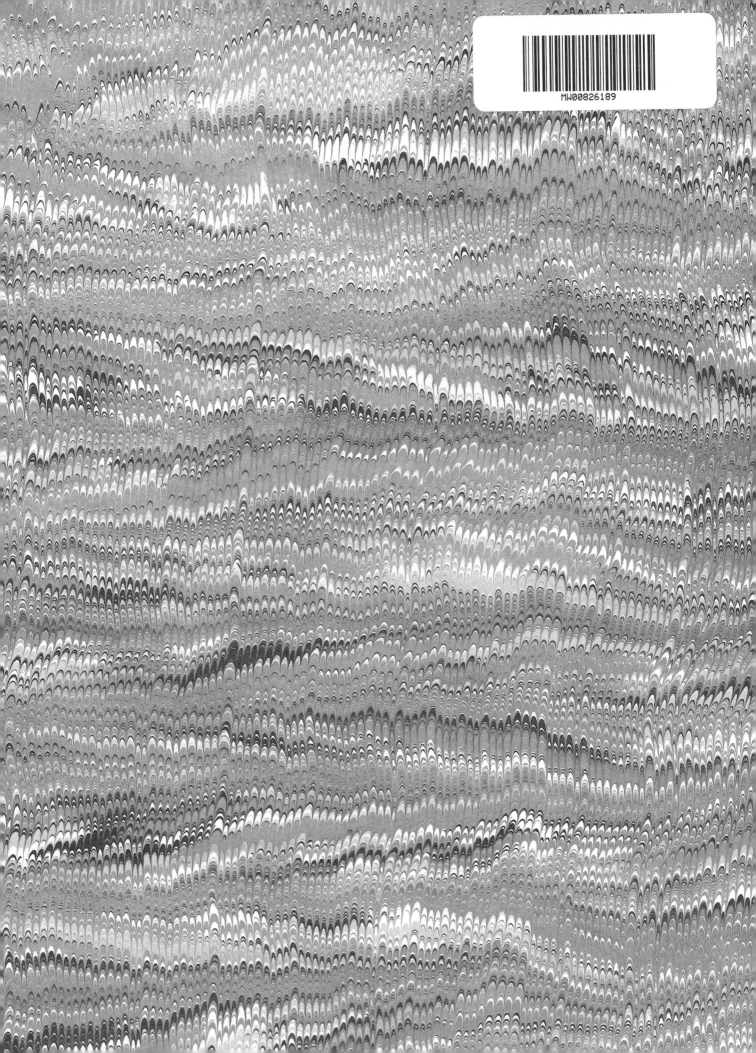

Skull & Crossbones Squadron

The Skull & Crossbones Squadron

VF-17 in World War II

Lee Cook

Schiffer Military/Aviation History
Atglen, PA

ACKNOWLEDGMENTS

A number of people have been involved since this book has been in the making. I would like to acknowledge the co-operation and assistance of all the members of Fighting Squadron Seventeen and their families who have provided documents, photographs, video and cassette tapes, personal interviews, and other valuable information to make this book possible.

I would like in particular to thank Tom Blackburn for the original idea and getting me started, Bill and Ginger Landreth for their continued help and support, "Andy" Jagger, Bill and Jean Popp, Walter and Maureen Schub, Roger Hedrick, Mills Schanuel, Mel Kurlander, Hal and Barbara Jackson, Jack and Alice Chasnoff, Dan and Ruthie Cunningham, Robert "Windy" Hill, Tom Killefer, Hap and Alice Bowers, Harold and Betty Bitzegaio, Jim and Vera Streig, Jim & Jan Dixon, Lennard Edmisten, George and Laurie Mauhar, Everett Lanman, Joy Anderson Schroeder, Deanna Beacham, Jamie Blackburn, Milly DeLeva, Boone Guyton, Alison Henning, Kraeg Kepford, Marc Okkonen, Therese Smith, Joyce Wharton, Elizabeth Cantrell, Del May, and Ray Ferguson.

Frank Olynk, Bill Semans (Kenwood Productions), David Weschler (RDR Video Productions), E.A.A. Library, Museum of Naval Aviation, Pensacola; Bernard F. Cavalcante, Kathleen M. Lloyd, Claudia Pennington (Department of the Navy), National Personnel Records Center (St. Louis), Louis Antonacci, National Archives at College Park, United States Naval Institute, Harry Bridges (Dare County Regional Airport Museum).

Aviation Artists- Nicholas Trudgian, Jim Laurier, Les Vowles, Sam Lyons, Jerry Crandall, Joseph Szady; Donna Bushman (E.A.A. Photo Dept.), American Fighter Aces Association, Bob Lawson, and Frank Aldridge.

Howard and Peta Cook, Derek and Audrey Barnett.

To my wife Sarah and daughter Charlotte for your sacrifices and putting up with me.

To anyone who has assisted me and I have missed, thank you.

Finally this is to express my sincere appreciation to all the courageous men alive and dead who went into Harm's Way. I hope that in some small way this book does you all justice.

Cover Artwork:

THE JOLLY ROGERS by Nicholas Trudgian: This painting shows a typical scene in the Solomons in 1943, when VF-17 accounted for 18.5 Japanese planes during the historic November Battle of the Solomon Sea. The day's fighting over, as dusk falls over the picturesque Pacific Islands, the Jolly Rogers return to their base at Ondongo. Some will land with just a few gallons of fuel left. The Jolly Rogers by Nicholas Trudgian. Reproduced by kind permission of The Military Gallery, Bath, England.

Book Design by Ian Robertson.

Printed in China.
ISBN: 0-7643-0475-5

We are interested in hearing from authors with book ideas on related topics.

Published by Schiffer Publishing Ltd.
4880 Lower Valley Road
Atglen, PA 19310
Phone: (610) 593-1777
FAX: (610) 593-2002
E-mail: Schifferbk@aol.com
Please write for a free catalog.
This book may be purchased from the publisher.
Please include $3.95 postage.
Try your bookstore first.

CONTENTS

Foreword

"TALLY HO! BANDITS! ONE O'CLOCK HIGH!"

That is what it's all about. That is the moment a fighter pilot trains for, hopes for, anticipates. This is no drill.
It is real.
Will he measure up? Everyone doesn't.
Will he survive? Everyone doesn't.
Will he be victorious?
Fighting Seventeen joined the air battle in the Solomon Islands in late October, 1943 and helped break the "Siege of Rabaul" in March 1944.
Battles won, enemies slain, losses sustained.
The Japanese knocked on the northern portals of Australia.
VF-17 helped to put an end to that.
Most of us thought the U.S. was a little tardy getting into saving the world.
But, thank god, a survivable outcome was won.
Lee Cook has surveyed all this through the medium of the JOLLY ROGERS.
Here is finally the chance to use the word;
indefatigable.
With skill and perseverance he has conducted research.
Through war diaries, personal interviews, photographs, archives and correspondence, Lee has extracted a story of men and machines at war.
No hotter tears have ever been shed than those shed in private by warriors who lose their comrades in battle.
There is no warmer handshake than the one exchanged 53 years after the fact between fighter pilots whose fast friendship was fused in the crucible of mutual combat.
Lee Cook knows this. He has stood among us.
He was one of us for a while.

William L. Landreth
Commander, U.S. Navy (ret.)
"Country"

Introduction

I shall try to explain how an Englishman managed to become involved with such a famous United States Navy Squadron and my reasons for doing this book.

I have had a lifelong interest in aviation and looking for a release from pressure at work I started to become more active visiting airshows.

It all started in the March and April of 1993. I saw advertised in 'Flypast' a limited edition print by Nicholas Trudgian called the "Jolly Rogers". I thought what a beautiful picture it was.

I really wanted to buy it but didn't get around to it. Fortunately I went to an air show at Coningsby on the 12th June. The first display tent I went into had the "Jolly Rogers" print already framed. I left the tent, but had to go back later on to buy it as my wife persuaded me to get it (she knew how much I wanted it).

My brother Howard's friend, Frank Aldridge, was regularly writing to fighter pilots in the U.S. and after speaking to him found out among his addresses was Tom Blackburn, the skipper of the Jolly Rogers (one of the pilots who signed the print).

I decided to write to Tom, not knowing what to expect as he was the first fighter pilot ace I had written to. I received a really good reply which encouraged me to write again as I was interested in finding out more about the squadron and whether it would be possible to write to some more people. He replied promptly and sent me a full roster of everyone who was still alive, and said to keep him advised of my progress.

The seed was planted!

I then wrote to everyone on this list. I again received many positive replies and my interest was starting to gain momentum. Every time I received a lead to follow up on I contacted more people and organizations, such as the National Archives, Museums, Department of the Navy, etc. I managed to obtain rare photographs, videos, microfilm, and many eye witness accounts of the action.

I knew the squadron were having a reunion in 1994, because when "Country" Landreth wrote to me in 1993, he did say they were getting together and in the back of my mind I wanted to go and meet them all. I then received news that Tom Blackburn had died. I felt at the time I couldn't stop now as I was progressing well with my research, and I strongly believed I would be letting him down.

I carried on writing to other members of the squadron, and received a reply from Bill Popp who suggested I should go to the reunion at Oshkosh and meet them. That was all the incentive I needed to go. I went to Oshkosh in July/August 1994 and met most of the surviving members of the squadron.

Jack Chasnoff had seen the information I had collected over the past year or so and said he would be very disappointed if I did not write a book on the history of the squadron. Another seed was sown!

Upon my return I persevered in pursuit of this goal. Every spare minute I had was spent researching, writing and following up any lead. Despite many obstacles and constraints, when I was invited to the squadron reunion in St. Louis in April 1996, I had a draft of the history to show the squadron.

My most memorable experiences of the squadron are to be made to feel welcome, and part of this elite group of people who have gone out of their way to assist me and adopt me in to the squadron. A family in every sense of the word.

Fighting Seventeen proved the F4U Corsair to the Navy and to Chance Vought as a carrier airplane.

To name but a few of their accomplishments:

First fighter bombers, increasing the endurance of the F4U, first F4U squadron to operate in action from a carrier. Many design modification changes which were adopted in later F4Us.

152 enemy planes shot down in 76 days. No bombers they escorted lost to enemy air attack. No ships covered lost. 13 Aces with "Ike" Kepford the leading Navy ace at that time with 16 kills. They were one of the top scoring squadrons in the Navy in World War II.

They took on the feared Japanese and helped defeat one of their island strongholds in the Pacific.

My only goal throughout this endeavor has been to perpetuate the memory of this famous squadron. To document and ensure in the future that they will be remembered for their many achievements. If in some small way I can attain this goal then I will be fulfilled. I have not set out to tell anything other than what happened. I have told it the way they have told me. Here it is. I hope you like it.

1

January 1943 - September 1943

VF-17 were commissioned on January 1, 1943 at N.A.S. Norfolk when Lt. Cdr. Tom Blackburn read his orders to 10 Ensigns and 8 enlisted men.

William "Country" Landreth was one of these ensigns.

"You're talking to one of the plank owners of VF-17. On the first of January, 1943, those that were sober enough to do so, reported for muster at eight o'clock in the morning. The skipper mercifully read his orders commissioning the squadron and said: "Muster will be tomorrow morning at eight o'clock. Dismissed".

Tom Blackburn was able to snag Lt. Cdr. Roger Hedrick as his executive officer.

"Tom and I instructed British students in F2A Brewster fighters at N.A.S. Miami in 1941-42 and when he was ordered to form VF-17 he drafted me as his executive officer".

Remembers Roger Hedrick.

Lt. Walter Schub instructed VN-11A in Jacksonville in 1941-42 with Lt. Ray Beacham and both joined VF-17 early in 1943.

Most of the pilots who were assigned to VF-17 were short of experience in combat type aircraft and had no combat experience.

Two exceptions were Lt(jg) Johnnny Kleinman and Lt(jg) Jim Halford who still had vivid memories of action in the early days of the Pacific war.

Although the squadron was destined to fly the new Chance Vought Corsair they had to fly whatever was available until the Corsairs were ready.

"Country" Landreth remembers this time:

"The Wildcat was a great airplane for 1938, but this was 1943. It was underpowered. Flying it out of Norfolk, which had short runways at that time with power lines at the end of the field, you'd crank on the power and the Curtiss Electric propeller would howl and growl and make a lot of noise and the airplane would just sit there and say, 'Who me?' Finally you'd get up to some kind of flying speed, hoist back on the darn thing, and hope it would come off. You had to crank the wheels up. From the side our guys like Hal Jackson and Danny Cunningham, fellas that were kind of short, you could see their heads bobbing when they were down on the crank, and the airplane was bobbing like a roller coaster. All the while they're trying to get the wheels up they would look up and see those wires getting closer and closer!"

One of VF-17's F4U-1s on th U.S.S. Charger during carrier landing qualifications in Chesapeake Bay. March 1943. Courtesy U.S. Navy photo. Robert L. Lawson Collection.

One of VF-17's F4U-1s about to touchdown on the deck of the U.S.S. Charger in Chesapeake Bay during the squadron's initial carrier landing qualifications. March 1943. Courtesy U.S. Navy photo. Robert L. Lawson Collection.

Dan Cunningham recalls flying the F4F:

"When I first went to VF-17 we had no planes. The skipper got 2 or 3 F4Fs. More and more of our boys were coming in, new pilots to the squadron. So he got us the duty of ferrying planes from Floyd Bennett, New York to San Diego. So we went up there as we had no planes to fly and got weathered in for 5 days. We went from coast to coast not more than 50 feet off the ground. We were hopping fences and telephone lines. It was great fun. It took us 15 days to go

from coast to coast. I wasn't carrying much dough so I called dad pretty near every night and said send me $50 as I was sending most of my dough home. So dad wired $50, then another $50. Eventually somewhere in West Texas I got stranded for 5 days with a hydraulic leak or something. I called him the last time and he said, 'I could taxi that plane across country in 15 days!' We finally got to San Diego. I remember one guy in a truck that I flew right down on and he opened his door, put his foot out on the running board and he's waving to me like crazy. I flew low next to trains and I don't know why but when you're flying low it's so much more fun than flying high. There's nothing like flathatting".

In February 1943 VF-17 received their first F4U's.

"It was bloody difficult because the airplane had undergone significant design changes while it was in the experimental stage and it had 2 bad crashes and the flight test people were extremely skittish about it.

"When we got the airplane in February 1943 the flight test data was available to us, but as far as handling characteristics and things to look out for it was very meager. We had to find out for ourselves to a large measure what to do, except for the information provided for us by Vought, especially by their chief experimental test pilot whose name was Boone Guyton. He was a very talented and articulate pilot who was invaluable in coaching us.

"The airplane was difficult because given the takeoff and landing attitude with the original canopy, the pilot visibility was essentially zero and was very much like Lindburgh's Spirit of St. Louis, looking out the side windows and through a periscope for his forward vision. We felt we were doing that with the Corsair for any takeoff and particularly for carrier landings. I recall the first carrier landing that I made aboard a jeep carrier out in Chesapeake Bay, U.S.S. Charger, which had a beam of about 70 feet and a length of

One of VF-17's F4U-1's on th U.S.S. Charger during carrier landing qualifications in Chesapeake Bay in March 1943. Courtesy U.S. Navy photo. Robert L. Lawson Collection.

The following pictures were taken while "Andy" Anderson and Jack Chasnoff were at one of the main Naval training bases, Corpus Christi, Texas. Jack and Alice Chasnoff in Miami, 1942. Courtesy Joy Anderson Schroeder.

450 feet. As I came up the groove to make a landing on the final stages of the approach the only thing I could see in front of me was the L.S.O. out on a platform to the side of the deck. When I got the cut signal from the L.S.O. Catwalk Cummings, I shoved the nose over to see what was in front of me which was a gross mistake because the airplane started going down like an elevator with no cable.

"In spite of my best efforts the thing hit with about a 10G impact and bounced about 20 feet in the air and came down with 2 blown tires and a very shaken and rattled pilot. The flight deck was essentially clear of people because when they saw me hit the first time everybody went scram into the catwalks.

"The airplane was not damaged, why I don't know. We put 2 new wheels and tires on it and continued the operation. This was typical of cut and try and find out making mistakes like my stupid one and just hope you didn't bust your butt learning.

"Unfortunately we did lose a lot of pilots in training. To a large measure, we were pushing them hard. They were fresh out of flight school. It was a damn difficult airplane to master. It was completely unforgiving if you made a mistake, if you let your airspeed get low at low altitude or if you banked too steeply there wasn't a god damn thing you could do about it. A number of fine guys got killed in the learning process.

"After 6 months working with it we had a reasonable mastery of it and from there on it was relatively smooth sailing operating the airplane". Recalled Tom Blackburn.

"Tom was an eager beaver, tough as hell and when he gave an order you did it. I respected that he led by example, he did it then said go do it. Inspires confidence. I was very grateful to get into a squadron like that and fly the hog. We loved the plane".

Said Dan Cunningham.

TEAMWORK

Roger Hedrick describes how important teamwork was to the squadron:

"We were trying to meld a team of rugged individuals, where we had a team that instinctively would react to the enemy. Certain conditions, positions even, so that each member of this team knew that he could count on the other one, knew what to expect of the other one".

"Andy" Jagger had this to say:

"Teamwork was very important and we had very intensive training in all sorts of things, gunnery, you name it and we were working on it, to as near perfection as we possibly could.

10 very intensive months of effort of all types and the very tragic part of that was that we lost more people in training than the 12 in combat. That was the sad part of training. The word safety in the war was unheard of. The expectation was that you were going to get killed 'or somebody was' and that was part of it. Really sad, but so true".

Tom Blackburn said one of his strongest recollections was the teamwork of the people involved wanting to work as a unit and pull together rather than as individuals. One of the things one has to look out for in the fighter business is the tendency for people to want to take center stage and forget about who is supporting and it's much more effective if the squadron, or division, or section of 2 aircraft as a minimum, worked as a team rather than have one person as the star.

"A fighter pilot to me was a man that was intelligent and energetic and sometimes the boys would be a little too exuberant and it was my job to quiet them down and ensure they performed the way we would like to have them in formation and so forth.

"Eventually we ended up with one of the greatest teams that I have ever been associated with. I think that the results that we achieved down in the Solomons will show that," said Roger Hedrick.

"Country" Landreth remembers Navy flight training.

"From all my reading, it seemed the most selective, the most difficult to get into, the best training-was carrier aviation in the Navy. It was the most demanding, the toughest. So my next thought was, gee, that's a pretty high level goal to try for. Then I thought, if I start at the bottom it'll take me a lifetime to get up to the middle, so what I'll try to do is start at the top and then if necessary I'll fall back down to the place where Peter's Principle will take me - the highest level of incompetence!"

Joy and "Andy" Anderson at Corpus Christi, Texas, 1942. Courtesy Joy Anderson Schroeder.

Jack Chasnoff and Joy Anderson at Corpus Christi, Texas, 1942. Courtesy Joy Anderson Schroeder.

Joy and "Andy" Anderson on the beach at Corpus Christi, Texas, 1942. Courtesy Joy Anderson Schroeder.

TAKING A CUT BUT STILL FLYING OFF CARRIER!

Jack Chasnoff had an unforgettable incident whilst training on carrier qualifications:

"This occurred at the time we were qualifying in carrier landings in the Corsair in Chesapeake Bay. We were stationed at Norfolk N.A.S. and were required to make a particular number of carrier landings in each type of plane we wanted to qualify in. The Corsair was the ultimate qualification for most of us. It was the end of our final part of Naval aviation training.

"The Charger was a small converted, I think perhaps a Liberty ship which had been converted into a carrier, and was considerably smaller than the standard fleet aircraft carrier. It was perfect for the duty of making itself available for budding young aviators to complete their carrier qualifications.

"The routine was that we flew out from Norfolk to where the ship was in Chesapeake Bay and awaited the signals to begin our landings, which were what we called 'touch and go' landings, because we landed one at a time, there were no planes parked forward. The deck was kept clear and each time we landed successfully the crew would disengage our tailhook and get us ready for an immediate take off so that we could fly the landing pattern again and make another landing.

"I was within one landing of qualifying, feeling that this was much easier than I had anticipated it to be. As I made what I thought was going to be my final approach for qualification, I got a signal that I was high and fast, and I took what I thought was the appropriate remedial action. It resulted in a cut signal from the L.S.O., so I cut the throttle, put the nose down and then pulled it back, but as it

turned out instead of being at the right speed to stall above the deck and catch a wire, I still had flying speed. The tailhook, fortunately for me, bounced between two wires. It didn't catch a wire. It bounced and went back up again. The plane bounced once and went back up again and I realized suddenly that that thing going past on the right hand side was the superstructure of the carrier. I was not only airborne, but flying over the forward part of the deck and in deep trouble!

"I have a vivid recollection of hearing the crash whistle sound. I thought that's me they're talking about. So the instant I realized it I jammed the throttle forward. I knew I needed full power to try to recover, and I jammed it forward so fast that it didn't catch. The throttle was all the way forward and the engine was not responding. So as quickly as I could I pulled the throttle back, paused for what I am sure was no more than a fraction of a second and then eased it forward until I felt the engine catch and then pushed it forward fast. The engine caught and I was almost literally hanging from the propeller at that point. The people on the ship told me later that they watched my plane begin to pick up speed as it sank, and they watched me sink beyond the bow and all of them thought they were going to hear a splash or see the wreckage as the ship went past. I have no idea of really how close I was to the water, but it must have been extraordinarily close. At any rate I had on full power, and after they had given up hope for me. They saw my plane staggering back up into the sky just barely making it.

"I did get airborne and they called me on the radio and told me to go back to base, which was a very welcome signal for me. I was not in shape to complete my qualifications that day.

VF-17 Pilots "Tuffy" Henderson, Jim Streig, Doug Gutenkunst, Lou Kelley, "Andy" Anderson, and Jack Chasnoff.Courtesy Joy Anderson Schroeder.

The following photos I believe were taken whilst the squadron was at Manteo, N.C. This would be from early April 1943. On the beach. VF-17 pilots Doug Gutenkunst, Jim Streig, Fred "Tuffy" Henderson.Courtesy Joy Anderson Schroeder.

Alice Chasnoff and friend at Nags Head Beach, N.C. Courtesy Joy Anderson Schroeder.

"They teased me about it afterwards and they tell me—I have no way of knowing whether this is true or not—that I flew all the way back to Norfolk with my tailhook, tailwheel, wheels and flaps down. It could well have been true because I was about as scared as I've ever been. All but paralyzed!!"

Dan Cunningham relates helping out a friend while on Navy Flight Training:

"I remember a guy who had been an enlisted Marine and he was going to go into the Marines again, but he couldn't shoot and he couldn't bomb. On fighter training using SNJs, you had to get 3 hits on the gunnery and 3 hits on the glide bombing. I got about 5 or 6 each on the first two times and he didn't have a hit at all. So I said. 'This is your last chance, so why don't we trade planes.' So I got in his and he got in mine. So I got him his hits. When we got to glide-bombing, I qualified the first hop and I hit some more on the second hop and he still didn't have a hit in the circle. I said, 'Let's do the same thing again,' and I went up and got him his hits, too. I told the skipper this when we were on a reunion and I said 'they'd have thrown his ass out if they'd knew about that wouldn't they.' He said, 'No, they would have thrown both of your asses out for doing that!'"

During the early days of training a number of young pilots were lost. Jack Chasnoff remembers losing a close friend "Tuffy" Henderson:

"I can tell you what happened to Tuffy. Tuffy was especially close to the Andersons and to Alice and me. He was one of the bachelors who befriended a couple of married officers and was a really wonderful guy. We all thought the world of him.

"He went out on gunnery run practice from Norfolk NAS with one of the new pilots in the squadron, I can't remember his name, but there were 5 or 6 people on this gunnery practice run.

"In the process of attacking the tow target apparently two of them started their approach to the target at the same time and they had a mid air collision and both of them were killed.

"As a matter of fact I succeeded to Tuffy's place in the line-up because shortly before that I had had appendicitis and I was out of action for a while. They flew me up from Manteo to have my appendix taken out, which is why I remember it so vividly. I couldn't fly for about a month and so I lost my spot in the line-up. I only got my spot back when Tuffy was killed and there was a vacancy.

"I ended up flying airplane number 20 which had his name stencilled under the cockpit. I remember so vividly that when we were approaching Pearl Harbor after we had gone through the Panama Canal. The skipper took me aside one day and he said.

'Jack, you're flying number 20.' I said. 'That's right.' He said, 'Please talk to your plane captain, I want to get Henderson's name off of there and yours on to there right away.'

So I did exactly as he told me. I spoke to my plane captain and the next day Henderson's name was gone and mine was stencilled on the side of the plane. I felt very close to Tuffy for that and many other reasons".

Dan Cunningham was on the flight when "Tuffy" was killed.

"We had a guy from Texas called "Tuffy" Henderson. Tuffy and I were taking 2 brand new kids assigned to us. We were doing simultaneous attacks on the tow plane. High side and overhead runs, and trying to get them co-ordinated at the same time. We did it, then the 2 kids were supposed to do the same thing. We made 2 or 3 passes and the kids got confused and didn't know what to do. I'm flying up there and I see Tuffy break off and I'm ready to go and I look at this kid and he's nowhere near catching us up, and he starts his run, too. So I called Tuffy and said, 'Look out, this kid's coming in too and I'm not breaking on the turn.' I don't know whether Tuffy heard me or not. But this kid's making a flat side and Tuffy's making a high side and they just went whoom!! All there was left was little flakes. I then called May Day. They hit head on at 400 miles an hour.

Don't leave much. Sad, as Tuffy was a good pilot".

"Bobby Mims had a good buddy of his, and Bobby got vertigo coming down through the clouds and this guy was on him all the way. Then Bobby finally pulled out and this guy couldn't and he went straight into the drink". Recalled Dan Cunningham.

"Country" Landreth also has vivid memories of losing a close friend:

"During those same days I had a dear friend, Bill Burnham, and this reminds me that there is not much done or said, it seemed to me, for recognizing the people that lost their lives in the course of our training period. We had suffered a lot of casualties that were not made much of in most of the writings about the squadron, including the skipper's book. One dear friend who died was Bill Burnham, who was with me through Opa Locka in Miami where we flew Brewster Buffalos and then we came up to Norfolk and we checked in to VF-41 to be commissioned. There came a day after we got our Corsairs when I was squadron duty officer and my friend Bill Burnham came to the office that day. He was just as white as a sheet. He was obviously sick and not feeling up to flying. But he was scheduled, as we regularly were, for high side, high altitude gunnery runs on a banner, and good old Norfolk of course has that milk bottle haze, where you go out and fly on the range and have a little blue spot at the top which is the sky and there's another little

blue spot down on the bottom, a little darker color which represents the ocean, and the rest of it is all haze, no horizon. I begged that guy, but Bill Burnham would not listen to me. I as much as begged him. I got up on the side of his airplane and told him he really ought to get down out of the airplane and get inside as he looked like he had the flu and was not fit to fly. But I found out later that he was a Christian Scientist and they don't believe in physical failures, you're supposed to reach out and get the spiritual power to overcome all these things. I'm sure he lost his life due to his religion because he was out making these high side runs where you pull quite a few G's and the people that were with him saw him pulling through and then the airplane faltered because when you pull too hard, particularly when you're in bad shape, not feeling well you will grey out. They saw his airplane falter and make a bad turn of some sort, and it was quite clear that he passed out long enough so that when he came back to he was mixed up as to what blue spot was the sky, and which one was the ocean, and he pulled back on the stick and he went in at high speed right into the ocean.

"I was best man at his wedding. He married a beautiful blonde girl from Miami. When we came through there he met her and later married her. That was just one of our casualties which ordinarily just doesn't seem to be spoken of much."

"Another casualty was Sam Carlton a real fine guy who used to be an engineer on a radio station out in my home state of Nebraska. Sam Carlton after we got moved on to Manteo took off and had an engine difficulty and made that urgently taught-against move to try to turn around and come back and save the airplane and land back on the airfield that he just left. He was at low altitude, didn't have the altitude to turn the plane around and spun in just at the edge of the field and made a big black ball of smoke and red flame and that was the end of Sam Carlton. That happened to be the third day of my time in hack which I had earned by going AWOL because Bob Keiffer, who probably you will see on early rosters and

Jack and Alice Chasnoff. Courtesy Joy Anderson Schroeder.

Robert Sidney "Andy" Anderson. Courtesy Joy Anderson Schroeder.

Alice Chasnoff, Mary Helen Kelley, Joy Anderson. Courtesy Joy Anderson Schroeder.

The Andersons' beach house Nags Head, N.C. Courtesy Joy Anderson Schroeder.

Naval Auxiliary Air Station, Manteo, N.C. Notice the water coming in on Runway Four. Courtesy Harry Bridges.

Naval Auxiliary Air Station, Manteo, N.C. Courtesy Harry Bridges.

was with me all through Kansas City E base, New Orleans, Miami, Corpus Christi and all through the squadron. He was going to marry one of my old girlfriends up in Norfolk which was quite a way from Manteo and before he left he got me to promise to be there and be his best man. We were standing duties of port and starboard duties, half the squadron had to be on board all the time, even on weekends. I thought for sure I could get someone to swap with me. I was going to have the duty on the day of the marriage on Saturday, but none of my shipmates would swap with me so I could go up there and I decided to go and see the skipper and he said. 'Come see me at 4 o'clock this afternoon and we'll take care of it'.

"I counted on the skipper being good for his word and I came to his office, knocked on the door and just as I walked into his office I hear this roar going down the runway and I looked out the window and there's the skipper taking off for Washington, D.C., where his family was. Well good old exec., now fine gentleman Roger Hedrick was then being very much the executive officer said, 'well, if you've got no relief you can't go.' I told him the skipper promised me and he said, 'go, get your relief and I'll turn you loose.'

"I couldn't find a relief so I took off anyway. I returned after carrying out my promise to my shipmate Bob Keiffer and his wife Pat and at muster on Monday morning here were all these guys in khakis and cut off trousers and Marine marching boots and pith helmets and rag tail uniforms of all kinds and here I was at the end with blues and gold stripes and white hat cover and at muster the skipper got down to me and said.

'Landreth, in my office!'

"I walked in and said. 'Reporting as directed sir'. He said. 'I understand you were AWOL over the weekend'. I said. 'Well sir, I, er'. He said. 'That's 10 days in hack'. He put me in hack and ordered me not to have contact with anybody or anything. I could go to the head across the passageway but I couldn't talk to anyone or have anything to read except Navy regulations or the bible, that's all. Then on about the 3rd day Sam Carlton spun in and that was the same day the skipper marched in and said. 'Your hack is over with'. I thought maybe it was because we lost a shipmate that day but I

think the real fact is he found out that nobody had been feeding me for 3 days. He had ordered me not to talk to anyone so I couldn't tell anybody I was hungry. So in effect I was not only incarcerated for 3 days but all I had for sustenance was water from the sink and it was one of those coincidences that Sam Carlton spun in on the same day". Recalled "Country" Landreth.

Bob Kieffer was one of the original members of the squadron "Country" Landreth recalls:

Bob Kieffer and I started flying yellow perils (N3N & N2S) at Fairfax Field in Kansas City. We followed the track together to New Orleans N.A.S. (Pool Base) then to Corpus Christi N.A.S. To finish our final training squadron, we were sent to Kingsville N.A.A.S. This was fighter training in SNJ aircraft. Nearly every cadet wanted to be a fighter pilot. Although we did not have fleet aircraft to fly, the tactics, formations and gunnery (one .30 cal.) were effective. We flew a lot, and finished with a commission and wings dating

An F4U-1 of VF-17 on the U.S.S. Charger in March 1943. Courtesy U.S. Navy photo. Robert L. Lawson Collection.

"Timmy" Gile leading a flight of F4U-1's off Manteo, N.C., in the spring of 1943. Courtesy U.S. Navy photo. Robert L. Lawson Collection.

from October 1, 1942. We each broke the training squadron record for most machine gun hits on a towed sleeve.

"We flew together on the same flights that day as I remember, and on the third flight of the day, our last hop in the Corpus Christi training, we were hot. Bullets were painted on the bullet nose with distinctive colored paints for each pilot so that the penetration of the cotton sleeve would show the hits. The ground crew counted the holes of each color, divided by 2-one in, one out-and the instructors stood around in disbelief that ONE of us broke the record, much less both of us. And by the same number of hits!

"After the wings were pinned on, we then went to Opa Locka N.A.S. (Miami) where we had the thrill of flying the Brewster Buffalo widow makers for so-called fleet preparation. On to VF-17.

"But there was no VF-17. We were attached to VF-41 temporarily, and then loaned out to the ferry command, where we flew F4F fighters to San Diego from Long Island.

"We stood up together on January 1, 1943, at the establishment of VF-17 in Hangar LP-2 at N.A.S. Norfolk, VA. Bob Kieffer was always intelligent, a real good friend and nice guy-got a nickname of "Sleepy", had a non-aggressive demeanor, and Tom Blackburn passed him off to another squadron, where he made a fine record as a carrier fighter pilot.

"I was dating a beautiful girl of the marrying kind in Norfolk, and at Bob's request got him a blind date with Pat's help. A few days later Bob asked if I minded if he dated Pat. I had decided not to marry during the war, said ok, and they married each other with me as best man.

"By then we were at Manteo, N.C. I had promised Bob to be in Norfolk for the wedding. I could not get a stand-by for that Satur-

day, went AWOL to get there, got back on Monday morning for muster and the skipper put me in "Hack" (see above).

"Cdr. Robert Kieffer U.S.N. (Ret.) and Pat Kieffer live in Coronado, CA. About 4 years ago Ginger, my sisters Jean and Erma, Bob and Pat and I were having lunch at the Mex. village in Coronado. For the first time, Bob and Pat learned that I went absent without leave to carry out my promise to be at the wedding, and had been punished for it. He picked up the check!!"

Wilbert Peter Popp describes his experience of Navy flight training:

"I went into active duty July 21, 1942 as an aviation cadet. I then went to pre-flight aged 20 for 13 weeks. Pre-flight was primarily physical training-no aviation involved. This was out of Moraga, California, near Oakland. After pre-flight I went to Los Alamedos N.A.S., California, near Long Beach where I went into the primary flight training program. There we flew the yellow peril M2S Stearman. My primary flight consisted of 6 phases: solo, basic flight, aerobatics, review, formation flight and night flying.

"This program lasted until January 1943. From there I went to Corpus Christi, Texas to finish my flight training and receive my wings. At Corpus we flew the SNV Vultee Vibrator with fixed landing gear and the SNJ Harvard. This training was directed to one's ultimate Naval speciality, ie. dive-bombing, torpedo bombing, patrol flying PBY, fighter pilot, reconnaissance flying the OS2U.

"I got my wings as an ensign on June 9, 1943 with my commission as an ensign dated June 1, 1943. My total flight time up to then was about 368 hours. From Corpus Christi I went to Melbourne, Florida for operational flight training in the Grumman F4F Wildcat, my first combat type of aircraft. At Melbourne, Florida we were organized in flights of 6 pilots for the entire program. Here I acquired an additional 60 hours of flight time in the F4F.

"Operational flight training consisted of formation flying, fighter tactics, air to air gunnery, night flying, cross country navigation hops, carrier landings and carrier check outs.

"This program lasted until the early September 1943. After 3 weeks leave en-route to my next duty station I reported to Norfolk, Virginia under C.A.S.U. 21. I was assigned to my first fighter squadron VF-17. My assignment to this squadron was purely accidental.

"My best friend through all our flight training was Clyde Dunn of Hiattville, Kansas. During Clyde's operational flight he was trained in the F6F Hellcat. During our interview at Norfolk the F6F flying time was entered in red because it was advanced.

"Because I had mentioned I had a cockpit checkout in the Hellcat that was also put down in red. The processing officer didn't know the difference. VF-17 was preparing to leave Norfolk for combat and due to operational mishaps was short of 2 pilots.

"Because Clyde and I appeared to have Hellcat time we were selected to join the Jolly Rogers. So instead of being re-assigned to a newly formed squadron somewhere on the East Coast we went with VF-17 on the U.S.S. Bunker Hill. This was in mid-October 1943. Neither of us had even seen a Corsair let alone fly it. We had not been carrier landing qualified in the Corsair. Therefore when the Bunker Hill left Norfolk into the Panama Canal up to San Diego, all Clyde and I could do was to observe operations and man stop clocks checking the pilots interval in the landing pattern. At Pearl Harbor I checked out for the first time in the Corsair, flying from Ford Island to Barbers Point doing touch and go landings. We got about 10 hours in the Corsair. I had my first Corsair flight on October 5, 1943."

"We flew the birdcages (the original F4U-1 cockpit canopy) up until we got deployed to the Pacific in combat, where we flew the 1A with a semi-bubble canopy.

I'll tell you, with that birdcage you couldn't see diddly-squat. But I'm eternally grateful we flew Corsairs; that was the best combat aircraft alive in the world at the time". Said "Country" Landreth.

Dan Cunningham had difficulty with the first F4Us. He relates his story:

"I couldn't see out of the old birdcage with the seat so low. So I used to use 3 parachute cushions. I put 2 on the seat. That would lift me high enough to see, but then my legs weren't long enough to give it full kick on the rudder, so I had to put one behind my back so I could do that. The skipper said. 'You're too short'. I think he was getting ready to bounce me. I said. 'I'll prove it to you'. So he said. 'Tomorrow morning we'll check out'. I said. 'Ok'. So I got in, put 2 on the seat then one behind me and he's standing on the wing with one foot in the hole underneath the cockpit and he said. 'Full right rudder, full brake'. I did full right rudder, full brake. 'Full left rudder, full brake'. He kept doing that and I kept hitting it all right and I said. 'See I am not having any problems'. He said. 'As long as the cushions hold out you're ok, but without them you're lost'. I said. 'No question about that'.

"So he's standing on the wing and I finally said. 'Give me a chance skipper I'll show you'.

"He was still shaking his head when he was walking away. I didn't know whether I was going to get bounced or he was going to keep me. With that new bubble canopy, we later got, I'm sitting as high as anybody. It was beautiful vision and it all worked out real well. He said later that he was glad he didn't bounce me!"

Upon reporting, the pilots found out that the "Bunker Hill" was not yet an aircraft carrier as only the keel had been laid—thus, each of these original men were considered "plank-owners." They were an anxious group of young men. They seemed to become a family in every sense of the word.

They grew close immediately and seemed to look out for one another from the beginning. They were flying planes that were not to be used in the war and they were so "hot"—flying under bridges and skimming the water that they were asked to leave Norfolk Naval Air Station in March 1943 and were sent for overhead gunnery practice and training to a little airfield at Manteo, North Carolina for the safety of Norfolk and the fleet!

"Some folks breathed a sigh of relief when the Jolly Rogers moved to Manteo in April 1943 to the Naval Auxiliary Air Station to practice at a nearby gunnery range". Said "Andy" Jagger.

Manteo, North Carolina is where the first colony was formed in America and is still a tiny summer place. It was mighty cold on the beach that March but the squadron held fast and got the "word" that VF-17 was going to get a new plane called the "Corsair" and that they would be the first to fly them. Several men got to go to the factory and flew prototypes and came back exclaiming their virtues. They could not wait!

It was while training in Norfolk and later Manteo that the reputation of the squadron grew and the name Blackburn's Irregular's was born."The older airmen have plenty of stories to tell. And some

Ens. F.A. "Andy" Jagger . Hook point failure. July 1943. Due to a design fault the tailhooks snapped when they came into contact with the steel drain channel's upon landing. If the hook caught an arresting wire they were lifted clear of the deck. If they missed a wire they caught the drain channel and snapped. After newly designed hooks were installed this problem was resolved. Courtesy U.S. Navy photo. Robert L. Lawson Collection.

A barrier crash on the U.S.S. Bunker Hill in July 1943. Courtesy U.S. Navy photo. Robert L. Lawson Collection.

folks who lived there in 1943 when the "hog fliers" were based in Norfolk have some stories to tell about them, too.

Roger Hedrick remembers his first impression of the Corsair:

"This was the new Chance Vought Corsair and we were all greatly impressed and thrilled with the fact that here we were flying something much faster than anything we'd been in prior to that time. Being an old fighter pilot myself I knew that speed was the number one thing I wanted in anything I was going into combat with".

Dan Cunningham recalls an interesting experience in the early days of the squadron.

"Up at the factory they were making 100 or so changes to the F4U. We had to fly them up there for these modifications. They had one of them ready to come back so Hal (Jackson) and I got into an SNJ. I was in the front seat and he was in the back, so I was flying. So I thought I would give him a good ride. I mean I really brushed the tree tops all the way. I was pushing down on the stick and he was pulling back. If I ever let go we would have spun in. He was pulling so hard it was difficult for me to push down. I picked up the hog and he flew the SNJ back. When we got back the leading edge of that silver SNJ was green as grass. The prop had hundreds of little nicks from twigs and that. They had to change the propeller and wash the hell out of it to get the stains off the wings. They said. 'You guys didn't fly too high on this hop did you!' We said. 'No we didn't!' Hal said he would never do that again".

Mel Kurlander while at Manteo recalls the following event.

"After about a week the skipper said we were going to fly combat air patrol and we sent out a challenge to any of the different squadrons in the area, feel free to come in from 6 in the morning to 6 at night. Well that didn't last too long because of a guy called "Jumping" Joe Clifton, who was well known in the Navy as a football player and later as a squadron leader. He was wild. He wouldn't

have to get on the radio to yell at a pilot, you could practically hear him! He came in with a group and unfortunately for him, evidently some of our guys had been out on gunnery runs and they came back and spotted these planes trying to sneak into the airfield and not get jumped. These guys went at them and somebody had not un-released their gun chargers and riddled "Jumping "Joe up the ass pretty good. He came down and ate out Tom and that was the end of anyone trying to come in and attack us. Same thing happened at Norfolk. We broke in at the mouth of the St. Johns river and went in singly. These guys had come in and caught a PBY, and started to make runs on it. Well when you are playing around and your guns are still loaded, they hit the PBY with someone important aboard. By the time we went on our shakedown cruise there must have been 10 guys on serious charges. People stayed away from us!"

Before the Jolly Rogers boarded the aircraft carrier Bunker Hill for the journey that would make them authentic American heroes, they raised a lot of hell in Manteo.

There was Ensign Howard "Teeth" Burriss, who, for fun and games, gunned his Corsair to 300 miles an hour, turned it upside down and buzzed at treetop height along one of our two-lane roads.

The motorists driving toward the plane pulled onto the shoulders to avoid what appeared to be imminent injury or death. A truck driver took no chances and drove into a ditch for safety.

"The admiral sure had me on the carpet for that one," recalled Jolly Rogers commander Tom Blackburn.

Blackburn's men picked up the nickname "Blackburn's Irregulars" before they were dubbed the Jolly Rogers. A group will get a name like that when they pull stunts like the one Robert H. "Windy" Hill did in his Corsair.

Hill, who flew in combat over the South Pacific with "Tar Heel Terror" painted on his tail, was from Beaufort, NC.

"My hometown of Beaufort, North Carolina is right on the ocean about 100 miles South of Manteo. So I went buzzing down along the coast at low altitude, came in over through the Beaufort Channel. Heading across the bay right towards the front porch of my home which was on the waterfront there, flew right over the top of the house as low and as fast as I could go. Then down the front street of the town right over the top of the buildings.

"My father came out of the building. I was wiggling my wings and he was waving. I went back, my mother was in the front yard. I made a simulated modified diving bombing run on her and had her running for the front porch." Remembers "Windy" Hill.

The Corsair was the Navy's newest fighter when the Jolly Rogers flew them. It was the first fighter to fly 400 miles an hour and picked up its nickname because as somebody said, the aircraft was 'about as cooperative as a hog on ice.'

The fold-wing plane also had a long, hoglike snout between the cockpit and propeller.

Blackburn was called on the carpet again for letting one of his aviators—Ensign Ike Kepford, later to become one of the squadrons 13 aces—alarm locals by engaging in a mock dogfight with an Air Force P-51 over downtown Norfolk. By then, Blackburn had nearly run out of explanations for the admiral.

Everett Lanman was one of the ground crew with VF-17 at Manteo. He has fond memories of this time.

"Some of the incidents that took place seem like yesterday, but over 50 years has lapsed and they will always stand out in my mind".

"In training we went down to an auxiliary airfield in Manteo, North Carolina and that is where the pilots were trained under Cdr. Blackburn. A few factory men worked alongside of us to repair the planes which at that time were new, all kinds of oil leaks (rocker boxes and pushrods) but eventually the problems were solved.

"We had a great time down there in Manteo and I remember being raided by VT-17 and VB-17 in mock raids and they would drop flour bags. We had the best pilots and best officers the Navy could offer.

"Some of the things that took place were really comical. The chief of police of Manteo said we could drive around on the island in an old 1935 car which had free-wheeling, but not to drive off the island. I remember going out through the main gate of the field and nobody knew how to control the car and as we went by the security shack instead of stopping we just waved!

"Another instance was when two fellows of the mech. gang came in one night feeling pretty good and outside of our barracks we heard a crash and we all ran out to see that the Model A Ford they were driving had gone over a telephone pole laying down which marked off our parking lot, so it was teetering on the log so we all lifted it off and no damage was done.

"In leaving the airfield to head back to Norfolk Air Station, as we passed the old car on the beach which had been set afire, we all stood up in the cattle car and saluted it!"

TRAINING

Dan Cunningham remembers the training as one of the main reasons for the squadron's success.

"I think the big thing about our squadron was that we were good because he trained the hell out of us. We had the best fighter plane in WWII and we had the best skipper the Navy ever put out and he worked us, and that work paid off because we knew what the heck we were doing, what we were supposed to do.

"He stressed gunnery and we were on gunnery hops every day in training. Sometimes 2 to 3 times a day. He worked us so hard at that, that we had to get good. I had nothing but admiration and respect for the great man that he is."

"We had to go up to the plant where they were producing them and we'd go up in groups of 4 or 5 and as they'd come off the line then they'd have them preflighted and tested then they would check us out on the airplane. When we first formed the squadron we had no planes or nothing. When we got the hogs we used to run into P-51s training in Florida and we could always tell whether we got a student or one of the instructors. If we got a student we'd wax his fanny, if we got an instructor we'd get a good tiff. We called it grab ass." Said Dan Cunningham.

"We did get a reputation for being a pretty rowdy bunch." Said "Country" Landreth.

"I suppose I was kinda soft hearted or soft headed with my guys. The reason I condoned and encouraged overly aggressive behavior, was that this was what was going to be required in a combat situation". Said Tom Blackburn.

Tom Blackburn had this to say of a fighter pilot.

"Got to have a hell of a big ego. He has to come on strong and have a lot of self confidence. Because he's basically a loner and it's his own skills and his own intelligence that mean the difference between living or not living".

It was at Manteo that "Andy" Jagger had a memorable experience.

"My one and only bail out from an airplane, and once was enough! It happened while the squadron was down in Manteo. We had an airfield all to ourselves. It was actually technically and officially an outlying field from the main Navy base at Norfolk.

"We were there for just a few months waiting for the aircraft carrier Bunker Hill to be commissioned. Then we went aboard it of course for our shakedown cruise down to the Caribbean.

"My experience was my very first night flight in a Corsair right after we had joined VF-17 from operational training down in Florida.

"We took off one night and were making touch and go's on the runway and a crosswind was pretty bad. It was kind of a stormy night with scattered thunder showers. I think it was in July. We had such a bad cross wind that the night flying duty officer, Chuck Pillsbury, took off in his Corsair and had us join up on him and the idea was to fly up to the main N.A.S. in Norfolk, where they had a mat, in other words a big circular area and you could land directly into the wind no matter which direction the wind was coming from. Well he didn't plan it very well, didn't file any flight plan or instrument flight conditions. He missed the turn. He flew north to the entrance to Chesapeake Bay and then turned left and should have got into the traffic pattern for the main N.A.S. Instead of that, because of the poor visibility, he missed the turn and he ended up over the eastern shore of Virginia, which is bounded on the east by the Atlantic Ocean and on the west by Chesapeake Bay. It was so late, actually after midnight, and we were running low on fuel and I got really desperate after him circling around. We were flying formation on him and I decided that I was going to have to leave our leader who was obviously lost and put on my landing light and try to find an open space down below in which to make an emergency landing after the engine stopped, which I expected to happen any minute. I circled around and I was really trying to anticipate the plane going out to sea after I bailed out. I didn't want it to crash into somebody's house. I did head out east toward the ocean and started to go over the side and realized that the plane was making a gentle turn to the right. So I got back in and trimmed it up again so it would go out over the ocean and, lo and behold, it continued to turn one way or another. Anyway, I was coming down in the chute when I saw and heard a big explosion and damn if it wasn't my airplane making a big hole in the ground in a farmer's field. I believe he was growing beans in that field and I think he was well paid for this damage to his bean pack by the Navy.

"But, actually the plane did crash so close to his house that it blew out some windows so I was very disappointed to know that my plan just didn't work out.

"The thing that I remember the most is that in coming down in a parachute at night you don't have the sensation of falling. It seemed as though I was just suspended in the air and the earth came up and hit me. I wasn't injured, I had a sore neck the next morning, but I was in pretty good shape.

"I realized I was in a potato field and where I come from in Long Island, potato fields were all over the place and I reached down and grabbed the earth and some potato plants and felt right at home.

"Pretty soon, and I didn't realize it, but there were people out looking for me. Once the people in the neighborhood saw there was wreckage all over the place but no sign of a body. So they were out looking for me and this car with the headlights going by near me didn't stop. But then it did stop and it turned out they had got stuck in a mudhole and I was able to run up and holler at him before he could get out. He took me to his house and I spent the night there and it was very kind of him to do that. He was a farmer who lived nearby and the next morning he took me over to where the plane had crashed and I didn't admit to anybody that I was the guy responsible for the windows being blown out of the guy's house.

"That's the story except that very afternoon a TBF had landed at a nearby airfield as I had called the skipper to tell him what had happened and he sent a TBF to pick me up. So the farmer drove me over to where the TBF was going to land and that's how I got back to the airfield at Manteo, NC."

Mel Kurlander describes one of his early experiences of carrier landings:

"Six pilots (1 Navy, 5 Marines) were on a carrier qualifying hop from Norfolk to Prince William in Chesapeake Bay. They were flying Wildcats, whose landing gear had the reputation of folding like an accordion if brought in too hot or high. Four of the planes had been wiped out, and the props had chewed up the deck.

*One of VF-17's F4U-1's flipping over on its back on the U.S.S. Bunker Hill in July 1943.*Courtesy U.S. Navy photo. Robert L. Lawson Collection.

"The fifth pilot decided he was too high, hit the throttle after taking a cut, and wound up hanging over the port side. He crawled down the fuselage and was on the deck as the carrier C.O. and the signal officer bore down on him. Without flinching, the pilot walked towards them, stated 'this deck is too small to land on,' and kept walking. The two officers were stunned at first, then started laughing and gave the pilot a pass.

"The six pilots then drew straws to see who would fly the remaining Wildcat back to Norfolk. The Ensign won—I know because I was that fifth pilot!"

Roger Hedrick recalls how he felt about the Corsair.

"I participated in some comparative fighter trials held at the Army Air Corps, Eglin Field, in May 1943 which gave me more confidence than ever that the Corsair was the best U.S. plane we could have taken to war.

"I flew a F4U-1 "Birdcage" model with the low seat and resulting poor visibility to Eglin and had flights in the P-38G; P-47C; P-51 A+B; F6F-3 Hellcat. In my opinion, none of them could have touched the F4U as to operations from a carrier against the maneuverable Jap fighters. I did however envy the P-38 and P-51 pilots their forward visibility when landing or taking off. The P-51 sans tailhook, stronger landing gear and folding wings was definitely a beautiful plane.

"My log book shows I had 2,900+ hours (approx. 2,500 in fighters) prior to my first aerial combat in November 1943. 225 hours which all pilots got in the F4U prior to sailing on Bunker Hill".

"My time in VF17 was one of the most exciting and rewarding times of my life. It was very stressful and there was a lot of grief mixed in with the joy and the pride, and at times I was sorely pressed to keep ahead of these guys and turn in a good enough performance so that I was leading them instead of them leading me". Recalled Tom Blackburn.

"I have often thought how lucky it was that I was assigned to VF17. They were a bunch of free spirited, high spirited pilots. The skipper taught us discipline and through his leadership and inspiration, he turned that group into a deadly fighting machine, that made records in the Pacific". Said "Windy" Hill.

On 24 May, 1943 the squadron flew under the Brooklyn Bridge en-route to Boston for U.S.S. Bunker Hill commissioning (CV-17). "Country" Landreth has vivid memories of this:

"On the way up to Boston to commission the Bunker Hill at the Navy yard the skipper took off the squadron. Everything that could fly took off without briefing and flew in formation. This would be in the spring of 1943."

"We kept getting lower and lower towards New York. I couldn't figure out why we kept letting down with that many planes in the formation. Must have been 25 planes. We were down near the water and I couldn't figure out what the skipper was up to. The next thing I know was I looked up and there was this great big dog gone suspension bridge looming up ahead of us.

"We kept staying low and it kept getting bigger and bigger and this giant cement pylon turns out it was lined up right in front of me and I was as low as I could get, as close to the airplane in front of me as I could get. I thought I was going to have to knock that pylon down before we got through.

We squeezed along and by not too big a margin we got that whole formation underneath the Brooklyn Bridge.

"I suppose to this day we are the only squadron that has flown in formation underneath the Brooklyn Bridge. That's one of the things the skipper and the squadron are famous for, but he never mentioned it in his book. It was difficult to get him to talk about it so he must have got his tail in a doorjamb or something over that. That was one of the wild things that we did. We got away with a lot of things that we shouldn't".

"Andy" Jagger also has memories of one incident:

"Tom Blackburn had the squadron perform a loop in formation. 8-12 of us in a big formation, Tom went up in a big loop-scared the hell out of me".

Dan Cunningham remembers another incident:

"Each squadron was assigned a cub, that they used to fly. One guy wanted to take it out and flathat or something. It was usually tied down, right behind where we parked all the hogs. He got it untied and got the motor started and with that the guy right in front of him decides to check his mags on his hog. With the power that the hog produces this damn cub lifts right up in the air from the airstream coming at him and then spins in on the wing. So we just razzed the shit out of this guy. We said. This son of a bitch can't even get off the matting and he spins in. We rode his ass pretty good for spinning in before he got to the runway".

SHAKEDOWN

VF-17 embarked on the U.S.S. Bunker Hill for their shakedown cruise to Trinidad on July 7, 1943.

As Tom Blackburn described in his excellent book the Jolly Rogers. "This was the perfect opportunity to practice group and squadron tactics and to learn to mesh with the ship's company".

"Andy" Jagger who was a young Ensign recalls one experience on the shakedown cruise:

"Coming aboard on the shakedown cruise and I was high and fast and I bounced right over the barrier and there were not too many airplanes up ahead.

"My section leader had landed and I was putting on the brakes and trying to avoid crashing into him. I did tear up his rudder but it didn't do any more damage to his plane and I'll never forget the surprised look on his face as he was climbing out of his airplane. He turned and looked and saw me coming at him and it was a look of horror on his face. Luckily I didn't do much damage.

"Where it all started was I was high and fast on my approach to landing and I got a signal from the L.S.O. that my hook was not down, so I reached over to put the hook down and my oxygen mask was there in the way and I was distracted momentarily to look at the oxygen mask and get it out of the way so that I could grab the lever to put the hook down. The next thing I knew I looked at the L.S.O. he was giving me a cut. Well he realized it and he told me afterward that it was his mistake to give me a cut when I was high and fast. I tried to get it down but hit and bounced. I probably bounced a couple of times because I ended up bouncing right over the barrier wire and I was really surprised when I went back down to the ready room and got an announcement over the P.A. system that Captain Ballentine, the skipper of the Bunker Hill, wanted me to report to him on the flight control area.

"Tom Blackburn, the skipper, being a real good skipper decided he would go with me. He wanted to stand by his pilots no matter what, and we stood there for a while until the Captain noticed us and he walked over toward me and I was expecting the worst of course. I thought well sure as hell this is the end of my flying career and much to my surprise he came toward me with his hand outstretched to shake my hand and he had a big smile on his face. He said, 'I don't know how you got in trouble, Jagger, but you did a good job in stopping it.' So that was a big surprise.

Tom Blackburn wrote me a little note later and gave it to me and it said, 'No matter how bad things are they could be worse. That was my souvenir from that situation".

"I can tell you about landing a Corsair aboard a ship. If you got it around and landed safely on board, you done it! It was a pretty good feeling of accomplishment when you got back home to the carrier again. During the approach you always wondered about whether you ought to open your cowl flaps or not, because if you open them you can't see, and if you close them the engine heats up. I had the advantage of being tall enough - I'm six-four - so I could kind of stick my neck up and see around that cowl.

"You know, though, speaking of carrier landings, a lot of these modern Navy aviators don't quite understand what it was like to take a cut where there was no alternative. There were the barriers and a pack of airplanes in front that could blow up and kill you. After World War II, I went through almost a ten year period where I was carrier-based flying A.S.W. (anti-sub warfare) Grumman S2Fs from straight and angled decks - over 350 total carrier landings.

"Angled-deck landings are a piece of cake compared to what we used to do. Most aviators who were raised on angled decks just don't know what they missed!"

"Country" Landreth recalls.

"On final approach to an aircraft carrier landing it was really difficult to see the landing signal officer. That big snout led us to start affectionately referring to it as a hog, and of course the leader was Big Hog". Said "Country" Landreth.

Everett Lanman was one of the ground crew on the Bunker Hill. He recalls the shakedown cruise:

"Back at Norfolk the ship came down and picked us up and we went on our shakedown cruise to Trinidad. Flight operations were every day and the skipper of our ship was the best one in the Navy (Captain Ballentine), who went on to make admiral.

"They found that the F4Us were too hot for carrier landings so we had a lot of engine and prop changes. One of the pilots of VF-17 on our shakedown cruise came over the flight deck and did a barrel roll and when he landed he had to report to the bridge. He was grounded for a few days. We went back to Norfolk and the ship went back to Boston".

AIR GROUP 17

Of greatest significance to the Navy's primary mission of defeating the Japanese was the introduction into the fleet of the first of the new Essex class carriers and their air groups equipped with new and more effective combat aircraft.

The Bunker Hill (CV-17) and its air group prepared for combat operations in the Pacific, by extensive practise during the summer of 1943.

The Bunker Hill was built in Bethlehem's Quincy, Mass., yard, launched on the first anniversary of Pearl Harbor and commissioned on May 25, 1943, Captain John J. Ballentine commanding. She was the fourth of the new Essex class carriers to be commissioned, and her addition to the Pacific Fleet was eagerly awaited. No time was wasted in going through the steps necessary to convert a brand new ship and crew into a fighting machine.

Her air group, Carrier Air Group Seventeen (CAG-17) had been commissioned on the first of January, 1943, at N.A.S. Norfolk with Commander M.P. Bagdanovich as air group commander. Its four squadrons-VB-17, VF-17, VS-17 and VT-17-trained through the spring to be prepared when the ship was ready. VT-17's Grumman TBF Avengers were typical of all torpedo squadrons being formed. However, the Curtiss SB2C-1 Helldivers of VB-17 and VS-17 (redesignated VB7 on March 1) and the Vought F4U-1 Corsairs of VF-17 were new to the fleet. VF-17 and VB-17 were to be the first Navy squadrons to take these types into combat.

For C.A.G.-17, Corsair and Avenger training went forward on schedule, however, Helldiver operations suffered from many problems which plagued the SB2C-1s during this period.

Following commissioning, the Bunker Hill underwent initial sea trials; and, on June 21, the first aircraft, a hook-equipped SNJ-4, operated aboard while the carrier was cruising in Massachusetts

Bay. On June 28, after CV-17 had reported to the Atlantic Fleet at Norfolk, the big day finally arrived as Lt. Cdr. F.M. Whitaker led VT-17's Avengers and Lt. Cdr.J.T. Blackburn, VF-17's Corsairs aboard for flight operations in the Chesapeake Bay operating area.

On July 1, VB-7 was merged into VB-17 to form a 36-plane dive-bomber squadron under VB-17's skipper, Lt. Cdr. J.E. Vose, and just over a week later, the squadron began operations from the ship in time to be ready for the shakedown cruise.

On July 13, the Bunker Hill and C.A.G.-17 departed the huge Naval Operating Base at Norfolk for their shakedown cruise to Trinidad. While in Trinidad, operations were conducted in the landlocked Gulf of Paria where German submarines were not a constant menace. Here ship and air group were extensively exercised to be ready for combat. On August 6, the Bunker Hill was underway for Norfolk, arriving on the 10th, and C.A.G.-17 returned to shore-based status while the ship and squadrons made their final preparations to go to war.

In September, ship, aircraft and men were ready to depart for the Pacific and the war. In Hawaii, VF-17 was replaced by F6F equipped VF-18: and on November 11, all the hard work and training made its first pay-off with C.A.G.-17's initial strike against the Japanese base on Rabaul. VF-17, meanwhile, went its separate way to combat success as a land-based Corsair fighter squadron in the Solomon Islands.

"Country" Landreth recalls Air Group 17:

"Bunker Hill (CV-17) C = carrier V = heavier than air. We had VB-17 Dive bomber, VT-17 Torpedo Bomber, and VF-173 squadrons that were going to be the hottest thing that ever went to sea. We had the first of the SB2C dive bombers replacing the old SBD which cruised at 120, dove at 120 and landed at 120. Very slow and difficult to escort, because you had to do a lot of weaving just to stay back on top of them. The SB2C was a much faster airplane. It had a sort of a habit of getting shot into the water in front of the carrier because the engine was not very reliable. It had a tendency to not quite carry the SB2C up in the air in front of the carrier with any kind of load whatsoever. We were once airborne with the relatively new TBFs and the brand new SB2Cs and we were the first successful carrier-based F4U squadron. The colorful Air Group Commander was then Commander (later Rear Admiral) Bagdanovich. He had painted on the side of his TBF (he was a torpedo plane pilot) 'The Sea Bag' and he was known as 'Bags' when he was not in the air.

"When we had the Air Group exercises we had a pretty dog-gone formidable Air Group on the Bunker Hill, of course breaking it up was traumatic for everybody. The Marines had all the Corsair parts down in the Solomon Islands, so that's where we went. We would have been a pretty hot Air Group if we had got to stay together".

Lt(jg) James A. Halford's (3.5 kills in VF-5 & 6 1942) plane on the U.S.S. Bunker Hill July 1943. Courtesy U.S. Navy photo. Robert L. Lawson Collection.

DESIGN MODIFICATIONS

As the first Navy squadron to take the Corsair into action VF-17 were responsible for many design modifications. The Engineering Officer "Butch" Davenport, along with ground crews, worked with Chance Vought Field Service Representatives, such as Ray DeLeva to improve many aspects of the first Navy Corsairs.

VF-17 were convinced the F4U was the ultimate carrier plane to take into action, despite many training casualties and the unforgiving nature of the plane to pilot error.

One of the major problems which required immediate attention was the landing gear oleo. Upon landing on a carrier the Corsair had a marked tendency to bounce high into the air, usually resulting in blown tires and a shaken pilot.

After taking unmodified F4U-1s on the shakedown cruise to Trinidad VF-17 were able to recommend major changes to the design. These included raising the pilot's seat to improve visibility, and the bubble canopy to replace the old birdcage, and a wing spoiler to improve the stall characteristics.

Before sailing off to war VF-17 received the new improved modified F4U-1A Corsairs which to a large extent they helped develop.

VF-17 were totally committed to the F4U and worked tirelessly in training and with Chance Vought to perfect the airplane before taking it into action.

Their record in the Pacific and the later success of other Navy squadrons proves that they were right to persevere and pioneer this airplane.

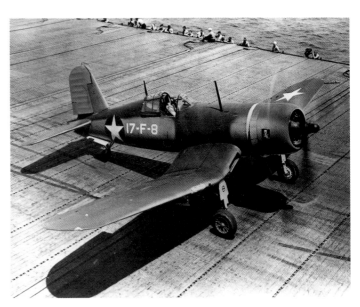

One of VF-17's F4U-1s on the U.S.S. Bunker Hill during her shakedown cruise in July 1943. Courtesy U.S. Navy photo. Robert L. Lawson Collection.

One of VF-17's birdcage canopy F4U-1s on the U.S.S. Bunker Hill during her shakedown cruise in July 1943. Courtesy U.S. Navy photo. Robert L. Lawson Collection.

2

First Tour
September 1943 - October 1943

LAND-BASED

On September 10, 1943, the Jolly Rogers left Norfolk for the adventure in the Pacific that was to make them immortal.

In September they went through the Panama Canal and arrived at Pearl Harbor on October 5, 1943:

"We had quite a bit of time on the carrier "Bunker Hill" (CV-17) before we were taken off just before going into combat. The supply line was all full of parts for Grumman airplanes in the fleet, and the Marines were operating Corsairs in the Solomons and they had all the parts down there. So when we got to Pearl Harbor in Hawaii, the Navy decided they couldn't support us". Said "Country" Landreth.

"We were all definitely dismayed and puzzled when orders were received detaching VF-17 from Air Group 17 and the U.S.S. Bunker Hill. These ordered us ashore at Pearl Harbor's Ford Island to await transportation to the Solomon Islands.

"We all had worked hard to overcome some of the early problems with the F4U and felt that the new F4U-1A model we received in September, just prior to embarking on board CV-17, had definitely been proven to be a superb carrier plane.

"We eventually learned that as the first F4U carrier-based squadron the logistic/supply chain was lacking in spare parts for the plane and more help was required for the landing at Bougainville and subsequent flights against the Japs at Rabaul". Said Roger Hedrick.

27 September
On this date VF-17 was composed of 43 officers and 14 enlisted men, and had a compliment of 36 F4U-1 aircraft.

28 September
Received ComAirPac secret dispatch directing VF-17, Lt. Cdr. J.T. Blackburn, U.S.N., commanding, upon arrival at Pearl Harbor to be detached from U.S.S. Bunker Hill and to prepare for early transportation to the South Pacific.

VF-17 was kicked off the Bunker Hill at Pearl Harbor because at that time it was the only squadron in the U.S. Navy qualified to land the Corsair on carriers.

The squadron had the option of staying on the Bunker Hill providing they would transfer to the Hellcat, which by unanimous vote the squadron chose to decline and stay with the Corsair. VF-17 was then assigned a duty with ComAirSePac Solomon Islands. From Pearl Harbor VF-17 went to Espiritu Santo on the U.S.S. Prince William known as the Pee Willie, primarily for transportation purposes only.

Tom Blackburn recalled his feelings on being land-based.

"We were extremely disappointed and so was the Bunker Hill because we were very much part of the team. They thought very highly of us. We were sent ashore not because the airplane was at that time defective in any ship-borne characteristic or because the landing officer of the ship and the higher echelons lacked faith in it. It was a straight logistic problem. We were the only squadron of

F4U-1A's of VF-17 on the U.S.S. Bunker Hill's flight deck going through the Panama Canal in September 1943. Courtesy U.S. Navy photo. Robert L. Lawson Collection.

Navy Corsairs to be operating in the Pacific to the west of Pearl Harbor. All the other fighter squadrons had Hellcats or Wildcats. It made no sense to try to supply 36 airplanes of one type and 500 airplanes of two other types and so the decision was very sensibly made to pull us off the Bunker Hill and put a Hellcat squadron on, send us down to the Solomons where the Marines were operating Corsairs, where the supply pipelines had Corsair parts (but we were always screaming for spares)".

Chance Vought service representative Ray DeLeva had much admiration for the squadron. "VF-17 proved the F4U to Chance Vought and they were very much indebted to VF-17 because it was through their efforts that we made it what it was for the Navy.

Chance Vought was very much enthused the way Fighting 17 handled that airplane. They showed the airplane could be a good fighting airplane, which turned out to be the best fighting airplane in the Pacific. The Japs feared that thing like the devil.

"My role was to get information to the factory to see what we could do to improve the airplane. There was always something that could be done to improve the airplane. My job was assisting ground maintenance people and pilots to find any innovation that could improve the plane.

"When the Bunker Hill came into Pearl they were detached. I never saw a more dejected group in my life. Because they thought they were going to lose the Corsair. But owing to the strength of Tom Blackburn, Roger Hedrick and the rest of the squadron, who were great enthusiasts of the airplane, very supportive of Chance

F4U-1A of VF-17 landing on the deck of the U.S.S. Bunker Hill on 14 September, 1943. Courtesy U.S. Navy photo. Robert L. Lawson Collection.

Vought I guess they fought to keep the airplane. I still say they were the scourge of the Japanese, just the sight of that airplane scared the hell out of them".

"Country" Landreth had an interesting experience when arriving at Pearl Harbor:

"When you're on the deck of a carrier you are always supposed to leave the tail wheel unlocked so that your plane could be moved around and twisted about through the traffic on the deck and as you taxi around or the planes get pushed around by the pushers the tail wheel has got to be unlocked and of course the law of the universe was that when you were heading for the beach that tail wheel had to be locked because when you landed it had to do a lot toward helping you roll out in a straight line when you got your tail wheel down and keep you from ground-looping that airplane.

So here we go to Pearl and they're launching us off the deck to go ashore on the North side of Oahu where Pearl Harbor is. We were being led off by flying the planes ashore rather than being off loaded by derrick.

"We broke up over the airfield but as we approached the airfield, this old Nebraska boy out from the middle of the United States had never seen anything as beautiful in the whole world. The blue-green waters of the bay, the surrounding green hills which came down to the water. The whole of the Pacific atmosphere was just something beyond belief, it was so lovely. In fact it was hard to keep your mind on what you were doing. But I came around after breaking up overhead, landed with a nifty little

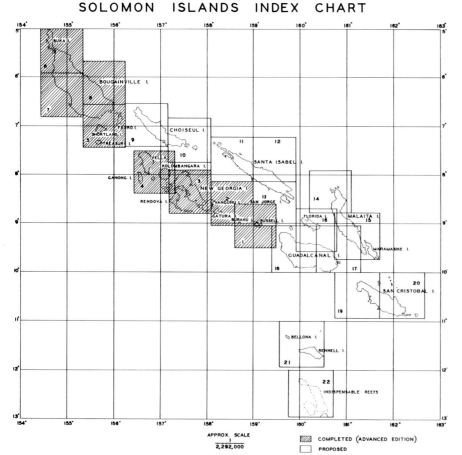

SOLOMON ISLANDS INDEX CHART

APPROX. SCALE
1
2,292,000

▨ COMPLETED (ADVANCED EDITION)
☐ PROPOSED

carrier approach landing and guess what? My dog-gone tail-wheel was not locked. I was very neat and deft and with skillful manipulation of the throttle and brakes I broke up the ground-loop after a 180º turn.

"That tail wheel when it touched the ground felt like a riveting hammer had been attached to the airplane as it spun around and the airplane ground-looped and usually you get a wing or a prop or something in a ground-loop. But I guess I have to give myself rather high marks for having got the airplane stopped in its rotation after 180º and there in front of all my squadron mates that landed ahead of me. I go rolling down the runway backwards! All I had to do to stop the airplane was add throttle. It was rolling down the runway about 35 miles per hour and I added throttle taxied off and parked the airplane and pretended like nothing had happened. I didn't scratch the wing or prop, and that's both fortunate and skillful and that's one of the primary things for which I was noted in the squadron at the time was successfully ground-looping the plane and didn't hurt anybody or anything!"

3 October-12 October
General organization and training operations at Ford Island.

5 October
The following 30 enlisted men transferred from U.S.S. Bunker Hill reported for duty:-

Baskin, C.R.	S2c	Hare, J.J.	AMM3c
Brandenburg, F.M.	AMM3c	Hoyle, B.C.	S2c
Craig, J.A.	S2c	Hyder, B.H. Jr.	AMM3c
Duke, G.C.	S1c	McCabe, T.A.	AMM3c
Edmisten, L.R.	AMM2c	Odem, F.R.	AMM1c
Emanuel, A.J.	AMM3c	Pitts, T.S.	AMM2c
Fehr, L.F.	AMM2c	Polite, F.	AMM2c
Fisher, T.B.	AMM3c	Rasmussen, B.	AMM3c
Flynn, E.W.	AMM3c	Shore, M.E.	S2c
Gafford, J.H. Jr.	AMM3c	Turner, J.R. Jr.	S2c
Gill, H.M.	AMM3c	Wert, E.M.	S2c
Glover, D.E.	AMM2c	Westphal, E.C.	AMM2c
Gober, E.W.	AMM1c	White, L.E.	AMM2c
Grogan, J.J.	AMM3c	Whitley, R.N.	S2c
Hamilton, R.A. Jr.	S2c	Wood, A.K.	AMM3c

7 October
Lt. H.A. March reported for duty from VF-24. "Dirty Eddie" March was a valuable addition to VF-17. He had seen combat action with VF-6 and shot down two enemy planes.

10 October
The following 8 enlisted men transferred from C.A.S.U. ONE reported for duty:-

Dineen, J.T.	AOM3c	Jacobs, E.W. Jr.	AM2c
Foutty, C.R.	AOM2c	Olaes, R.J.	AOM3c
Green, D.C.	AMM2c	White, M.A.B.	AMM1c
Grochowski, N.R.	AMM2c	Yager, WM.	AMM2c

The following 6 enlisted men transferred from C.A.S.U. TWO reported for duty:-

Barak, L.T.	AOM2c	Sarnecki, J.A.	AMM2c
Parker, W.L.	AMM3c	Simoneaux, N.F.	AMM3c
Rankin, D.M.	AOM3c	Sletterink, D.G.	AMM3c

The following 9 enlisted men transferred from C.A.S.U. FOUR reported for duty:-

Bretz, K.G.	AMM2c	Landry, M.R.	AMM3c
Cox, B.L.	AMM2c	McLaughlin, D.D.	AMM3c
Homewood, E.A.	AMM2c	McLean, E.R.	S1c

Jamison, W.A.	AMM3c	Taylor, R.E.	AMM2c
Jordan, L.W.	AMM3c		

12 October
Received ComAirPac secret dispatch to Comfightron 17 to embark, with squadron personnel, aircraft, and material, on the U.S.S. Prince William for transportation to the South Pacific, to report upon arrival at destination to ComSoPac for duty in that area.

13 October
Lt. D.A. Innis, reported for duty from VF-24. "Stinky" Innis reported to VF-17 with previous combat experience and a credit of one Japanese Zero shot down.

The U.S.S. Prince William with 45 officers and 67 enlisted men of VF-17 aboard for transportation, got underway at 0730.

13 October-25 October
On board the U.S.S. Prince William; daily routine of ground training for officers and enlisted men.

25 October
Disembarked from the U.S.S. Prince William at Espiritu Santo and reported to ComAirSoPac. Thirty-six F4Us were catapulted between 0930 and 1130. Remainder of personnel and material of VF-17 were put ashore by lighter at Espiritu Santo between 2000 and 0600 (26 Oct.). Received secret dispatch from ComFairSouth to Comfightron 17 directing the squadron to proceed to Henderson Field with ground echelons on October 26, and report to ComTask Force 33 for duty.

Lt. L.F. Herrmann (MC), reported for duty from ComFairSouth Pacific.

26 October
In accordance with ComFairSouth order, the following 34 pilots flew VF-17 F4Us to Henderson Field, take-off at 1130; arrival at 1515:-

Lt. Cdr. J.T. Blackburn	Lt(jg) M. Schanuel
Lt(jg) D.H. Gutenkunst	Lt(jg) R.S. Anderson
Ens. F.J. Streig	Lt(jg) D.C. Freeman
Lt(jg) T. Killefer	Lt. C.D. Gile
Lt. T.R. Bell	Lt(jg) D.G. Cunningham
Lt(jg) E. May	Lt(jg) P. Cordray
Lt. S.R. Beacham	Ens. B.W. Baker
Ens. D.T. Malone	Lt. J.A. Halford
Lt. J.M. Kleinman	Lt(jg) J.M. Chasnoff
Lt(jg) C.W. Gilbert	Lt. L.D. Cooke
Lt(jg) G.F. Bowers	Lt(jg) H.M. Burriss
Ens. R.H. Hill	Lt. M.W. Davenport
Lt. C.A. Pillsbury	Ens. I.C. Kepford
Lt. W.J. Schub	Ens. M.M. Kurlander
Ens. R.R. Hogan	Ens. T.F. Kropf
Lt(jg) R.H. Jackson	Lt. H.A. March
Lt. Cdr. R.R. Hedrick	Ens. J.O. Ellsworth

Ensign G.F. Hall, Ensign W.P. Popp, Ensign C.H. Dunn, G.H. Lampe, AMM2c and T.A. McCabe, AMM3c were ordered to temporary duty with operations, Bomber strip one, Espiritu Santo.

ONDONGO-PLACE OF DEATH

William "Country" Landreth at Pearl Harbor. October 1943, VF-17 outward bound at Ford Island. Courtesy William Landreth.

27 October
As directed by ComAirSols the above listed 34 pilots flew from Henderson Field (take-off at 0600; arrival at 0730) to Ondongo, New Georgia, and reported to ComAirSols for duty.

Pilots from the squadron flew 3 combat air patrols (20 sorties) over the Treasury Islands. All patrols negative.

The bulk of the squadron material, and the following 7 officers and 65 enlisted men were transported form Espiritu Santo to Henderson Field (take-off 0230; arrival 0615), from Henderson Field to Munda (take-off 1430; arrival 1600) by S.C.A.T., and from Munda to Ondongo by boat, arriving at 2100:-

Officers
Lt(jg) B.D. Henning
Lt. L.F. Herrmann
Lt. D.A.Innis
Ens. F.A. Jagger
Ens. L.M. Kelley
Ens. W.P. Meek
Ens. W.C. Wharton, Jr.

Enlisted men

Barak, L.T.	AOM2c	Jamison, W.A.	AMM3c
Baskin, C.R.	S2c	Jordan, L.W.	AMM3c
Brandenburg, F.M.	AMM3c	Kern, C.J.	AEM2c

Fighting 17, Pearl Harbor, prior to going into action. Although it was thought this photo was taken at Espiritu Santo no steel hangars were ever near to the Espiritu Santo area. The date of this photo is from 7 October, 1943, when Harry March reported for duty and before 13 October, 1943, when Don Innis reported to VF-17. This is the reason Don Innis is missing from this group. Front Row: Schub, Wharton, Gile, Killefer, Kropf, Jagger, Cordray, Davenport. 2nd Row: Burriss, Baker, Jackson, Kleinman, Hedrick, Blackburn, Hogan, Bowers. 3rd Row: Cooke, Anderson, Meek, Malone, Chasnoff, Schanuel, Ellsworth, Beacham, Freeman, Cunningham, Kurlander, Hill, Keith, Landreth, Bell. Top Row: Dunn, Gutenkunst, March, Halford, Gilbert, Henning, Kelley, Kepford, Streig, Pillsbury, May, Hall, Popp. Missing: Innis. Of the forty-three pilots manning the squadron prior to first combat, ten were killed while serving with VF-17. Courtesy Walter Schub and Joyce Wharton.

Bretz, K.G.	AMM2c	Landry, M.R.	AMM3c	Green, D.C.	AMM2c	Turner, J.R. Jr.	S2c
Cantrell, G.G.	AOM1c	Mauhar, G.	AMM1c	Grochowski, N.R.	AMM2c	Wert, E.M.	S2c
Condit, R.K.	AMM1c	McDonough, G.J.	AOM1c	Grogan, J.J.	AMM3c	Westphal, E.C.	AMM2c
Cox, B.L.	AMM2c	McLaughlin, D.D.	AMM3c	Hamilton, R.A. Jr.	S2c	White, L.E.	AMM2c
Craig, J.A.	S2c	McLean, E.R.	S1c	Hare, J.J.	AMM3c	White, M.A.B.	AMM1c
Dineen, J.T.	AOM3c	Meeteer, H.U.	Y3c	Homewood, E.A.	AMM2c	Whitley, R.N.	S2c
Duke, G.C.	S1c	Morfeld, E.R.	AMM1c	Hoyle, B.C. Jr.	S2c	Wood, A.K.	AMM3c
Edmisten, L.R.	AMM2c	Murray, B.	ACMM(AA)	Hyder, B.H. Jr.	AMM3c	Yager, Wm.	AMM2c
Emanuel, A.J.	AMM3c	Neil, J.L.	PR2c	Jacobs, E.W. Jr.	AM2c		
Engler, E.O.	ARM2c	Odem, F.R.	AMM1c				
Engler, H.E.	ARM2c	Olaes, R.J.	AOM3c				
Fehr, L.F.	AMM2c	Parker, W.L.	AMM3c	**28 October**			
Fisher, T.B.	AMM3c	Pitts, T.S.	AMM2c	Pilots from the squadron flew 5 combat air patrols over Ondongo			
Flynn, E.W.	AMM3c	Polite, F.	AMM2c	(24 sorties), and 2 combat patrols over the Treasury Islands, (16			
Foutty, C.S.	AOM2c	Rankin, D.M.	AOM3c	sorties). All patrols were negative.			
Furze, G.F.	AOM1c	Rasmussen, B.	AMM3c	Four pilots escorted a PBY-5 (Admiral Halsey aboard) from			
Gafford, J.H. Jr.	AMM3c	Sarnecki, J.A.	AMM2c	Munda to the Russell Islands.			
Gill, H.M.	AMM3c	Shore, M.E.	S2c				
Glover, D.E.	AMM2c	Simoneaux, N.F.	AMM3c	**29 October**			
Gober, E.W.	AMM1c	Sletterink, D.G.	AMM3c	Twenty-four pilots escorted (medium cover) B-25s and PV-1s on a			
Goyette, C.H. Jr.	AMM1c	Taylor, R.E.	AMM2c	strike against Buka and Bonis airfields. No enemy aircraft were			

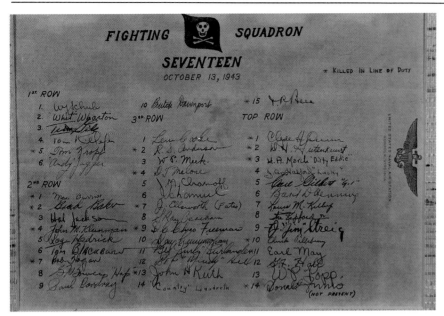

Signatures of all Fighting 17 pilots. Pearl Harbor, October 1943. This is dated 13 October, 1943, the day Innis reported for duty. Courtesy Walter Schub and Joyce Wharton.

was probably a derelict it did not burn. No A/A encountered.

Twenty-three pilots escorted (medium and high cover) 72 SBDs and 24 TBFs in a strike on Kara airfield. After the bombing attack 4 F4Us led by Lt. Cdr. Hedrick strafed shipping in Tonolei Harbor. Five small barges and one large barge were damaged. The strafing runs were made from a low altitude—about 50 feet. Moderate A/A (light automatic) fire was encountered, as the attack was evidently a surprise.

Twenty-four pilots went on a strafing mission against shipping in Tonolei Harbor.

The attack was made from the N.E. over a hill of 1,000 ft. 12 F4Us split off and went down the eastern shore. The other 12 took the western shore. The western flight strafed 6 barges, the eastern flight strafed 3. Altitude about 40-50 ft. Two landing barges were set on fire, and 8 were damaged. A/A fire from light automatic weapons was fairly intense. The A/A positions were on the hills surrounding the harbor. All the flight returned safely.

Seven pilots escorted a Dumbo (PBY) up to a point S. of Munia Island to rescue a P-39 pilot in the water. When the Dumbo landed it came under artillery fire from Ballale Island. Lt. Halford led his division (4 planes) down and strafed gun positions on the island.

Since they came down on the Island out of a rain squall they achieved surprise, but as the A/A gunners were already firing at the PBY on the water they were in a position to direct intense fire at the fighters. However no hits were sustained; and the F4U'=s did considerable damage to personnel (gunners), and to one Betty on the Runway. After their pass they regained altitude and escorted the Dumbo back to base.

encountered, and A/A fire was light and erratic. The F4U pilots reported numerous bomb hits on both Buka and Bonis—on the strips and in the revetment area.

Two combat air patrols over the base were flown (8 sorties) with negative results.

Four pilots escorted a PBY from Segi to the northwest tip of Santa Isabella Island and return. The mission of the PBY (to pick up survivors) was accomplished.

Twenty-four pilots were assigned as cover for a P-38 photographic plane whose mission was to photograph Kara, Kahili, and Ballale airfields. The P-38 was unable to take off and the F4Us proceeded to Tonolei Harbor, Bougainville, to strafe shipping. Lt. Cdr. Blackburn led 3 divisions down into Tonolei Harbor in elements of pairs. One 80-ton steamer and one landing barge were strafed. Both were out in the harbor. The steamer was set afire and seen to explode; the barge was severely hit—believed sunk. These 3 divisions then retired to the S.E. and returned to base.

The 4th division (Lt. Kleinman) broke right after entering the Harbor and strafed 2 landing barges and 4 80-ton steamers.

One steamer was set afire forward, and the landing barges were believed badly damaged. The flight then reversed course and headed south and strafed a third landing barge as it was proceeding to Ballale Island. The flight then returned to base.

A/A fire was moderate, both light automatic and 90mm. The greatest concentration was on Ballale Island, but some was noticed on the eastern side of Tonolei Harbor.

30 October

Eight pilots escorted 12 TBFs in a strike on Sangegi point, Choiseul Island. The TBFs bombed the shore north of Bambatana.

Lt. Beacham and Ens. Malone made 3 strafing runs on a Zeke on the shore 3 miles N. of Bambatana, Choiseul Island as the Zeke

31 October

Seven combat air patrols were flown over Ondongo (36 sorties) all of them negative.

F4Us of VF-17 at Munda, New Georgia at the start of the first combat tour. Courtesy Lennard Edmisten.

3

First Tour
November 1943

FIRST AIR COMBAT

This month was to be VF-17's introduction to air combat. November 1, brought an end to the training, waiting and tensions that had been building since heading out to the South Pacific.

1 November
The following 8 pilots made contact with about 28 Zekes and 12 Vals while on patrol over U.S. ships in Empress Augusta Bay, Bougainville.

Lt. Cdr. J.T. Blackburn   Lt. T.R. Bell
Lt(jg) D.H. Gutenkunst   Lt(jg) E.May
Ens. F.J. Streig   Lt. S.R. Beacham
Lt(jg) T. Killefer   Ens. D.T. Malone

The F4Us took off, made normal rendezvous, and proceeded to Empress Augusta Bay. The flight was orbiting Cape Torokina at 25,000 ft. when an enemy formation, estimated at about 40 Zekes and Vals, was sighted over Mt. Sugarloaf. The Vals were at about 16,000 ft., the Zekes at 18,000 ft.

Lt. Cdr. Blackburn dived on the leading Zeke from about 21,000 ft. When the formations were 2,000 ft. apart, the Zekes apparently saw the F4Us and dropped their belly tanks. The leading Zeke executed a right chandelle, Blackburn fired and hit him but did not destroy him. Blackburn recovered to the left, looked for his wingman, and in the process made a diving head-on run at a Zeke on his port bow. The Zeke turned up 20° and returned fire with 7.7s and 20mms but broke sharply at 200 yds. to the right and down.

Hits were observed on port wing and fuselage of the Zeke which trailed white smoke. The 7.7mm hit on Blackburn's left wing probably occurred on this run. On recovering from the run Gutenkunst was sighted above, and to the south of the melee and rendezvoused with Blackburn. The Japs turned right 90° and headed towards Empress Augusta Bay and they re-entered the melee. Blackburn made a run on a Zekes' tail (he at 16,000 ft., the Zeke at 15,000 ft.), he began firing at 200 yards, and when at 100 yards the Zeke burst into flames and went down. The pilot did not jump.

Tom Blackburn describes his first kill:

"I had a flight of 8 Corsairs as part of the combat air patrol over Empress Augusta Bay. I spotted the enemy flight off to the North East from us at a distance of 25 miles.

"As we got within about a mile coming in 30 degrees off their course, the Jap fighter leader spotted us and honked around in as

Tom Killefer, Ondongo, November 1943. Courtesy Lennard Edmisten.

Dan Cunningham at Ondongo, November 1943. Courtesy Lennard Edmisten.

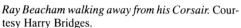

Ray Beacham walking away from his Corsair. Courtesy Harry Bridges.

Harry "Dirty Eddie" March and "Country" Landreth. Courtesy U.S. Naval Historical Center / M.W. "Butch" Davenport Collection.

tight a turn as he could, to counter our attack. I fired at him and as far as I could tell I didn't hit him.

"I turned and went back into the mad scramble of airplanes and picked up a Zero and bore in on him to point blank range. When he blew up I was close enough to get gasoline and hydraulic fluid on the windshield of my airplane. When I got that first flamer the sensation was almost identical to my first piece of ass".

Blackburn then headed north, picked up Ens. Malone (the wingman of his second section) northwest of Cape Torokina and both pursued the Japs northwest. Lt. Cdr. Blackburn believed that at this point the Vals jettisoned their bombs, no damage being done to their targets, the transports.

Shortly after this, Blackburn saw what he believed to be one F4U headed southeast pursued one mile astern by a Zeke. The friendly plane was zig-zagging at 5,000 ft. Blackburn attacked the Zeke from above and in front but missed. The Zeke continued his pursuit and over Cape Torokina began firing. Blackburn, then 700 yards astern, fired on the Zeke who broke away, turned left and headed north at 3,000 ft. Blackburn followed (beginning his chase at 15 miles astern) slightly below the Zeke. He closed to 100 yards, pulled up to the Zeke's level and fired. The Zeke burst into flames and crashed into the water. During this entire action Malone was flying wing on Blackburn.

The pair then patrolled under orders from the F.D.O. The remainder of the flight had no tactical significance.

To resume the account of the initial attack, Ens. Streig and Lt(jg) Killefer, the second section in Blackburn's division followed Blackburn down on the leading group of Zekes but missed on their

first pass and pulled up to 17,000 ft. Streig located a Zeke in the left flanking formation at 14-15,000 ft. He and Killefer made a 60° deflection high side run, the Zeke burst into flame at the root of the right wing and crashed. The section then turned back to Mutupena Pt. sighted a Zeke over Mt. Bagana heading north, got directly on his tail and fired at a range of 250 yards.

The Zeke caught fire and crashed. The pilot was seen to bail out. Streig and Killefer then followed another Zeke north, almost to Buka, but could not overtake him. The section then returned to base.

In the initial attack Lt(jg) Gutenkunst, Blackburn's wingman, saw a Val leave the formation and reverse course. He followed him, fired at long range and believed he scored several hits. The Val, however, continued on course. Gutenkunst then rendezvoused with Blackburn at 18,000 ft., east of the melee. As Blackburn attacked the group Gutenkunst saw a Zeke below him and fired on him. The Zeke turned head on and fired. At that moment Gutenkunst looked back and saw another Zeke on his tail. He turned west and took cover in a cloud. He climbed to 25,000 ft., orbited for 15 or 20 minutes, saw no planes and returned to base.

Again during the initial attack Lt. Beacham observed 2 Zekes making gentle S turns below 1,000 ft. on his port bow. By this time the Jap formation had been broken up.

Ray Beacham was credited with the squadron's first kill, he describes the action: "I broke out of formation," Beacham said, "and I sure did hear plenty about that later from the skipper."

"During the dive I fired at the Zero every time I caught him in my sights. I don't know where I hit him but he went down in flames.

Then I started climbing up to join the rest of the squadron. I was below the fighting level when two more Zeros came after me. They managed to damage my right wing but I got away and headed back home".

He made a high side run from 13,000 ft. and fired at 300 yards, his angle of fire being 60° above the Zeke. The Zeke rolled over in a steep dive. Beacham rolled with him and followed him down. He had a straight run on the Zeke's tail and after a one second burst the Zeke exploded. Beacham recovered at 2,500 ft. and headed out 10 miles, climbing to gain altitude. He was climbing to 13,000 ft. in an attempt to re-enter the melee when 2 Zekes came down head on out of the sun. The leading Zeke fired, hitting Beacham's plane. The second Zeke turned to get into position on his tail. Beacham skidded, rolled over on his back, dived straight down followed by the Zekes to 5,000 ft. He leveled out at 2,500 ft., poured on the coal and returned to base at 13,000 ft.

Lt. Bell and Lt(jg) May, (the 1st section in the 2nd division) attacked the Zekes after Blackburn's division had made its first pass. At the time the Japs were in no discernible formation. Bell (with May following) made a beam attack on a Zeke, got in a 45° deflection shot and saw a flash of flame aft of the cockpit. The flame died down and the Zeke rolled over slowly into a steep glide and disappeared. The section made a similar run on a second Zeke but did not hit him. They then climbed to 25,000 ft. and resumed patrol. No further contacts were made and they returned to base.

The following tactical comments were reported after this mission.

Zekes were providing close cover for Vals, in one layer only, proceeding at slow speed (estimated 170 m.p.h. true).

F4U formation could have wrought more damage if it had sliced through after group of Zekes into the Vals and out through lead Zekes since the Japs were going very slowly and could not have stayed with F4Us. Jap formation disintegrated as result of first pass. F4U speed was excessive (350 kt. ind.) for type of attack made (on covering fighters) but would have been correct for slice through entire formation.

Lack of aggressiveness of Zekes was notable as was their lack of cohesion. Only F4Us attacked by Zekes were singles - two out of four wingmen failed to stay in formation. F4Us markedly outperformed Zekes in everything but maneuverability. Zekes looked brand new.

This was the first engagement with Japanese planes for all pilots on the flight.

Blackburn shot down 2 Zekes and damaged 2 Zekes; Beacham shot down 1 Zeke; Streig shot down 1 Zeke; Killefer shot down 1 Zeke; Bell damaged 1 Zeke; Gutenkunst damaged 1 Zeke.

Two F4Us were slightly damaged.

At the conclusion of a negative 2 hour patrol over U.S. ships in Empress Augusta Bay, Bougainville, Lt. Halford led his division

Tom Blackburn in Corsair "Big Hog" running up on line. Courtesy U.S. Naval Historical Center / M.W. "Butch" Davenport Collection.

Tom Killefer in "Teeth" Burriss' plane early in the first tour. Courtesy U.S. Naval Historical Center / M.W. "Butch" Davenport Collection.

back to base, he being low on oxygen. The following pilots (4 out of the 8 on patrol) dived on Jap barracks and other buildings on the north shore of Kulitunai harbor, Shortland Island:

Lt. L.D. Cooke
Lt. M.W. Davenport
Lt(jg) H.M. Burriss
Ens. I.C. Kepford

As they came down fast out of the overcast their attack was a surprise. They made one strafing run and withdrew low on the water. Because of the high speed of the F4Us as they passed over the target no results of the strafing could be observed. Medium A/A fire was intense, but none of the F4Us were hit. The division then returned to base.

After a negative 2 hour patrol over U.S. ships in Empress Augusta Bay, Bougainville, Lt. Kleinman led his division, the following 4 pilots out of the 8 on patrol to Shortland Island, approaching from the N.W. He dived from about 1,000 ft. to tree top level and strafed the south shore of Kulitinai Bay. Huts and A/A positions were the target.

Lt. J.M. Kleinman
Lt(jg) C.W. Gilbert
Lt(jg) G.F. Bowers
Ens. R.H. Hill

Several barracks were left smoking. Medium and light A/A was intense, and one plane was hit by a 7.7 shell. Damage was negligible.

The following pilots on patrol over U.S. ships in Empress Augusta Bay, Bougainville, intercepted 9 Zekes and 7 Vals:

Lt. Cdr. R.R. Hedrick	Lt. C.D. Gile
Lt(jg) M. Schanuel	Lt(jg) D.G. Cunningham
Lt(jg) R.S. Anderson	Lt(jg) P. Cordray
Lt(jg) J.M. Chasnoff	Ens. B.W. Baker

Hedrick's and Gile's divisions took station as high cover over Empress Augusta Bay. Cocker Base reported bogies S.E. of Cape Torokina. Hedrick saw an enemy formation over the island and turned to intercept it.

A force of about 9 Zekes were spotted at 23,000 ft. Hedrick took his flight up sun, got in a position 1,500 ft. above the Zekes and came down in an easy 20° dive. He fired into a Zeke's fuselage (using only 4 guns as his generator had gone dead on the flight up) and saw him burst into flames and crash.

"I swung out West to get up sun from them. As I got closer I saw that red meatball on the wing of one of those babies and I said "by god this is it. We're here and now we can get a little revenge for what these guys have been doing to our shipmates.

I opened fire using the point of aim, the intersection of the wing root and the fuselage. As this Jap planes wingspan filled 50 mils in my gunsight, I pressed the trigger maybe 2 seconds and he went up in a ball of fire." Recalls Lt. Cdr. Roger Hedrick.

All Zekes still carried belly tanks when attacked.

At his first burst 5 Zekes rolled sharply to the right and down. After completing his attack, Hedrick chandelled, looked for his wingman, but could not find him. He climbed to 25,000 ft., returned to the flights' appointed rendezvous, circled for 20 minutes and then returned to base. At no time did his transmitter function, and as mentioned before, his generator was not operating.

Lt(jg) Schanuel, Hedrick's wingman, fired at the Zeke on the right of the plane shot down by Hedrick, but missed. He pulled up into the sun and made a wide circle to the left at 25,000 ft. He heard Cocker Base reporting bogies and saw 7 Vals at about 15,000 ft. heading S.W. out of Empress Augusta Bay. He made a beam run on the leading Val, opened fire at 225 yds., missed, but hit the leader's wingman.

This plane was seen to stream white smoke, but remained in formation. Schanuel then went to the rendezvous and circled for 45 minutes. On his way back to base he strafed Ballale Island.

Lt(jg) Anderson, the leader of Hedrick's second section, made a run from dead astern at a Zeke in the second pair of the Jap formation. He over-led him and when the Jap saw the tracers he executed a split S . Anderson pulled up and looked for his wingman. He could not find him and started back to the rendezvous. He could get no pressure above 15,000 ft. so returned to base. He had been able to use only 2 of his guns.

Lt(jg) Chasnoff, Anderson's wingman, shot at the Zeke flying wing on the plane attacked by Anderson. The Zeke executed a violent right turn. Chasnoff dove after Anderson, picked up another Zeke, fired, and may have hit it. At this moment the Zeke he had originally attacked reappeared on his tail. He dove away and rejoined Gile's division over Empress Augusta Bay.

#33-Lonesome Polecat. As aircraft were lost or damaged, Butch Davenport's plane #33, was wrecked and was replaced new with #9, his final plane. Courtesy U.S. Naval Historical Center/M.W. "Butch" Davenport Collection.

Robert "Andy" Anderson. Courtesy Joy Anderson Schroeder.

Lt. Gile, leader of the second division, and his wingman, Lt(jg) Cunningham, dove on a pair of Zeros to the left of the pair attacked by Hedrick.

Gile got one in his sights, lost him, and found another immediately. At this time he was in a 45° dive, speed about 270 knots, altitude 18,000 ft. As his tabs were trimmed for 200 knots and he was bouncing in the slip stream, he had great difficulty in keeping his sights on the target. Bullets were all around the Zeke, and several incendiaries were seen to hit the wings, but did not burn. Gile went past the Zeke, almost hitting him with his right wing. The Zeke dove into a cloud and was not seen again. Gile then went to 20,000 ft. and patrolled over Empress Augusta Bay. He was joined by Cunningham, Cordray and Baker.

Lt(jg) Cunningham, Gile's wingman, followed Gile down in his firing run on the Zeke. When Gile went past the Zeke, Cunningham took his place and fired, but despite the fact that he saw bullets hitting, the Zeke did not burn.

When the enemy disappeared in a cloud, Cunningham climbed, rejoined Gile, and went on patrol. He 'pancaked' with 15 gallons of gasoline left in his tank.

Lt(jg) Cordray and Ens. Baker, the second section in Gile's division, dove on a pair of Zekes from the original formation. Cordray, with Baker on his wing, fired at the leading Zeke. The second one pulled out and turned on their tails.

They dove to 1,000 ft., headed west for 5 minutes and climbed into the sun to 29,000 ft. They came down to 25,000 ft. over Empress Augusta Bay, rejoined Gile, and went on patrol. At 1,500 ft. they left station and 'pancaked.' Baker had no gas left when he landed.

The following tactical observations were reported after this mission:

This engagement demonstrated the ability of the Zekes to work as pairs. In two cases the wingman of the Zeke being attacked pulled out and came in on the tail of the attacker. Also the Zekes in this engagement showed a tendency to turn right instead of left as had been previously reported. The Zekes looked brand new.

This was the first engagement with enemy planes for all pilots in the flight.

Hedrick shot down 1 Zeke; Schanuel damaged 1 Val; Gile and Cunningham damaged 1 Zeke. None of the F4Us sustained any damage.

After a negative 2 hour patrol flying high cover over landing forces in Empress Augusta Bay, Bougainville, the following 8 pilots left station and proceeded S.E. to Shortland Island.

Lt. J.A. Halford	Lt. L.D.Cooke
Ens. J.O. Ellsworth	Lt(jg) H.M. Burriss
Lt(jg) J.H. Keith	Lt. M.W. Davenport
Lt(jg) W.L. Landreth	Ens. I.C. Kepford

From 1,000 ft. they dived on Kulitunai Bay, strafing 140-foot landing barge (which fired at them with 2 MG's) and 118-foot boat. Both craft were at the south shore of the bay.

The flight withdrew over Poporang Island and Faisi Island. Intense light and medium A/A fire was encountered from these islands. Lt(jg) Keith, leader of the second section in the 2nd division, was hit on this withdrawal, his plane was seen to stream black smoke. He flew for about 2 minutes (altitude 75 ft.) and made a water landing about 15 miles S.E. of Faisi Island. He was seen to climb out (apparently uninjured) and swim away, but apparently without his life raft.

Keith's wingman, Lt(jg) Landreth turned on his emergency I.F.F. and circled for 5 minutes, then returned to base. Lt. Halford, the division leader, and his wingman circled once and headed for

Jack Chasnoff on Ondongo late in 1943. Courtesy Jack Chasnoff.

Paul Cordray VF-17 ace with 6 kills at Ondongo, November 1943. Courtesy Lennard Edmisten.

Barakoma airfield (Vella Lavella Island). He called Barakoma 5 times asking that a Dumbo be sent for Keith. When he landed at Barakoma he found it was too dark to send a Dumbo. He asked that

a rescue boat be sent from the Treasury Islands. This could not be done either.

Halford and his wingman remained at Barakoma overnight and returned to Ondongo the next morning. The area where Keith went down was carefully searched for the next 2 days by F4Us; but no trace of Keith could be found. He was reported as "Missing".

"Country" Landreth recalls the loss of his close friend: "The way we lost Johnny Keith was one of those silly, terrible accidents. Like most accidents, fatalities or casualties, they are the apex of several things going wrong together.

"On my first combat flight, beginning the late afternoon of November 1, 1943, I was flying Johnny Keith's wing. We went out on a fighter sweep over Kahili Airstrip on Bougainville.

"The flight leader invented an idea on the way back. We were going near the Shortland Islands on our way back from Bougainville back to Ondongo. This guy says, 'we'll spread out and go low on the water and come in from the north.' There was a harbor there. The theory was that there would be some landing craft or barges bringing supplies in hidden amongst the trees, or anchored out in this little lagoon. We won't come in the direction of our base, we'll be coming from the other direction. We'd get low on the water, spread out, and pop out over that ridge right into the harbor, and shoot up everything that was a good target, a decent target of any kind whatsoever.

Dan Cunningham and Hap Bowers in "Command Car", New Georgia, 1943. Courtesy U.S. Naval Historical Center / M.W. "Butch" Davenport Collection.

Tom Blackburn taxiing out in "Big Hog". Munda, November 1943. Courtesy U.S. Naval Historical Center / M.W. "Butch" Davenport Collection.

L-R. *"Dirty Eddie" March, Tom Killefer, "Big Jim" Streig, Ondongo, November 1943.* Courtesy Lennard Edmisten.

*"Big Jim" Streig and his groundcrew.*Courtesy Lennard Edmisten.

Tom Blackburn at Ondongo, November 1943. The bullet holes from Roger Hedrick's accidental attempt to shoot Blackburn down have been recently patched. Courtesy Lennard Edmisten.

"Boy, were they waiting for us! I'll tell you, they saw us from I don't know how far out, but when we popped out over that ridge I've never seen anything like it before or since. At about 200 feet or 300 feet, our altitude, 40mm explosions like a flat black roof! I'm telling you, they must have had those guns set on instantaneous - automatic. Every gun that was around the whole harbor just fired straight up in the air - all these black bursts of 40mm fire. It didn't look like 5-inch stuff. It was thick and intense - and we were right in the middle of it with all our airplanes - eight, as I recall, but it could have been twelve.

"I left Johnny for a moment; I thought I saw something along the shoreline. It looked suspiciously like a barge or something, and I whipped around to focus on that and I strafed the entire shore, including this suspicious-looking area. I turned back on the line, joined back up on Johnny, and while I'd been gone, he got a piece of this anti-aircraft fire. He was streaming white smoke-which is engine oil vapor—I knew right then that Johnny was not going home that day.

"I flew right on his wing and his airplane was working all right. We were in communication by hand signals and radio, but it was just a matter of time before he would run out of oil and his engine would seize. We withdrew from the island, and Johnny knew he was going to have to make a water landing. He was in trouble. As his airplane slowed down I stayed right with him, right down to the water as he made a good water landing.

"Now here's the way you get killed. Procedures! You're going to make a water landing? Ditch the hood! Two red handles, in, down - it's gone. At least get the canopy locked back, with your elbows.

"But Johnny wasn't a very big guy and not a very strong guy, and he didn't do emergency procedure. You've got to get the gosh-darn canopy off so it can't hurt you, can't damage you, can't trap you. I'm sitting there watching this. He would push it back and it would slide back - but it wouldn't lock. Then he'd fiddle with his (microphone) cord, cinch up his shoulder straps and seat belt and the canopy would slip forward, then he'd push it back again, then

he'd do something else, then push it back - but it never locked. Because it wasn't locked, it slid forward and closed when he hit the water!

"The airplane, of course, floats for a little while nose down, but it went down pretty quick. He had most of his ammo and quite a bit of gas left, so it was a heavy airplane. He didn't have much time, and when he hit the water, now he's locked in. So he sort of half-way panicked and he opened his canopy and tried to get out - but you've got your parachute, your boat, your survival gear hanging on you, trying to get out of a narrow opening. He decided he's not gonna make it that way. So he unsnaps his parachute and boat, he gets out through the narrow opening, stands on the wing root and decides to reach back into the airplane to pull the stuff out - and the airplane sank. He was left with his Mae West life-jacket in shark-infested waters, right off the coast of a Japanese-occupied island - with night-time falling—I stayed with him, and two other guys climbed to altitude to call for a Dumbo; all the while knowing that open-sea landing at night is not what PBYs do. As slow as they are, they could not get there before night time.

I stayed until it was dark. The next morning we went out pre-dawn looking for Johnny - a whole bunch of airplanes flying all over the area. We never found him. So I lost my best friend the first day in combat. It was a little difficult to handle that.

"The flight leader got in trouble with the higher-ups for what they called 'jousting with anti-aircraft.' They said that's a non-profit proposition. That island was bypassed. All they had was ammunition on that island; they didn't have any food. So we flew by and gave them a nice target. That was dumbness!

"I knew Johnny all the way through flight training and our squadron training and out to the Pacific. Johnny was a slight individual and one of the finest gentlemen that ever walked around in a pair of shoes. He didn't have a mean bone in his body, and didn't have a very aggressive attitude.

"I always kind of thought he was probably too polite and too generous of heart, and would have been a good patrol plane pilot!

He wouldn't go swimming over at the swimming pool at the Officers' Club with you, and it took me six months to find out that he thought he was too slight of build and he had knobbly knees and he didn't want anybody to see him in a bathing suit! That kind of tender-hearted guy is usually not mean enough to be a good fighter pilot." Four F4Us escorted a Dumbo (PBY) to Zimoa Island and back. The mission of the Dumbo was to land supplies and pick up wounded.

Eight F4Us made a reconnaissance flight over Kara, Kahili, and Ballale airfields. All fields reported operative.

2 November
Four F4Us were assigned to fly patrol over friendly forces in Empress Augusta Bay, Bougainville.

Lt. Cdr. J.T. Blackburn Lt(jg) D.H. Gutenkunst
Ens. F.J. Streig Lt(jg)T. Killefer

Many bogies reported, but the Fighter Direction from Cocker Base and Dane Base (F.D.Os for Empress Augusta Bay) and Lion Base (cruiser Task Force) was so poor that no contacts could be made. The F.D.O.s failed to give vital information concerning bearing, distance, altitude, and course of bogies.

While proceeding on a vector west of the bay the flight observed the U.S. Task Force 39, distance about 20 miles. The ships fired on a flight of F6Fs passing over them.

A few minutes later a force of Vals (number uncertain) attacked the ships. Because of poor vectoring the F4Us were unable to close with the enemy, who retreated to the S.E. No ships were hit by the Vals. The flight left station and headed for Shortland Island. They came down from the north and at tree-top level strafed barracks on

Faisi and Poporang Islands. Moderate A/A fire was encountered (light, heavy and medium), and on the withdrawal Lt(jg) Killefer's plane was hit. A 20mm shell exploded in the cockpit, exploding the oxygen bottle.

Killefer suffered a painful shrapnel wound on the left leg. Both legs and his left forearm suffered first and second degree burns.

All planes returned to base.

Tactical comments reported after this mission were as follows:
The need for *good* Fighter Direction is obvious.

Four F4U's searched the area south of Shortland Island for Keith for 2 hours but with negative results.

Twelve F4Us formed part of a fighter escort of an SBD-TBF strike at any Jap shipping found on the S.W. coast of Bougainville Island. Two divisions remained with the bombers, who went as far north as Buka without finding any targets. They then escorted the bombers back to base. The third division of F4Us,

Lt. C.D. Gile
Lt(jg) D.G. Cunningham
Lt(jg) P. Cordray
Ens. B.W. Baker

led by Lt. Gile, lost the bombers. This division crossed Bougainville at Empress Augusta Bay, turned south and came down on Kara Airfield. They strafed 3 houses at the N. end of the strip and left them smoking. The division then turned east to Tonolei Harbor.

At the end of the harbor they turned S.S.E. and came in looking for barges. None were found, but one medium A/A gun was silenced on the east shore of the harbor.

All strafing was done at tree-top level. Light A/A fire was intense.

L-R. *Davenport, Cooke, Hogan, Gutenkunst in front of Hog Hollow, Ondongo, November 1943.* Courtesy Lennard Edmisten.

L-R. *Hal Jackson, "Ike" Kepford, Paul Cordray at Ondongo, November 1943.* Courtesy U.S. Navy photo. Robert L. Lawson Collection.

Two aces, "Big Jim" Streig behind "Ike" Kepford. Courtesy U.S. Navy photo. Robert L. Lawson Collection.

2nd Division of "Butch" Davenport's flight en route to Bougainville. Courtesy U.S. Naval Historical Center / M.W. "Butch" Davenport Collection.

Eight F4Us flew a 2-hour negative patrol over Empress Augusta Bay, Bougainville.

On return they made a reconnaissance flight over Kara, Kahili and Ballale airfields. All were reported operative.

Two negative 2-hour patrols (16 sorties) were flown over Empress Augusta Bay, Bougainville.

3 November

Two negative 2-hour patrols (14 sorties) were flown over Empress Augusta Bay, Bougainville.

One negative 3-hour patrol (4 sorties) was flown over Munda.

Sixteen F4Us were assigned as cover for an SBD strike on Kahili. Because of bad weather the bombers were unable to reach the target.

4 November

Eight divisions of F4Us (only 27 planes, as 5 were unable to take off because of engine trouble) made rendezvous with 60 SBD's and 18 TBFs over Baga Island and then proceeded to target, Kahili airfield, Bougainville. After the successful bombing attack 9 F4Us (3 divisions) escorted the bombers back to base.

Lt. Cdr. Blackburn and Lt. Pillsbury led their divisions north to Matchin Bay.

Lt. Cdr. J.T. Blackburn	Lt. C.A. Pillsbury
Lt(jg) D.H. Gutenkunst	Lt. W.J. Schub
Ens. F.J. Streig	Ens. R.R. Hogan
Lt(jg) T. Killefer	Lt(jg) R.H. Jackson

The divisions swung east to the shore at about 50 ft. altitude. They made one pass at the landing barges and sank them. Two planes confirmed their run and passed over Chabai Plantation, silencing an A/A gun and strafing barracks. The remaining 6 planes strafed an 80 ft. wooden boat, swung inland, then out again, and made 2 passes at a 150 ft. coastal steamer. It was seen smoking. On the second pass Blackburn's plane was hit in the left wing by light A/A and seriously damaged. The 2 divisions then returned to base.

Tom Blackburn remembered this action: "I got clipped and completely terrified when up against some light Japanese shipping at the north end of Bougainville Island. There were some outlying islands with anti-aircraft emplacements which we strafed first, then we pulled up over these islands strafed the Jap shipping in the harbor and then we had to cross the shoreline which was fairly heavily armed.

"I have a very vivid recollection of instead of having 6 guns firing against the heavy A/A on the shoreline, having 5 guns jammed and only one operating so it was going pop! pop! pop! I caught a couple of bullets on that one. The horrible shock of not having cleared my guns and having one gun shooting instead of 6 stays with me to this day.

"One bullet that was apparently meant for me went through the left wingtip and creased the top of the canopy over the top of my head. I wasn't aware of it at the time else I would have been even more scared."

After the bombing attack Lt. Bell led his division north to a point just west of Buka at 20,000 ft. altitude. He observed a bombing attack by B-24s. Many hits observed. He then led his division back to base.

After the bombing attack at Kahili, Lt. Cdr. Hedrick and Lt. Gile led their divisions N.W. to Empress Augusta Bay.

Lt. Cdr. R.R. Hedrick	Lt. C.D. Gile
Lt(jg) M. Schanuel	Lt(jg) D.G. Cunningham
Lt(jg) D.C. Freeman	Lt(jg) P. Cordray
Ens. B.W. Baker	

Then they cut N.E. across Bougainville to Arawa Bay on the N.E. coast and headed north to Cape Mabiri. All 7 planes made passes at a 150 ft. cargo vessel at Cape Mabiri and set it afire. One mile north of this point they made 2 passes at a fishing steamer heavily loaded with gear and left it smoking. About 2 miles north of this Hedrick's section made one good run on a landing barge full of equipment, and sank it. The flight then turned and proceeded south along the coast to Loluei Point, where they strafed a schooner at anchor and set it afire. Further south at Cape Friendship they strafed a good sized fishing boat and left it smoking. The divisions then returned to base.

All the above strafing runs the F4Us opened fire at about 500 yards. All strafing done at very low altitude 200 to 20 feet. Loading was 2 A.P., 1 Tracer, 1 Incendiary.

No A/A fire was encountered.

One negative 2-hour patrol (4 sorties) over Munda was flown.

Twelve F4Us escorted a Dumbo (PBY) to Kahili Bay, Bougainville, to pick up a survivor in the water. Mission accomplished according to plan.

5 November
Three negative 2-hour patrols (16 sorties) were flown over Munda. Three negative 2-hour patrols (24 sorties) were flown over Task Force 38 (U.S.S. Saratoga, Princeton, CL and DD screen).

6 November
Four divisions of F4Us (14 planes, as 2 failed to take off) escorted 5 B-25s from Baga Island to Matzungen Island. At a point one mile S.E. of the latter island the B-25s made 4 low bombing and strafing runs on 3 ships. One 150-ton AK exploded and sank, one DE type sank, and an 80-ton AK blew up and sank. Three of the above mentioned divisions returned directly to base.

Lt. J.M. Kleinman	Lt. J.A. Halford	Lt. H.A.March
Lt(jg) C.W. Gilbert	Ens. J.O. Ellsworth	Lt(jg) W.L. Landreth
Lt(jg) G.F. Bowers	Lt. L.D. Cooke*	Lt. D.A. Innis*
Ens. R.H. Hill	Lt(jg) H.M. Burriss	Ens.W.C. Wharton

*Returned early because could not find flight.

The 4th division, led by Lt. Davenport,
Lt. M.W. Davenport
Lt. W.J. Schub
Ens.R.R. Hogan
Lt(jg) R.H. Jackson
which had been flying high cover, headed S.E. at 2,000 ft., speed about 200k.

At a point 10-15 miles offshore, bearing 240° from Cape Moltke, Bougainville Island, the division observed a Betty at 300 ft. altitude on an E.S.E. course one mile to the east of them. They turned to intercept it; the Betty apparently spotted them and turned north. Davenport made the first run, followed by Schub and Hogan, although these attacks were practically simultaneous.

All made low, high side runs. Davenport made 3, Schub 4, Hogan 2, and Jackson made one long run on the Betty's tail. All runs were pressed home to the limit. At the conclusion of Jackson's run the Betty burst into flames and crashed into the sea.

During the action the Betty took evasive action, S-turning in order to give the dorsal gunner good shots at the fighters. No other turret was seen to fire.

Walter Schub recalls this mission: "Returning from combat air patrol over Empress Augusta Bay we had finished a 3.9 hour on the high cover and getting prepared to go back to base on Ondongo. our four planes heading south and approximately 10 miles off the coast of Empress Augusta Bay-about 4.00 p.m. The division make up consisted of Davenport and his wingman (the division make up was an impromptu one as my wingman was Bob Hogan rather than Whit Wharton, my regular wingman). Hal Jackson was flying wing with Davenport. In any event we were finished with our escort mission and were in a loose formation (just our four planes) and cruising along about 200 knots.

It had been a quiet day, no enemy aircraft were sighted. As we were leaving the vicinity of Empress Augusta Bay I was checking the area behind us when I noticed a reflection some distance behind and further out from Empress Augusta Bay. In making a turn to the west for a better observation, I felt we should investigate it. As I and my wingman were turning, I contacted Davenport and appraised

him of the situation. Sure enough it was a Japanese Betty medium bomber, and they were making tracks or turning hard to get away from us. The Betty was jettisoning different things out of the plane to lighten the load to escape. They were so low that our four planes couldn't really shoot it down in a hurry. We were taking our time.

"With the Betty heading into the sun and at an altitude of 300-500 feet, we were very much restricted as to the type of run to use. The situation dictated that we attack from the rear and above. Unfortunately the other three didn't back off and let me take care of it-seeing as how it was my find. I do believe my first run on it was fatal (for the Betty of course), but we all did get some gunnery practice.

"During this situation the Betty headed toward the water, the right wing dipped and they were getting out of control, no fire or flame. I did notice at this time that 4 Japanese people aboard the Betty were jumping out of the aircraft and they went 1-2-3-4 with no parachutes on and went into the water.

"Unfortunately, as was mentioned in Tom Blackburn's book, the Betty crew was subjected to a certain amount of suffering. I saw four of them jump before the Betty nosed down to the right and cartwheeled as it hit the water. No parachutes were observed and no reports were received as to crew recoveries. We circled a couple of times, saw no indication of anyone alive or in need of help. So we turned around and went home.

"We did make about five passes each. Conditions of sun and altitude, available time and fuel led us to minimize the odds of our getting shot down. I had the reputation of not losing anyone that flew with me-as was brought out in later squadrons."

Two negative 2-hour patrols (16 sorties) were flown over Empress Augusta Bay, Bougainville.

Two negative 2-hour patrols (8 sorties) over Munda were flown.

Eight F4Us escorted a Dumbo (PBY) to Empress Augusta Bay, Bougainville and return.

VF-17 Ready Room. Schub, Davenport, Chasnoff, March, Kepford, Blackburn, Wharton (kneeling), Kurlander (kneeling), Streig, Hogan. Ondongo, November 15, 1943. Courtesy U.S. Navy photo. Robert L. Lawson Collection.

7 November

One negative 2-hour patrol (8 sorties) was flown over Munda.

Two negative 2-hour patrols (16 sorties) were flown over Task Group 31.6.

Sixteen F4Us escorted B-25s and PV-1s in a strike against shore installations at Atsinima Bay, Bougainville Island. The B-25s went in to attack the shoreline. The leader veered out to sea and bombed (1 bomb) what the F4U's identified as 2 U.S. PT boats. The boats were about 5 miles off shore. The F4Us at 4,000 ft. The bombs missed wide.

The bombers then made many low bombing and strafing runs (at 75 to 100 ft. altitude) on the beach at Atsinima Bay. The attack lasted 35 minutes. The F4Us could not see any targets and hence could not estimate damage done.

At the conclusion of the attack the F4Us escorted the bombers back to Baga Island.

8 November

Three negative 2-hour patrols (24 sorties) were flown over Empress Augusta Bay, Bougainville.

Twelve F4Us were assigned to fly escort on B-25's in a strike against shipping in Matchin Bay. Because of the extremely bad weather surrounding the base and the early hour (dawn), none of the fighters were able to find the bombers. Seven returned to base. The following 5 pilots

Lt. Cdr. J.T. Blackburn

Lt. H.A. March

Ens. W.C. Wharton

Ens. F.J. Streig

Lt(jg) T. Killefer

left Baga Island, the rendezvous point and took a N.W. course to a point at sea 50 miles S.W. of Buka. By this time the weather had cleared.

They turned E. into Matchin Bay (no shipping seen) and Blackburn, March and Wharton took a course of 310° to Minan Island, swung right on a course of 40° to the Buka strip. Just before passing Minan Island they had observed a transport-type plane (probably a converted Ruth) circling to land.

The three flew right along the Buka strip (altitude 50 ft.), strafed a Zeke parked on the S.W. end of the strip, and strafed personnel on the edge of the strip. By this time Blackburn and March were on the tail of the Ruth, who was half way up the strip, altitude 10 feet. Both planes had perfect shots (range 200 to 25 yards), and the Ruth, hit in the wing roots and motors, burst into flames and crashed. No dorsal turret was observed, and so it was assumed the plane had been converted to a transport.

The 3 F4Us turned sharply to the south and were joined by Streig and Killefer, who had passed over Bonis Airfield. All five searched the N.E. coast of Bougainville for shipping, but with negative results.

At the southern tip of Bougainville the weather turned bad. The flight swung over Ballale Island (the strip seemed operative), and moderate light and heavy A/A fire was encountered. On the withdrawal from Ballale Killefer's plane was badly hit by a 20mm shell in the starboard wing. They then returned to Ondongo.

Whit Wharton standing next to his Corsair. Courtesy U.S. Naval Historical Center / M.W. "Butch" Davenport Collection.

A flight of 6 F4Us (2 of the original 8 were unable to take off)

Lt. Cdr. R.R. Hedrick	Lt(jg) D.G. Cunningham
Lt(jg) M. Schanuel	Lt(jg) P. Cordray
Lt(jg) R.S. Anderson	Lt. C.D. Gile*
Lt(jg) J.M. Chasnoff	Ens. B. Baker*

*Returned early.

took station over Empress Augusta Bay to fly high cover over the landing forces there. They were orbiting at 25,000 ft. over Cape Moltke. The F.D.O. at Cocker Base vectored them out to intercept a large bogey. Their first vector was 220°.

They held this course for a few minutes, then were vectored on 170° then back to 221°. Very shortly after this vector Lt. Cdr. Hedrick, the flight leader, saw through the clouds to the S.E. of the flight, about 15 miles off shore, 24 Zekes and Hamps and 15 Vals on a Northeasterly course. The fighters were about 22,000 ft., the bombers at 12,000 ft. Hedrick turned to intercept them as they were obviously heading for the ships in the bay. After he had turned the F.D.O. gave the bogey course as 110°.

Robert "Andy" Anderson recalls this day: "You were scared when you first made contact on a mission but once you got going it was just so exciting and exhilarating. It's probably wrong to say it was fun. It was almost fun.

"When I was a kid I used to read these pulp dime magazines about the W.W.I. exploits of Rickenbacker, Luke. They talked about a Lufbury circle and that's where a group if they were under attack, will go into what amounts to a tail chase; they'll circle. You're covering the guy ahead of you and you're trying to gain altitude.

"This actually happened. One day we were out, Roger Hedrick was leading the division and we jumped a bunch of Jap fighters and it really struck me; I was really surprised to see them use this maneuver because it was a W.W.I. tactic. Very surprising!"

Hedrick chandelled across the enemy formation to get into position, and the Zekes immediately formed a loose Lufbury circle. In the attack Hedrick lost sight of his wingman. He picked a Zeke on the far side of the circle, made a high side run, and hit him. The Zeke dove straight down through the clouds, with gas streaming from the plane. By this time the Zekes were in the clouds; Hedrick went in to find them, with no success, and headed N.W. at full speed to cut across their course. After their first attack they had turned, and were apparently retiring.

The action now developed into a running fight up the S.W. coast of Bougainville, almost as far as Buka. Hedrick spotted a six-plane division at about 12,000 ft. He began his run and the Zekes turned in towards him and he hit one of them on an opposite-course run. Pieces flew from the Zeke's engine, but he flashed by too quickly to determine the extent of damage. Hedrick made several passes at the remaining Zekes, and finally caught one as he (Hedrick) was recovering from a chandelle. He saw his bullets go in astern of the engine.

Shortly after this he was joined by the second section of his division (Lts(jg) Anderson and Chasnoff); and a little later by his wingman, Lt(jg) Schanuel. The reformed division continued N.W. after the Zekes. Hedrick made a run on a single Zeke; and at that moment his second section saw 10 Zekes and Hamps (the action was still going north), and went after them. Hedrick and Schanuel were soon after joined by a pair from the other division (Lts(jg) Cordray and Cunningham) and all four continued north after the Zekes; but in spite of several passes they were unable to get any definite hits. Cordray and Cunningham were separated from Hedrick's section after 2 passes.

"Combat lasts about a split second long. If you don't get them and you try and look for them, there's nobody there. It just happens so fast and is over so quick. It's usually real fast action, then you're the hell out of there". Recalls Dan Cunningham.

At a point about due west of Buka passage, Hedrick turned back. He joined Schanuel off the southern end of Bougainville. Schanuel landed at Barakoma, Vella Lavella, out of gas. Hedrick returned to Ondongo.

Schanuel followed Hedrick down in his original attack on the Lufbury circle. He saw a straggler outside the Jap formation and got on his tail. He fired at 100 yards from dead astern, and the Zeke caught fire and went into a steep dive through the clouds. Schanuel was now at 20,000 ft. He headed due east, climbing to gain altitude, and at 25,000 ft. was over Empress Augusta Bay. He circled for a few minutes, saw 3 F4Us (Hedrick, Anderson, and Chasnoff), and joined them.

This reformed division went west to gain altitude, and then turned on the Zekes again. Hedrick dove on a Zeke with Schanuel on his wing. Schanuel fired but over led. Immediately after this he saw a Zeke coming in on his tail. He pushed over and escaped the Zeke's fire. In his dive he fired at another Zeke but saw his tracers going underneath the plane. He pulled up sharply, climbed, and looked for Hedrick. He saw no other F4Us and headed for home. On the way he was joined by Hedrick. Schanuel landed at Barakoma, Vella Lavella, with 7 gallons of fuel in his tank. After refueling he returned to Ondongo.

In the initial attack on the Jap fighters the second section of Hedrick's division (Lts(jg) Anderson and Chasnoff) followed him down (distance 500 yards) in his dive on the Lufbury circle. The section fired on a Hamp, who turned out of the circle. Anderson and Chasnoff followed. Anderson was dead on his tail, and fired from 500 to 150 yards astern until the Hamp exploded.

By this time the Jap circle had broken and Zekes and Hamps were all over the sky.

Anderson and Chasnoff (working as a pair) made 8 or 9 passes, each pass being preceded by a chandelle. They got on the tail of one Zeke, had him in their sights, fired; but he turned into a cloud.

Hedrick then called them to join up with him, and the division was again complete. When Hedrick made his run on a single Zeke, Anderson and Chasnoff turned away to attack a flight of 10. As they were pursuing the flight they saw a single Zeke heading for a cloud, and started after him. The Zeke did a split-S as Anderson fired. Anderson circled and went after him. At this time only one gun was shooting. Chasnoff followed Anderson. The Zeke turned left, Chasnoff started a run—but only 2 guns were firing and his sight went out. The Zeke disappeared in a cloud.

Zekes were again observed heading north and the pair started after them. The chase went on for about 30 miles, with the F4Us starting 3 miles astern of the enemy and gaining on them all the time. A new bogey was reported on course 295°. Anderson and Chasnoff turned and made contact with this group of Zekes. They fired at one, who disappeared into a cloud. At this moment 2 Zekes came down on Anderson's tail. He did a split-S and the Zekes followed him. Chasnoff started an S after them, when he was jumped from behind by 4 Zekes. His rudder cable was shot away. He nosed over and dove for the clouds below with the Zekes after him. His extremely high speed allowed him to escape them. He then found Anderson and the pair proceeded back to base at 3,000 ft.

During the attack on Chasnoff, Anderson was still under attack by the 2 Zekes who had followed him down in his split-S. He saw many tracers passing over his wings, and realized he was bore sighted. He was then at 6,000 ft., heading S.E. He nosed over, lowered his seat, and pulled away at 320 knots. He then joined Chasnoff and returned to base.

NARROW ESCAPE

Jack Chasnoff had good reason to remember this mission.

"The only narrower escape I had than the carrier landing was the incident over Bougainville when 'Andy' and I had chased a Zero back toward Rabaul thinking that we were going to out fly him and be in a position to shoot him down. Suddenly we were attacked by 4 Zeros from above. In jest, I said when telling the story that we had these 4 Zeros cornered for a moment or two!

"They were firing at us and Andy saw them first and did a split-S to get out of the way, and as I started to do exactly the same thing, just as I rolled over on my back their fire hit the tail section of my plane and severed the control cable for my rudder. I had no idea what had happened, except that I heard a sound like a sledgehammer hitting my plane when those bullets hit and I thought my tail had been shot off, because the rudder pedal just collapsed under my foot. I was in the process of giving it full left rudder and suddenly the rudder pedal went all the way to the firewall. I looked up and I could see all 4 of them with their 20mm cannon winking. Apparently they had sighted in with their tracer bullets and the

Roger Hedrick and his plane. An exceptional fighter pilot and Naval Officer. Courtesy U.S. Naval Historical Center / M.W. "Butch" Davenport Collection.

7.7mm guns that they used and had pushed the switch that they carried to cut the cannons in when they thought they were getting hits. I could see these cannons winking at me and knew that things were not the way I wanted them to be!

"I was in a dive at the time and I really hit the panic button and decided that the only thing for me to do was get out of the airplane. Well I forgot that in order to get out of the airplane one of the first things you have to do is open the hatch and the second thing is to release your safety harness. I didn't do either. I was about to claw my way out through the canopy, when I began to realize that they were not hitting me anymore. I looked back, saw that they were following. I looked ahead and saw a cloud and I figured I'm going to wait until I get through that cloud before I bail out because I didn't like the idea of being a target for 4 hungry Zeros.

"I went into the cloud in a very steep dive, came out of the cloud down below and decided it was time to level off, and to my amazement, when I pulled back on the stick the plane began to recover. The tail section was intact, the elevators were working fine. I pulled out of the dive and began plans to bail out in somewhat more organized fashion. I called the Mayday signal and opened the hatch, undid the safety harness. I looked back and they were not chasing me anymore. I thought it over, decided well the smart thing for me to do is to fly as close to my base as I can and then bail out, and I headed back toward the base.

"I discovered that I had control of the plane. On the way back I met Anderson who was looking for me. He joined up on me and I asked him to look at my tail section. He told me that it was apparently all there, which was very reassuring to me.

"He joined up on me, this time he was on my wing, and we started back toward the base. Our route took us over a small island, I think it was called Treasury Island, which had a heavy enemy anti-aircraft installation. We all knew about it and all avoided that island.

"This time I was so involved with my own private thoughts about what had almost just happened to me that I took a course that was leading me directly over this island. I noticed as we got closer to this island that Andy was moving off to the right and increasing the distance between us. I wondered about it a little but I kept on a steady course because I knew I was headed back toward our base. After a minute or so of this with Andy moving farther out to the right, he picked up his microphone and said to me, 'What's the matter Jack, you want to get your ass shot off!'

I suddenly came to my senses and slid off to the right to join up on Andy.

"I would have flown directly over it at relatively low altitude and I would have been a sitting duck if he hadn't pointed out to me that was a pretty stupid thing to be doing. Anyhow I told Andy to land first because I was afraid of what was going to happen if I tried to land.

"I was debating between bailing out or trying to make a landing. I opened the hatch again and that slipstream was so strong that I didn't think that I really wanted to undertake to bail out of the airplane. The more I thought about it the more I decided I'd rather they scrape this airplane off the runway than have to fish me out of the sea. So I got permission for a straight-in approach and I discovered as I made my approach that I could in fact maintain a little rudder pedal with the tab control. The tab was working although the rudder cable itself was not. I screwed the tab control to put on as much left rudder as I could and I countered that with actual right rudder because my right rudder pedal was working and I was able to make a landing. I could hardly taxi because both of my feet were so far forward to reach the brakes that I had to lower the seat and I couldn't see very well to taxi. Fortunately my plane captain met me as the plane slowed down and he directed me in. Looking over the wing I could see where he was.

"The whole thing was a very harrowing experience for me. If you are making a list of harrowing experiences I think it belongs on the list!"

In the initial attack on the Zekes in the Lufbury Lts(jg) Cordray and Cunningham (the only pair in the second division who had taken station) stayed up as directed by Lt. Cdr. Hedrick. Their altitude was 29,000 ft. They saw 6 Zekes slightly above them and to their left. The F4Us scissored and none of the Zekes made an attack.

As these Zekes turned away Cordray decided to lead the pair down into the fight below him. They went down in S turns, and saw 4 Zekes at about 20,000 ft. and one straggler. Cordray and Cunningham sneaked up behind the straggler, and at 150 yards Cordray opened fire. A puff of smoke was seen on the Zeke's fuselage.

Cordray had to pull up abruptly to avoid collision with the Jap, and Cunningham got on the Jap's tail. He stayed on him during 3 shallow S turns. The Zeke began to give out black smoke and disappeared into a cloud.

Dan Cunningham recalls his first kill: "On the way home we ran into a stray and got him and joined back up and one time I think I was with Paul and he made a run on him and he thought he was smoking. I blasted him, but I wasn't sure I got him either. So we stayed there and watched him go into the water. I said to Paul. 'What do you want to do, Share him'. He said. 'No it's yours'. I think that was my first one. As a wingman you don't get a lot of shots. If you are a section or a division leader you get a hell of a lot more shots".

Cunningham rejoined Cordray and almost immediately they were attacked by 12 to 15 Zekes. The Zekes worked in pairs, and the attacks were apparently co-ordinated. The F4U's scissored and began climbing from 16,000 ft. to 21,000 ft. They were then above the Zekes and made several passes. As Cordray was recovering from a pass he saw what he took to be an enemy plane, and started towards it. Cunningham recognized it as an F4U and called to Cordray not to shoot.

They then joined up with the new plane (Hedrick) and his wingman (Schanuel) and with them made 2 passes (see above). After the second pass they lost Hedrick's section. They then saw 2 Zekes below them (at about 15,000 ft.) on their port quarter.

Cunningham attacked, the leading Zeke turned in towards him, and Cunningham fired into him on an opposite course run. The Zeke burst into flames as he swept past. Cunningham pulled up in a

L-R. *"Andy" Anderson and "Timmy" Gile. Ondongo, November 1943.* Courtesy U.S. Naval Historical Center / M.W. "Butch" Davenport Collection.

right chandelle, and with Cordray, followed the burning Zeke for several thousand feet—until it was obvious the plane was destroyed. As their gas was running low they turned home and landed a few minutes after Hedrick.

Dan Cunningham remembers this mission.

"I was up with Rog and his 4 and then Paul Cordray was supposed to have his 4 but only 2 of us were there. I mean 1 besides Paul and that was me. So instead of having 8 we had 6.

"They had bogies coming in and he tore out there to beat the band and there was a whole raft of them coming. As soon as they said buster, I thought my God here we go. It was a little bit twitchy as they say and you tend to make a doughnut out of your parachute. You know what I mean, its a little tightening.

"Well, Paul was on him and was diving and he overran him. Then I Jumped over and got on him and he caught on fire, then went on in."

Schanuel shot down one Zeke; Anderson shot down one Zeke; Cunningham shot down one Zeke, and with Cordray damaged another Zeke. Hedrick damaged three Zekes. Chasnoff's plane was hit by 7.7s from a Zeke, which shot away his rudder cable. All planes returned safely to base.

The following report was submitted by Lt. Cdr. R.R. Hedrick after this mission.

TACTICS ON ESCORT MISSIONS

The Jap fighter planes are using 6 plane divisions with the sections flying a flat ABC. The high cover planes have been 10,000 feet above the bombers they were covering, with no medium cover in evidence. When cruising the fighter planes fly a straight course, holding their positions on the bombers until our planes are sighted.

The divisions were in the following positions when observed: one slightly ahead, two on each flank, and one astern of the bombers. Another division, not sighted by me, was reported to have been 5,000 feet above and down sun from the main fighter formation.

The main force of high cover planes have been at 22,000 feet and the bombers at 12,000 feet on both occasions observed (November 5th and 7th). It was reported that the Jap fighters providing low cover joined up with the bombers, and when our planes attacked, the fighters would sometimes pull up in a loop and come back on our planes with good results for the Japs.

When the Jap fighters sight our planes the divisions go into column and start sweeping S turns; and when any division is attacked others tail in, forming a loose Lufbury circle. The entire group of Jap fighters remained on the defensive throughout a thirty minute fight, making no attempt to climb or launch an attack of their own, even though the odds were at least 5 to 1 in their favor. Even when our planes were split up with one plane making runs on from 4 to 6 of them, they remained on the defensive. Although we made at least twenty head-on runs on which we fired, the Japs did not attempt to pull up or push over even slightly to return the fire.

When a run was started on a plane in a Jap division, the entire division (in column) would turn toward the attack and the individual plane fired on would usually roll over sharply to the right and go down in a vertical dive, with the remaining planes continuing the turn and in a position to follow our fighter down if he should follow the Jap plane into his dive. If not followed down, the Jap plane would pull back in a steep wing over and rejoin his division (Good chance to catch them at top of wing over.)

On two occasions when the top cover was not sighted by our pilots, they held their altitude (at 22,000 ft.) until our planes had made some runs on the bombers and were well split up before coming down out of the sun to attack our planes.

It is the opinion of the writer (Hedrick) that the Japanese have gone in extensively for formation flying, which they do well, and that either their pilots are very inexperienced or have definite orders not to make any maneuver which would make formation flying too difficult—unless they are actually attacked. The sections (2 planes) never split unless one is attacked, in which case he rolls over as given above.

9 November
One negative 2-hour patrol (4 sorties) was flown over Munda.
Eight F4Us flew a negative 2-hour patrol over Task Group 39.
Four negative 2-hour patrols (23 sorties) were flown over Empress Augusta Bay, Bougainville. At the conclusion of the third patrol the following pilots, as directed, strafed the mouths of the Laruma and Jaba Rivers where Jap troop concentrations were reported. The flight made numerous strafing runs, flying at tree-top level, but no actual targets were observed.

Lt. Cdr. R.R. Hedrick	Lt(jg) D.G. Cunningham
Lt(jg) M. Schanuel	Lt(jg) P. Cordray
Lt(jg) R.S. Anderson	Ens. B.W. Baker
Lt(jg) J.M. Chasnoff	Lt. C.D. Gile*

*Returned early -engine trouble.

No A/A fire was encountered. It is believed that a Jap sniper stationed at the top of a coconut palm fired on the flight and succeeded in hitting the windshield of Ens. Baker's plane. Baker strafed the tree with approximately 1800 rounds and thereby chopped it down.

After strafing for about ten minutes, the flight returned to base.

10 November
Two negative 2-hour patrols (8 sorties) were flown over Munda.

Twenty-four F4Us took off from Ondongo and made rendezvous with the SBDs and TBFs off West Cape, Choiseul Island. The formation proceeded up along the N.E. coast of Bougainville with the F4Us flying at altitude from 15,000 to 21,000 feet.

When the formation arrived at Buka, there was an overcast 8/10 cover. The bombing attack was fairly successful, several hits being observed on the runway and revetment areas.

After the attack the F4Us as directed, proceeded down the N.E. coast of Bougainville at about 5,000 feet to search for enemy shipping. No shipping seen, but one pilot reported a possible seaplane ramp on the west side of Bakawari Island.

RETURN TO THE BUNKER HILL

11 November
The following pilots acted as cover over Task Force 50.3 (U.S.S. Bunker Hill, Essex, Independence, and DD screen) east of Bougainville:

Lt. Cdr. J.T. Blackburn	Lt. Cdr. R.R. Hedrick	Lt. C.A. Pillsbury	Lt. T.R. Bell
Lt(jg) D.H. Gutenkunst	Lt(jg) M. Schanuel	Ens. R.R. Hogan	Lt(jg) H.M. Burriss
Ens. F.J. Streig	Lt(jg) R.S. Anderson	Lt(jg) R.H. Jackson	Ens. I.C. Kepford
Lt(jg) T. Killefer	Lt(jg) J.M. Chasnoff	Lt. L.D. Cooke	
		Lt. J.M. Kleinman	Lt. C.D.Gile
		Lt(jg) C.W.Gilbert	Lt(jg) D.G. Cunningham
		Lt(jg) G.F. Bowers	Lt(jg) P. Cordray
		Ens. R.H.Hill	Ens. B.W. Baker

Tom Blackburn had vivid memories of this day: "I was told 2 days beforehand, highly classified that we would be flying out from Ondongo to land aboard the carriers out in the Solomon Sea for their raid against Rabaul.

"We had taken the arresting hooks off the aircraft to lighten them and I had to go back and tip my hand somewhat by telling the maintenance gang to install the hooks and check them out to see if they worked properly. It didn't take any great genius to figure out that some carrier operations were coming up. I had to keep my yap shut as far as the squadron was concerned until the night before and then I was able to brief them as to what our commitment was. That was: me to take 12 planes to land on and operate from the Bunker Hill; and Rog to take 12 to land and operate from the Essex which were the two big carriers involved in that raid.

We went out as a 24-plane unit, got over the ships, everything was blacked out of course, but we were able to locate them with radio signals. We were overhead about 5 o'clock in the morning and we operated as a combat air patrol over the ships.

"As dawn broke they launched their first strike of the day into Rabaul which was about 200 miles from the carriers."

George Mauhar was the Crew Chief at the time of this mission. He describes his part in it:

VF-17 ace "Timmy" Gile at Ondongo, November 1943. Courtesy U.S. Navy photo. Robert L. Lawson Collection.

"We operated out of Ondongo. We got there and about a week or so later the Engineering Officer Davenport, said, 'We don't need tailhooks anymore. Take anything out that will lighten the planes.' The crew took all the tailhooks off and laid them alongside the revetment, and the gun heaters. They didn't require those so we took them out. About 2-3 weeks later Davenport said, 'We're going to have to put the tailhooks back on.' They needed to land aboard carriers to refuel to support a mission to Rabaul.

"I thought, oh my God, what did we do with all the tailhooks. They were laying out there all rusting. I got the crew together and said we got to put those hooks on. We found them all. They were laying in mud, water, etc. We had to test them by putting the planes in a flight attitude and then use a scale to test the pull on them so they didn't bounce when they land. We got them all on and, fortunately they all worked".

"Rabaul being out of the range of our bases at Ondongo at that time, none of our planes could get to Rabaul and back home. So a task force was sent in". Roger Hedrick remembers.

"Operating off the carriers Bunker Hill and Essex the squadron's mission was to provide cover for the carriers while their squadrons escorted bombers to Rabaul. We flew out in early morning darkness through rain squalls to rendezvous with the Carrier Task Force of the Bunker Hill, Essex and Independence and 9 destroyers, who were steaming towards the giant base at Rabaul to launch a strike by their air groups on Rabaul". Said Robert "Windy" Hill.

Roger Hedrick again recalls:

"We circled overhead and watched while they launched the strikes from those 3 carriers. We were well aware of the fact that as we landed aboard ship, that we were there for one reason; to protect this task force from what was going to be a large raid coming in by the Japanese from Rabaul. They were going to do everything they could and here they had an opportunity to get 3 of our carriers. So we knew that we could expect everything they could throw at us would be coming our way shortly."

Dan Cunningham relates his part on this eventful day:

"It starts at the top. He (Tom) was great. He was one that did it then said go do it. He had the most hours of flying in the whole squadron. He always volunteered for the pre-dawn missions. I remember one time the day we were going to land on the carrier they had to put tailhooks on our planes. The strike was going in to hit Rabaul and we went out to rendezvous with them so that as soon as they launched the strike force we went in and landed, and had lunch. About the time they were due back they launched us to protect them while they took their own boys aboard. I was flying along and I looked down and I was flying on 2 P-40s. I just joined up on the exhaust of the P-40s. I turned on my I.F.F. to find the ship. Eventually I found them and landed. I ended up with a different lot and not on the Bunker Hill. We refueled and then they launched us. I mean they brought everything the Japs had. A hell of a lot of airplanes flying around.

There were 5 of us together and they vectored us out after a bogey. One plane for 5 of us. He led us down to the water full throttle staying behind him. Jim finally blasted him and then we had to climb full throttle again. We used so much gas. I kept leaning back my mixture as I was using so much gas. One time this worm starts to come out of my cowling. I had burned out the exhaust. I had leaned it so thin and run it so hot. I eased off a little so I didn't blow my engine. By the time we got home there couldn't have been more than vapors in the gas tank".

The action as far as VF17 was concerned may be divided into two operations. The first consisted of a 24 plane cover (plus 12 F6Fs from VF33) over Task Force 50.3 (Bunker Hill, Essex, Independence, and destroyer escort) from dawn until it was necessary to land aboard and refuel. During this period the carriers launched their strike on Rabaul. The second operation was to fly cover over the Task Force while it landed its returning planes and retired to the south. It was during this second operation that the Japs in four waves, attacked the Task Force.

Twenty-four F4Us took off from Ondongo between 1700 and 1720. One plane was forced to return because of a late take off and consequent failure to find the others.

Lt. Kleinman's flight found the ships at 1815, but the others overshot. As the visibility was poor (broken clouds at 1,000 to 3,000 ft.) and for some reason the Bunker Hill and Essex did not have their YE equipment turned on, Lt. Cdr. Blackburn's and Lt. Cdr. Hedrick's flights did not find the carriers until 1900.

During their search, however, these flights were actually within 15-20 miles of the Task Force.

The carriers launched their planes between 1945 and 2045. At 2130 the shore based fighters began to land aboard the carriers (11 F4Us aboard the Essex, 12 F4U's aboard the Bunker Hill, and 12 F6Fs aboard the Independence) and completed the landing operation in 15 minutes.

Tom Blackburn remembers landing back on the Bunker Hill again:

"We landed aboard, refueled and re-armed and had breakfast. After eating from an Army mess with spam, battery acid and scrambled eggs made from powdered eggs which was something less than superb. We had linen tablecloths, orange juice, corned beef hash and poached eggs and if you excuse the expression 'living like white folks.'

"One of the notable things about this was that we had not made any carrier landings since before leaving the states in early September and we put 12 on the Bunker Hill and 12 on the Essex without getting waveoffs. Every approach was right the first time so that we got a cut and there were no blown tires and scraped wing tips. No damage whatsoever and the people on the ships couldn't believe that we could turn in such a smooth performance after 2 months lay-off.

"After a couple of hours aboard ship we were launched when the strike group was coming back from Rabaul, took up position over the carrier task force to defend against enemy air attack. The returning strike group landed back aboard and the Japs, as expected, followed the returning strike with a dive-bombing and torpedo attack covered by fighters. They sent in approximately 100 aircraft and we were their principal opposition, 24 of us plus 12 Hellcats which were based on a light carrier.

"The 36 fighters were the opposition to the incoming Jap strike. The melee was beyond description. The carriers had to land their airplanes while the Japs were pressing home their attack. Anti-air-

"Butch" Davenport in the cockpit of his Corsair, with one of his ground-crew. Courtesy Lennard Edmisten.

craft fire was not suppressed because there were friendlies around. The anti-aircraft fired at anything that was in the air, including us of course, and it was in the course of this action, that if memory serves me correct Kepford got 4 kills. I got one kill.

"In any event we lost one airplane and the pilot was recovered, we had bullet holes in quite a few including mine. But the carriers received no damage whatsoever, and after the action was over a few people were so low on gas that they had to land on the carriers to refuel so they could get home."

The fighters were refueled and rearmed, and took off from the carriers at 2330. Lts(jg) Gilbert and Bowers were sent back to Ondongo as Gilbert's guns would not charge. Lt(jg) Killefer's starter was broken and he did not take off until 0245, at which time he could not find the other fighters and, after a futile search, returned to Ondongo. That meant that at midnight 20 F4Us were covering the Task Force.

At 0030 the first real bogey was reported. At this time Royal Base (the main F.D., based aboard the Essex) had vectored 4 of the 5 F4U divisions far out from the Task Force after a bogey which turned out to be the shore-based F6Fs; Red Base (based aboard the Independence) thus had one division of F4Us under his control. This division (Lt(jg) Cordray, Ens. Baker, Ens. Streig, Lt(jg) Cunningham) was vectored out (330° at 20,000 ft.; 157° at 23,000 ft.; 60° at 23,000 ft.) and at about 0045 Ens. Streig spotted a Tony on his port bow on an opposite course and at the same level. Streig (with Cunningham on his wing) immediately turned and pursued the Tony in a 30° dive, overtaking him rapidly.

The Tony levelled at 10,000 ft., then pushed over in a 45° dive to 200 ft. Streig levelled out behind him and fired from 300 yards astern. After a short burst the Tony exploded. The division then reformed and climbed to about 20,000 ft. The action had occurred about 10 miles north of the Task Force.

"Big Jim" Streig recalls this action: "I was on a combat station at about 20,000 feet northeast of the carrier and the radar picked up a bogey coming in from the northeast. I was sent out to intercept him and investigate and I had a four plane division. We caught up with the bogey and he immediately dove and headed for the water and we took off after him and chased him down to an altitude of about 500 feet and then made a run behind him and blew him up on the water. He didn't get back but he had already radioed our position to the Japanese.

It was the first Jap in-line engine Tony shot down in the South Pacific Islands."

Dan Cunningham was Streig's wingman on this eventful day:

"The flight control officer on the ship knows who's up there and where, and he would vector us out. They'd pick them up way out and we'd supposed to get them before they got to the carriers. There was a single fighter coming in, finally we see him and we all dove down and Jim Streig who happened to be leading it and we followed him all the way down to the water and then finally he shot him and he blew up.

"Then we had to climb like heck because by that time there's jillions of them coming out after us. It got so bad that you didn't have to be vectored as they were already in sight and we were after them."

For the next 2 hours Cordray's division orbited over the ships or pursued negative bogies. At about 0230 Red Base sent them out on a vector of 340° at 23,000 ft (at this time the F4Us had been in the air for 3 hours). When the division was about 15 miles from the Task Force the enemy force was sighted off the starboard beam on a S.E. course. It consisted of 3 groups of Vals and Kates (40-50 aircraft) at 18,000 ft., and about 50-60 fighters (Zekes, Hamps and Tonys) stacked from 20,000 ft. to 25,000 ft. Cordray immediately called Royal Base and the other F4U divisions.

Royal Base replied that the planes sighted were friendly and that Cordray should continue on out on a course of 340°. Just as Cordray's division started to obey this order they saw the bombers push over, and turned after them. Cordray and Baker attacked one group of fighters and Streig and Cunningham attacked a different group, both attacks being simultaneous.

"Big Jim" Streig again describes his part in this eventful mission: "As we were climbing back weaving in and out of the clouds and we looked up to the left and we saw these square-wing-tipped planes and I thought to myself, the F6Fs are up there. All of a sudden I realized the F6Fs were on the deck and there weren't any up there.

"We looked again and we saw the whole Japanese force coming in from Rabaul and Buka toward the carriers and at that time I was about 15-16,000 feet. I called the C.I.C. (fighter control) on Bunker Hill and told them to hold their hats because the shit was about to hit the fan! We immediately pulled up and started to climb and got above them and intercepted them and I got one more and two more probables and started running out of fuel and had to go back to the beach. They couldn't take me on the carrier because there was so much going on. My wingman at that time was Danny Cunningham and he had thrown an exhaust stack through his cowling and gone back and I was up there by myself.

"So I headed back toward Ondongo and managed to reach Vella Lavella got in the landing pattern and landed and I was going down on the taxiway and my engine quit. I just got back, thank goodness. One of the boys dropped in the water on the other side of the island.

A rare photo of "Ike" Kepford in plane #7 early in the game. Most of the photos of Kepford were with plane #29. Courtesy U.S. Naval Historical Center / M.W. "Butch" Davenport Collection.

It was quite a fiasco that day. There was probably close to 150 airplanes coming out to intercept the task force. We were airborne for about 3.5 to 4 hours of which about 2.5 hours was hectic combat before I left it. Some of it still went on after I departed but I had made 2 climbs to altitude and used a lot of fuel."

When attacked the Zekes turned towards the F4Us. Streig shot at 2, missed, did a chandelle to the left (losing his wingman in the process) and made a head-on run at 3 Zekes who dove out away from him. Streig saw another group of 8 or 12 Zekes at about 24,000 ft., and nearer the ships. He climbed to 26,000 ft. and made a high side run on a Zeke, coming in on his tail in a 20° dive. He saw his bullets go into the cockpit. The Zeke pulled up sharply, went into a spin and crashed into the water. Several Zekes and Hamps were now on Streig's tail and he climbed, using full power, to 28,000 ft. The Zekes stalled out at 26,000 ft. From his altitude advantage Streig made several passes at the Zekes and Hamps, all runs being head-on. He caught a Zeke breaking away and shot a foot and a half off his rudder, and fired at a Hamp, seeing pieces fly off a wing. After this last pass he turned home and landed at Barakoma, Vella Lavella at 0435 with 15 gallons of gas (Cunningham was forced to leave Streig immediately before Streig shot down his second plane. He returned to Ondongo, pancaking at 0450).

Cordray and Baker made an attack on 2 Zekes, as Streig made his second attack.

Cordray missed, chandelled to the left, and lost Baker, who had chandelled to the right. Cordray made a second run (high side from 25,000 ft. to 20,000 ft.) and put a good burst into a Zeke's engine. He lost sight of the Zeke, but it was probably destroyed. He made one more pass at the Zekes without getting a chance to shoot, pulled up and found Baker in the clouds. They headed for home; Cordray landed at Barakoma at 1545 with his gas gauge registering zero (he had 70 gallons when the fight began), Baker made a water landing nearby.

Baker had more luck than Cordray on their initial pass at the 2 Zekes. Cordray fired at the leader and missed, but Baker got several good bursts into the wingman, saw his bullets go into the Zeke's engine and the plane go down in flames. Baker looked for Cordray, couldn't find him, but saw 10 Zekes. As he was climbing away from them the ships fired on him and he had to dive out of danger.

He climbed again and made 2 more passes on Zekes. After his second pass he joined up on Cordray and started for home at 120 k indicated. To lighten his plane Baker fired all his ammunition. Just over Wilson Strait his engine stopped. He nosed over, picked up 130 k and brought the plane down on the water in a stall, time 0500. He had no trouble getting out of the plane (which floated for 5 minutes) and by great good fortune a Dumbo landed just beside his plane. He was taken ashore at Barakoma.

While Cordray's division was being controlled by Red Base (U.S.S. Independence) the other four divisions were under the control of Royal Base (U.S.S. Essex). They orbited at different altitudes and were sent on several vectors from 2330 until about 0230. At this time they were vectored out at 14,000 ft. on a course of 180°. When they were about 10 miles from the Task Force, Lt. Cdr. Blackburn, leading the first division, saw a Tony on his starboard beam headed north at 10,000 ft. next to a large cumulus cloud. The Tony apparently sighted the F4Us, for he dropped his detachable wing tanks, and started a steep dive and a gentle turn into the cloud. Blackburn overtook him very rapidly (his rate of closing being about 60 or 70 k). He fired at a range of 350 yards, but missed. He closed to 250 yards, fired, and saw the left wing root catch fire. The Tony spun into the water in flames.

Tom Blackburn describes the engagement: "As dawn broke they launched their first strike of the day into Rabaul which was about 200 miles from the carriers. After the strike was clear we had one Jap snooper, a Tony fighter. The fighter director on the Essex vectored us out. I shot down this Tony, I had to race Kepford to get to it first, but that was the only opposition that we had at that time, if you can call that opposition. The poor bastard didn't have a chance with 24 Corsairs after him!"

The four divisions then reformed and were told to orbit base at 22,000 ft. At about 0245 they were vectored out 20 miles on a course of 340° and told to orbit.

At about 0300, seeing heavy A/A fire from the Task Force, they turned and headed towards the ships at full speed. Blackburn saw 2 F4Us make runs on 2 Zekes and miss. He and his wingman started after the Zekes, who saw them and went into a steep dive.

Blackburn followed the Zeke section leader, who did a right half roll at 8,000 ft. Blackburn pulled out at 6,000 ft. He saw the Zeke below him at 500 ft., headed for a cloud 3 or 4 miles away. Blackburn closed from above, fired at about 500 yards and missed. He closed to 300 yards, fired again, and saw smoke stream from the right wing. At this point the Zeke entered the cloud. Through gaps in the clouds Blackburn got in 2 more bursts, then his windshield fogged up and he broke off. At this point he was alone, his wingman having lost him.

Blackburn saw 4 Tonys above him at 5,000 ft. (he at 1,500 ft.) so he re-entered the cloud. One Tony followed and Blackburn turned in the cloud and the Tony broke off. As Blackburn came out of the cloud he saw 2 F4Us on his port beam (Hedrick and Schanuel). Hedrick, mistaking Blackburn for an enemy, fired a short burst, then perceived his mistake, and the 3 F4Us joined up.

Tom Blackburn remembered this incident:

"What I saw was groups of Japanese aircraft emerging from both sides of a huge thunderhead. It consisted of about 40 Jap fighters and what looked to be 30-35 Jap dive bombers. So I set up on the leader of the Japanese fighter flight, feeling that if I could knock him down this would be a maximum disorganization. Unfortunately when he saw me coming early enough he dove out and I got sucked into following him. I couldn't catch him and he pulled into a cloud and I levelled out at around 3000ft. I'd lost my wingman in the process and the windshield and the canopy were so cold from the altitude that they fogged over to absolutely solid.

"So I ducked into a cloud to give the glassware a chance to warm up and once that happened I stuck my nose out of the cloud again and spotted 6 Japanese Tonys who saw me come out of the cloud. The flight leader was rocking his wings and starting into a dive mighty close. I was terrified I had the impression of being killed any minute. I hooked the plane around as tight as I could and ducked back into a cloud. I really expected to be nailed then so I came out of the cloud and as I did I saw 2 Corsairs and the lead Corsair's guns opened up."

The lead Corsair was none other than Roger Hedrick, who remembers: "I spotted one Jap Zeke trying to head back to Rabaul and I took after him. Just as I got into firing position he goes into a big cloud. I chased him into another one, out he came, I chased him back and I thought he was coming out again and it was a full deflection shot, the plane was coming out crossing ahead and I was squeezing the trigger, and my God that's a Hog."

"It was a beautiful shot 3 bullets through the accessory section and 3 behind the armor plates at the back of the seat." said Tom Blackburn.

"Low and behold who's in this plane and what plane is it but "Big Hog" Tommy Blackburn, and old Tommy's giving me this hey you lousy shot. Thank God I was a lousy shot."

They swung around north of the Task Force, saw no A/A or enemy planes, and returned to Barakoma, being joined by Burriss over the Treasury Islands. All 4 landed at Barakoma at 0440.

Lt(jg) Gutenkunst, Blackburn's wingman, followed Blackburn down after the 2 Zekes. He picked the Jap wingman, fired at long range, but lost him in the clouds. Gutenkunst climbed to 12,000 ft., saw the ships' A/A fire, and looked for the enemy attack. He saw 6 Kates, low on the water, heading north, but too far for him to reach. The A/A fire ceased, he joined up on Anderson and Chasnoff, and returned to Barakoma, landing at 0530.

Lt. Kleinman and Lt(jg) Burriss, the second section of Lt. Cdr. Blackburn's division, turned back towards the Task Force with the other F4Us when they realized that the enemy attack had been launched. They were spiraling down looking for enemy planes and saw 2 Zekes at 10,000 ft. but too far away to attack. They went down to the water and almost immediately Burriss saw a Betty pursued by a group of F6Fs. Burriss turned abruptly to intercept (losing Kleinman) and closed in on the Betty. He got in a long burst from 7 o'clock level and the Betty went into the water.

Burriss pulled up to the left, saw another F4U at 3,000 ft. (Lt. Cooke) and joined up. The pair spotted a Kate making a run on a ship. Each made 2 beam runs.

Cooke broke them off, but Burriss made another beam run, chopped back on his throttle and ran right up on the Kate's tail. At about 1,000 yards from the ship the Kate burst into flames and went into the water.

Burriss pulled up and saw a Kate heading north right on the water. Burriss came down in a beam run and simultaneously an F6F made a beam run from 9 o'clock. The Kate struck the water and exploded. Burriss then climbed to 6,000 ft. but saw no enemy

"Chico" Freeman with his F4U-1A, L.A. City Limits. Courtesy U.S. Navy photo. Robert L. Lawson Collection.

planes. He joined up on Gile and being low on gas, headed for home. He landed at Barakoma with 25 gallons at 0430.

When Burriss broke off to attack the Betty, Kleinman saw about 8 Kates at 500 ft. heading for the Task Force. He made one unsuccessful run on the leading plane, recovered in a quick wing over, got on his tail, fired, and the Kate caught fire and crashed into the water. This took place just inside the destroyer screen, and the Kate had not dropped her torpedo. Kleinman continued in over the screen, saw another Kate to his left, and made a beam run from 4 o'clock. As he was recovering for a second pass he was hit by a 40mm shell from one of the ships. The shell exploded and blew up his instrument panel, wounding him in the face. Kleinman turned to get out of the screen and was jumped by 2 F6Fs. They made head on runs, and hit his wing. Since he had no instruments, Kleinman navigated by the sun back to Barakoma, landing at 0445.

Lt. Pillsbury's division (Lt. Pillsbury, Ens. Hill, Ens. Hogan, and Lt(jg) Jackson) turned towards the Task Force when they heard it was under attack.

Pillsbury's section stayed high until they saw a torpedo attack about to be launched.

They headed for 2 Kates but lost them in the clouds. They went back to 18,000 ft. on the west side of the Task Force and saw a dive bombing attack on the east side.

As they were too far away to intercept it they dove to the water in an attempt to find torpedo planes. They went over the screen, and just beyond Hill got on the tail of a Kate. He fired a long burst and the Kate caught fire and crashed into the water.

Robert "Windy" Hill remembers this engagement.

"After flying from our land base, Ondongo, New Georgia, for about 150 miles, our 23 F4U Corsair fighters rendezvoused with the carriers before first light.

"We then provided combat air patrol until the carrier air groups had been launched for an attack against the large Japanese Naval base at Rabaul. Immediately afterwards we landed aboard the Bunker Hill and the Essex, where we refueled and were airborne again while the carrier aircraft were returning from their strike on Rabaul.

"Japanese fighters, dive bombers, and torpedo bombers, in excess of one hundred, followed the returning Navy aircraft and commenced their attack on our fleet.

"Suddenly the sky was filled with a mass of turning, twisting, climbing, diving aircraft. It was a fantastic sight. The air seemed to be filled with black puffs of bursting five-inch A/A shells. Japanese aircraft were exploding and hitting the ocean engulfed in flames. It was a wild free-for-all, a survival of the fittest.

"I had plunged into this melee frantically seeking to intercept an enemy plane. Finally, I spotted a Kate torpedo bomber heading toward the Bunker Hill. I went into a high-speed dive, approaching from the left rear, ignoring the wall of anti-aircraft fire from our carriers that was exploding near the bomber. As I centered the Kate in my gun sight and commenced firing, I could see tracer bullets coming toward me from the enemy's rear-seat gunner. My bullets were hitting now, though, and suddenly the Japanese plane burst into a mass of flames, slowly turned upside down, and crashed into the ocean.

"I had just killed my first human beings—so how did I feel? I was engulfed in a wave of euphoria: I had just saved some mothers' sons, some wives' husbands, some little children's fathers aboard the carrier, from being blown to smithereens or incinerated—burned to a crisp in a holocaust of fire and explosions. I yelled with excitement—a modern version of the famed 'rebel yell' heard at Gettysburg.

"There is nothing more exciting or thrilling than aerial combat, where you kill the enemy pilot before he can kill you. Its not like a ball game where if you lose you can play again tomorrow. If you lose in this arena, there is no tomorrow!"

Hill and Pillsbury rejoined at 5,000 ft. and as Hill had only 62 gallons of gas, headed for Barakoma at 140 knots. Over the Treasury Islands Hill realized he could not make it, so he prepared for a water landing. At 400 ft. his engine cut off, he nosed over, and landed 250 yards off the south shore of Sterling Island at 0500. His plane spun around on the water, but floated for 30 seconds and he got out easily.

He inflated his life jacket and jettisoned his parachute. He got in his life raft and paddled to shore. A New Zealand battery sighted him and phoned for a boat. The boat was unable to locate him. He then tried to make a landing in his raft, but the strong surf and currents prevented him. He was finally picked up by a Higgins boat.

Robert"Windy" Hill has clear memories of this incident: "Finally, my fuel state required me to head for home. Flying across a seemingly endless expanse of ocean, I soon became concerned about whether or not I had sufficient fuel, because I was using fuel more rapidly than normal. I was afraid I had been hit and was slowly leaking gas.

"My emotions were on a roller coaster ride. Shortly before I had been to the heights, and now I had plunged to the depths as I was finally forced to accept that I wasn't going to make it to my base airfield.

"So what was I going to do? Drifting in a one man life raft across the empty Solomon Sea had little appeal for me.

"When you find yourself in this type of situation, you realize that there is no one in the whole wide world who can help you. You have to depend strictly on your own resources and abilities. You've got to rise to meet the occasion or no one will ever know what happened to you. You will be listed as an M.I.A.

"I decided to change course and head for Treasury Island, hoping to get near land before my gas was exhausted. I reviewed the ditching procedure (a euphemism for a controlled crash in the ocean). I told myself, 'Let's not screw this up because you only get one chance.'

"Finally the moment of truth arrived—and, considering this was my first water landing, it wasn't half bad.

"Immediately after hitting the water, I rapidly executed that most famous of military maneuvers known as: 'Let's get the hell out of here!' As I swam away, I watched my airplane disappear beneath the ocean's surface in about twenty seconds.

"I knew that New Zealand forces had landed on this island on October 27, but I didn't know how much territory they controlled, so I didn't know what kind of reception committee I would find ashore.

"A ragged looking man suddenly appeared out of the jungle as I floated a little ways offshore in my raft. My heart skipped a beat at first because I thought he was Japanese, but he semaphored the message, 'Help is on the way.' (Honestly, I really did read the semaphore). Shortly thereafter a boat came alongside and picked me up.

"That night, my New Zealand hosts who had rescued me provided me with a hammock, which I hung between two trees in the jungle.

"As I lay there with a rain shower coming down, I reviewed the events of the day. I recalled how I had left a safe, comfortable job as a junior gunnery officer aboard a battleship because the duty was not exciting enough for me—I wanted to be a Navy fighter pilot and be where the action was, so I resigned my commission in order to take flight training as an aviation cadet. 'Well,' I thought, 'Your desire for action was certainly granted today. In fact, you might have experienced a little more action than you really had in mind.' Finally I dropped off to sleep—thankful to be alive still—and slept like a baby".

Meanwhile Pillsbury had made radio contact with Terrier Base (Treasury Islands station) and had given him Hill's position. He then returned to Barakoma, landing at 0515 with 27 gallons. His was the last F4U to land.

When Hogan and Jackson (the second section in Pillsbury's division) heard the contact report they headed towards the Task Force at about 16,000 ft. They saw 6 Zekes at about 20,000 ft. The Zekes made no attempt to attack, but stayed up doing slow rolls.

"Andy" Jagger, "Duke" Henning, Bill Popp. New Georgia, 1943. Courtesy U.S. Naval Historical Center / M.W. "Butch" Davenport Collection.

Jackson then saw a single Zeke at his own altitude. The Zeke turned towards him and Jackson made a head on run. He saw his bullets go into the engine (his own right wing was hit by 2 7.7s) and the Zeke broke off and went into a steep dive. Hogan saw it crash into the water.

"Hal" Jackson recalls: "We took off real early, 0230 in the morning. After the air group took off we landed aboard, my group on the Essex and then they refueled us and everything then we took off and the Japs came back and weren't expecting to see any fighter cover.

"There were about 36 of us out there waiting for them. I think all of us shot down at least one or two Japs that day. I got one that day. After that we broke off and had to fly back to Ondongo and about 3 or 4 ran out of gas 5 or 6 miles before they got back.

"The first time I saw a Jap airplane I burned up all six of my guns. I got on his tail and fired until the plane exploded."

The section joined up and as Jackson had only 200 pounds of oxygen and 80 gallons of gas they headed for Barakoma, landing at 0440 with about 20 gallons each.

Lt. Cdr. Hedrick's division (Hedrick, Lts(jg) Schanuel, Anderson and Chasnoff) also turned towards the Task Force when the attack began. They approached, losing altitude (18,000 to 12,000 ft.) and saw 4 Zekes pursued by F4Us. Hedrick and Schanuel attacked one who dodged, and headed north. He was in a 45° dive with Hedrick on his tail when the latter fired (at 300 yards). Just as the Zeke entered a cloud it began to burn. Hedrick and Schanuel then joined with Blackburn (see above) and returned to Barakoma.

Lts(jg) Anderson and Chasnoff, the second section in Hedrick's division, spotted 2 Zekes before Hedrick saw his. They blipped their guns but were unable to attract his attention. They made a run (they at 20,000 ft., the Zekes at 17,000 ft.) and Anderson saw his incendiaries hitting the cockpit of one of the Zekes. Both Zekes pulled up in a loop. Chasnoff waited and fired at the Zeke (already hit at the top of his loop). The Zeke rolled out and started a dive, at which point Chasnoff lost him.

The pair then heard Royal Base reporting a torpedo attack. They went to 15,000 ft., saw no planes, and began to call Royal Base for information. They called repeatedly, but never received any answer. By this time the attack seemed to be over, so they headed for home, being joined by Gutenkunst and Cooke.

Chasnoff, Cooke, and Gutenkunst landed at Barakoma at 0430 with 15 gallons each.

Anderson landed at Ondongo at 0435 with 35 gallons.

Lt. Bell's division (Lt. Bell, Ens. Kepford, Lts Gile and Cooke) broke up just before the enemy attacked. Bell and Kepford (Bell with 130 gallons and Kepford with 120 gallons) headed for home at 0246.

Gile and Cooke heard the attack announced and spiralled down to water level about 2 miles north of the Task Force. They headed west and started a run on a Kate attacking a destroyer. They saw the Kate shot down by A/A fire and made a run on another. Gile was too fast and overran, and at this point lost his wingman.

He picked up a Kate heading for the Bunker Hill, made one run, pulled up too high and too fast, but chopped back his throttle and made another pass from 250 ft. He got in 2 bursts, saw the Kate

catch fire, gave it another burst and saw the Kate explode. During this run the A/A fire was intense. Gile saw another Kate going west and headed after him. An F6F got in first, and Gile turned back towards the ships. The attack seemed to be over, and the ship-borne fighters in the air, so Gile joined up with Burriss and both returned to Barakoma, landing at 0430. Gile had 20 gallons left when he landed.

When Gile separated from Cooke the latter climbed to 12,000 ft. He saw the second torpedo attack developing and went down to intercept. He made one run, missed, and climbed to 11,000 ft., where he joined Anderson and headed home, landing at Ondongo.

Bell and Kepford, as stated above, had headed for home at 0246. They saw the ships begin firing, turned back, and let down fast. They entered the fight over the Task Force just after the dive bombers had pushed over. Bell and Kepford followed them down (the Vals recovered very low, about 50 ft.) beyond the destroyer screen. The Vals were in 2 loose columns; Bell picked the port column and Kepford the starboard. The Vals kept their diving brakes down and were jigging, but Bell came down on one, saw it crash, picked up the plane ahead and after a very short burst set it afire and saw it go in.

The attack seemed to be over (in reality it was only the first wave) and Bell again started for home. He was 15 miles from the Task Force when he looked back and saw a second attack. He turned but was too late to intercept. He was then very low on gas, so he gave the Bunker Hill a deferred forced landing signal. The carrier began clearing the deck, when the third attack came in. Bell was unable to make any definite runs (he was at 3,000 ft.) and after the attack had been beaten off he joined up with Kepford and landed aboard the Bunker Hill at 0420. He refueled and rearmed, took off at 0545 and landed at Ondongo at 0700.

Everett Lanman one of the original groundcrew who stayed on the Bunker Hill when VF-17 were detached at Pearl Harbor remembers this engagement.

"In our first action at Rabaul our old Jolly Roger squadron helped protect us, which they sure did. They landed aboard the ship for refueling and I remember one of the pilots had his guns firing before his wheels were retracted, many of the pilots scored more than one victory, that was how thick the Jap planes were".

Ens. Kepford broke off from Bell when they attacked the Vals. He got his first Val on a high side run and saw him go down in flames. The Vals then headed for a rain squall. Kepford made a flat side run from 500 ft. and after a short burst the Val exploded. Just as he made this pass 2 Zekes made runs on him but missed. Kepford pulled up into a right turn and headed for another Val. The Val went into a rain squall with Kepford after him. The Val turned and Kepford made a full deflection shot and saw the Val explode. He turned right out of the rain squall and on an opposite course run on a fourth Val saw his bullets hit the wing.

Kepford then joined up with Bell and headed home. About 15 miles from the Task Force they turned back to meet the second Jap attack. Kepford rocked his wings and got through the A/A fire. He spotted a Kate coming up aft of the Bunker Hill. He cut across and tried to get on the Kate's tail. As the A/A bursts were bumping him around he had difficulty in keeping his sights on, but finally he

Butch Davenport on right, with one of his groundcrew.
Courtesy Lennard Edmisten.

closed to 50 feet, fired and saw the Kate roll over and go into the water. The rest of his flight parallels Bell's. Kepford's actions on this mission earned him the Navy Cross.

The following tactical comments were reported after this eventful mission.

The most obvious tactical comment must concern the failure of the Fighter Director aboard the Essex to put the covering fighters in a position where they could intercept the enemy attack. Had the Fighter Director aboard the Independence had all divisions under his control instead of only one division, he could have had 32 fighters over the enemy before their attack could have been launched. As it was the Essex Fighter Director vectored 16 fighters out 30 miles from the Task Force to intercept 12 friendly planes, and when the enemy was sighted ordered *all* fighters to continue still farther out on the same vector. It was only when the Task Force was actually under attack that he summoned them back.

This truly remarkable tactical error may have been caused by some defect in the Essex's radar, but whatever the cause, it should be remedied speedily, for only the ships' A/A and great good fortune prevented the first Jap attack from succeeding.

The overall success of the operation demonstrates the feasibility of using carrier trained but shore-based fighters as cover for an attacking carrier Task Force.

The F4Us in particular showed remarkable endurance. Most were in the air for 5 hours, with a long fight after the 3rd hour. The ability of shore-based fighters to make a night flight and find the force to be covered in the dark would be considerably increased if the carriers turned on their YE.

As far as the enemy tactics are concerned nothing particularly new was reported. Of interest is the previously reported ability of Jap fighters to work in pairs and in 4 and 6 plane divisions.

The detachable tanks carried under the Tonys' wings may be a hitherto unreported feature. It will be noted that these tanks were not dropped simultaneously, the left tank being jettisoned before the right.

The Vals' use of dive brakes when attacked during their retirement is perhaps a new evasive tactic. Several pilots reported that they tended to overrun the Vals.

8 out of 20 VHF radios failed completely and others performed badly, due mainly to no test equipment or spare parts.

VF 17 pilots shot down 18, and damaged 7 enemy planes, the score sheet being as follows:

Blackburn shot down one Tony and damaged one Zeke; Hedrick shot down one Zeke; Jackson shot down one Zeke; Cordray damaged one Zeke; Streig shot down one Tony and one Zeke and damaged one Zeke and one Hamp; Gile shot down one Kate; Chasnoff and Anderson teamed up to damage one Zeke; Kleinman shot down one Kate and damaged another Kate; Bell shot down two Vals; Kepford shot down three Vals and one Kate and damaged one Val; Hogan shot down one Zeke; Baker shot down one Zeke; Hill shot down one Kate; Burriss shot down one Kate and one Betty and teamed up with an F6F pilot to shoot down another Kate.

"Later we heard confirmation from the task force commander they were extremely pleased with the performance of Fighting 17." Said Roger Hedrick.

The carriers were not damaged. The defeat in the Solomons stunned the Japanese. They withdrew their warships from Rabaul, allowing the U.S. to build an airstrip on Bougainville.

12 November
Sixteen F4Us escorted a Dumbo (PBY) with Admiral Halsey aboard from Rendova Island to Cape Torokina, Bougainville, and return.

Thirteen F4U's (3 of the originally scheduled 16 were unable to take off) left Ondongo and made rendezvous with 42 SBDs and 24 TBFs over Baga Island. Altitude 12,000 ft.

The formation proceeded directly to Kara airfield, Bougainville, passing over Molla Point. The bombers were at 12,000 ft., the fighters 14,000 ft. The F4Us reported the strike as successful, with several hits on the runway.

No A/A fire was encountered at Kara, but some of light intensity was met over Kahili. Altitude of the bursts was 10,000 ft.

The weather over the target was fair: scattered cumulus at 4-5,000 ft., cumulo stratus at 12,000 ft. Visibility fair.

The F4Us escorted the bombers back to Baga, then returned to base.

13 November
Three negative 2-hour patrols (24 sorties) were flown over Empress Augusta Bay, Bougainville.

Three negative 2-hour patrols (20 sorties) were flown over the damaged U.S.S. Denver.

14 November
Three negative 2-hour patrols (24 sorties) were flown over Task Unit 31.5.5.

Two negative 2-hour patrols (8 sorties) were flown over Munda.

Eight F4U's made rendezvous with 54 SBDs and 8 TBFs over Baga Island.

An early photo of "Chico" Freeman with aircraft #7. He later went on to fly number 34. Courtesy U.S. Naval Historical Center / M.W. "Butch" Davenport Collection.

Altitude 12,000 ft. Because of extremely bad weather over the primary target (Kara Airfield, Bougainville) the bombers struck Ballale Island.

Their targets were apparently A/A positions and supply areas, as no bombs were seen to hit the runway.

A/A fire was intense, but none of the bombers or F4U's were shot down.

The fighters escorted the bombers back to Baga, then returned to base.

Four F4Us covered a Dumbo (PBY) to Treasury Islands and return.

15 November
Two negative 2-hour patrols (12 sorties) were flown over Munda.

Eight F4Us were assigned as high cover over U.S. forces in Empress Augusta Bay, Bougainville.

Lt. C.A. Pillsbury	Lt. M.W. Davenport
Lt. W.J. Schub	Lt(jg) D.C. Freeman
Ens. R.R. Hogan	Lt. S.R. Beacham
Lt(jg) R.H. Jackson	Ens. W.P. Meek

At the conclusion of the patrol, they were directed to strafe ground installations at Chabai Plantation. They left station and proceeded up the S.W. coast of Bougainville, 20 miles inland, flying very low. All eight swept across the target area in line abreast, and strafed A/A positions and houses (presumed barracks and storehouses). Two houses were set afire, and at least 2 A/A positions were silenced.

Light and medium A/A fire was of moderate intensity. The 40mm bursts were at a very short distance from the guns, the Japs apparently having a very short time fuse.

After sweeping over Chabai, Lt. Pillsbury led his division north over Buka and Bonis airfields. Pillsbury himself turned S.E. and crossed the Bonis runway. As he did, his plane (left wing) was struck by a 7.7mm. bullet and a 37 or 40mm shell.

The other three members of his division continued N. over the Buka strip, strafing A/A positions, and turned E. out to sea. As the planes were passing over the coast, Lt. Schub's plane was hit by a 37mm or a 40mm shell. The shell passed through the fuselage just below the vertical stabilizer and did no serious damage. Pillsbury's division re-formed and proceeded down the E. coast of Bougainville and thence to base.

A/A fire over Buka and Bonis was moderate. No planes (other than 3 wrecks) were seen.

After strafing Chabai, Lt. Davenport's division swung right and proceeded down the E. coast of the Island searching for suitable targets. Nothing was found until Kuriki Island, where they strafed a 60 ft. tug-type craft (in good condition) on a reef and set it afire. The division returned to base after searching the rest of the coast.

Eight F4Us were assigned as escort for 6 B-25's in a strike on enemy shipping around Bougainville Island.

The F4Us made rendezvous with the bombers (only 4 appeared) over Baga Island.

The formation proceeded at a low altitude up the S.W. coast of Bougainville, passed in close to Buka Passage, then went north of Buka Island, turned and proceeded down the N.E. coast. Two B-25s dropped one bomb each on a hulk with no bottom beached on the east side of Dambach Island. One bomb was 200 yards short, the other was 200 yards long. Shortly afterwards a B-25 dropped two bombs near a small wreck on the beach near Kessa Plantation. Two bombs were dropped on a beached 60 ft. hulk on Moto reef. Two bombs were also dropped on the west tip of Bakawari Island. One bomb hit the water off shore, the other struck the point of land aimed at, uprooting several trees.

All bombing was done at low altitude, 100-200 ft.

After the conclusion of the last attack the F4Us escorted the bombers as far as Baga Island and then returned to base.

Eight F4Us were assigned to fly a 2 hour patrol over U.S. forces in Empress Augusta Bay, Bougainville.

Lt. H.A. March	Lt. D.A. Innis
Ens. F.A. Jagger	Ens. W.C. Wharton
Lt. L.D. Cooke	Ens. J.O. Ellsworth
Lt(jg) H.M. Burriss	Ens. L.M. Kelley

At the conclusion of their patrol they were directed to strafe barges or other targets in the Chabai area (Matchin Bay). When the flight went off station the weather to the north was bad (thunder showers and heavy clouds) so they cut across Bougainville and started down the N.E. coast.

At the foot of Arawa Bay four planes strafed an A/A position. The flight continued south and passed over the Keita strip, four planes strafing a building at the end of the runway. The flight then swung east over the water, turned, and came in on a 40 ft. barge which was just backing off Banaru Reef. The barge was set afire.

All strafing was done at tree-top level.

All planes returned safely to Ondongo.

One negative 2-hour patrol (8 sorties) was flown over Empress Augusta Bay, Bougainville.

16 November

Four negative 2-hour patrols (32 sorties) were flown over Task Unit 31.6.

One negative 2 hour patrol (4 sorties) was flown over Munda.

A flight of eight F4Us made rendezvous with 18 SBDs over Baga Island at 8,000 ft. and escorted them N.W. to the mouth of the Jaba River in Empress Augusta Bay.

The bombers made their first run from the east, swung out over the bay, and returned for a second run. They made 6 in all. After the first run Lt. March thought the attack had been concluded and led his division S.W. to pick them up for the retirement. He never found them and returned to base.

Lt. Gile's division remained over the bombers at 7,000 ft. until their attack was over and escorted them back to base.

As the targets were not visible to the escorting fighters, no estimate of damage could be made.

The weather over the target was good; high scattered clouds at 15,000 ft., low scattered at 1,500 ft; visibility good.

Eight F4Us escorted a Dumbo (PBY) to Empress Augusta Bay, Bougainville and return.

Four F4Us searched the water around Elo Island for a missing P-40 pilot with negative results.

17 November

Two negative 2-hour patrols (16 sorties) were flown over DesRon 23.

Two negative 2-hour patrols (24 sorties) were flown over Empress Augusta Bay, Bougainville.

Eight F4Us were assigned to cover a B-25, SBD, TBF strike on Buka and Bonis airfields, the F4U's being assigned especially to the B-25s. Rendezvous was made over West Cape, Choiseul Island at 12,000 ft. and the formation proceeded up the N.E. coast of Bougainville to the target.

The B-25s bombed the Bonis strip, they bombed from about 10,000 ft., while the F4Us were at 17,000 ft. Coverage was good. Moderate heavy A/A was encountered. It was accurate as to altitude, but trailing. Weather over the target was good.

*Ray Beacham "The Kitty Hawk Kid" sitting in his Corsair.*Courtesy Harry Bridges.

The B-25s left the target and headed south along the S.E. coast of Bougainville at about 10,000 ft. Lt. Innis and Ens. Wharton were at the rear of the formation covering 3 B-25s, one of which had been hit in the left engine and was streaming smoke. Innis saw 4 Zekes at 12,000 ft making a turn in towards the B-25s. The F4Us did wing overs and came down on the Zekes, who went into column and split-S'd. Innis and Wharton were able to make 2 passes each, but without observing any hits. The Zekes disappeared to the north and the 2 F4Us resumed cover.

They escorted the bombers as far as Vella Lavella and then returned to base.

One negative 2-hour patrol (4 sorties) was flown over Munda.

ANDERSON'S RESCUE

Although VF-17 had numerous distinguished engagements one of the most memorable missions was the rescue of Lt(jg) Robert S."Andy" Anderson.

16/17/18 November 1943

A flight of eight F4Us were assigned to fly cover over U.S. shipping in Empress Augusta Bay. While still some distance from the bay they heard bogey reports from Cocker Base and put on full speed. When they arrived on station they were immediately vectored out by Cocker on a course of 270° (their altitude was 25,000 feet) for 30 miles, then on course 315° for about 10 miles. No contact was made and the flight returned to Empress Augusta Bay.

Cocker Base then reported that the ships were under attack and directed all planes to intercept the enemy. The F4Us chopped down to 6,000 feet and when they were about 10 miles off Cape Motupena saw the enemy (bearing 230° 8 miles distant from Cape Torokina) heading N.W. The enemy were evidently in 2 groups.

Lt. Cdr. Roger Hedrick's division broke left and attacked one group (3 Kates and 4 Zekes) and "Timmy" Gile's division broke right and attacked the second group (5 Kates and 5 Tonys).

Hedrick's division closed rapidly on the Japs. Hedrick made a run from dead astern on a Zeke, who made a slight climbing turn to the left and exploded. He then made two passes at another Zeke, but missed and saw Jack Chasnoff shoot it down.

Hedrick then turned back to look for more enemy planes, saw none, but did see a pilot parachuting down (Anderson). He circled the pilot, by now in the water, and signalled Chasnoff to join up. The pair then headed for Cape Moltke. Hedrick calculated the distance and bearing and turned south to Cape Torokina, and, since his radio was unreliable, dropped a message giving Anderson's position. He then returned to relocate Anderson, but could not find him. During the search he was alone, Chasnoff having disappeared over Cape Torokina. Hedrick then left the area and returned to Ondongo.

Lt(jg) Mills Schanuel went down with Hedrick in the attack on the Zekes. He made a stern run on a Zeke who rolled away and was seen by Anderson to burst into flames and crash into the water. Schanuel turned left and got another shot at a Zeke, who disappeared under his wing. He then climbed up into the sun and at 23,000 ft joined up on 4 F6Fs (Hellcats). He saw a group of F4Us heading south and started to join up with them. Realizing that they belonged to another flight which had been on a strike escort, he broke away and searched for Anderson, then headed home to Ondongo.

Robert "Andy" Anderson recalls the action.

"I was in Roger Hedrick's division and we'd taken off before daylight that day and were flying cover for a landing on Empress Augusta Bay for the 3rd Marine division. I think they landed on the 1st November and this was on the 17th.

We'd been on station maybe 10-15 minutes and a flight of Jap

VF-17 Ready Room.
L-R. *Jim Streig (leaning) Hap Bowers, Tom Blackburn, Dan Cunningham (head in hands), Tom Killefer, Ike Kepford, New Georgia 1943.* Courtesy U.S. Naval Historical Center / M.W. "Butch" Davenport Collection.

Zeros and dive-bombers came down and we attacked. My wingman and I broke away and attacked some of the fighters and I was chasing one firing; as I was following this guy down, first thing I knew I saw tracers going by my own airplane. I could feel my own airplane getting hit and I broke away and looked the airplane over for damage and I couldn't see anything.

"I saw another target and took off after him, as I was firing I started to get smoke in the cockpit, so I broke off the attack and there was fire in my right wing. The cockpit was getting smoky. So I broke off the attack and Jack Chasnoff who was my wingman at that time, as a matter of fact he was all during my time with VF-17. But it was getting so bad that I decided I was going to abandon the airplane.

"So I started to bail out and as I remember the attack started out at fairly good altitude as we had our oxygen masks on. I started to climb out of the airplane and I couldn't shake myself loose from my oxygen mask and my headphone extension cord. So I had to get back in the airplane and disconnect them, and from then on the sequence of events is rather blurred, but my wingman tells me that I rolled the airplane over and dropped out. My parachute opened about the time I hit the water. I must have been quite low. Jack said he estimated my altitude was under 800 feet.

"How I got that low I have no idea. I hit the water and got my raft out and climbed into it and waved to the guys, told them I was in good shape, assumed they would come back and look for me, and of course they did."

Chasnoff followed Anderson down in the latter's first run. He pulled up to the right as Anderson recovered and got a good burst into a Zeke. He saw pieces of the engine fly out and the plane smoke (the Zeke was seen to crash into the water).

On this mission Jack Chasnoff scored his first victory. He describes the action: "The first plane I shot down I did the very same thing as "Andy" Jagger describes his first kill. I followed it down to the water long after it had burst into flames and was obviously destroyed. I joined up on it, I had a little extra speed and joined up on it and just flew wing on that airplane until I watched it crash and explode in the water. That was a dumb thing to do, but you're hypnotized by it.

"It was over the Bougainville the day Anderson was shot down. I got two that day, but the first one was the one that as it turned out hit Anderson's plane.

"We were in a fairly steep dive from altitude trying to intercept these planes and apparently we got them in view and were chasing them but there were some which we had overshot and as we were diving at a fairly steep angle this Zero pulled up underneath us and fired at Andy and I saw that happen.

"Anderson when he knew he was hit pulled violently off to the right and up. He immediately began to gain altitude and I watched this airplane which having shot Anderson down put its nose down and started to dive. I was in this fairly steep dive and I made what turned out to be almost a full deflection shot and could see the tracers hitting the top of the fuselage and the canopy and it went from there right into the water. Then I pulled up looking for Anderson

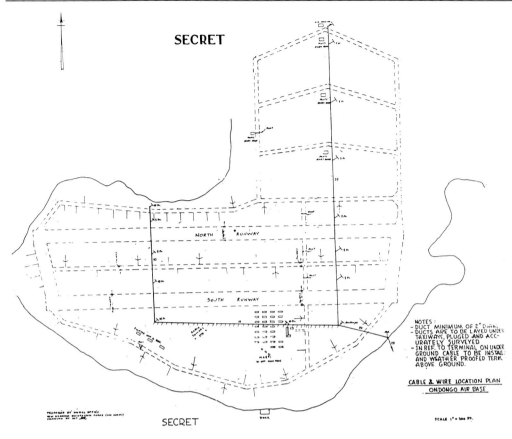

SECRET

NORTH RUNWAY

SOUTH RUNWAY

NOTES:
- DUCT MINIMUM OF 2" DIAM.
- DUCTS ARE TO BE LAYED UNDER TAXIWAYS, PLUGED AND ACC-URATELY SURVEYED
- IN REF. TO TERMINAL ON UNDER GROUND CABLE TO BE INSTALL AND WEATHER PROOFED TERM. ABOVE GROUND.

CABLE & WIRE LOCATION PLAN
ONDONGO AIR BASE

SCALE 1" = 300 FT.

SECRET

Chasnoff lost Hedrick over Empress Augusta Bay and headed back to locate Anderson. He searched for an hour and a half but with negative results. During this time rescue boats from Cape Torokina were in the area on the same mission. He radioed the rescue boats that he was low on gas and was returning to base.

As stated above, the second division (Lt. Gile, Lt(jg) Dan Cunningham, Lt(jg) Paul Cordray, and Ens. Brad Baker) broke right in the initial attack. Gile got on the tail of a Kate, low on the water, who eluded him in a climbing turn. Cordray and Baker followed this Kate and Cordray, in a stern run, shot him down (the Kate exploded).

The division then climbed to 12,000 feet about 10 miles north of Cape Torokina. At this time they saw the bombers returning from the Buka strike. Five minutes later they saw a group of 10 Tonys and Zekes at 8,000 feet, proceeding N.N.E. over Point Tosair.

and couldn't find him. As I was looking around for him I saw this other plane that really just crossed my line of vision in the perfect spot. I fired at it and as I described earlier, I followed it down to the water.

"After shooting that plane down I pulled up to the left and I saw Anderson in a very steep dive with his plane burning, trailing smoke. I began hollering at him on the radio, Bail out! Bail out! At that moment I wasn't positive it was Anderson and I was hollering F4U pilot Bail out! Bail out!

"I thought he was too low to bail out, because I was above him by this time. I thought it was too late, but at the very last moment I saw his 'chute blossom and he hit the water. I think he must have hit at almost the same time. He had spinal injuries, a broken ankle and some broken ribs. I think probably from the impact of hitting the water the way he did. He just barely made it".

Chasnoff then saw another Zeke to his right and got in a long burst. He pulled up to gain on Anderson when the latter started a run. Chasnoff followed him, saw Anderson shoot and miss. Chasnoff throttled back, fired and saw his bullets go in and the Zeke catch fire. He recovered to the left and, over his right shoulder, saw Anderson roll over on his back and bail out. Chasnoff saw the 'chute open at about 1,000 feet and he circled it as it went down. He saw Anderson land in the water apparently uninjured.

Hedrick then signalled him to join up. The pair circled twice and then headed for Cape Moltke. They made a right turn and came down to Cape Torokina.

The Zekes were at 7,000 feet and the Tonys at 8,000 feet. It may be that the Japs regarded the Tony as their best fighter and felt that the 4 flankers are sufficient protection against an attack from above.

The division crossed above the Japs and went down to attack from the starboard side. Cordray tried a full deflection shot at a Tony and missed. Cordray then climbed, looked for Baker but could not find him*. He continued his climb in 3 circles with 2 Tonys climbing inside him. At 10,000 feet the Tonys broke away to the right. Cordray reversed and got on the tail of the rear Tony. He fired a short burst, the Tony began to burn, and exploded when he hit the water.

The other Tonys had disappeared so Cordray climbed and headed north. He joined up with 2 F4Us (Marines) and saw Zekes heading N.W. The 3 F4Us gave chase but could not overtake the Zekes. They gave up the chase and saw 3 Tonys low on the water heading north (this was about 45 miles N.W. of Cape Torokina). The 3 F4Us made individual passes. Cordray got on the tail of a Tony who took violent evasive action, making 4 flipper turns to the right. After the fourth turn Cordray was able to close to 200 yards. He fired and the Tony crashed into the water.

Cordray then rejoined the 2 Marines and proceeded to the Shortland Islands, where he broke off and returned to Ondongo.

*Baker was never seen again.

Gile and Cunningham pinched 4 Zekes in the center of the formation. Gile made 3 identical passes, each pass being followed by a left chandelle (200 feet gain each time). He shot down a Zeke on each pass. All 3 Zekes caught fire and exploded.

The section seeing no more enemy planes, returned to patrol Empress Augusta Bay then returned home to Ondongo.

Hedrick shot down one Zeke; Chasnoff shot down two Zekes; Schanuel shot down one Zeke; Gile shot down three Zekes; Cordray shot down one Kate, and two Tonys. Baker was presumably shot down as he was not seen after the beginning of the action. Anderson's plane was set afire and he bailed out.

Recovery of Lt(jg) Anderson
Merl "Butch" Davenport describes the action and recovery of Lt(jg) Anderson: "My fondest memory is the recovery of Anderson, who had been shot down in an engagement that involved the loss of several Marine pilots and Anderson and another Pilot from our squadron Brad Baker.

This engagement had taken place late afternoon and they were all presumed to have been lost, although Jack Chasnoff, Anderson's wingman, had seen him go into a parachute.

"It just happened that I learned through the skipper Tom Blackburn of an intelligence that they had up at Bougainville that the Japanese were coming down from Rabaul very early in the morning and were conducting strafing operations against the Seabees and Marines that were on this landing at Bougainville.

"I really liked to fly at night and I got clearance from Tom Blackburn to organize a 4 plane flight up to Bougainville, taking off from New Georgia very early in the morning with the intent of intercepting these Japanese strafing missions.

"My division of four F4U's left Ondongo at 0325 18 November 1943.

"While on the way to Buka at 0425, I sighted a light in the water which appeared to be held in our direction without blinking. My division circled the light once at an altitude of 1,000 feet. During this circle a lightning flash revealed nothing about this spot but the light in the water.

"After investigating by flying low and using the landing light, the object was found to be small enough to be a pilot afloat in the water. At this time, my division decided to leave the objective of the rest of the flight.

"I then called Dane Base, told them we had sighted this light and asked him to take a bearing while I kept my emergency flash on and circled close by. When this had been accomplished, the division continued circling for a short time before the light blinked out. We had planned on remaining close by, so when this happened, I made a half minute square (flying straight for a half minute before making a 90° turn) about the spot using 1650 R.P.M. and 25"Hg. manifold pressure.

"The light did not reappear after a long interval so we decided to return to Dane Base for patrol—for our secondary mission.

"At daybreak, I requested the bearing of the light from Dane Base (295° distance 32 miles) and proceeded out from Pt. Easy. At

the end of the required time, nothing was sighted except numerous gas belly tanks, etc. We turned back and re-covered the area to Pt. Easy. As soon as we reached this point, since we were sure of the bearing, we took the same heading out again for seven minutes at 160 knots. At precisely this time, Ens. Ike Kepford, my section leader, sighted the pilot in his raft. This was at 0600.

"As soon as the pilot in the raft had been checked for comfort, and Dane Base had been called, the division split up making a big circle about the spot in the water, each at a different level up to 3,000 feet. At this altitude I used 1300 R.P.M. and 27" Hg. manifold pressure with 10° flaps, maintaining my flight level with 90-110 knots indicated.

"By this time Dane Base had contacted the rescue boat Janie only to find it short of fuel and unable to make the pick-up. Dane then arranged for a PT boat and, at my request, called Base for a flight of our planes to relieve me.

The division continued to circle and finally Ens. Kepford and his wingman Ens. Kurlander returned to Barakoma for lack of fuel, leaving myself and Ens. Freeman to await relief. The latter had 110 gallons of fuel and I had 125 gallons at this time".

"Butch" Davenport described his wingman: 'Chico' Freeman was born and raised in San Francisco and on the tail of his airplane he had a big sign 'L.A. City Limits.' He was incorrigible, but a wonderful guy. But he wrote a poem as he was sure that in that life raft was one of our pilots. He wrote a poem and put it in a bean bag and dropped it over the side, and by God it landed within arm's reach and Anderson (we didn't know it was Anderson at the time) picked this thing up and read the poem."

"Since no relief arrived, we covered the spot until the PT boat arrived and picked up the pilot and raft at 0900.

"Ens. Freeman and I then headed for home at 1600 R.P.M., 24"Hg. manifold pressure, 120 knots, landing at Ondongo at 1005 with 28 gallons of fuel remaining. The total time of the flight was six hours and forty-five minutes."

Due to Davenport experimenting with fuel saving techniques on routine missions he was able to stay airborne for this length of time which further enhanced the operational capabilities of the Corsair.

"It was on the way back that we established radio contact with the Catalina and found out the name of the pilot, which was Anderson. They brought him back to a dug out hospital that they had on New Georgia.

"I didn't see Anderson, I don't know why but I didn't see him after. A couple of people went over to visit him in the hospital. He was flown back to Guadalcanal and then the States. He was badly injured. One of them said, 'Andy, you can thank God for that flashlight that you had.' Anderson said 'I don't know what you're talking about, I didn't have a flashlight.'

"So here's the irony. One of the other pilots that had been shot down had a flashlight and his efforts resulted in the saving of Anderson. This is the irony and the aspect of fate is the hunter. You can't understand these things why they occur this way."

"Andy" Anderson remembers: "It really seems providential that they saw a light and they found me. Pretty good luck."

As soon as it was learned that Anderson had no light, Lt. Davenport and Ens.Wharton went up to search for the second pilot. They took off from Ondongo at 1640, 18 November, 1943, and began searching at 1730. They searched until 1840. This search included not only the area between Cape Torokina and Sandinsel Island but also the coast from Kuraio Mission to Cape Torokina. No sign of any pilot was seen.

Davenport and Wharton landed at Ondongo at 2000.

"They shipped me back to the States. I was on convalescence status for about a year, I was on limited flight duty. Then our skipper, Tom Blackburn, was starting to form a new air group to go aboard the Midway. I managed to get hold of him and get re-assigned to this new air group. We were training on Cape Cod when the war ended. So I became a civilian again." Anderson recalls.

Five negative 2-hour patrols (40 sorties) were flown over Task Unit 31.6.

Ens. C.H. Dunn and Ens. W.P. Popp having in accordance with orders, completed their temporary duty with Fighter One, Espiritu Santo, reported for duty with VF-17.

Wilbert Popp recalls this time:

Mel "Kurly" Kurlander. Courtesy Mel Kurlander.

"The squadron was hoisted aboard a converted oiler, the Prince William for transportation to the South Pacific. We landed at the major staging base in Espiritu Santo and because Clyde and I had only 10 hours of flight time in the Corsair, Blackburn sent us to the Marine field on Espiritu to get additional hours in the F4U.

"Clyde and I were temporarily attached to the Marine headquarters squadron whose pilots were then assigned as replacement pilots to "Pappy" Boyington's Black Sheep Squadron.

"Just before leaving to rejoin VF-17 on Ondongo I met the great "Pappy" Boyington. During my time on Espiritu I also had the pleasure of seeing Charles Lindbergh give a demonstration on taking off with a Corsair on a short field - I believe 850 feet with a maximum bomb load.

"Clyde and I rejoined the squadron in the middle of November 1943 at Ondongo and took part in the air activity-much of which was in the Bougainville area—including the invasion of Bougainville. Toward the end of 1943 we were relieved from Ondongo, returning to Espiritu for R & R. We also spent one week in Sydney Australia".

19 November
Five negative, 2-hour patrols (40 sorties) were flown over Empress Augusta Bay, Bougainville.

One negative, 2-hour patrol (8 sorties) was flown over Munda.

20 November
Four negative, 2-hour patrols (30 sorties) were flown over Task Unit 31.5.1.
One negative, 2-hour patrol (4 sorties) was flown over Munda.
Eight F4Us were assigned as cover for an SBD-TBF strike on Mosigetta, Bougainville. The rendezvous was to be over Baga Island at 12,000 ft. Eight F4Us took off but could not find the bombers at the rendezvous. The flight then proceeded to the target area through bad weather (squalls and low clouds) and one division, finding no bombers, returned to base.

The other division (Lt. Cooke's) found 7 TBFs off southern Bougainville. When these returned the second section covered them, while Lt. Cooke and Ens. Popp went north to find other bombers, heard talking on the radio, but were unsuccessful. They turned south and, as directed, came down on Kara to observe its condition. The field seemed perfectly serviceable. The section strafed a Betty (in good condition) parked on the edge of the strip and set it afire. The attack was evidently a surprise as Cooke and Popp came in out of a rain squall. No A/A fire encountered. The section then returned to base.

21 November
Three negative, 2-hour patrols (24 sorties) were flown over Empress Augusta Bay, Bougainville.
Two divisions of F4Us were assigned as cover over U.S. forces on Cape Torokina, Bougainville. They were to be on station for 2 hours. When they arrived Dane Base vectored out the P-39 low cover to intercept them. This forced a breach of radio silence by the F4Us.

Dane then directed the flight to climb to 20,000 ft. on a vector of 260° to intercept bogies who were reported to be at 10,000 ft. or 16,000 ft. Lt. March led his division out 25 miles on this vector, but Lt. Davenport (who could not establish radio contact with Dane) remained over Cape Torokina at 3,000 ft. Three bombs were dropped in the water off a nearby island, and Dane Base summoned March back to Cape Torokina. His division turned and dove at full speed.

At 13,000 ft. they passed a Tony on opposite course, but their speed was too great for them to turn and engage. The Tony was later shot down by the P-39s.

Meanwhile the second division (Lt. Davenport, Lt(jg) Freeman, Lt. Beacham, and Ens. Jagger) were at 2,000 ft. on the edge of a cloud, and to the west of Cape

Torokina, thus being in the dark. They saw the bomb splashes and headed in towards Cape Torokina on a course of 290°, and saw 6 Zekes, slightly below them and 500 yards off their starboard beam on a course of about 150°.

The Japs were not going particularly fast and Davenport swung his division in a 180° turn on their tails. As he made his turn the Japs saw him, dropped their belly tanks, and four of them shifted into a column preparatory to forming a Lufbury circle. Davenport and his wingman (Freeman) climbed in a sharp turn to get into position and began their runs.

Davenport picked the leader of the 4 Zekes and came in on a flat side run. He closed to very short range and saw his bullets going into the cockpit- (the pilot bailed out, injured, and was picked up by a PT boat.

Davenport then saw a Zeke at 1,000 yards making a beam run (90° deflection) at him. He turned into him but passed below him without getting his sights on. He completed a 360° turn, and saw a Zeke above him in a climb. He started after him, saw he could not catch him, and rolled over on his back and down. At that moment he saw a Zeke on an F4U's tail (Jagger). He went after him, and fired. The Zeke pulled up and Davenport lost him. He then turned back and saw a Zeke above him on his left, and on an opposite course. He turned in and fired and saw the Zeke start smoking and crash into the water. He then joined up on Freeman and they circled the Jap in the water. They went back on patrol over the bay and then headed back to base.

In the original attack Freeman took an interval of 200 yards on Davenport and followed him down, choosing the third Zeke in the column as his target. He saw the second Jap firing on Davenport, so he made a beam run and got his bullets in the Zeke's engine. The Zeke crashed into the water.

The third and fourth Zekes were then on his tail. As they closed to about 75 yards and commenced firing, Freeman kicked his plane into a skid and one Zeke passed by on his port beam. He tried a sharp bank to the left, saw a Zeke still behind him, kicked hard left rudder and went into a half spin to the left. This maneuver shook the Zeke off.

Freeman saw Davenport not far off on the tail of a Zeke. He turned to join up, looked back, and saw a Zeke start a run on him. He made a high, sharp chandelle to the left and turned 180°. The Zeke went straight ahead (N.E.) and Freeman completed a full turn

Tom Blackburn in a Japanese officer's hat 15 November, 1943. Courtesy U.S. Naval Historical Center / M.W. "Butch" Davenport Collection.

and headed after him. He caught him just west of Mt. Balbi, fired a short burst from dead astern and saw flames in the cockpit. The Jap pilot apparently tried to bail out, for Freeman saw a 'chute come out of the cockpit and whip itself to pieces on the tail. The Zeke crashed into the jungle.

Freeman then turned back, joined up with Davenport and resumed patrol.

At the time the Zekes were sighted Lt. Beacham (with Ens. Jagger on his wing) was out far enough on Davenport's left so that the Zekes passed between him and Davenport's section. Beacham climbed in a fast chandelle and came down on the Jap formation. He shot at a Zeke, who did a split-S. Beacham turned sharply but could not catch him. He climbed and turned back to the scene of the action. He saw 2 Zekes, one of them came at him in a head on run, fired a short burst, then broke off. The others went into an extraordinarily steep climb. Beacham followed this Zeke in his climb and, just as the Zeke was about to stall out, fired at about 50 yards. He saw hits on the engine and fuselage and the Zeke spun out (1-1/2 turns) but recovered in a diving spiral.

Beacham headed back to the fight and saw a Zeke low on the water, heading west.

He gave it full throttle and got on the Zeke's tail. He cut his throttle and fired at a range of 100 yards dead astern. The Zeke crashed into the water and Beacham turned back. He saw a chute in the water, which he circled. He perceived it was a Jap (his life jacket was black) and heard Davenport call the PT boat to come pick the Jap up. Beacham then joined up and resumed patrol.

Ens. Jagger was fairly far out on Beacham's wing when the action started. He was unable to follow Beacham's chandelle, so climbed and came down on the formation by himself. He made several passes but all his shots went wide. He tried to join an F4U making a left turn, and just as he moved over the F4U fired at a Zeke crossing his path. Jagger's turn put him on the tail of the Zeke and he saw his bullets go in.

The Zeke started to smoke and dove in a tight spiral. Jagger followed him down from 2,500 ft. to 1,000 ft., firing as he went. The Zeke burst into flames and crashed into the water.

"Andy" Jagger remembers his first combat victory:

"A friend of mine was sick and had a fever and a touch of the flu. I volunteered to take his place. Being the fresh-ensign I had not heard that expression never volunteer.

"We took off in the blackness of night and we were not allowed to have running lights on. You flew on the exhaust flame of your leader and that's the best way to get vertigo which was later found out. I wasn't feeling too well after a while. "Butch" Davenport was the division leader. It turned out we 4 planes shot down 6 enemy airplanes, and one of the survivors of those 6 enemy airplanes turned out to be a Japanese Lieutenant who was the flight leader and he had been sent down to find out why so many of his airplanes had not returned home after VF-17 had taken its toll for quite a few flights!

"Somehow or another I forgot to charge my guns or charge them fully or properly, because I will never forget trying to shoot down an enemy plane with one of the six guns firing and that was very embarrassing. I guess I was extremely lucky because the one gun managed to do it.

"The other mistake I made was to follow him down and I was so excited about it I forgot a cardinal rule, that you are not supposed to be separated from your section leader. Here I was following down this plane, shooting at it, and when he crashed in the water I should have immediately started looking around and to join up with my section leader. I circled around looking at this wreckage in the water. I was just captivated by the idea that I had shot down an enemy plane. I was so excited and wrapped up in the fact that I got one that I circled him almost gloating over it!

"It was the first Jap I had shot down. I came to my senses and then looked around for Davenport's flight, which I left which was a bad thing to do as you are most vulnerable when you are by yourself. It took me a while to catch up with him."

Jagger then joined up on March's division (his assigned place) and resumed patrol.

Tactical comments reported after this successful mission were as follows.

The success of this operation can be explained by the fact that it had been carefully planned. The enemy had made two previous dawn attacks, and Lt. Davenport had studied the reports of these. On the evening before this flight he went over all the available intelligence data, and decided that the best place for an interception was slightly inland from Cape Torokina at an altitude of 2,000 ft. This would enable him to catch the Japs as they came down over the mountains behind Empress Augusta Bay. The position also had the advantage of being on the dark side.

Davenport and March agreed that the latter's division should stay up as cover, and in a position to meet any different type of attack. Lt. Davenport also believed that the Jap attack would come just at dawn and planned to be on station before that time.

Events proved him to be correct. Had he arrived on station at the time assigned him, he might very well have been too late. Had he gone out and up with March on Dane's vector he would certainly have missed the interception. As it was the entire operation was carried out exactly as it had been planned.

The previously reported tendency of the Japs to form Lufbury circles is of interest, as is their recent adoption of formation flying. It should be noted that in this action the Japs were eager to engage the F4Us.

It should be stated that after 5 major contacts with the enemy, in which 46 enemy planes were destroyed, pilots of the squadron were more than pleased with the raised cockpit-type F4U-1. They regarded this new type as greatly superior to the old low cockpit type.

Davenport shot down two Zekes; Freeman shot down two Zekes; Beacham shot down one Zeke; Jagger shot down one Zeke. One of the F4Us was hit in the oil cooler by a 7.7 shell.

PILLSBURY'S DISAPPEARANCE

Six F4Us (2 of the original 8 had been forced to return early because of the illness of one of the pilots) left station over Empress Augusta Bay, Bougainville after a 2-hour patrol. As directed, the F4Us searched the Monuito-Kahili trail for strafing targets.

Lt. C.A. Pillsbury   Lt. W.J. Schub

Ens. R.R. Hogan   Lt(jg) C.W. Gilbert

Lt(jg) G.F. Bowers

Ens. R.H. Hill

Lt. Schubs' division could not find Monuito mission itself, but strafed huts and bridges along the trail, leaving several huts smoking. Then they returned to Ondongo.

Lt. Pillsbury and Ens. Hogan also searched the trail. They found and strafed five trucks. Just before they reached Kahili, Hogan, cut right to avoid passing between Kahili and Kangu Hill. At about 3 miles off shore he looked back and saw Pillsbury flying low on a S.W. heading one mile west of Kangu Hill. Hogan turned to join up but could not find Pillsbury. He circled Noile Point, calling Pillsbury on the radio, but could not see him or get radio contact. He returned to base, stopping to orbit at several points en route.

Walter Schub describes what happened.

"My division was in close vicinity to Chuck Pillsbury during our mission to strafe targets of opportunity along the Monoitu-Kahili Trail. I did see Chuck's plane ahead of me, but I delayed in following him for fear the enemy ground troops would be ready and waiting for more Corsairs to come down the same slot and bang! bang!

"After a few circles in the area (away from the trail) I commenced to track north along the trail. We strafed some bridges and huts, and other indications of habitation. Suddenly about five miles ahead and somewhat to the left was a barrage of anti-aircraft fire, but this barrage was bursting just above the trees-two hundred to five hundred feet. It would be about the height of our strafing runs. I kept saying to myself-I've never seen A/A fire fused to detonate at such a low altitude. As soon as I saw the A/A burst I turned my division hard right and got out of there. I'm still not convinced that it wasn't A/A fire (I am aware that a rifle bullet was allegedly blamed for Chuck's death).

"Chuck was one fine person. A senior Lieutenant and third in command after Hedrick."

Hal Jackson recalls the loss of his friend.

"I lost a really good friend called Chuck Pillsbury, it was four days after "Andy" got shot down on the 21 November, 1943. Many years later I met his nephew who's head of a museum in Fort Worth and he told me they found his body and plane in 1970 just west of Kahili airfield. They found Chuck's body and he was still in the cockpit there, and they brought him back and buried him."

Searchers were immediately sent out with negative results. Searches were also made during the following 2 days, again with negative results.

As Hogan saw no A/A fire, it is presumed that Pillsbury's plane was hit by light machine gun fire and crashed.

Four F4Us made a 2-hour search of the area where Pillsbury was presumed to have gone down. Negative.

22 November

Sixteen F4U-1s from Ondongo, but on scramble alert at Barakoma, Vella Lavella, were assigned to cover an SBD-TBF strike on Kahili airfield, Bougainville. The F4Us made rendezvous with the bombers over Baga Island at 12,000 ft. They escorted them to the target, being stacked from 16,000 ft. to 18,000 ft.

Bomb coverage was reported as good.

A/A fire was moderate in intensity.

After the attack, the F4Us escorted the bombers back as far as Baga Island.

Eight F4U's returned to Ondongo; the remaining 8 returned to Barakoma.

Four F4Us escorted a Dumbo (PBY) to the Treasury Islands and return.

One negative 2-hour patrol (8 sorties) was flown over Empress Augusta Bay, Bougainville.

23 November

One negative 2-hour patrol (4 sorties) was flown over Munda.

Fifteen F4U's made rendezvous with 24 B-25s and 6 PVs over Baga Island. They escorted the bombers in 2 groups (11 B-25s in one, 12 B-25s and 6 PVs in the other) to Chabai Plantation, Bougainville. The first group bombed from 8,500 ft. and the second group went in low. Bomb coverage was reported to be excellent.

Medium and heavy A/A fire was moderate to intense. At least one B-25 was hit, but did not go down over the target.

At the conclusion of the attack the F4U's covered the bombers as far as Baga Island.

Four F4U's searched the area where Pillsbury was presumed to have gone down. Negative.

One negative, 2-hour patrol (8 sorties) was flown over Empress Augusta Bay, Bougainville.

24 November

Two negative, 2-hour patrols (16 sorties) were flown over Task Group 36.1.

Twenty-four F4Us made rendezvous with SBD's and TBF's over West Cape, Choiseul Island, at 6,000 ft. They proceeded up the N.E. coast of Bougainville, and the bombers attacked Tarlena Plantation and Chabai Plantation from north to south.

Bomb coverage was reported as exceptionally good, with several large fires started in the Chabai area.

Medium and heavy A/A fire was moderate.

At the conclusion of the attack the F4Us escorted the bombers back to base.

These tactical comments were reported after this mission.

On the return trip, several SBDs, who had not dropped on the target jettisoned their bombs in the water. As they passed directly over Poperang Island, an excellent target, it would have been more economical if they had dropped their bombs there.

Four F4Us covered a PV-1 to Empress Augusta Bay, Bougainville, and return.

Lt(jg) R.S. Anderson was detached and admitted to Naval Base Hospital, Munda, New Georgia, for treatment.

25 November

One negative, 2-hour patrol (4 sorties) was flown over Task Group 39.

26 November

Three negative, 2-hour patrols (24 sorties) were flown over Empress Augusta Bay, Bougainville. At the conclusion of the first patrol the following pilots proceeded to Soraken Island, Matchin Bay, to strafe shore installations. Few suitable targets could be observed on the plantation, but huts on 3 islands just west of Soraken Plantations were thoroughly worked over, and several set afire.

Lt. Cdr. R.R. Hedrick	Lt. L.D. Cooke
Lt(jg) M. Schanuel	Lt(jg) H.M. Burriss
Lt(jg) P. Cordray	Ens. J.O. Ellsworth

No A/A fire was encountered.

On return the flight flew over the Shortland Islands to look for float planes, but none were seen. What may be a new strip under construction was observed on Morgusaia Island.

At the conclusion of the third patrol, a flight of 8 F4Us proceeded down the N.E. coast of Bougainville to search for strafing targets. Lt. Bell's division flew low along the coast, while Lt. March kept his division at 8,000 ft. for cover.

Lt. T.R. Bell
Lt(jg) E. May
Ens. I.C. Kepford
Ens. M.M. Kurlander

Mel Kurlander describes one early dawn mission.

"Ike and I were going on an early dawn attack and we were to rendezvous around an island about 5 miles away with 'Butch' and 'Chico'. We got up to the island and it's dark and we have our running lights on and our rendezvous was always counter-clockwise.

"We're making our formation trying to catch up with the other 2 planes who had taken off before we had, and we kept seeing planes going the wrong way, different lights.

"We couldn't figure out what was going on. So finally we went back to the base and then we all figured out that the Japs were rendezvousing at the same island that we were. They were going one way we were going the other!"

Their first target was a long warehouse on the beach about one-half mile south of Cape Puipui which was strafed and set afire. The division crossed the Cape and set fire to another warehouse at Rankama. The F4Us swung inland and came down on Kieta Airfield. They raked a line of 10 sheds on the edge of the (unserviceable) strip, and set one afire. The flight then gained altitude and returned to base.

27 November
Eight F4Us escorted 5 B-25s from Baga Island to Queen Carolina Harbor, Buka Island. The first attack was made on a wreck beached on a reef off Mitau Islands. Two bombs were dropped, but both were about 200 yards wide. The bombers then bombed and strafed a decayed jetty about a mile N.W. of Cape Dunganon. Several bombs fell near the jetty.

The bombers turned south and strafed a Japanese infantryman on a small pier opposite Pazsu Island. The infantryman had a rifle, and when last observed, was still firing.

The B-25s continued south and at Burunatui Plantation launched repeated attacks.

Many bombs were dropped and all the bombers made strafing runs. It was reported that a great many trees were uprooted.

About 10 minutes after the last attack the bombers were able to join up, and were escorted home by the F4Us.

No A/A fire was encountered. Weather over the targets was clear. All bombing done from low levels.

L-R. *"Timmy" Gile, "Big Jim" Streig, Tom Killefer, Doug Gutenkunst, Tom Blackburn, at Ondongo, November 1943.* Courtesy U.S. Naval Historical Center / M.W. "Butch" Davenport Collection.

Sixteen F4Us escorted 23 B-25s in a strike on Buka airfield. The F4U's made rendezvous with the bombers over Baga Island and proceeded to the target. The B-25s made their runs in 2 waves from N.E. to S.W. The first wave dropped their bombs on Buka Passage, but the second wave got good coverage of the strip. The bombing was done from 12,000 ft. while the F4Us were at 15,000 ft. Heavy A/A fire was meagre and inaccurate and came from the tip of Sohanne Island. At the conclusion of the attack the bombers proceeded down the N.E. coast of Bougainville.

They strafed installations at Arawa Bay, and a large house just south of Chinatown at Aieta. No A/A was encountered.

28 November
At the conclusion of a negative, 2-hour patrol over Empress Augusta Bay (Task Group 31.7) 12 F4U's proceeded to Motopena Point as directed to strafe a radio tower reported there.

Lt(jg) Robert "Hal" Jackson. Courtesy National Archives.

Lt. Cdr. J.T. Blackburn   Lt. C.D. Gile
Lt(jg) D.G. Cunningham   Lt(jg) D.H. Gutenkunst
Lt. M.W. Davenport   Lt(jg) T. Killefer
Ens. C.H. Dunn   Ens. T.F. Kropf
Lt(jg) D.C. Freeman   Lt(jg) E. May
Lt(jg) C.W. Gilbert

The destruction of this tower was regarded as being of primary importance, and all the pilots had been instructed to rake the area, even if no target was visible.

This the 12 F4U pilots proceeded to do. They made numerous runs over the point and each expended about 1,200 rounds of ammunition. Nothing could be seen except dense jungle. Lt(jg) Gutenkunst's plane was hit by what was probably machine gun fire (no tracers were seen) in the right wing. His oil cooler was punctured, pressure dropped , and on the return to base he was forced to make a dead stick, water-landing in Wilson Strait, just off Barakoma airfield. He was unhurt and was immediately picked up by a crash boat.

The rest of the F4Us returned to Ondongo.

After the strike these tactical observations were reported.

Since the radio tower on Motupena Point was regarded as such an important target, it was strange that those in charge of the operations on Bougainville made no attempt to discover its exact location. It would have been a simple matter to have sent either a photographic plane or a reconnaissance plane over the area, since there were always at least 24 VF in the vicinity.

The result of such a photographic or reconnaissance mission would probably have led to the conclusion that the radio tower was too well hidden to permit its being efficiently strafed. If destruction of the whole area was desired it could have been done more efficiently by the 4 DDs then available in Empress Augusta Bay, or by an SBD or TBF strike. As it was, 12 F4Us expended about $7,200 worth of ammunition-probably without concrete results-and one F4U (approximate cost $135,000) was lost.

Four negative, 2-hour patrols (31 sorties) were flown over Empress Augusta Bay, Bougainville.

A flight of 7 F4Us (the 8th took off late and was unable to find the others), at the conclusion of a negative, 2-hour patrol over Empress Augusta Bay, headed north with the intention of strafing Chabai Plantation.

Lt. Cdr. R.R. Hedrick   Lt. L.D. Cooke
Lt(jg) M. Schanuel   Lt(jg) H.M. Burriss
Lt(jg) P. Cordray   Lt(jg) G.F. Bowers
Ens. J.O. Ellsworth

On arriving at Matchin Bay it was discovered that Chabai was obscured by rain.

The flight therefore strafed Soraken Plantation (an alternative target) setting 3 camouflaged huts afire. One hut burned particularly fiercely, and the dense black smoke seen led to the conclusion that it contained oil.

The flight also strafed huts on the 3 small islands west of Soraken Plantation.

Lt. Cdr. Hedrick and Lt(jg) Schanuel flew past Sohanna Island and saw what might have been a float plane on the north tip of the island.

All strafing done at low levels.

No A/A fire was encountered.

At the conclusion of a negative, 2-hour patrol over Empress Augusta Bay a flight of 7 F4Us proceeded as directed, to strafe ground installations between Monoitu Mission and Kahili in southern Bougainville.

Lt. T.R. Bell   Lt. W.J. Schub
Ens. W.P. Meek   Lt(jg) W.L. Landreth
Lt(jg) R.H. Jackson
Ens. M.M. Kurlander

Lt. Bell's division located Monoitu Mission and found that two houses near the mission had already been destroyed, but that the Mission itself was still intact. They made several runs on the Mission and left it burning fiercely. No A/A was encountered.

Lt. Schub, Lt(jg) Jackson, and Ens. Meek covered the Monoitu-Kahili trail and strafed 4 bridges. The bridges, although hit, did not burn.

As Schub made a run on 4 huts at Shishigatero an A/A gun (probably 40mm.) fired at him at a range of about 75 yards.

All planes returned to base.

Ready Room. Group of ten personnel in front of Ready Quonset, New Georgia. L-R. Back Row: *Jack Chasnoff, "Hap" Bowers, "Duke" Henning, Hal Jackson, "Chico" Freeman, "Windy" Hill.* L-R. Front Row: *"Andy" Anderson, Bob Hogan. I believe the last two are Johnny Kleinman and Lou Kelley.* Courtesy U.S. Naval Historical Center / M.W. "Butch" Davenport Collection.

29 November

Four F4Us escorted a Dumbo (PBY) to Empress Augusta Bay, Bougainville, and return.

Eight F4Us escorted a Dumbo (PBY) to Kieta Harbor, Bougainville, and return.

At the conclusion of a negative, 2-hour patrol over Empress Augusta Bay, Bougainville, the following pilots, as directed, strafed a line 500 yards inland from a directional arrow on the beach.

Ens. R.R. Hogan
Ens. D.T. Malone
Ens. C.H. Dunn
Ens. W.P. Popp

This area presumably contained Jap machine gun posts and troops. The F4Us strafed, though they could see no targets. They were then directed by Dane Base to strafe a line 200 yards inland and 250 yards west of the arrow. At the conclusion of this mission the F4Us returned to base.

30 November

Four negative, 2-hour patrols (24 sorties) were flown over Cat Base (2 DDs) in Empress Augusta Bay, Bougainville.

One negative, 2-hour patrol (4 sorties) was flown over Munda.

Eight F4Us were assigned as high cover over an SBD-TBF strike on the Jakohina, area. The F4Us made rendezvous with the bombers over Baga Island at 12,000 ft. and proceeded to the target. Bombing lasted 15 minutes.

Coverage was reported as particularly good, the area covered being that between Kahili strip and Kangu Hill.

Heavy A/A fire was meagre at the fighters' altitude (14,000 - 16,000 ft.) but intense at lower altitudes. It was accurate in range but inaccurate in altitude.

After the attack the F4Us escorted the bombers as far as Baga Island, then returned to base.

4

End of First Tour
December 1943

1 December
On this date VF-17 was composed of 42 officers and 66 enlisted men, and had a compliment of 34 F4U-1 aircraft.

Two negative, 2-hour patrols (16 sorties) were flown over Empress Augusta Bay, Bougainville.

REST AND RECREATION-AUSTRALIA

2 December
Wilbert Popp recalls his first combat tour: "My first combat tour on rejoining VF-17 stationed at Ondongo, was in November 1943. My total flight time up to then was 385 hours, with about 27 hours in the Corsair. This was a combat air patrol over our base. My first actual combat was a strike to Mosige on Vella Lavella. Most of this phase of VF-17's tour of duty was over Bougainville and Green Island. We left Ondongo on December 3, 1943, flying up to Espiritu Santo over Guadalcanal, referred to as 'Cactus' over to Espiritu referred to as 'Buttons'. At Espiritu we were housed and supplied by C.A.S.U. 11. During that time we received replacement pilots, new planes and additional training. We also had R & R at Sydney, Australia".

On this date VF17 was relieved by VF33.

The defeat in the Solomons stunned the Japanese. They withdrew their warships from Rabaul, allowing the U.S. to build airstrips on Bougainville, Piva Yoke fighter strip and Piva Uncle light bomber strip. While the new airstrips were constructed the squadron received 2 weeks much needed rest and recreation in Australia.

The following 34 pilots flew F4U-1 aircraft from Ondongo to Fighter One, Guadalcanal, take-off 0830, arrival 1030:-

Lt. Cdr. J.T. Blackburn	Lt(jg) T. Killefer
Lt. Cdr. R.R. Hedrick	Lt(jg) W.L. Landreth
Lt. S.R. Beacham	Lt(jg) E. May
Lt. T.R. Bell	Lt(jg) M. Schanuel
Lt. L.D. Cooke	Ens. C.H. Dunn
Lt. M.W. Davenport	Ens. J.O. Ellsworth
Lt. C.D. Gile	Ens. R.H. Hill
Lt. H.A. March	Ens. R.R. Hogan
Lt. W.J. Schub	Ens. F.A. Jagger

Lt(jg) G.F. Bowers	Ens. I.C. Kepford
Lt(jg) H.M. Burriss	Ens. T.F. Kropf
Lt(jg) P. Cordray	Ens. M.M. Kurlander
Lt(jg) D.G. Cunningham	Ens. D.T. Malone
Lt(jg) D.C. Freeman	Ens. W.P. Meek
Lt(jg) C.W. Gilbert	Ens. W.P. Popp
Lt(jg) D.H. Gutenkunst	Ens. F.J. Streig
Lt(jg) R.H. Jackson	Ens. W.C. Wharton

3 December
The above listed pilots flew F4U-1 aircraft from Fighter One, Guadalcanal to Pallikulo Airfield, Espiritu Santo, take-off 1015, arrival 1415.

3 December-5 December
The remaining 6 officers, 66 enlisted men, and squadron gear was flown from Ondongo to Pallikulo Airfield, Espiritu Santo by S.C.A.T.

4 December-5 December
The above listed 34 pilots and Lt. D.A. Innis, Lt. L.F. Herrmann and Lt(jg) J.M. Chasnoff were flown from Espiritu Santo to Sydney, Australia, by S.C.A.T.

5 December
Lt(jg) R. Mims reported for duty. Mims was an original member of VF-17 and had sailed out with the squadron in September, but due to appendicitis did not make the first tour.

5 December-16 December
Extensive work on aircraft, checks, engine changes, etc.

Dan Cunningham (7 kills), one of VF-17's thirteen aces. Courtesy U.S. Navy photo. Robert L. Lawson Collection.

Lou Fitzgerald with his F4U Corsair. Courtesy U.S. Naval Historical Center / M.W. "Butch" Davenport Collection.

6 December-14 December
Rest and Recuperation Australia and induction of new pilots.

The Australians rescued from the Japanese onslaught gave the squadron a very warm welcome.

Roger Hedrick has clear memories of being in Australia.

"The people were exceedingly friendly, I remember vividly the Australia hotel. We used the term snake pit once or twice up in the States. I was bunking with Lem Cooke in an apartment. We had a high rise overlooking Sydney harbor. But as we started out of the hotel, lo and behold here were two young ladies walking in. They looked very attractive, so we did a 180 and followed them in.

"We had a wonderful time that evening dancing and so forth. Then it seems to me they decided they could come in and perhaps help us cook a meal now and then, which they did."

"Later on these two girls came out with nothing but panties on, lined up arm in arm just as if they were in a chorus line. Lem and I were in the sack trying to catch up on some sleep, and they wanted us to get up and go out to the horse races or some stupid thing. Here they come, and believe me they got our attention!"

Roger Hedrick recalls another incident.

"We were in a restaurant. While we were eating, in old khakis looking pretty scraggy. People were looking, waiting to ask us something, but didn't have the nerve, and didn't want to interfere with us. So I finally stood up, looked at them and said, 'Folks, we're winning. They started applauding and that was a big help to our morale, too."

Dan Cunningham has fond memories of VF-17's time in Australia:

"We go down to the Sydney hotel and there would be 10 or 12 of us in there drinking beer and we run them out of beer. So we said how about some ale, they said yes we got ale.

"So we end up running them out of ale. So they said, 'did you ever try stout.' You're supposed to put half stout and half beer. No beer, no ale, only stout; and that kinda broke up the party".

"Windy"Hill was another who made the most of R & R:

"After a couple of days non-stop round-the-clock parties with various girls, I was going to take an afternoon off and relax and go to this musical show they were having in Sydney. This young lady, who was the female star of the show, came out on the stage. When I saw her I was smitten!

"After the show was over I go to the stage door, slipped the old guy on the door some money, got him to take a message up to the young lady, saying I would like to take her to dinner that evening.

"The word came back, thank you very much but she had a date for that evening. Well I wasn't about to be shot down in flames that easily. So I sent another message back up saying I would like to just meet you and tell you how much I'd enjoyed your performance. Well what performer can resist something like that.

"I introduced myself. I turned on all the charm that I possessed. I pulled out all the stops. She smiled at me, she said I have a date for this afternoon, but would you like to meet me here tomorrow afternoon.

"The next afternoon I was there with an armful of roses. Just like I'd seen Clark Gable do in the movies when he was romancing somebody. I had a taxi outside with the taxi driver standing there holding the door open for us. We got in, went up to her apartment, had a few drinks, got to know each other, cooked a few steaks for supper.

"Well this became kind of a daily routine. When I got back to Espiritu Santo I purchased the latest issue of Yank magazine, turned to see who the pin up girl was and lo and behold there smiling at me was this lovely girl I had just kissed goodbye in Sydney".

Mel Kurlander remembers his time in Sydney.

"Everyone was assigned by the Red Cross different apartments. 3 of us roomed together and what we tried to do was find an area with some gals left over. "Windy" Hill met up with a beautiful gal, Miss Sydney, and had a couple of friends to set me and "Country" up with. We were at the stage door, three Americans all with a dozen red roses for these girls. Three Americans walking off with three beautiful Australian girls.

"Windy" wanted to marry this girl. The women were great there. I was taking some uniforms over to the laundry and I bumped into a girl and asked her where the nearest laundry was and she said, 'I can do it for you'. She said. 'Let me have it'. Lo and behold she ironed them when she brought them over. She wouldn't even let us buy her a drink.

She said. 'You guys have done so much for us it's the least I can do'".

REPLACEMENT PILOTS

8 December
The following officers reported for duty from ComFairSouth:-
Lt(jg) J. Miller
Ens. J.M. Smith

10 December
The following officers reported for duty from ComFairSouth:-
Lt(jg) H.J. Bitzegaio
Lt(jg) J.W. Farley
Lt(jg) C.L. Smith

Harold Bitzegaio remembers joining the squadron:

"When I joined the squadron I had never flown an F4U. I had about 2 weeks of indoctrination before I was in combat. I was in an F4F squadron out there originally then went back to the States in F6Fs and then was transferred to F4Us (VF-17).

"The F6F was brand new and I was very reluctant to leave F6Fs. I thought I was being downgraded. Later on I had 3 jugs shot out over Japan and flew the F4U almost 300 miles with 3 cylinders gone with the crankcase out. No hydraulic fluid - no flaps landing on the carrier".

13 December
The following officers were flown to Tontouta, New Caledonia by S.C.A.T. to ferry five F4U-1s to Pallikulo Airfield:-
Lt(jg) H.J. Bitzegaio
Lt(jg) J.W. Farley
Lt(jg) J. Miller
Lt(jg) C.L. Smith
Ens. J.M. Smith

15 December-16 December
All officers having been on leave in Sydney, Australia were returned by S.C.A.T.

17 December-31 December
Mel Kurlander had a close call when he returned from Sydney. He describes the event:

"When we got back from Sydney the first night the commanding officer gave us orders to fly formation. We hadn't flown formation for 2-3 weeks. We still had hangovers from Sydney. So Tom just told us to taxi out, take off and come back and land. I really almost killed myself. We had some smoke pots on the coral strip, and a tower built of bamboo 3-5 stories high. I was taking off and I started drifting and losing the flares on my right wing. I'm thinking I'm going to go right into that tower. I had just about enough flying knots. I might have had 70-75 knots. I started pulling back and dropping the wing down. I'm practically spinning in. Just before I hit the deck I was able to straighten it out. I bent the left wing and then taxied down to the end. I'm about, at most 6 feet, from chewing up the end of a B-17 I think. Some guys had been flashing me and they jumped on to each wing and got me back to where our planes were parked. All new overhauls for our planes had just been done. I was flying Carl Gilbert's plane. He's in grabbing breakfast and asking who bent the wing on his plane. No-one knew I had done it".

Walter Schub remembered that from December 16 to January 22, 1944 the order of the day was routine rear area Instrument refresher and misc. training flying.

"Andy" Jagger recalls being at Espiritu Santo:

"This was an island in the rear no longer in the combat zone a long way from Bougainville. We were mainly inducting 4 to 5 new replacement pilots into the squadron. Practicing things we had got rusty on. While here we were taken on survival training, led by

Group of VF-17 pilots at Ondongo 1943. This photo was taken between 22 December, 1943 and 5 January, 1944. Back Row L-R. Ellsworth, Cordray, Freeman, Gile, Unknown, Hedrick, Kepford, Landreth, Unknown, Hill. Front Row. L-R. Cooke, J.M. Smith, Cunningham, Fitzgerald, Wharton, Schanuel. Courtesy U.S. Naval Historical Center / M.W. "Butch" Davenport Collection.

some experts and taken into the jungles of Espiritu Santo. None of us were ever exposed to survival in a jungle".

17 December
The following officers were assigned F4U-1s which they ferried from Tontouta, New Caledonia to Pallikulo Airfield:-
Lt(jg) H.J. Bitzegaio
Lt(jg) J.W. Farley
Lt(jg) J. Miller
Lt(jg) C.L. Smith
Ens. J.M. Smith

18 December
Lt. J.A. Halford and Lt. J.M. Kleinman were detached.

21 December
Mel Kurlander describes an incident shortly after Sydney:
"He didn't go for all the spit and polish unless it was called for. We wandered around in sandals, tennis shoes, socks, cut off shorts. I came back from Sydney with an Aussie hat. I was flying with this Aussie hat on with the skipper and I then had my flying hat over the top. He turned round and looked at me and I thought he was going to reach out through the cockpit and get me by the neck and drop me. He was so pissed off. I never did that again!"
The following officers reported for duty from ComFairSouth:-
Ens. K.P. Babkirk
Ens. J.R. Travers

22 December
Ens. L.A. Fitzgerald reported for duty from ComFairSouth.

29 December
During night-flying operations at Fighter Strip One, Espiritu Santo, an F4U-1 flown by Lt(jg) C.L. Smith struck a tree. Lt(jg) Smith was able to gain sufficient altitude to bail out and was recovered with only minor injuries. The plane was destroyed.

5

Blackburn's Irregulars

Due to the exploits of the squadron around Norfolk and Manteo early in 1943 they were given the name "Blackburn's Irregulars". Many of the pilots were high-spirited and eager for action of any sort. This led to a number of stories and incidents as follows:

"Country" Landreth said that being called "Blackburn's Irregulars:" "was overdone a little bit. In some cases I think that was true. We had some pretty tough guys to handle. In the case of myself and several others that came from Corpus via Miami, we were raw ensigns with no experience, and we were sent to that squadron because it was being commissioned at the time we were available.

"You have to be aware that everybody that came out of Corpus Christi wanted to be a fighter pilot. Some are selected and some are not selected. As it turns out, Bob Keiffer and I set a record in the Training Command the last day of our training in the number of hits on the sleeve. We both had the same identical number of holes in that sleeve, and both broke all the records they had before in the SNJ. I feel then, and still do, that may have had a lot to do with us going to the premier fighter squadron in the Navy.

"VF-17 was the first successful carrier-based Corsair squadron - and there wasn't any fighter pilot that didn't want to fly the Corsair, the best airplane in the world. Among other things, it meant you had the best chance of survival because of performance and what-not".

"Country Landreth describes Tom Blackburn:

"He demanded top performance, he demanded you to be there on time ready to fly, he expected you to be an expert formation flyer, he didn't tolerate any lack of discipline in the air. He was inclined to be lenient about things on the ground until you crossed that invisible line. He didn't have a lot of spit and polish attitude. We had our inspections, we went through all the other drills. He tried to make us Navy people as well as fighters.

"He was certainly a party man himself. I learned early that you don't go ashore with the skipper's group and try to stay up with him, because it was a useless task. He'd be the last one standing, and he'd be the guy that would be there first the next morning.

"He was a young-looking slender fella'. In fact, more than one Ensign, reporting for duty, went to the squadron ready room, and (seeing Blackburn) said, 'Hey, fella'. Where's the skipper? I'm re-

porting for duty.' Blackburn would say, "Yeah? You're looking at 'im!"

Mel Kurlander recalls his skipper:

"We were known by a variety of names, VF-17, "Skull and Crossbones", Whistling Death (by the enemy), eventually Jolly Rogers and "Blackburn's Irregulars" (by the Navy hierarchy).

"Apropos to the latter, we had just returned from R & R in Sydney to Espiritu Santo, and the C.O. (Army) ordered us to fly

A different view of ten personnel in front of Ready Quonset, New Georgia. L-R. Back Row: *Jack Chasnoff, "Hap" Bowers, "Duke" Henning, Hal Jackson, "Chico" Freeman, "Windy" Hill.* L-R. Front Row: *"Andy" Anderson, Bob Hogan. I believe the last 2 to be Johnny Kleinman and Lou Kelley.* Courtesy U.S. Naval Historical Center / M.W. "Butch" Davenport Collection.

night formation. Tom told us to take-off, fly around the strip, land and give the plane a down-check.

"The next morning we had a sneak inspection. The squadron was in full array, baseball caps, Aussie hats, skivvy shirts, shorts, sandals, tennis shoes, no socks and a few Aussie fleece boots.

The C.O. arrived in a jeep and Tom threw him a salute. This Army officer took one look at us, jumped back into the jeep and left. We never heard from him again.

Blackburn, with his sly fox sardonic half-smile (which we all knew) must have been thinking 'don't ever mess around with my pilots.'

"Tom Blackburn was a one-of-a-kind skipper".

Two articles were published during and after the war about VF-17 and give a clear indication of how the name "Blackburn's Irregulars" was born.

BLACKBURN'S IRREGULARS

They made training-field commanders wake up screaming. Squadron leaders damned them, his thoughts became unprintable. So one man took them and whipped them into the finest aerial team in the U.S. Navy.

Once there were a lot of guys nobody wanted. So one man tamed them by a judicious blending of compulsion and persuasion into the finest aerial fighting team in the United States Navy.

For their squadron's battle insignia, they chose the pirate death's-head, and, whatever you may think of the originality of their choice, it admirably suited the wild, to-hell-with-regulations behavior of their early training days.

They christened themselves the Skull and Crossbones Squadron. Official Navy documents record them as VF-X, commanded by Lieutenant Commander John Thomas Blackburn, of Washington, D.C. Other fliers and the gold-bricked victims of their exuberance called them Blackburn's Irregulars-and the name stuck. Not only did it go well with their insignia, but it defined their origin-a nucleus of pilots transferred to Blackburn from other squadrons the leaders of which had decided that life without them would be much less complicated.

The leaders wanted men they could handle, not cocky youngsters who couldn't seem to remember that regulations applied to them, too! Spit-and-polish was more to their taste than aerial horseplay. They sent their mavericks away. Blackburn took them.

Now they are heroes, and everybody wants them-chambers of commerce for testimonial banquets, war plants for worker-incentive speeches, and the Navy as shining embodiments of "the highest traditions of the service." Oh, they're a joy and a treasure now, all right, but they would gladly trade the pallid present for the robust and unruly past when they were a pain in the neck to the admiral.

The admiral didn't love them. He said to the only man who did, "If you can't handle those hellions, I'll find someone who can."

A bad Bet for the Japs
To which Lieutenant Commander Blackburn made the kind of reply you'd expect from a devoted but slightly astigmatic parent. He said, "Admiral, from past performance it would look as if I can't handle those fellows, and I respectfully submit sir, that nobody in the Navy can. I can promise you that I shall do my best, sir. I further promise you that when we get into action, these boys will harass the Japs as effectively as they are harassing you and me right now."

That wasn't a promise. It was a prophecy. As this is written, Blackburn's Irregulars have shot down more Japanese airplanes than any other fighter squadron in our armed forces. Their score, in 76 days of combat flying, is 154 enemy planes destroyed in the air and two on the ground; five small ships and sixteen barges sunk with their cargoes of troops or supplies.

In one five-day period, it knocked down 60.5 Jap planes (credit for one plane is shared with another squadron) for what probably is an all-time record for any fighter squadron.

It has 13 aces—more, at this writing, than any other Navy squadron. On five separate occasions, individual pilots each shot down four Japs in the course of one furious action. In nine weeks, on two tours of duty, it flew the amazing total of 7,192 combat hours for an average of something over 200 for each of its 24 pilots.

Only 20 planes and 12 pilots were lost to enemy action. Three of the losses resulted from anti-aircraft fire. In other words, the squadron made the enemy pay nearly eight planes for every one he shot down.

But what really makes the boys swell with pride are two facts:

1. No ship for which it provided air cover—and it flew 90 such missions—was ever hit by bomb or aerial torpedo.

2. Not a single bomber from any squadron it protected on nearly 40 raids was lost to Japanese aircraft.

Rear Admiral J.J. Balantine is shown with four of the thirteen aces of the crack Corsair squadron known as "Blackburn's Irregulars". L-R. Lt. Harry March, (5 Jap planes); Lt. Cdr. Roger Hedrick (9); Adm. Ballantine, now chief of staff, Air Force, Pacific Fleet; Lt. Cdr. J.T. Blackburn, (11); and the No. 1 Navy ace (at that time), Lt(jg) Ira C. Kepford, (16). Courtesy U.S. Navy photo. Robert L. Lawson Collection.

Lt(jg) Ira C. Kepford poses by the cockpit of a Vought F4U Corsair in March 1944. Flying this type of plane with Fighter Squadron 17 in the Solomon Islands in November 1943-February 1944, he shot down 16 Japanese planes, to become the Navy's then leading ace. Courtesy National Archives.

Defense, obviously, is the primary function of a fighter squadron. But to defend effectively it frequently must fight offensively. It must destroy or disperse the enemy before he can strike at ships or bombers. In this respect, the record of VF-X is perfect.

Other fighter squadrons in our Armed Forces may have been as good. None could have been better.

Ace of the Squadron

One of the men who helped make that perfection was Ike Kepford. His full name is Ira Cassius Kepford. You've got to know him pretty well before he'll tell you his middle name. His home is Muskegon, Michigan. He is twenty-four years old. At Northwestern University he was a blocking halfback who knocked guys down so Bill De Correvont, the All-America, could score touchdowns. He was good enough to make the second All-America himself. The squadron's top ace, he knocked sixteen Jap planes into the Pacific. The Navy recently awarded him the Distinguished Flying Cross.

Death, as every flier knows, has its favorites. Ike was one of them. If this were not so, he wouldn't be back in the States, taking things easy. He would be resting on the bottom of the Pacific somewhere between Rabaul and the China coast.

When death gave Ike his second holiday, he was headed for China knowing full well that he'd never get there from Rabaul in a Corsair, even at 400 miles an hour.

Anyway, he figured the Zeros would tag him before his gas tanks emptied. He didn't like the idea any better than you would, but he figured he'd been living on borrowed time since, during a Rabaul raid a couple of weeks earlier his ship had taken some hits which fired a wing and exploded all the machine-gun bullets in it-some of them through the cockpit. None of these bullets hit him. So, with the burning wing, he left Rabaul and landed at his base on Bougainville on one wheel.

This is how Ike got into his second predicament over Rabaul. The squadron moved in for a strike at the key Jap base last February 19th. In the original melee of Jap and American planes, he got one Zero. As he was pulling away from the falling Jap, he spotted a seaplane just off the water. He gave it a short squirt and set it afire.

Ike was no waster of ammunition. His father taught him to shoot as soon as he could hold a shotgun. As far as anyone knows, no fighter pilot has approached his record of four kills and one probable in a single action with 75 bullets per gun.

In going after the seaplane, Ike exposed his tail. Now three Zeros were on it, two on one side, one on the other. He called over the radio to the rest of the squadron:

"Chalk up two for Ike. Three Zeros have me pocketed. This looks like the works."

All he could do was to make a straightaway run for his life. He got down as close to the water as he dared. The Zeros were firing. He could see their tracers all around him. He used his water injector, a device that makes a 2,200 to 2,300-horsepower engine out of one with a normal top rating of 2,000. He gained about 100 yards on the Zeros. Their shots now fell just to his rear (The Irregulars were the only Navy Squadron flying Vought Corsairs, the gull-wing fighter equipped with the mechanism that sent a tiny squirt of water into the fuel mixture for extra power in emergencies. The effect of the water jet is similar to the effect of fog or damp night air on the performance of automobile motors).

Ike couldn't pull up. Zeros climb too fast. If he turned, that would give the Japs the kind of shot they were praying for. So he kept straight on, lifting just enough to clear the islands, then down again over the water on a beeline for China.

There is no more terrible strain in the world than a chase like this. After five or ten minutes of it, the pilot's nerves usually begin to go to pieces, and his engine heats up to the point of fire. Ike stood it for between twenty and thirty minutes. His engine smelled warm, but it wasn't burning, as he turned into the single Zero.

The Jap turned to follow, but he was over-anxious. He forgot how close he was to the water. A wing tip caught on a wave. He spun over and over, then vanished in a quick dive. He presented Ike with his third kill for the day.

A little before three o'clock that afternoon, a lone Corsair came down on the landing strip on Bougainville, and the most humble, God-fearing man in the world unsteadily climbed out. He was Ike. All other pilots of the squadron had long since returned and had given him up for lost. They wanted to know what had happened.

He tried to tell them, but was so unnerved that he couldn't so much as lift his hand to point out on a map where he had been.

They gave Ike a drink of brandy and sent him to bed. It was nearly noon the next day when he got up.

On that February 19th raid, the Irregulars were opposed by from 50 to 75 enemy planes. They got 16 of them without loss to themselves. Not since that day have the Japanese dared send an airplane against our squadrons from Rabaul, once one of their most formidable bases.

The Irregulars first learned they were to have the place to themselves when they returned to Rabaul three days later. As they exercised their will in the skies, a falsetto voice was heard on their radios. Some thought a Jap was speaking. Others surmised one of the Irregulars was having a joke. Anyway, the voice said, "Sorry, no airplanes today. Please drop your bombs and go home."

With a carrier-task-force attack on Rabaul—the first large-scale assault on the base—the United States Navy celebrated last Armistice Day. The Irregulars went along to help cover the carriers. They shot down 18 Japanese planes and shared a nineteenth with another squadron. Not a pilot was lost, although two planes went down in the water. No carrier was damaged.

"We flew out to the carriers from our base on New Georgia Island." Blackburn related. "It was the first time that air cover had ever been provided for carriers from the beach while planes were being launched. After the striking force had started for Rabaul, we landed aboard and had breakfast of orange juice, eggs and steak. It had been a long time since we had a breakfast like that.

"We were airborne again while the dive bombers and torpedo planes were being recovered. The Japanese counter-attack came while we were up. That was the most exciting thing I have ever seen. Down below, ships of the Navy zig-zagged a crazy pattern of wakes. The air was filled with airplanes and anti-aircraft fire. You can't imagine how much stuff our ships were throwing up. It didn't seem possible that we could be flying through it after Japs and not being hit. Burning Japs were dropping all over the place, and our blue fighters were flying among them. You wouldn't have thought there would be room for all that stuff up there. In the water, there were pools of flame. That's where the Japs were dying.

The End of the Attack

"Then suddenly it all stopped as if someone had uttered a command. A few bonfires sputtered out in the sea. Everywhere there was silence.

"The squadron put in an average of 10.5 combat hours per man that day. The planes we lost went down for lack of fuel. Two of the boys flew to the carrier for refueling. The rest of us took a chance and made it back to base, although some of our tanks had about a pint of gas left."

"Many of our planes were badly shot up. A 20-millimeter shell exploded, literally, in the face of Lieutenant John M. Kleinman. It didn't faze him, but it blew out his instrument panel. Here he was miles from nowhere and no instruments to show him the way home. He took a look at the sun and guessed a course. He held it, and I'll be damned if it didn't get him back. I'll never know why. Kleinman

was later sent to Melbourne as an instructor. He was killed in a crash there."

A story is told about one of the Irregulars that reminds me of Charles Lamb's tale about the Chinese who burned down the house to get roast pork. During a strafing raid on Bougainville, a Jap sniper took a pot shot at the plane of Ensign Bradford Baker, of Spokane, Washington. The bullet hit Baker's windshield. It made him so mad that, at the first opportunity, he cut loose with all his guns at the sniper's tree. He didn't hit the sniper but he did cut down the tree.

On most occasions, however, members of the squadron got more than a single Jap for their .50 caliber ammunition. One day an attack was scheduled on Buka, northwest of Bougainville, where the Japs had an airfield. The Irregulars were to have met a flight of B-25s about fifty miles from the island, but the rendezvous point was curtained by a heavy storm, and no contact could be made with the bombers. Pressing through the storm, planes of the squadron finally emerged into clear weather close to Buka.

Blackburn decided that the least they could do would be to strafe the place. As they were moving in low for the attack, the Irregulars saw a Japanese transport coming down for a landing. Lined up alongside the runway was what looked like a reception committee of Japanese officers. Judging from the display of gold braid on their uniforms, they were gentlemen of rank who must have been expecting a personage of major importance.

An Unexpected Welcome

Three of the squadron got into the transport's landing circle, and when the big plane was about ten feet from the ground, two of them cut it to pieces with their machine guns. A liberal sprinkling of lead was also fired into the official greeters. So taken by surprise were the Japs, that the Irregulars were a mile away before the enemy was able to get as much as one anti-aircraft gun into action.

The Japs have been so successful in using bad weather to hide attacks or to cover troop movements that sometimes storms make them overconfident. That's the way it was one day last October when a squall covered Tonolei Harbor in the Rabaul area. In a leisurely fashion, they were running in some troop barges when the Irregulars beat down through the rain to have a look. They ruined eight barges.

Roger Hedrick. Bougainville, February 1944. Courtesy Lennard Edmisten.

Like every good team, the Irregulars were adept at working out new plays.

Some of their tactics can't be detailed without showing the Japs how to save their necks. Blackburn and his pilots, for example, devised a new type of high-altitude cover. The first time they used it, they cut down eight Zeros, and not a Jap got close enough to fire a shot at our bombers. They also discovered that a certain form of aerial display actually bluffs the Japs out of closing for a fight.

One of their favorite tactics they called the Statue of Liberty because it reminded them of the old football play. To execute the play with a fighting squadron, you need a big hill. There was such a hill near a Jap airfield in the Solomons area. For quite some time, the Irregulars made daily attacks on the field, climbing over the hill each time they came in, and again on their way home. The Japs were in the habit of chasing them as far as the hill and then turning back.

One day, the Irregulars scooted to the side of the hill instead of going over it.

The Japs as usual, turned for home, but our boys kept on going round the hill. They were back at the field just as the Japs were landing, and gave them a very nice going-over. The Japs fell for the Statue of Liberty three or four times before they got wise.

Perhaps the most convincing evidence of the squadron's greatness as a team is the relatively even distribution of its 154-plane score through its members. Only two pilots failed to get a plane, and each of them was credited with a "probable." Next to Kepford, Blackburn owned the highest score. He had eleven. Lieutenant Commander Roger R. Hedrick of San Gabriel, California, the squadron's executive officer, was third with nine.

The other aces were: Lieut. Oscar I. Chenoweth, South Miami, Florida; Lieut. Clement D. Gile, Pittsburgh; Lieut. (jg) Earl May, Milwaukee; Lieut. (jg) Howard McClain Burriss, Granville, Ohio; Lieut. (jg) Dan G. Cunningham, Chicago; Lieut. (jg) Paul Cordray, Dallas; Lieut. (jg) Robert Mims, Dallas; Lieut. Merl W. Davenport, Detroit; Lieut. (jg) Frederick J. Streig, Watsonville, Calif; and Lieut. Harry A. March, Jr; Washington D.C.

Blackburn had his squadron on two tours of combat duty. The first tour from October 27 to December 1, 1943, found them on New Georgia Island. After a rest period in Australia, they put in a second hitch, of a month, from a base on Bougainville whence they assisted with the neutralization of Rabaul.

It was for the squadron's work during the first tour, however, that Blackburn was awarded the Distinguished Flying Cross. The Navy liked the way the Irregulars covered the Marine landings at Empress Augusta Bay on Bougainville. It liked their teamwork and, in the citation, gave Blackburn credit as playing coach.

On that last point, no member of the squadron will argue. When they got to the Pacific, only four pilots had ever seen a Jap plane. Yet, in their first action they showed they were a polished team. They got that way in training. They got that way because Blackburn

allowed as much freedom as was needed-and no more-to a bunch of self-assertive individualists.

They had little use for regulations. He wasn't a spit-and-polish man himself.

They liked to dive down in formation onto a field and watch the little yellow training planes scatter. That's called buzzing the field. Blackburn liked to do that too. They liked to buzz the homes of their girls, their maiden aunts and assorted other citizenry in areas adjacent to their training bases. Blackburn could go along with that, also, but, as squadron commander, he "had to be respectable and try to make the others the same."

The squadron had several training bases, because buzz-happy field commanders frequently found it necessary to transfer it to save their nervous systems.

Finally they were banished to a small field in North Carolina, forbidden to engage in further buzzing and instructed to fly within sight of the field at all times, so that any violation of the no-buzz order could be immediately detected. They reacted by notifying every other squadron within flying distance of them that they would be on patrol over the field for four hours every morning.

Their dispatch read: "Combat air patrol on station from eight until noon. Visitors welcome."

Every squadron in the area accepted what was readily recognized as a standing invitation to go dogfighting.

Caught in a Dogfight

One day a squadron of torpedo planes flew 275 miles to engage them. It so happened that they arrived while a little target plane was flying near the Irregulars. Suddenly, the little plane was caught in the middle of scores of diving, climbing, thundering aircraft.

The target pilot will never understand how he survived.

After it was over, the boys felt so good, they dropped dummy bombs all over the flying field.

Blackburn condoned this, if he was not himself a conspirator. Between sessions of buzzing and dogfighting, his men were getting hour after hour of solid combat training. He drilled them on gunnery-deflection shooting. For six months the squadron did practically nothing but shoot, until as Blackburn said, "I had a lot of guys who could cream them. I mean our guys could really shoot."

He also hammered into their heads the doctrine that the job of a fighter pilot is to protect bombers and shipping, and that only by team fighting is the job done.

"I told them that if any of them started off by themselves to become little heroes, I would find out about it sooner or later, and I would ground every man who forgot what his job was," he recalled.

Blackburn never found it necessary to ask for the shift of any pilot he obtained by transfer from another squadron.

"Only those people were transferred from the Irregulars who wouldn't play on the team and who didn't have the necessary insanity," he said.

BLACKBURN'S IRREGULARS

The truck driver, wheeling his big trailer rig along the highway outside of Norfolk, Va., had had a busy day. If his foot was a trifle heavier on the gas than usual, it was only because he was so close to home with a long, straight stretch of concrete in front of him. There wasn't another vehicle in sight in any direction.

"Hey, Jake," the assistant driver said, "I think somebody wants to pass us."

"What the hell are you talking about? There's nobody. . ."

The words died in his mouth as he checked his rear-view mirror. Tearing down the highway after them, about 20 feet off the pavement, was a dark blue, inverted gull-winged monster, growing more tremendous by the second. Suddenly, with a terrifying surge of sound and air pressure, it overtook and skipped over the truck, giving only a brief glimpse of pale blue underside.

"It's one of those goddam Navy hotshots!" the driver raged, taking out his frustration by leaning on his horn. "They got the whole sky to fly their goddarn Corsairs in and they gotta use the highway too! If I coulda caught his number, I'd report him. I'd get him grounded for life. I'd. . ."

"Maybe you'll get your chance now, Jake," the assistant said. " I think he's coming back."

Far down the highway, the big F4U had dipped its wings and looped gracefully to the left. But instead of flying away, it stayed in the loop until it had described a complete turn. And now it was coming back up the highway at better than 300 miles per hour and even lower than before. The gleaming propeller seemed almost to touch the concrete.

"For God's sake, that crazy fool's gonna ram us!" the driver screamed and sent the rig careering off the road, through a fence and into a field. The Corsair, never swerving from its beeline path, roared past the spot where the truck had been, the pilot waving gaily. Just to make the sight a bit more unnerving, he was flying upside down!

The truck driver didn't get the squadron number, but the identification was no mystery to Navy authorities when the complaint was filed. Within an hour Lieutenant Commander J. Thomas Blackburn, commander of Fighter Squadron VF-17, was on the carpet again. In the best Annapolis tradition, he sucked in his breath and took it as a fiery rear admiral raked him fore and aft over the latest escapade of one of his men.

It was Burriss this time, Ensign Howard M. Burriss of Granville, O. He was the wildest one of the lot. It was Burriss who was fascinated with Mach 1, the speed of sound. When he joined the squadron, he had loudly announced that he intended to hit the speed of sound some day. Since this was roughly double the top speed of a Corsair, nobody had been too worried about it. So one day Burriss had taken his plane up to 25,000 feet and put it into a screaming dive. He hadn't quite attained Mach 1, but he did manage to hit 600 m.p.h., wrinkling the wings, buckling the fuselage and scaring the hell out of himself. He was so scared that now he was buzzing trucks upside down.

"And if you can't control those hellions, I'll find someone who can," the admiral was saying. There was a momentary silence and then Commander Blackburn got in his stock reply. "Sir, I'll do my best to keep them in hand. I can promise you that when we get into action, those boys will harass the Japs as effectively as they are harassing you and me right now."

Tommy Blackburn sighed as he replaced his cap outside the admiral's office.

He had expected to be chewed out, just as he had expected all the chewings that had gone before and all the rest that were sure to come later. It was a hell of a way to go into combat - to volunteer to command the most goofed-up fighter squadron in the whole damned Navy.

Squadron VF-17 was made up of what the Navy politely called "high-spirited" fliers. It was a euphemism meaning there was nothing wrong with their flying ability but they were just too wild to be handled under conventional discipline. They were the mavericks of the Navy-flathatters, buzzers, dogfighters, party brawlers, heavy drinkers and insubordinates. In normal times they would have been court-martialed and discharged, but this was 1943 and the Navy needed every good pilot it could get. But the brass decided it was more expedient to assemble all the bad actors into one mass headache rather than have them scattered around all over. Tom Blackburn, himself a perfect example of Annapolis discipline, had the unenviable job of trying to weld them into a fighting unit.

When VF-17 was formed and commissioned at Norfolk on January 1, 1943, Blackburn was assigned ten blackballed ensigns and two fliers with combat experience, Lieutenant Commander Roger Hedrick and Lieutenant Harry March. Commander Hedrick was named executive officer. No sooner had the ensigns been assigned to their first Corsairs than the complaints started coming in.

Norfolk residents raged bitterly over the shattered windows in their homes, caused by stunting Corsairs that pulled out of dives so close to the ground that the people below could smell the fumes of

Three of the squadron's leading aces pose by a Vought F4U-1A Corsair fighter, after their unit left the combat zone , 22 March, 1944. L-R Roger Hedrick (9 kills), Tom Blackburn (11 Kills), "Ike" Kepford (16 kills) the then leading Navy ace. Courtesy U.S. Navy photo. Robert L. Lawson Collection.

Tom Blackburn sitting in "Big Hog". Courtesy U.S. Naval Historical Center / M.W. "Butch" Davenport Collection.

their exhausts. A group of inspecting officers had to hit the deck when two of VF-17's planes came flat-topping over the field one day. One of the admirals jumped to his feet, brushed dirt from his dress blues and fumed, "Commander Blackburn, I consider this maneuver most irregular!"

That's how the outfit got its nickname—Blackburn's Irregulars.

If Ensign Burriss wasn't bad enough, there was Ensign Ira C. Kepford. He had been on the black-list since the day he first soloed at Glenview, Ill. He had taken the occasion to stage a dogfight with another fledgling over the crowded Arlington Park race track. Since both dogfighting and flying over crowded race tracks were forbidden, the Navy brass tolerated Kepford's conduct only when it learned that he had performed a virtually impossible outside loop in the SNJ advanced trainer.

Dogfights were Kepford's big weakness. One day when he was flying at prescribed height over Norfolk, minding his own airspeed, he came across an F6F marked with the Royal Naval Air Force insignia of Great Britain. Kepford playfully peeled off and got on the "enemy" tail. When the Englishman responded with a perfect chandelle, the ensign delightfully pressed the dogfight and soon the two planes were barreling all over the Norfolk skyline, shattering windows in every section of the city.

When Kepford landed, his mechanic said, "Ike, you're in for it this time. The skipper wants to see you on the double."

In Commander Blackburn's office, Kepford stood at attention while the patient C.O. looked him over and asked, "Did you win?"

"Yes, sir."

"Good. Now get to your room. You're confined to quarters for thirty days."

Burriss and Kepford were particular problem children, but each of the other men who were added to the roster of three dozen fliers also had some special dubious "qualification." Lieutenant Clement D. Gile had been an instructor in Miami with Commander Blackburn; he was a hot pilot but he had a weakness for all-night parties. Ensign Robert Mims was a Texan who was always getting into fistfights. Ensign R.H. Jackson liked to go out on the town. Lieutenant (jg) Tom Killefer hadn't been able to get along with the skipper of his previous squadron.

Blackburn kept his eyes peeled for good men who were in the doghouse in other units. Even in 1943 he had little trouble "acquiring" the Navy's black sheep from commanding officers who were happy to get rid of them. In VF-17 the oddballs were right at home. They chose the pirate's skull and crossbones as their battle insignia. What the choice lacked in originality, it more than made up in appropriateness.

Son of a Navy captain, Tom Blackburn himself was a man eager to start shooting in earnest. His leadership was intuitive as well as traditional. His judgment told him he shouldn't try to put out the fire in his "Irregulars"; he should try merely to confine it. He held the reins loosely but he knew when to yank them tight. He was genuinely intolerant of only one thing—bad gunnery.

He called Gile in one day and asked, "Have a good time in town on leave?"

Gile answered tentatively, "Yes sir."

"Your gunnery shows it!" Blackburn shot back.

Gile had no more leaves until his gunnery improved. Blackburn had them shooting, shooting, shooting, in a dedicated test of his conviction that success in war breaks down to one essential question—how accurately can you fire at the enemy? Woe was unto the Irregular whose ammunition color didn't register enough times in the gunnery sleeve.

Lumping so many free spirits together was not going to change their stripes—and Blackburn knew it. Girl friends' houses continued to be buzzed, havoc being wreaked on the fragile glassware. Citizens near the training field were in constant fear of having an F4U come unexpectedly down upon them out of the blue. Primary base fliers in the area, equipped with only elementary trainers, were scattered at times by whole formations of diving, supposedly friendly aircraft. Always, endlessly, there were dogfights.

The aerial horseplay eventually found the Irregulars banished to an obscure field at Manteo, N.C., an unsuspecting little town of 1,500 people. They were forbidden to engage in further buzzing and instructed to fly within sight of the field at all times, so that any violation could be immediately detected.

A few days later, an announcement was sent to every squadron within flying distance of them. It read: "Combat air patrol on station from eight until noon. Visitors welcome. VF-17, Manteo N.A.S."

Every outfit in the vicinity translated this into an invitation to come over and dogfight. One day a squadron of torpedo planes flew 275 miles to engage them. They arrived just as VF-17 was about to break off and land, with its little Piper Cub target—tower among them. Instantly the air was a wildly angling swarm of thundering, swooping airplanes. In their midst was the tiny yellow Cub, making its own passes at the "enemy"—something like the furry, plump rabbit turning on the huge, hungry wolf.

The Irregulars won the battle and felt so good afterward that they dropped dummy bombs all over the field.

But despite these diversions, VF-17 was acquiring solid training, both in combat and aerial discipline, as unlikely as the latter sounds. For six months they piled up endless hours of purposeful flying. In surprise moments of formation flying the skipper would turn tightly into his wingman to test his nerve as well as his technique.

They never let up on the deflection shooting drills until one day Blackburn bragged that the enemy didn't have a chance. "I've got some guys who can cream them."

It came time for overseas orders. When they arrived, Kepford, still confined to quarters and uncertain about rules and regulations in this situation, stayed in his room, momentarily forgotten, and managed to make the ship by only ten minutes.

There was still opportunity, however, for more hell-raising, Irregulars style, as they reached San Diego on their way westward. At a Marine base party, the inevitable

"Who's better, Marines or Navy?" argument erupted. This perennial discussion, spirited enough when lubricated by liquor, developed even more fireworks with Irregulars around. Somehow an admiral at the party was cast on the side of the Marines and an Irregular spun him around and challenged him, fists raised. The atmosphere suddenly became very thick with rank and the other Irregulars quickly hustled out their brave buddy. Luckily for him, he got only probation.

At San Diego they also invited some girls out to the base for a party and then discovered that the ladies didn't want to go home.

"Big Jim" Streig with his plane #3. Courtesy U.S. Naval Historical Center M.W. "Butch" Davenport Collection.

Gallantly, the Irregulars decided the only thing they could do was lock the bungalow during the day and pull down the blinds. For two-and-a-half days the girls stayed. The Irregulars reacted with surprising modesty to the comments of other flyers at the base. "The girls must like us," they said, simply.

Aboard ship, the night before they were to cross the Equator, they stole out in the dark and ripped open a huge, canvas tank of water that was to be used for their initiation the next day. Decks were flooded and there was general consternation and anger, which was reflected in the relish with which the "Shellbacks" performed the rites on the VF-17 "Pollywogs." But the Irregulars had such a good laugh it lasted clear through the ceremony.

Although they were Navy and carrier-trained, the Irregulars became land-based at Ondongo, New Georgia, on October 27, 1943. War came to them in full force over Empress Augusta Bay on November 1, only five days later.

At eight that morning, eight of them were guarding U.S. ships in the bay when they got their first look at the Japs. But it was an unequal look. There were 40 Japs-28 Zekes (fighters) and 12 Vals (bombers). The Corsairs were at 21,000 feet, the Japs at 18,000. Eager Tom Blackburn and seven of his irrepressible Irregulars dived.

The Jap formation disintegrated and the melee began. Blackburn pointed his nose at the leading Zeke, who executed a right chandelle. Blackburn fired and hit him, but he didn't go down. Blackburn recovered to his left and looked around for his wingman, Lieutenant (jg) Doug Gutenkunst of Milwaukee, WI. In the process, he made a diving head-on run at another Zeke, saw his hits bring white smoke, but took a few 7.7's from the Jap in return. He chased a third Zeke and fired at 100 yards. The Zeke burst into flames and crashed into the water.

Ensign Jim Streig of Watsonville, CA, and Killefer, keeping their section intact, missed in that headlong first pass, but they quickly picked out another Zeke, made a 60-degree deflection run and saw it explode at the right wing root. They sighted another, heading away, got onto his tail, opened fire at 250 yards and saw it begin burning. The Jap pilot bailed out.

Lieutenant Sheldon Beacham, of Kittyhawk, N.C., noticed two Zekes making gentle S-turns 1,000 feet below. From 13,000 feet he pushed over in a hasty, long plummet. When he loosed his guns, one Zeke rolled over in a steep climb. Beacham rolled with him and followed. In just one second the Zeke blew up. As Beacham climbed to rejoin the general fight above, two Japs jumped him out of the sun. The first sent bullets into Beacham's plane, the second turned to position himself on his tail.

Beacham skidded, rolled over on his back and dived straight down. He leveled off at 2,500 feet, jammed the throttle forward and escaped. Gutenkunst, busy pumping lead into a Val, also found himself scissored between two eagerly firing Zekes; he whipped into the safety of a cloud.

It was to be a busy opening day. That same afternoon, in a somewhat more equal match—nine Zekes and seven Vals to eight Irregulars—Commander Hedrick, leading a high cover patrol, spotted the enemy before the latter saw him and his friends. They went up-sun and came down in an easy 20-degree dive. Hedrick, able to use only four guns because of a generator failure, fired into a Zeke's fuselage, watched it burst and crash. In the resulting dogfight, the Irregulars learned of the Japs' ability to work in pairs. When the leader was attacked, the wingman peeled off and returned on the tail of the attacker. The dogfight ended in a standoff.

But the Irregulars had won their first day's aerial combat, 6 to 0. If the Japs were surprised, it might have comforted them to know that a few American admirals were, too.

But that same day Lieutenant (jg) J.H. Keith, of Bronson, KS, was hit by anti-aircraft fire on retiring from a strafing run. His plane, streaming black smoke, came down 15 miles from enemy land. The remainder of the flight agonizingly watched him leave the plane—without a life raft—and start swimming. They circled, steadily radioing for aid for their downed mate. But it was too dark to get a Dumbo (seaplane) search organized.

Back at Ondongo, intelligence officer Lieutenant Basil (Duke) Henning, of Louisville, KY, wrote down the poignant phrase, "missing in action." And the demanding, self-critical Blackburn wrote down: "F4U formation could have wrought more damage if it had sliced through the rear group of Zekes into the Vals and out through lead Zekes, since the Japs were going very slowly and could not have stayed with F4Us." He also noted: "F4Us markedly outperformed Zekes in everything but maneuverability."

War now became a daily affair. Killefer was hit by a 20-mm. shell, wounded by the shrapnel and burned on the leg. Blackburn's plane, too, was punctured by an anti-aircraft shell while strafing Jap shipping from as low as 20 feet, but both made it back.

One day, extremely bad weather prevented a rendezvous with a group of B-25s the Irregulars were supposed to protect in a shipping raid. Unwilling to return to base without doing anything and always looking for a fight, Blackburn took four pilots with him through the sour weather, hoping to find action at the Japs' airstrip at Buka. They emerged in clear atmosphere and quickly made ready to strafe whatever they could find. As they dropped toward the deck they spied a Jap transport in its final landing leg. Alongside the runway they could see what appeared to be a reception committee.

The mass of gold braid indicated a very important passenger aboard the transport.

As Killefer and Streig stood by Blackburn took March and Ensign W.C. Wharton, of Greenwood, SC, with him into the traffic pattern. With insolent aplomb they strafed a Zeke parked on the end of the strip and shot up the personnel there. By now they were on the tail of the transport, halfway up the strip and only ten feet from the ground. Blackburn and March shot it down in flames. They loosed more lead into the official greeters and were a mile away before the enemy could put a single anti-aircraft gun into action. Still eager, all five made passes at the Japs on Ballale airfield against intense anti-aircraft fire, and again Killefer stopped a 20-mm. shell and again made it home.

Duke Henning's aircraft action report about the transport kill included the wry observation: "Enemy plane had no opportunity to show its performance."

Elsewhere the same day, six other Irregulars found a pack of trouble. It was 4-to-1, with 24 Zekes opposing them. But they knocked down three and stayed whole themselves—and they learned more about Japanese tactics. The Japs were going in for rigid formation flying. They flew in a loose Lufbury Circle and fought only defensively.

One of them would chase an attacking American only if the latter went in blind pursuit of a Jap. The Navy boys really had to earn their kills.

On Armistice Day, VF-17 took off sleepy-eyed, in a day just a few hours old, to augment the first large-scale assault on mighty Rabaul. They flew cover over the Carrier Task Force until the strike had been launched. Then they landed aboard the Bunker Hill and the Essex and breakfasted lavishly on orange juice, eggs and steak. It had been a long time since they had had that kind of chow. When it was time for the strike to return, the 20 Irregulars went up again, to intercept any possible enemy counter-attack. The weather was foul, solid overcast at 24,000 and heavy squalls on three sides of the force. They were sent on what turned out to be a fruitless vector, when suddenly they got an urgent recall. Enemy aircraft closing in on the fleet.

By the time the Irregulars neared the fleet, the Jap dive and torpedo bombers had pushed over into their runs—Kates, Vals and Bettys. Zekes, Tonys and Hamps protected them, about 100 all told. The fleet gunners were throwing metal frantically.

Heedless of anti-aircraft fire from their own ships' guns, the Irregulars went barreling after the Jap planes in their straining Corsairs. It was a hectic, thrilling, deadly sight.

"Big Jim" Streig and Tom Killefer at Ondongo, November 1943. Courtesy U.S. Navy photo. Robert L. Lawson Collection.

Everyone was right on the ocean. In a screaming effort, Ike Kepford caught a torpedo bomber off the bow of the Bunker Hill just as the Jap was ready to drop his fish, and shot it down. Gile overtook and eliminated a Jap closing in on a cruiser. Procedure and tactics were discarded. This was free-for-all survival; war at its most selfless. The only aim: Go after the Jap plane that was bearing in on a ship—even if you were caught between both American and Jap guns.

As Blackburn remembered the fight later: "It was the most exciting thing I have ever seen. Down below, ships of the Navy zig-zagged a crazy pattern of wakes. The air was filled with airplanes and anti-aircraft fire. You can't imagine how much stuff our ships were throwing up. It didn't seem possible that we could be flying through it after Japs and not be hit. Burning Japs were dropping all over the place and our fighters were flying among them. You wouldn't have thought there would have been room for all that stuff up there. In the water there were pools of flame. That's where the Japs were dying."

Suddenly it all stopped, as if on command. A few lingering bonfires sputtered out in the sea. Everywhere there was silence. Not a carrier had been hit. Not an Irregular pilot had been lost; two planes had gone down, but only for lack of fuel. Two others had landed on carriers to refuel. Now VF-17, many of its planes badly

"Butch" Davenport and plane captain #9 at Bougainville 1944. Courtesy U.S. Naval Historical Center / M.W. "Butch" Davenport Collection.

shot up and fuel supply low, turned for the flight back to base, regrouping haphazardly. Some of the planes made it home with a pint of gasoline left.

The squadron turned in an average of ten and a half combat hours per man that day. They shot down 18 Japanese planes and shared a 19th with another squadron.

Eleven of the 20 Irregulars had been credited with kills. Ike Kepford, the mad flat-hatter, had picked off four of the Jap bombers. Burriss, the reformed truck-buzzer, eliminated two and helped an F6F carrier pilot take out another. Streig put down a Tony and a Zeke. Lieutenant Thaddeus Bell, of Seattle, Wash., added two more bombers to the VF-17 score.

The Irregulars' wrath never diminished. During a strafing raid on Bougainville, a Jap sniper sent a bullet into the windshield of the plane of Ensign Bradford Baker, Spokane, Wash. The lead lodged freakishly in the glass and Baker became so incensed that he peeled back and cut loose with all his guns at the sniper's tree. He didn't hit the Jap, but he cut down the tree.

Blackburn was proving to be as ideal a leader as the unit's training in the States had promised. He led with skill, ingenuity, courage and understanding. Hedrick, the executive officer, was spit-and-polish Navy but he was a hot pilot, too. Gile, older than the majority but bowing to no man in enthusiasm at party time, went into battle with the mature dedication of one who had early foreseen war. He had enlisted in 1940, soon after leaving Yale and long before Pearl Harbor. Lieutenant Merl W. Davenport of Detroit was called "Mother" for his solicitude. Streig was contemptuous of Jap bombing raids and refused to trade his comfortable cot for a foxhole until the night the Japs dropped a phosphorus bomb. In the huge, bright light, Streig could be seen bursting out of his tent, leaving a perfect silhouette in the canvas. March obeyed an urge to scratch and became known as "Dirty Eddie." Burriss was "Teeth." Jackson, a few flickers of gray in his hair, had the happiest routine. To ease the tension of war, he would ask the flight surgeon for a nip of brandy. A little went a long way with Hal. In a half hour he would be stiffly asleep. On a good day, Jackson would manage four naps. Killefer was held in great respect. So too, was Duke Henning, the articulate intelligence officer.

Ike Kepford's accurate gunnery made them all marvel. No complicated gun sight could improve on his instinct for knowing exactly where to send a bullet to meet the moving target he wanted to hit. Superior reflexes went with that gift. In a scramble one day, Hedrick burst out of a cloud. Ike, believing he was a Jap, shot instantaneously; then realizing the plane was American, he quit in the next second. On the ground they counted only six rounds shot out of each of Kepford's six guns—just 36 bullets. There were 12 bullet holes in Hedrick's plane.

A few days later eight of them were aloft early in the morning over Empress Augusta Bay, flying ship cover. Twenty-nine of the other side—12 Zekes, nine Tonys, eight Kates—dove into view. With professional dispatch the two four-plane divisions broke away; each division then split into two sections, to fight in four pairs. Gile and Lieutenant (jg) Dan Cunningham, Chicago, pinched four Zekes. Gile made three identical passes, each pass followed by a left chandelle with a 2,000-foot gain each time. He shot down a Zeke on each pass. It had taken Tim, who had once been chewed out for his gunnery, only a minute to do the triple.

Meanwhile, Lieutenant (jg) Paul Cordray of Dallas, with wingman Baker, dropped to the deck after a Kate. In a stern run, Cordray shot and the Kate exploded.

Cordray climbed and noticed two Tonys climbing inside his turn. He kept going up. At 10,000 feet, the Tonys broke away. Cordray quickly reversed himself and got on the tail of the rear Tony. A short burst did it. He picked out another Tony, who took violent evasive action, making four flipper turns to the right. After the fourth turn, Cordray closed to 200 yards and fired. His third victim crashed into the water.

The Irregulars claimed four other planes in that action. But Baker was never seen again. Lieutenant (jg) Robert S. Anderson's plane was set afire and his cockpit filled with smoke. He figured his speed was 300 knots and tried to nose up to reduce it, so he could bail out safely. But the nose wouldn't lift nor would his flaps lower. He managed to pull his hatch open, flipped the plane on its back and bailed out-fracturing an ankle, breaking a rib and injuring his back. His life jacket wouldn't hold him up in the water, but he managed to free his chute and inflate his raft. Other Irregulars circled protectively overhead and radioed for rescue boats. But eventually they had to leave and the boats couldn't find him.

At 4:25 the next morning "Mother" Davenport was proceeding up the west coast of Bougainville with a division for a dawn strafing attack against Buka. He sighted a steady light in the water. "Turn on your landing lights," he directed. "That could be Andy."

The four dropped low at the water and picked out what they thought might be Anderson's raft. On that assumption, Davenport spoke again: "We'll delay the mission and circle." He turned on his emergency radio call and asked a nearby American base for a bearing. He noted it and continued on his patrol.

As soon as they were finished, Davenport took the division back to search for Anderson. Making use of the bearing information he had been given earlier, Davenport found the object the second time over the course—and it was Anderson. No rescue boat was available, so they circled until one section was forced back because of fuel shortage. But Davenport and his wingman, Lieutenant (jg) Chico Freeman of Los Angeles, managed to stay on station. Davenport was just barely hanging in the sky, trying to conserve fuel. He was using but 1,300 r.p.m., with ten degree flaps and an indicated airspeed between a mushy 90 and 110 knots. A PT boat picked up Anderson at nine o'clock. When Davenport and Freeman finally landed, Davenport had only 23 gallons of gas remaining and they had been in the air for six hours, 45 minutes. Even the Vought Corsair people couldn't believe it when they were told about it.

But Davenport wasn't through thinking. Two nights later, poring over intelligence reports of two successive dawn attacks the Japs had just made, he told Henning, "They're coming over the same way, the same time—right at dawn. The best place for an interception is slightly inland from Cape Torokina at 2,000 so we can catch them as they come down over the mountains behind the bay. That way we also have the advantage of being on the dark side. But we've got to be on station before dawn."

Part of Butch Davenport's flight of eight planes while on combat air patrol over Bougainville 1943. #34 L.A. City Limits flown by "Chico" Freeman, later killed on the U.S.S. Bunker Hill in VF-84. Courtesy U.S. Naval Historical Center / M.W. "Butch" Davenport Collection.

That's the way it worked. Six Zekes unsuspectingly came down the path.

Davenport and Freeman bagged two each, Beacham one and Ensign Frank Jagger of Southampton, N.Y., the last one. As if that weren't enough, the Irregulars learned from a survivor that the Jap flight had been headed by an Army major, sent along to find out why the Japs were losing so many planes.

These were just some of the big innings in a constant existence of challenge, both offered and accepted. The tour lasted from October 27 to December 1, with the squadron averaging 140 combat hours per week. When they weren't in pilot-to-pilot dogfights they escorted bombers, protected ships of the fleet, and strafed Japanese craft and bases. They gained respectability in sensational fashion. The Navy liked the way the Irregulars covered the Marine landings at Empress Augusta Bay on Bougainville so well it awarded them a unit citation, with Blackburn receiving the Distinguished Flying Cross in addition. The turn of events was something of a revelation for an outfit that had started out with only two combat veterans and a motley collection of intractable individualists.

It wasn't all perfect. There were losses, and they were almost always outnumbered. The fatigue of constant combat was terrific. So when December came, they were sent to Espiritu Santo for a rest. An 11-day leave in Australia was included.

They had lost none of their off-base touch.

Burriss proved most ingeniously equipped for shore leave. There were girls in Australia and he made a date with one. "I've got a surprise for you," he promised. He knew his austerity. He arrived for his date with an armload of American toilet paper and his date grinned as she would not have had he bought roses or candy. In those days it was all but impossible to get such fancy toilet tissue.

To fill in for its losses, VF-17 picked up replacements worthy of the Irregular tradition. One, Lieutenant (jg) Harold Bitzegaio, of Terre Haute, Ind., had come from a squadron famed for its parties. At one of them, in San Diego the night before the ship sailed, festivities ended with champagne glasses being hurled against the walls. Bitz once had slow-rolled over his field, forgetting his safety belt was loose, and smashed the rearview mirror with his head. His cruise box, full of about 100 bucks worth of booze, which he had lovingly shepherded from the States, was still with him when he showed up for duty with the bristling Mims, who had missed the first tour because of an injured back.

They were to go back on January 24, 1944, to a new base at Piva Yoke airfield on Bougainville. But Blackburn had a worrisome problem. A squadron collection had bought enough beer to load a five-ton truck. Blackburn had stowed it in the king-size Quonset he and Hedrick shared at Ondongo. How to get it to Bougainville? They had been around enough to know that if they put it aboard ship they would never see it again. Finally, one of the younger Irregulars spoke up:

"Skipper, we've had eight of us take on as many as 75 Japs. Since we'll have all 36 on this hop, why not just 200 rounds per gun for four guns, and fill the other four ammo cans with beer?"

They did even better than that. Allowing themselves 200 rounds in only the two inboard guns, they stuffed more beer in the gun heater boxes and the two outboard guns. On the leg from Guadalcanal to Bougainville, Blackburn took the squadron high into the cold altitudes. When they landed at hot, thirsty Bougainville, each pilot turned to the Marine plane captain who climbed onto the

wing to help him out, handed the enlisted man a can opener, and said, "Here's your church key; let's have a cold beer."

The Irregulars were in.

They were also in for a hail of fire. The United States stepping-stone strategy for the islands in the Pacific now called for neutralizing Rabaul. But Japan was protecting its vital base with a sky-filling armada, a curtain of bullets and shrapnel and a fierce determination.

On the 26th day of January, 30 Irregulars went up to escort Navy bombers striking at Lakunai airfield, New Britain. Between 50 and 60 Japs were waiting. Their brown paint, with the Rising Sun emblems, stood out starkly in the noon brightness.

The SBDs and TBFs approached at 14,000 feet; the F4Us were at 19,000. The Japs were ranged over the target area from 15,000 to 21,000 feet. When the bombers went into their turn to the target, the Japs jumped. But few of them got through the cover to the bombers. Blackburn had ordered a high cover to remain aloft, to guard against a trap. He took nine of the Irregulars into the scrap, engaging 30 to 40 of the foe. Weaving, shooting, climbing, turning, stunting, the two sides mixed freely. As Gutenkunst knocked one Zeke flaming into the water, his eye caught another making a low-side run on him. Doug yanked the stick, turned in sharply, and converted the positions into a high-side run of his own with a full deflection shot at close range.

Down the Jap went. Three Zekes made a run in column on Hedrick from above, rolling over from an opposite course into a split-S. Hedrick turned a tight 180 degrees to escape. When three others went after the bombers, Hedrick went after them. The leader

Roger Hedrick, Bougainville, February 1944. Courtesy U.S. Navy photo. Robert L. Lawson Collection.

Corsair "Big Hog" running up on line. Courtesy U.S. Naval Historical Center / M.W. "Butch" Davenport Collection.

zoomed into a loop to double back and arrive on Hedrick's tail. But Hedrick rose after him, caught the Jap at the top of the loop and just did get out of the way as the falling Jap went by, burning fiercely.

Killefer, busy with a Zeke, looked back to see another Jap shooting at Lieutenant (jg) J.W. Farley, of Cedar Rapids, IA, Tom immediately turned toward Farley's pursuer and fired desperately to help. But as he turned away, he saw Farley go into the water.

Lieutenant (jg) Robert Hogan, Denver, Colo., and Jagger found themselves being jumped by six Zekes plunging at them. Jagger was hit in both wings by 20-mm shells, but he swung violently to the right and moved out of the line of fire. Hogan didn't make it. Other Irregulars thought he might have bailed out; a parachute was seen to open in that position. Ensign Robert Hill, of Beaufort, N.C., at 16,000 feet was also caught by 20-mm shells. He went into a spin but managed to recover after tumbling more than a mile. His left aileron was badly damaged, and he headed for home alone.

There he discovered he couldn't use his flaps to land. He had to come in fast, bounced and flipped over. He went to the hospital with a severe head gash.

The Irregulars were not a happy group that night. They had knocked down nine, but had had their worst day. Two of their own were gone and a third was in the hospital.

It didn't get any better the next day. With Marine F4Us and Army P40s, they rallied over B-25s striking at Lakunai again. Sixty to 70 Japs were out, in a pressing aggressiveness that found the Irregulars continually having to knock an enemy off the tail of a buddy. This time the Japs, in a change of strategy, waited until the bombers were retiring—then slammed into the protecting fighters.

Bell and Bitzegaio found themselves in a savage struggle. Bitz destroyed one Zero and sent smoking a Hamp that was making a run on Bell. But the fight had carried them to within 200 feet of the anti-aircraft pattern—and into the range of a dozen other Jap planes. They hastened to climb, the enemy flocking after them. Bell didn't make it. Bitz's plane took a 20-mm hit. He skidded, fell out, split-S'd and reversed his course. Still there was a Jap at his back. Bitz yelled into the mike: "Help, someone!"

"Coming, Bitz!" It was Kepford streaking over. Kepford had been standing by with a division at high cover for just such emergencies. He and his wingman, Ensign D.R. McQueen, Homewood, ILs, were picking on 20 Japs when they heard Bitz's call. Down into the arena they went and Ike turned his guns on the Zeke firing on Bitzegaio.

Cunningham also chalked up two, getting the first in a column run with Kepford's division and the second when, pouring on the coal to join a fight over Cape George, he digressed a moment to pick off a lone Zeke he spied below, near the water.

A high-side run sent the Zeke turning turtle, his prop windmilling as he went into the ocean.

Streig and Mims, while relishing the Zeke they had just combined to burn in the belly, looked around to discover that they were surrounded by seven other Japs and in the worst possible position. The Japs were above and astern. They edged closer to Streig. The unintimidated Mims swung into the line behind the closest and quickly started a blaze. Streig broke sharply to port, losing Mims in the process but undertaking his own offensive by going after a Jap

VF-17 Ready Room. L-R. "Big Jim" Streig, "Hap" Bowers, Tom Killefer, Tom Blackburn, "Ike" Kepford, Dan Cunningham, New Georgia, 1943. Courtesy U.S. Naval Historical Center / M.W. "Butch" Davenport Collection.

he saw below. He scored. Alone now, he spotted eight Zekes taking off from their Rapopo airfield. He made a beam run on the nearest, and as the pieces flew by him he turned tail and headed back for the retiring bombers, making an engine quivering 310 knots at 1,000 feet.

Mims' evasive action had carried him far afield. A little farther on, he saw eight to ten unsuspecting Jap planes, their wheels down, circling over the water off their Malaguna airfield, apparently making ready to land. Despite the odds, Mims couldn't resist the temptation. He made a roaring pass, shot one into the water and fled.

Burriss and Jagger were jumped, as the bombers went in, by several Zekes. Burriss stopped a 20-mm in the accessory section. But Burriss continued after one of his tormentors, bore into 50-yard range and exploded his quarry. Jagger, meanwhile, went after another Zeke, rolled with him through the Jap's maneuvering and added one more victim. But Burriss' plane was crippled. His oil pressure dropped. When it quit, oil came out of his propeller governor and the prop suddenly surged to 3,300 r.p.m.

Burriss chopped the throttle and the prop stopped. He was only 1,000 feet above water, 120 miles from Cape Torokina, with a dead plane. He called Blackburn: "Big Hog, I'm going to have to go in" (Their F4Us were "hogs" to the Irregulars, and Blackburn, of course, as their leader, was the big one).

Burriss opened his hatch, popped his flaps at 500 feet, slowed to 120 knots, leveled off at ten feet, and skimmed in across an eight-foot swell. He scrambled out onto the wing without any trouble as the plane sank almost immediately. His wrapped chute kept him afloat until he could undo the harness and inflate his raft. Jagger and three Marines circled above him. Blackburn came over, too. Killefer radioed Dane Base for a Dumbo, and Burriss' friends watched over him until the Dumbo arrived an hour later.

Five other Irregulars had added kills, to make a total of 16 for the day, but they had come back without Bell and they had lost Burriss' plane. Four other planes had been damaged by the Japs.

The third day, the odds came up—20 Irregulars to 50-70 Japs. But despite that, they let none through to the bombers. They shot down 14 and lost no one to the other side. Mims was hit in the windshield and oil-cooler in the first attack, then chased a Zeke from 13,000 feet almost to the ground, firing most of the time. The wily Jap went into a roll and Mims lost him, but he noticed another Zeke nearby at 1,000 feet. Mims fired until his guns, as well as the Jap plane, were smoking. Only one gun continued to function and a Marine pilot on nearby duty came in to help finish the job.

Killefer ended up a run to find himself in the TBF formation. Spying a lone Zeke low on the water trying to sneak into the bombers, Killefer went after him, discovered that only one of his guns was working—but still sent the Jap down. Hedrick, also plagued by gun stoppage, followed a Zeke into an Immelman, shot him at the top of the desperate maneuver, then circled the parachuting Jap in salute.

There seemed a little let-up the next day, when ten Irregulars had to take on only 18 Japs. Disaster had threatened when only two planes of a projected four-plane cover were able to get off the ground at Piva Yoke. But those two were Kepford and Burriss, the deadliest shooters in the squadron.

At 30,000 feet, they spotted 12 Zekes below them at 24,000. They pushed over and in perfect teamwork, first one, then the other protecting tails, they made high sides, overheads and sharp chandelles between passes. They never let the surprised, boxed Japs get away. The whole action lasted only ten minutes and they accounted for an incredible four Zekes apiece!

The mortal combat continued, with ceaseless nervous tension. On the fifth day the morning B-25 escort ran into 30 Japs; the afternoon TBF escort of 15 encountered 30 more. The first group got two, while saving themselves and the bombers. The second claimed eight—but paid a price.

Four of the pilots flew both missions, including Blackburn, Kepford and Gutenkunst. In the afternoon Blackburn, leading the high cover, spotted 20 Zekes joining up over Simpson Harbor. In the charge he came down on the top pair and blew out one Zeke. Seeing two others starting runs on two F4Us, he turned his nose up, hurried to gain altitude, connected and followed his prey in a diving spiral, still shooting. The plane caught fire and the Jap bailed out.

It was a no-let-up fight for Blackburn and wingman Gutenkunst, alternately firing at someone or being ambushed, once by as many as 12 Zekes. But the Japs were scoring, too. While Lieutenant (jg) Mills Schanuel, St. Louis, and Lieutenant (jg) T.F. Kropf, Wamego, KS, sneaked up on one group of Zekes, three others turned the tables on them. Schanuel rolled over and dove through a cloud layer to escape. He waited underneath the clouds for Kropf, but Kropf never appeared—and never made it back.

Kepford eluded a dozen Zekes making expert approaches at him, then knocked a Zeke off Beacham's tail. He fought his way through a sky crowded with Japs to join the bombers in their runs. But a Tony did a split-S and made a run on him. Ike's right wing was badly hit, but he kept firing with his left wing guns and set the Tony afire while his own right wing burned from the explosion of ammunition cans. His own machine-gun bullets flew everywhere around him, including the cockpit, but miraculously missed him. His mates radioed: "Bail out, Ike, bail out!"

"No. I'm going to try to make it back to base."

Ike figured he was too near enemy territory for rescue and preferred the longer odds on getting back.

With the burning wing, he left Rabaul for Piva Yoke. There the right wheel wouldn't extend. He landed on the left one. The plane ground-looped viciously and was a total wreck. Kepford walked away. "The shoulder harness bruised me a bit," he said, when asked how he felt.

The grinding battle continued. Beacham's plane was riddled with shrapnel. His hydraulic system went out and there was six inches of gasoline in his cockpit from a broken fuel line. He didn't dare land at base, so he radioed that he would set down in the water. It was dark and one wheel hung to trip him, but he made a good landing near a crash boat. Despite the rigid shoulder straps, Beacham was thrown forward and broke his nose. But he climbed out groggily and was rescued. Returning to Piva Yoke, the Irregulars found the strip closed because of Kepford's crash on the runway. The long afternoon fight had carried into the night and the traffic circle was horribly congested. Gutenkunst collided with a Marine pilot and both crashed to their deaths.

Insignia of VF-17 with 130 Jap flags, on Bougainville, in the Solomons. Courtesy National Archives.

In the five days of air combat, the Irregulars had shot down 60 and one-half planes, probably an all-time record for a single fighter squadron in the history of warfare. They had lost four planes, and the next day they suffered another loss that put a dark lining around their magnificent effort.

Burriss and Jagger flew medium cover at 14,000 feet for a TBF strike on Tobera. The Japs, abandoning their tactic of waiting until the American bombers had started their run or were retiring, this time came in early from 24,000 feet to intercept.

In their first pass, one of them hit Burriss, setting his plane smoking. As he prepared to make a water landing, another Zeke made a run on him. Jagger drove the Zeke away, but in so doing lost sight of Burriss, who, despite his predicament, had his plane under control and appeared ready for a successful water landing in enemy territory. But no one saw him make it.

A Dumbo searched for him in vain. The next morning, despite awful weather, the Irregulars turned out 40 planes into the teeth of the enemy to help another Dumbo look for him, for two hours. But Burriss was never seen again.

There was no rest on Sunday, February 6, as Blackburn, Mims and Bitzegaio, at high cover, challenged a whole squadron of 25 Japs for a violent 15 minutes of action. With a speeding series of runs and recoveries that were a model of daring and discipline, they

Groundcrew on "Butch" Davenport's F4U-1A. Courtesy U.S. Navy photo. Robert L. Lawson Collection.

decimated the group. Blackburn destroyed three Zekes, one Hamp and probably destroyed two more Zekes; Mims destroyed two Zekes, one Tojo, and probably destroyed two Zekes; Bitzegaio destroyed a Hamp. Total 12. Blackburn hounded one plane for 4,000 feet in a diving spiral to erase him. Bitz scored his between blackouts, caused by the abrupt stick yanking. Mims lost his oxygen and flew around drunkenly. Bitz came as close to him as he dared, trying to determine the trouble. He radioed Blackburn: "Skipper, I think Bobby's hurt."

But descent to lower altitude cleared Mim's head. They went home, but not before the skipper chalked up another in an unlikely little scene. The pilot of a lone Hamp apparently had quit work for the day and was cruising along unconcernedly, a cigarette lit and feet cocked on the instrument panel. Blackburn quietly crawled up his tail, shot and hit all sides of the cigarette—and the Jap.

Several times the Japs staged fake dogfights among themselves at a distance, in hopes of suckering the Irregulars away from the bombers they were mothering. No one bit. "Nobody is going to start out by himself to be a little hero," Blackburn had said back in the States and the irrepressible ones had listened. They flew in a wave, in order to sweep all the sky they could. And they stayed at least in a pair at all times.

On the ground they were blithe about their victories. They refused to split a destroyed plane among themselves; they flipped a coin for the credit because they didn't want to be bothered with fractions. They developed a taste for warm beer, though at times they ingeniously cooled it with pressure from CO2 fire-extinguisher bottles.

They kept their eyes open and learned something on nearly every flight, even a quiet cover over Navy Task Force 39. Henning noted that day's action in the log book thus: "Cover TF 39. Negative, except that all pilots reported beautiful, light-colored, big-breasted native women on Tami Island."

On February 19, 25 members of VF-17 pointed their noses again towards Rabaul, to find the sky full of the Rising Sun. There were from 50 to 75 enemy planes out to challenge them.

Just before the contact, Kepford dove on a float plane, the most succulent target available to a fighter pilot, and blasted it as it putt-putted along—then looked back to see two Zekes and two Tojos on his tail, bracketing him. He had cheated death once recently; now it looked as though his number was up. He swore he would go struggling. He dived for the sea hoping the heavier air there would grant him more speed. The Zekes climbed too well to risk a climb.

Ike suddenly dumped his flaps and backed off the throttle, and one of the Zekes overran him. Ike shot him down, but three Japs remained. Kepford radioed: "Chalk up two for Ike. Three Zeros have me pocketed. This looks like the works."

He flew for his life. The instinct for preservation and his training took hold. He grew very methodical, this man who loved dogfights.

He could see the Japs' tracers all around him. He jammed the throttle full forward and turned on the water injection, which made a 2,300 horsepower engine out of a 2,000-rated one. When the engine began shuddering, he eased off a little on the water. He experimented with the flaps, begging for more speed.

AMM3c L.W. Jordan uses a spray gun and stencil to add more "kill" markings to VF-17's scoreboard, bringing the total to 154. These Japanese aircraft were shot down in aerial combat over the Solomons. Note that censor has deleted the squadron number from the photo. Courtesy National Archives.

The tracers continued by. He was gaining by inches but he couldn't win. For one thing, he was headed toward China. Gas exhaustion would down him, even if the Japs didn't. The strain was enormous, minute after terrifying minute. Once he glanced down toward his sneakers; they were green. They were supposed to be white. He thought agonizingly. "I'm seeing things; I'm really going haywire" (He had unknowingly stepped into dye marker earlier and the sweat from the heat of the day and the flight for his life had discolored the canvas shoes).

Ike thought if he could get close enough to the water he might make a sudden left turn, present himself as a momentary target to the lone Jap there, and maybe the Jap would miss. Ike turned violently; the Jap, engrossed and hungry for the fat target now, dropped his wing, too—into the ocean—and cartwheeled to his death.

Now one of the two remaining Japs peeled off. But the angry fourth still pursued, though Ike now was headed home. Kepford racked his brain to figure some way out of his plight. He fired away all but ten seconds of ammunition to lighten his plane. He switched from wing fuel tanks to the main, so the plane would keep its trim and he wouldn't have to change pressure on the stick. He crept painfully ahead and when that last Jap finally turned back Kepford had had death at his back for 23 minutes.

He landed to the sound of cheers from Marines, sailors and Irregulars lining the runway. They had given him up for dead. He was crying with relief. The flight surgeon rescued his nerve ends with copious supplies of brandy until Kepford could sleep—and then he slept the clock around. While he did, Duke Henning wrote up the day's score: Irregulars 16, Japs 0.

Cunningham had contributed four of those and Lieutenant O.I. Chenoweth, of Miami, FL, three, when just the two of them, with the usual Irregular disregard for safety, barreled into 16 Japs. Cunningham plucked three from F4U tails, saving three American lives while he was making his three kills.

This would be the last formidable front the Japs would present at Rabaul; in fact, the last the Irregulars would see of an enemy plane in the air during the remaining two weeks on Bougainville.

There came more time now for poker and closer attention to beer and a few other potions. A beer run to Guadalcanal was established. Once, Ensign George Keller of New York City, trying a short cut, took an anti-aircraft hit that exploded a case of beer on him and the turkey he was carrying on his lap. Blackburn punished him by not letting him have any turkey at chow that night.

The war correspondents discovered them and helped them celebrate. Bitz wrote in his log: "Got up with a slight hangover this morning. Too many correspondents with liquor."

Blackburn's Irregulars had shot down more Japanese airplanes than any other fighter squadron in the Armed Forces. Their score, in but 76 days of combat, was 154 enemy planes destroyed in the air and two on the ground; five transport ships and 17 barges sunk with their cargoes of troops and supplies. The Irregulars boasted 13 aces—more than any other Navy squadron. In nine weeks they had flown the amazing total of 8,577 combat hours, an average of 224 per regular pilot. Only 20 planes and 12 pilots were lost to enemy action. Four of the losses were from anti-aircraft. These figures meant that the Irregulars had made the foe pay with nearly eight planes for each one they had lost.

That was the measure of their courage and skill. The measure of their discipline was reflected in another startling statistic: Not a ship for which the Irregulars provided air cover—and they flew 90 such missions—was ever hit by a bomb or torpedo. Not a single bomber from any squadron they protected on nearly 40 raids was lost to Jap aircraft. It was an amazing record of responsibility for men who had been tagged as the most irresponsible in the naval service.

Kepford led the squadron—and the whole U.S. Navy—with 16 planes; Blackburn was next with 11. Then it was Hedrick, 9; Gile, Chenoweth, and Lieutenant (jg) Earl May of Milwaukee, each with 8; Cunningham and Cordray, 7 each; Davenport and Mims, 6 each; Streig, 5.5; and March 5. The missing Burriss was the unlucky 13th. Of the pilots who had completed both tours only two didn't have a kill and both of them had "probables."

There had been only one award ceremony on the island, but now medals and lionization awaited the gang. Henning was given extremely short notice to write up citations but he responded in typical Irregular fashion. Duke rounded up two others who could type. Schanuel, a former newspaperman, was one, Duke told them, "You use 'intrepid,' 'extraordinary' and 'heroic'. I get the others." Having divided the superlatives fairly, the three typed out the citations in two hours.

There were Navy Crosses, Silver Stars, Distinguished Flying Crosses and Air Medals in abundance—and Purple Hearts and posthumous awards. The Navy sent the Irregulars back to the States for Chamber of Commerce testimonials and for worker-incentive speeches at war plants. They were, the Navy said, shining examples of "the highest traditions of the service."

Then came the peace and all but a half dozen of the Irregulars—still free, unregimented spirits—attacked civilian life.

Kepford answered a newspaper ad in San Diego placed by the Rexall Drug Co., wanting "young men to learn retail selling." Fourteen years later Kepford is president of the Ligget Drug Co. of New York, with some company-owned stores doing a $70-million-a-year business and servicing another 600 affiliates. He lives in Greenwich, Conn., with his wife and two youngsters. He collects guns, hunts and thinks he still owes Mims a little money from a poker game that went on for six weeks.

But Mims doesn't really need it, unless to buy a tank of gas for the pink, air-conditioned Cadillac he rides in. He went back to Dallas—in oil, of course—turned independent promoter and made his mint. Jackson went home to Texas too, back to Denton. He chose law and has served two terms in the Lone Star State's legislature.

Killefer and Bitz also went from Blackburn to Blackstone. The former Rhodes scholar, has exhibited the same brilliant, analytical mind that impressed the Irregulars; he is a member of a major law firm in Washington, D.C. In the height of the recent Cold War, Killefer flashed the old Irregular spirit. He closed off his law practice, despite his family-man status, and marched into a government office. "I hear," he said, "so much talk about the threat of Communism, about how we need people with experience and a wish to do something for our government. Here I am; where can I serve?"

Washington bundled him off to Europe for two years, in a secret, still unpublicized activity.

Bitz headed back to Terre Haute, IN. Now he's an up-and-coming attorney, president of the Wabash Valley Pilots Club, and a leader in the successful fight to build an auxiliary airport at Terre Haute.

Gile, as lean as he was in those hot days in the Solomons—and obviously as enterprising—is assistant vice-president at J.P. Morgan & Co., in Wall Street. He catches the train at Rye, N.Y., where Mrs. Gile and four daughters await his daily return. Another pillar of his community, Duke Henning is a professor at Yale University and master of Saybrook College there.

Cunningham went into life insurance selling and now is a member of the Million-Dollar-Roundtable, the class fraternity of the premium entrepreneurs.

Davenport heads a successful aviation engineering corporation in Detroit.

Of those who stayed in, there is enough gold braid to create a sunrise and much sense of responsibility. Hedrick is a captain. Streig, Beacham and Landreth are full commanders. Chenoweth was, too, until he resigned to join Chance Vought Aviation—the firm that made the old F4Us.

Blackburn? He's a four-striper, closing in on admiral. He made the first landing on the super carrier Midway and launched planes from her deck while going down the Hudson River. His crew flew a weapon off the Midway in the first Navy operational suitability test of an atomic weapon. He is now acting assistant chief of staff for Navy Aviation in the Pacific.

All of which seems an unlikely ending to the tale, considering those early days when the United States Navy thought the Irregulars were the flyers most likely to be court-martialed. Today, the

Lt. Cdr. Tom Blackburn discusses the successful operations of his unit, VF-17, in the central Solomons during the November 1943-February 1944 period. VF-17 also known as the Skull and Crossbones squadron and Blackburn's Irregulars was credited with shooting down 154 Japanese aircraft. Photo taken after Blackburn's return to the U.S. Courtesy National Archives.

mark of the Irregulars is still on them—an alertness and quickness, a seemingly carefree attitude that fails to hide the lode of judgment and knowledge. The unafraid spirit still shows.

They're still good for a laugh, too. Why, for instance, doesn't Kepford pilot a plane nowadays?

"The procedure around the airports annoys me," he says.

Procedure was always a horrible word to an Irregular.

Members of squadron with Lt. Cdr. Tom Blackburn in center. Courtesy National Archives.

6

Second Tour
January 1944

1 January
On this date VF-17 was composed of 49 officers and 71 enlisted men, and had a compliment of 36 F4U-1 aircraft.

1 January-23 January
Rear area training.

3 January
Lt(jg) R.L. Mills and Ens. H.B. Richardson Jr. reported for duty.

5 January
Lt. O.I. Chenoweth reported for duty. "Oc" Chenoweth was credited with a Zeke from his previous combat tour with VF-38 in the Solomons area. Lt. L.D. Cooke detached.

8 January
Ens. K.P. Babkirk and Ens. J.R. Travers detached.

9 January
The squadron moved to Turtle Bay Airfield, Espiritu Santo.

10 January
Ens. J.C. Dixon and Ens. D.R. McQueen reported for duty.

11 January
The following officers reported for duty:-
Ens. E.E. Beeler
Ens. M.W. Cole
Ens. P.E. Divenney
Ens. G.M. Keller, Jr.

13 January
Ens. L.M. Kelley detached.

15 January
Lt(jg) J.M. Chasnoff detached.

17 January
Ens. G.F. Hall detached.

18 January
Lt. L.T. McQuiston reported for duty.

19 January
Lt(jg) C.L. Smith detached.

21 January
Lt(jg) T.F. Kropf was forced to make a water landing because his engine cut out. He was recovered immediately but the plane was destroyed.

22 January
Lt(jg) E.C. Peterson, Jr. reported for duty.

Lt(jg) R. L. Mills at Bougainville 1944. Courtesy National Archives.

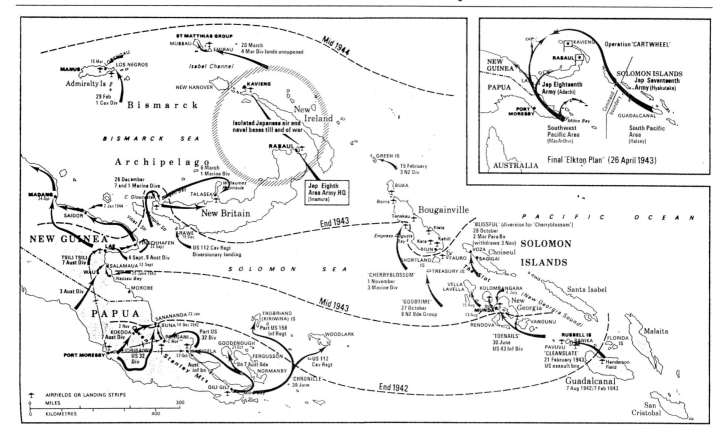

24 January

The following 34 pilots flew F4U-1s from Turtle Bay Airfield, Espiritu Santo to Piva Yoke Airfield, Bougainville, B.S.I.; take-off 0900, arrival 1700:-

Lt. Cdr. J.T. Blackburn
Lt(jg) D.H. Gutenkunst
Lt(jg) F.J. Streig
Lt(jg) T. Killefer
Ens. W.P. Meek
Lt(jg) R.R. Hogan

Ens. D.T. Malone
Lt(jg) G.F. Bowers
Ens. R.H. Hill
Lt. T.R. Bell
Lt(jg) H.J. Bitzegaio
Lt(jg) E. May

Lt(jg) R.H. Jackson
Lt. M.W. Davenport
Lt(jg) D.C. Freeman
Lt. S.R. Beacham
Ens. L.A. Fitzgerald
Lt(jg) D.G. Cunningham
Lt(jg) R. Mims
Lt. Cdr. R.R. Hedrick
Ens. J.O. Ellsworth
Lt(jg) P. Cordray
Lt(jg) J. Miller

Ens. W.P. Popp
Lt(jg) I.C. Kepford
Ens. M.M. Kurlander
Lt. H.A. March
Lt(jg) C.W. Gilbert
Lt(jg) H.M. Burriss
Ens. F.A. Jagger
Lt. W.J. Schub
Ens. W.C. Wharton
Lt(jg) W.L. Landreth
Ens. C.H. Dunn

INTO RABAUL

VF-17 returned to combat when the new Bougainville airstrip was ready, which extended the reach of the American air assault. Most of the island was occupied by the enemy and Fighting 17 would now face its greatest challenge, flying missions over Rabaul.

"Country" Landreth recalls flying in for the second tour:

"By January 24 the Seabees got two airstrips, Piva Yoke and Piva Uncle, right near the beach of Empress Augusta Bay (Torokina, Bougainville). We used Piva Yoke as a base to fly to Rabaul every day. The Marines just took enough area around there for the airfields. They didn't want the whole island; the Japanese were all over the island.

"We relieved VMF-214-Pappy Boyington's "Black Sheep" squadron—on station. We flew in, they flew out, just about two weeks after Boyington had been shot down and captured".

Wilbert Popp recalls returning for the second tour:

"Early in 1944 we returned to combat on Fighter #2 on Bougainville. Most of our action was then over Rabaul. My best friend Clyde Dunn was later lost on a mission over Rabaul as a replacement pilot for one of our pilots who feigned an injury. Perhaps you can tell I'm still bitter about it.

"During our missions over Rabaul I witnessed some of the greatest flying I ever saw, namely by New Zealanders who had fought with the R.A.F. over London and now flew low cover over Navy bombers flying the Curtiss P-40 Kittyhawks".

24 January-26 January

The remaining officers and all enlisted men and squadron gear were flown from Espiritu Santo to Piva Yoke Airfield by S.C.A.T.

Tom Blackburn and the Skipper of VF(N)-75 Gus Wildhelm at Bougainville early in 1944. Courtesy U.S. Navy photo. Robert L. Lawson Collection.

Tom Blackburn describes the differences between the two tours of duty.

"The fighting started on 26 January and was of an entirely different character than we had had before. It was a hell of a sight more hazardous. In previous activities flying over Empress Augusta Bay the carriers we had been the hunters. Now when we were going into Rabaul we were the hunted".

Roger Hedrick recalls action over Rabaul.

"By the time we took off with the 225 mile trip to Rabaul, en route the Japanese on the island behind us at Bougainville would radio over to their friends at Rabaul telling them exactly how many planes were coming. We could see the dust cloud rolling up off each field as the airplanes took off to get up and climb above us.

"On the first tally ho of each flight somebody would see a bandit. Bandits high 11 o'clock that's when all your aches and pains would disappear and that oxygen mask quit cutting into your face and the ache your ass had from sitting on your parachute and rations was gone.

"Your only thought was 'I've got one job to do and that's to get that guy before he gets me or gets to the bombers.'"

"Country" Landreth remembers missions to Rabaul.

"We'd go up and challenge the Japs who had over 100 airplanes every day. We'd get there about 11 o'clock in the morning. There would be a great big dogfight right up there over the harbor at Rabaul".

25 January
Sixteen F4Us searched the area south of Cape St. George, New Ireland, for downed pilots with negative results.

60 ENEMY PLANES IN FIVE DAYS

26 January
Thirty two F4Us were assigned to cover the SBDs in a joint SBD-TBF strike on Lakunai airfield, New Britain.

Lt. Cdr. J.T. Blackburn	Lt. Cdr. R.R. Hedrick
Lt(jg) D.H. Gutenkunst	Ens. J.O. Ellsworth
Lt(jg) F.J. Streig	Lt(jg) G.F. Bowers
Lt(jg) R. Mims	Ens. R.H. Hill
Lt(jg) T. Killefer	Lt(jg) P. Cordray
Lt(jg) R.R. Hogan	Lt(jg) J. Miller
Lt(jg) J.W. Farley	Lt(jg) R.H. Jackson
Lt. M.W. Davenport	Lt(jg) D.T. Malone
Lt(jg) D.C. Freeman	Lt. H.A. March
Lt. S.R. Beacham	Lt(jg) H.M. Burriss
Ens. M.W. Kurlander	Ens. F.A. Jagger
Lt. C.D. Gile	Lt. W.J. Schub
Ens. J.M. Smith	Ens. W.C. Wharton
Lt(jg) D.G. Cunningham	Lt(jg) W.L. Landreth
Ens. L.A. Fitzgerald	Ens. C.H. Dunn

Thirty planes (2 failed to take off) made rendezvous with the bombers west of Taiof Island at 6,000 ft. The approach was made on an original course of 317° crossing New Ireland, going way over Duke of York Island, and reaching Crater Peninsula at Nordup, where a left turn was made into the target.

The bombers approached at 14,000 ft. with the fighters stacked to 19,000 ft. Jap fighters (estimated to be from 50 to 60 in number) were in the air around the target at altitudes from 15,000 ft. to 21,000 ft., and as the bombers began their turn, the Japs came down to attack the formation.

Few of the Japs were able to get through the fighter cover to make successful runs on the bombers. With the exception of the high cover the fighters followed the bombers in their dives, weaving when possible, by divisions, and if divisions were separated, by pairs. As the heavy A/A was accurate and intense, and as the Japs, with altitude advantage, had the F4Us at an initial disadvantage some of the medium and low cover had to break away from the bombers.

Lt. Cdr. Blackburn (at 16,000 ft.) first sighted a group of the enemy over Duke of York Island at about 10,000 ft. to 15,000 ft. This group did not attack, nor did a second group of 9 Zekes seen over Rapopo at 15,000 ft., on a south easterly bearing.

But 12-15 Zekes sighted over Rabaul, attacked the medium and low cover from 21,000 ft. Blackburn himself made contact as the formation was retiring from the target. He was at 4,000 ft. over the channel off Rapopo. He made a head-on run, scored hits on a Zeke's engine, made a quarter roll to the left and hit him in the left wing. The two planes crossed, and the Zeke dove out; headed northwest and went into the water off Matupi Island. This kill made Blackburn the squadron's first ace.

Shortly after this Blackburn and his wingman (Lt(jg) Gutenkunst) were attacked by two Zekes.

The Zekes made unsuccessful low side runs and disengaged.

A single Zeke was then seen following a single SBD low on the water, but when Blackburn and Gutenkunst headed towards him, the Zeke dove away. The pair caught up to the SBDs off Cape Gazelle. As they began their weave, Gutenkunst broke off to attack a Zeke low on the water. The Zeke turned away, but Gutenkunst caught another Zeke nearby, got on his tail, and sent him flaming into the water. As Gutenkunst disengaged, a Zeke came in from his side in a low side run. Gutenkunst turned in, made a high side run, got a full deflection shot at close range and the Zeke went down in flames. Blackburn and Gutenkunst resumed their weave, and although many Zekes were in the vicinity, no further attacks were made on the formation.

Lt. Cdr. Hedrick sighted his first Zekes midway between Duke of York Island and Lakunai. His flight was at 19,000 ft., the Japs were at 22,000 ft. The group engaged his flight and Hedrick got one shot at long range. As he recovered he saw 6 more Zekes in column above and behind him. He turned towards them and they rolled over and dove away. As Hedrick pulled up his wingman lost him (his second section had broken off after the initial attack) and he found himself alone at 12,000 ft. directly over Rabaul. He saw 3 Zekes 300 ft. above him on opposite course.

They rolled over and made overhead runs in column; Hedrick made a 180° turn and passed close by them. Hedrick then started down to the rally point 5 miles east of Cape Gazelle. He was over the channel at 6,000 ft., still astern of the main SBD formation when 3 Zekes dove past his bow in pursuit of the bombers. Hedrick followed and the leading Zeke, perceiving this, zoomed up. Hedrick caught him at the top of his zoom, fired and the Zeke's left wing root caught fire, and as Hedrick pulled clear the Jap went down.

Hedrick then joined up with a Marine F4U and scissored over the SBDs. He got shots at two more Zekes who disengaged. The rest of the flight was uneventful.

Tom Blackburn standing beside "Big Hog". Courtesy U.S. Naval Historical Center / M.W. "Butch" Davenport Collection.

Group at Bougainville L-R. *Bill Popp, Hal Jackson, John Smith, "Timmy" Gile, Mills Schanuel, Don Innis, "Ike" Kepford, Roger Hedrick.* Courtesy U.S. Naval Historical Center / M.W. "Butch" Davenport Collection.

Lt(jg) Cordray, leading the second division in Hedrick's flight, spotted the enemy when Hedrick did. As the Zekes came down Cordray missed on a stern shot and saw a Zeke hit his wingman, Lt(jg) Miller. Miller spun but recovered, and he and Cordray scissored down to 6,000 ft. As they were following the bombers to the rally point (5 miles east of Cape Gazelle), they spotted 8 more Zekes to the south of the bombers' formation. Cordray got on the tail of one Zeke and gave him a long burst. He pulled up in a sharp turn and lost sight of the Zeke. Another pilot, who observed the action, saw this Zeke crash in flames. Immediately after this Cordray got a head-on shot at another Jap, though he could not estimate the damage inflicted. He was then joined by Miller and they went home with the SBDs.

Miller went in with Cordray to attack the 8 Zekes south of the rally point. He got on a Zeke's tail (losing Cordray in the process) and fired until the Zeke began to blaze. He pulled up, dived on a Zeke, fired into him, and the Zeke peeled off smoking. Miller then headed for the bombers, eluding a Zeke who made a run on him, joined his division and headed home.

Lt(jg) Killefer, leading the second division in Blackburn's flight, was following the SBDs down in their dive when he saw a group of Zekes 4,000 ft. above, coming down on him. He made an unsuccessful snap shot at a Zeke diving past him and he and his wingman (Lt(jg) Farley his second section had become separated) continued down under the A/A and caught up to the SBDs low on the water as they were coming out into Blanche Bay. He headed after a Zeke to his left, looked back and saw another Zeke on Farley's tail, Killefer turned towards him, fired and missed; as he turned away saw Farley's plane go into the water. At the time he saw a Zeke pulling up slowly in a 70° climb. Killefer made a 100° deflection shot and saw the Zeke pass under the bombers and crash into the water. Killefer then pulled up, and joining Blackburn and Gutenkunst, escorted the bombers home.

Lt(jg) Hogan and Ens. Jagger, the second section of Killefer's division followed Killefer down in his dive and were jumped by 5 or 6 Zekes. The Zekes had apparently begun their dive before the F4Us and had a considerable speed advantage. Jagger had two on his tail, and was hit in both wings by 20mm. shells. He broke sharply to the right to get out of their fire. At about this time Hogan must have been hit. It is possible that he bailed out, as a parachute was seen about this position.

Lt. Gile's division was at 16,000 ft. over the bombers as they made their pushover when they were jumped by a group of Zekes. They dove out, recovered at about 7,000 ft. and Gile headed for a melee over St. George's Channel off Rapopo. Gile made passes at 4 Zekes, and in a quarter stern run from 8 o'clock, set the fourth afire. Gile looked for his second section, could not find them, so he and his wingman headed out after the SBDs. Twelve Zekes followed and one closed the range on Smith, Gile's wingman, got on his tail, shot and hit him. Gile chandelled to the right and made a run on the Zeke who disengaged, made a 180° turn and headed back towards Rabaul. Gile and Smith joined up, and as the latter's plane had a hydraulic failure, the pair returned to base.

As the SBDs were about to turn into the target Lt(jg) Landreth and Ens. Dunn, the second section of the division covering the last group of SBDs, spotted 2 Zekes chasing 4 F4Us. They followed one Zeke up as he was climbing after an F4U and both fired until their air speed dropped off. The Zeke barrel-rolled out and Landreth stayed with him, still firing. Dunn's engine cut out on the roll and he dropped behind. When Landreth last saw the Zeke it was going down in a spiral, streaming black smoke. Landreth rejoined his first section just before the bombers pushed-over, and was joined by Dunn over the rally point. On the retirement several Zekes began runs on the formation but when Landreth and Dunn turned into them the Japs disengaged.

Ens. Hill was at about 16,000 ft. over Rabaul just before the SBD's made their run. He was following his section leader down when he was hit by 20mm. shells from the starboard quarter. He went into a spin and only managed to recover at 9,000 ft. His left aileron was badly damaged and the empennage was almost shot away. He headed for home, alone, as he could find no one to join up on, remaining airborne with the greatest difficulty. When he arrived over the field (8,000 ft.) he put down his wheels and flaps but found that with his flaps open his nose dropped off.

Accordingly he tried a landing without flaps, but bounced and flipped over. His head was severely gashed and he was hospitalized.

"Windy" Hill at Bougainville taxiing his F4U-1A. Courtesy U.S. Navy photo. Robert L. Lawson Collection.

"Windy" Hill remembers the mission.

"On the 26th I was part of a flight which was to provide protective cover for an SBD/TBF strike against Lakunai Airfield, Rabaul.

"As we approached the target area and the bombers commenced their attack, the division I was in was jumped by eight Zekes attacking from above us out of the sun. I weaved violently to the right and nearly had a head-on collision with a Japanese fighter. Seconds later I heard an explosion and felt my plane shudder under the impact of 20 mm hits. My cockpit filled with smoke, and I fell off into a diving turn, out of control, at about 16,000 feet.

"I was frantically trying to regain control of my aircraft, but my flight controls were not responding—I thought I was on fire due to the smoke and started to bail out. But as my hand grabbed the canopy release handle, the thought crossed my mind: those people down there don't treat their prisoners very well, so I had better wrestle with my Corsair a little longer.

"Slowly I began to regain control, and finally I was in level flight. I then took stock of my condition and saw that my left aileron and most of my tail surfaces were damaged, with the remnants flapping in the breeze.

"I headed alone for Bougainville, about 150 miles away, flying at 3,000 feet, so I would have sufficient altitude to bail out if my aircraft became uncontrollable.

"Approaching our home base at Empress Augusta Bay, I tested the plane in landing condition. I found that I could maintain control with the wheels down, but when the flaps were lowered, the nose started dropping.

"I switched to the bomber landing strip, which was longer, and I felt I could make a flat, high-speed landing and grease it on the pierced steel matting. As I went floating down the runway, I had to ease off a little power. Even with the stick back against my belly, the nose dropped slowly, the prop struck the ground, and I went skidding down the runway, tail first and inverted at 125 knots, demolishing the Corsair.

"They pulled me unconscious, with severe gashes in my head, from the plane and took me to the hospital (This was in the day of cloth helmets). Within a week, however, I had recovered and was back in action, flying with a very tender, bandaged head which I would slowly ease into my helmet for each flight.

"During the time I was in the hospital, I became friendly with two of the corpsmen and asked them if they would like some brandy. They thought that was a marvelous suggestion, so one afternoon I eased out of the hospital and returned to my tent at the fighter strip. I took a bottle of brandy I had stashed away and went back to the hospital.

"That night, after lights-out, the three of us went to the beach and opened our treasure. Just as the evening was getting a glow on,

"Butch" Davenport's plane after "Windy" Hill's crash landing. Courtesy U.S. Navy photo. Robert L. Lawson Collection.

"Butch" Davenport's plane wrecked at Bougainville. Courtesy U.S. Navy photo. Robert L. Lawson Collection.

Ready to go:March, Gilbert, Schub. Wharton, Jagger, Bitzegaio. VF-17 ready room January 1944. Courtesy U.S. Navy photo. Robert L. Lawson Collection.

...here was an enemy bombing attack on the nearby air strips. Washing Machine Charlie was doing his thing.

"It was a great show. People were diving into fox holes for protection, tracer bullets were filling the air, bombs were exploding, fires were blazing, and the "boom, boom" of anti-aircraft fire was pounding.

"So what did we do? Well, we decided it called for another drink and continued to sit on the beach. It was too good a show to miss seeing.

"Besides, we rationalized, the bombs would probably be dropped on the airfield, not off in the boondocks by the beach where we were sitting. How great our youth is, that time in life when you feel immortal—you think that you will live forever".

Heavy A/A from the Lakunai area was intense and accurate, both in range and deflection. Phosphorus bomb bursts were observed at about 5,000 ft. It was the impression of the pilots that these bombs were either dropped by planes or shot up by A/A as markers, as there were no planes near the burst.

About fifty or sixty Japanese fighters intercepted the formation over St. George's Channel. Blackburn destroyed one Zeke, Gutenkunst destroyed two Zekes, Killefer destroyed one Zeke, Cordray destroyed one Zeke and damaged one Zeke, Hedrick destroyed one Zeke, Miller destroyed one Zeke, Gile destroyed one Zeke and Landreth and Dunn shared one probable Zeke.

Farley and Hogan were shot down over St. George's Channel. It is possible that Hogan may have parachuted. Hill's plane was badly hit by 20mm fire and crashed on landing. Hill was slightly

injured. Two other F4Us were slightly damaged by 20mms and 7.7s. Miller was slightly wounded by shrapnel. No bombers were lost to enemy aircraft.

Lt. Walter Schub relates his part in the mission.

"When we returned from Australia and first started on our raids to Rabaul, my division was scheduled to fly low (close) cover over the bombers into maybe Lakunai Airfield. On returning from the strike Tom Blackburn was contacted by the flight leader, a Colonel, the overall coordinator (I don't know whether Army or Marine) who told Blackburn that VF-17's close cover did one hell of a job in protecting the bombers and that division should be kept on that assignment. He said, 'He's good I'd keep him there.' So that's where I got stuck, which meant I couldn't leave the close cover and go chasing after Japs. This of course gave my division an 80% assignment of close (low) cover—which meant we were to stay with the bombers and not stray too far off. This too, set us up for our share of A/A fire as it was directed at the bombers. When we did get a snap shot at a Zero going down through the formation we didn't have the opportunity, usually, to follow it down to see it crash (to claim a kill it was required to see it blow up in front of you or to see it crash into the sea).

"In fact I had one Marine pilot come in and wanted to know whose plane was in such and such and I took a snap shot and he said 'Boy you really knocked that guy down. I really didn't know much about it except that I shot several times. I figure maybe 8-10 planes but who cares as long as they go down. I still had no evidence of shooting these down as I had to stay with the bombers, so I couldn't confirm them. My formation warded off many planes from the bombers.

"This requirement was impossible for us to comply with—we had no "aces" in our division—but we didn't get separated from each other and we didn't lose anyone. I had the reputation of not losing anyone that flew with me—as was brought out in later squadrons".

"My division was Whit Wharton, Country Landreth (section leader) and variable 4th (Landreth's wingman). As combat losses came up, wingmen were shifted around—promoted to higher positions, etc."

27 January

Five divisions (20 F4Us) were assigned as cover on one of 2 B-25 squadrons striking Lakunai airfield, New Britain. Four more F4Us from the squadron made a part of the cover on the other bomber group.

Lt. Cdr. J.T. Blackburn	Lt. T.R. Bell
Lt(jg) D.H. Gutenkunst	Lt(jg) H.J. Bitzegaio
Lt(jg) F.J. Streig	Lt(jg) E. May
Lt(jg) R. Mims	Ens. W.P. Popp
Lt(jg) T. Killefer	Lt(jg) I.C. Kepford
Lt. O.I. Chenoweth	Ens. D.R. McQueen
Ens. J.C. Dixon	Lt(jg) D.G. Cunningham
Lt. H.A. March	Ens. L.A. Fitzgerald
Lt(jg) H.M. Burriss	Lt. W.J. Schub
Ens. F.A. Jagger	Ens. W.C. Wharton
Lt(jg) W.L. Landreth	Ens. C.H. Dunn

The B-25s were at 12,000 ft., with the fighters stacked to 19,000 ft. The formation approached over Cape St. George and Duke of York island to Crater Peninsula where a left turn was made over the target. The retirement was down over the channel.

From 60 to 70 Jap fighters intercepted the strike as the bombers were leaving the target. They did not attack the B-25s but were exceptionally aggressive in their runs on the F4Us. They were first observed climbing over Lakunai, and down on top cover as the bombers began their retirement. The fight continued to the rally point (5 miles east of Cape Gazelle) and a few Zekes continued on the flanks of the formation in the hopes of picking off stragglers.

Heavy A/A was intense and accurate, most coming from the Lakunai area, though some was observed from Rapopo.

The Japs first attacked the top cover. Lt. Bell kept his division together, and they turned with the enemy. A Zeke started a low beam run on Bell's wingman, Lt(jg) Bitzegaio, but he turned in and got a good head-on shot. The Zeke's ammunition can blew up, he caught fire, and rolled away. By this time they were 200 ft. over an A/A pattern and the division was forced to jink. Bitzegaio saw a Hamp pulling up on his port, got a half deflection shot, and the Hamp pulled through and rolled away smoking. Another Hamp made

an opposite course run on Bell, Bitzegaio pulled out, turned and got a full deflection shot. Twelve Zekes and Hamps were then observed above and below. Bell pulled up in a right turn, Bitzegaio to the left. At this moment Bitzegaio's plane was hit by a 20mm (Bitzegaio kept this 20mm shell as a souvenir of this mission and had it with him at the VF-17 reunion in 1994!).

He skidded and fell out, then split-S'd and reversed course.

A Zeke was on his tail, he called for help, and Kepford shot the Zeke down. Bitzegaio looked for Bell, couldn't find him (it is highly probable that Bell was shot down just after Bitzegaio was hit) but saw his second section trailing the bombers. He joined up, climbed to 10,000 ft. and came home with the formation.

Wilbert Peter Popp saw Bell being shot down and recalls the action:

"It was on 27 January 1944. We were on a strike escorting bombers on an attack over Lakunai Airfield on Rabaul. Lt(jg) Thaddeus Richard Bell from San Francisco, graduated University of Washington was leading our four plane division. I was Tail-end-Charlie. None of us saw the Zero who made an overhead dive on our division. Normally the Tail-end-Charlie would be the obvious target, however he hit Bell. Bell went straight up and flipped over

Harold Bitzegaio at Bougainville in January 1944. Courtesy U.S. Navy photo. Robert L. Lawson Collection.

"Ike" Kepford and "Duke" Henning at New Georgia 1943. Courtesy U.S. Naval Historical Center / M.W. "Butch" Davenport Collection.

on his back and came straight down in a vertical dive. We never saw his final dive but unfortunately it was fatal.

Thad was a great, great guy."

Lt(jg) May, leader of the second section, kept with Bell until the latter made his right turn. He got in several unsuccessful shots, then saw a P-40 below him tailed by 3 Zekes. He went straight down, made a beam run from 4 o'clock and saw the Zeke roll over and crash into the water. May recovered at 5,000 ft. and rejoined the formation during the whole of this action Ens. Popp was on May's wing.

Lt(jg) Kepford, leading the second division of the high cover was also jumped on the first attack. They made their first runs in column on 6 Zekes 5,000 ft. below them. Kepford got one, Cunningham a second and McQueen a third.

Dan Cunningham flew with Ike Kepford on many occasions. He recalls this mission.

"I was on one hop with Ike, leading his second section. When we joined up with the bombers we normally split into 2s and started weaving. We never did. We were in pretty close formation and I'm working my ass off to hold my position and my wingman was doing the same but twice as hard. I'm watching him so tight that I didn't see what was ahead of us. All of a sudden Ike's shooting, his wingman's shooting and I'm right behind a Jap. I started shooting and my wingman started shooting. He went right up the ass of 4 of them with 4 of us and we blew the 4 of them out of the sky. I thought that was the neatest thing I had seen. But he was that kind of a guy. He didn't break us up because he saw the 4 Japs. I enjoyed flying with Ike, he was a good pilot and a good shot and guts! Aggressive, he wanted to win. Whatever he did he wanted to win. That's why he was so successful and a helluva nice guy".

They climbed back to 19,000 ft. and the division separated into pairs—Kepford and McQueen made several passes on about 20 Zekes without success. Kepford then heard Bitzegaio call for help, made a high side run on the Zeke and saw him burst into flames. He and McQueen climbed again, and Kepford saw a Zeke on another F4U's tail and probably destroyed him. The pair made a series of runs, ending at 8,000 ft. They then found the bombers who were just leaving the rally point. On the way back, they beat off 2 attacks by a division of 6 Zekes.

Lt(jg) Cunningham and Ens. Fitzgerald, the remainder of the second division left Kepford after Cunningham got his first Zeke. They were attacked by a Zeke from astern and split-S'd away. They used full power and got over the bombers at the rally point. On the retirement they saw a flight south of Cape St. George. As they headed toward it Cunningham saw a single Zeke below him. He made a high side run, the Zeke rolled over smoking with his prop windmilling and went into the water. He and Fitzgerald then rejoined the bombers.

When the Japs attacked the medium and low cover, Lts(jg) Streig and Mims dove away and lost the Zekes. Climbing back to 14,000 ft. they pulled up on the tail of a Zeke and got a good burst into his belly. The Zeke burned.

4 Zekes were seen above and 2 or 3 above and astern. This group came down and got on Streig's tail. Mims turned in on one of

"Big Jim" Streig, ace with 5.5 kills. Courtesy U.S. Naval Historical Center / M.W. "Butch" Davenport Collection.

them, and with a burst from dead astern, set him afire. Streig had broken left and down (losing Mims in the process) and saw a Zeke below him at 3,000 ft. He made a high-side run, saw the Zeke burn, and crash, and pulled up to 5,000ft. Tracers went by him and he dove to 1500 ft. He climbed to 5,000 ft. and headed for Cape Gazelle. He saw 7 or 8 Zekes climbing from Rapopo Airfield at 1500 ft. He dove on the nearest Zeke and made a beam run. Pieces flew from the plane, he fell off to the right, and crashed near the field. They then put on full power and headed for the retiring bombers making 310 knots (indicated) at 1,000 ft. He joined up on Mims and headed back to base. After Mims and Streig were separated the former dove for the water. He saw 8 or 10 planes (blue grey in color) circling slowly with their wheels down, right on the water off Malaguna Airfield (Mims was unable to identify the type). He got on one's tail and it crashed into the water. He then headed for Cape Gazelle and joined up on Streig over the bombers. Lt. Chenoweth, leading the second section of a division in the medium cover, was weaving 2,000 ft. over the bombers on their retirement when he saw 6 Zekes diving down from the vicinity of Rapopo. The leader made a run on Chenoweth's wingman, (Ens. Dixon) but did not fire. Tracers went by his wings, Chenoweth split-S'd to the left and picked the Zeke up on the turn. Both were on their backs and Chenoweth, firing from almost dead astern, saw his bullets go and the flame smoke and Chenoweth kicked up to the right to avoid the P-40s and saw the Zeke go into the water off Praed Point. He could not find Dixon, so he called him on the radio and established contact. He poured on the coal and came back over the bombers, joining up on 2 Marine F4Us.

Lt(jg) Gilbert, flying wing on a division leader in the medium cover, caught a Zeke's 20mm as the bombers were leaving the target. He split-S'd out and as he rolled over caught a Zeke in his sights. Both planes were diving steeply and Gilbert fired into the Zeke's tail until it burned. He recovered at 12,000 ft. and looked for his section leader without success. Japs were all over the sky so he dove out to the center. As he was off Cape Gazelle 4 Zekes made runs, but when he turned into them they disengaged. But another Zeke came in on his tail and he was hit again.

"Butch" Davenport in front of the squadron scoreboard. Courtesy U.S. Naval Historical Center / M.W. "Butch" Davenport Collection.

He joined up on 2 P-40s and picked up the bombers off Cape St. George.

Lt(jg) Burriss and Ens. Jagger were jumped by several Zekes just as the bombers were going into the target. Burriss' plane was hit by 2 20mm. shells in the accessory section, he dove and got on the tail of a Zeke who jinked forward and down with Burriss behind him. Burriss closed to 50 yards and saw him catch fire and go down. Meanwhile Jagger, got on the tail of the Zeke who shot Burriss. The Zeke rolled, Jagger stayed with him firing all the time. He saw him smoke, but did not wait to see him go down as he was anxious to join up with Burriss (Burriss in his recovery from his

run saw the Zeke go down in flames). Burriss was at full throttle and Jagger did not join up until they were off Cape Gazelle. Burriss' oil pressure was dropping, and he kept his speed to 160 k. His oil pressure finally went down to zero, oil came out of his prop governer. He chopped back on his throttle and his prop stopped. All this time he was at 1,000 ft. He opened his hatch and prepared for a water landing. At 500 ft. he popped his flaps (indicating 120 k.) leveled off at 10 ft. and skimmed in across an 8 ft. swell. He got out on the wing without any trouble and the plane sank almost immediately. His chute kept him afloat in a sitting position.

He undid his harness and inflated his raft. Before going in he had called Blackburn, as had Jagger, and 3 Marines circled Burriss, Blackburn arrived and circled until the Dumbo (called by Killefer on Dane Base just as Burriss went in) arrived and dropped a smoke bomb. Burriss was picked up after almost an hour.

Lt. Schub's division was bottom cover on the first B-25 squadron to go in. As the bombers dropped, he saw 5-7 Zekes about 2,000 ft. above. The leader dived and released a phosphorous bomb which burst about 500 ft. above the formation. Schub got a 90° deflection shot at the second Zeke coming down, and probably destroyed it. The third Zeke looped and rolled, diving behind the bombers. The F4U split-S'd away, turned and came back over the B-25s. No further attacks were made on the formation.

Cunningham destroyed two Zekes, Chenoweth destroyed one Zeke, Bitzegaio destroyed one Zeke, and probably destroyed two Hamps, Gilbert destroyed one Zeke, Burriss destroyed one Zeke, May destroyed one Zeke, Kepford destroyed two Zekes and probably destroyed one Zeke, McQueen destroyed one Zeke, Jagger destroyed one Zeke, Schub probably destroyed one Zeke, Streig destroyed two Zekes and shared another Zeke with Mims, who also shot down one Zeke and one unidentified aircraft.

No bombers were lost to enemy aircraft.

The following pilots escorted B-24s in a strike on Lakunai airfield:

Lt. M.W. Davenport	Lt(jg) D.C. Freeman
Ens. H.B. Richardson	Ens. E.E. Beeler
Lt. S.R. Beacham	Lt. Cdr. J.T. Blackburn
Ens. M.M. Kurlander	Lt(jg) D.H. Gutenkunst
Lt. C.D. Gile	Lt(jg) T. Killefer
Ens. J.M. Smith	Ens. W.P. Meek

The enemy attempted no interception. Heavy anti-aircraft fire was meager and inaccurate.

One negative shipping search (4 sorties) was made northeast of New Ireland.

28 January

ROVING HIGH COVER

This was the first mission that Roving High Cover was used. This was a small flight of between 4-6 planes flying at high altitude ahead of the main strike. The aim being to jump the Japs before they began attacking the main force. This caused the Japs to become disorganized and minimized the amount of Jap fighters getting through to the bombers.

Due to the amount of Jap planes encountered on these Roving High Cover missions they began calling them the "Gravy Train."

Twenty F4Us were assigned as partial cover on the TBFs in a joint SBD-TBF strike on Tobera Airfield, New Britain.

Lt. Cdr. J.T. Blackburn	Lt(jg) G.F. Bowers
Lt(jg) D.H. Gutenkunst	Ens. G.M. Keller
Lt(jg) F.J. Streig	Lt(jg) P. Cordray

Lt(jg) R. Mims

Lt(jg) T. Killefer

Ens. W.P. Meek

Lt(jg) D.C. Freeman

Ens. P.E. Divenney

Lt. Cdr. R.R. Hedrick

Ens. J.O. Ellsworth

Lt(jg) J. Miller

Lt(jg) R. H. Jackson

Lt(jg) D.T. Malone

Lt. H.A. March

Lt(jg) C.W. Gilbert

Lt(jg) E. May

Ens. F.A. Jagger

Rendezvous was made west of Taiof Island and the formation went in on a course of 277° over Kabanga Bay, south of the target, and turned right.

The bombers made their runs from east to west, and retired to the rally point over Kabanga Bay. The close and medium cover (12,000 ft. to 16,000 ft.) went down with the bombers in their dives. A roving high cover of 6 F4U's came in at 32,000 ft. About 40 or 50 Zekes and Hamps intercepted the strike as they were about 10 miles SE of the target, but none of the Japs got through to the bombers.

The high cover disorganized at least part of the enemy's attack, and the low and medium cover was strong enough to turn back all fighters who got through to them, accounting for at least 9. Lt. March shot down a Zeke in what was apparently his first attack on the TBF cover - March was at about 15,000 ft. over Kabanga Bay in the approach, weaving over the bombers with another division. About 8 Zekes came down in a dive on the second division. March turned in, and up, and got a good burst into a Zeke who was recovering in a wingover. The Zeke was seen to crash in flames. Lt(jg) Gilbert, March's wingman, got in a snap shot at another Zeke and saw pieces fly from his tail. Almost immediately afterwards a Zeke began a run on March but pulled away and over on his back. March pulled up his nose, fired and set the Zeke afire. At this point the bombers went down in their dive with March and his division over them. Zekes made several attacks on the formation during the retirement, but disengaged when the fighters turned towards them.

Lt(jg) Mims, number two man in Blackburn's division in the lower cover, was hit in the windshield and oil cooler on the initial attack. Mims broke to the right, got a 90° deflection shot on a Zeke, followed him from 13,000 ft. almost to the ground firing most of the time, but lost him as the Zeke went into a roll. Mims was west of the field and headed for the rally point over Kabanga Bay. He was at about 100 ft. when he got on the tail of a Zeke. He fired a good burst (4 guns) and saw the Zeke begin smoking. He fired again, and only one gun worked, and as he pulled up a Marine F4U finished off the Jap. Mims then climbed, joined another F4U and, since his oil pressure was dropping, headed home. On landing his plane was caught in a slip stream and nosed over. Lt(jg) Gutenkunst, leading the second section of Lt. Cdr. Blackburn's division in the low cover, got his first shot at a Zeke climbing at the formation just after the bombers' loads dropped—Gutenkunst was at 2,000 ft. He nosed over in a head-on run at the Zeke, who fell away and into the water. During the retirement Gutenkunst saw a Zeke chase an F4U low on the water. Gutenkunst started his run and the Zeke made a 180° turn and headed back inland. Gutenkunst followed, made a beam run, ending dead astern, and saw the Zeke blow up. He rejoined the bombers, by this time well rallied, and escorted them home. Ens. Divenney went down with Gutenkunst in the latter's run on the Zeke. A Zeke got on Divenney's tail, and he broke away and lost sight of Gutenkunst—Divenney, then at 6,000 ft., saw a Zeke go by, got on his tail and fired until the Zeke caught fire. As he pulled up another Zeke went by in a run and Divenney got a full deflection shot and saw the Zeke go into the water. He was then jumped by three Zekes. He went to the deck and joined a nearing F4U. The pair rejoined the formation and went back to base. Lt(jg) Killefer and Ens. Meek, part of the medium cover, became separated from the rest as they went down with the bombers. A Zeke made a high side run on Killefer, but pulled away. Another Zeke made a run, the pair split, and Killefer got on the Zeke's tail. He missed, and Meek, from a position slightly above Killefer, came down and fired at close range from astern. The Zeke caught fire at the wing roots and went in. Immediately afterwards a Zeke jumped Meek who split-S'd away, losing Killefer in the process. Meek joined up with a Marine in the SBD cover and came back to base with that formation. When Meek did his split-S, Killefer was about 1,000 yards behind and 1,000 ft. above the bombers. He joined up with Lt. May and the pair scissored. A Zeke got very close on May's tail (but did no damage), Killefer turned in, and the Zeke disengaged. Killefer saw another Zeke behind him, turned, and the Zeke turned up and away, but quite slowly. Killefer closed fast, fired from 200 yards, and saw the underside of the Zeke's wing catch fire. Killefer confirmed his burn and found himself in the middle of the TBF formation. He saw a Zeke heading for the bombers low on

Paul Cordray on the wing of his plane. Courtesy U.S. Navy photo. Robert L. Lawson Collection.

Group of VF-17 pilots at Bougainville 1944. Courtesy Lennard Edmisten.

"Hal" Jackson at Bougainville 1944. Courtesy Hal and Barbara Jackson.

"Duke" Henning, Tom Blackburn, "Ike" Kepford relaxing after a mission. Courtesy U.S. Naval Historical Center / M.W. "Butch" Davenport Collection.

the water, started after him, got on his tail, fired, and although at the end of the burst only one gun was firing, the Zeke rolled over and went into the water. By this time the bombers had rallied. Killefer took position over them and escorted them home.

The high cover approached the target area at 30,000 ft. As the bombers made their attack Lt. Cdr. Hedrick saw Zekes coming in from the seaward. Twelve Zekes at about 24,000 ft. were in a loose column, breaking off separately and making runs in formation. Hedrick's flight (6 planes) came down, also in column first, and Hedrick made 4 passes, but with only one gun firing. After the third pass a Zeke got on Hedrick's tail and he zoomed up. Just as the Zeke appeared to be stalling out, Lt(jg) Cordray, came up behind him and fired a long burst. The Zeke caught fire and fell away. Cordray and his wingman lost Hedrick as they recovered. After several passes Cordray saw a Zeke 300 ft. below him. He made a beam run, closed to extremely short range and fired. Pieces flew from the Zeke, he burned, and went down. Hedrick finally got 4 guns working. He was ten miles astern of the retiring bombers at 4,000 ft. when he saw a Zeke 2 miles away, closing slowly on the bombers. The Zeke nosed over at an F4U low on the water and Hedrick fired, but at too long a range. The Zeke pulled up in an Immelman and Hedrick followed. He closed to 100 yards and fired at the left wing root and engine. The pilot bailed out, and the plane caught fire. Hedrick strafed the chute, but believes that his shots bracketed it.

"One particular fight that I'll never forget over Rabaul". Remembers Roger Hedrick.

"We had had a big melee and I was split up and had no wingman. Normally the Japs would chase us about 20 miles off shore back towards Bougainville and then they would pull back. Once in a while we would look back and see their victory rolls or whatever there.

"This time I saw one character doing that and I was so incensed that I said 'I'm not going to let him get away with that.' So by myself I went back and shagged after him. I bounced him and I shot him down. The plane burned and he parachuted out. I came around in a big circle while this fellow was coming down in his chute. I thought to myself there's one rascal that isn't going to be back shooting at us tomorrow. As I approached him I did squeeze the trigger. However I was going so fast I didn't realize, but he was standing still and first of all I damn near ran into his canopy. But I got close enough that I could look at him and he raised an arm to me. I did not actually hit him, but I would have if I could have.

"It wasn't until about 10 seconds later that 3 of the other fellows, his friends, jumped me. That was, I think, the really one time that I experienced real terror.

"Here I had them on both sides behind me and I had 225 miles over water to get home. They were making runs at me and I was not doing much dodging because I knew I had to get acceleration, get out far enough ahead of them out of range. We did have a slight speed advantage over them. So I kept going, but this couldn't have lasted very long, but to me it seemed like eternity.

"They pulled off and went back in line low on fuel. I took out the little canteen I had and swallowed that and lit up a cigarette and believe me I never tasted anything better in my life".

Lt(jg) Miller, Cordray's wingman, followed Hedrick and Cordray in their initial passes. After Cordray's first hit, he and Miller were alone.

A Zeke made a high side on Cordray, Miller turned in on a head-on shot, and saw pieces fly from the Jap's engine. The pair then dove on 5 Zekes, each taking one. Miller's Zeke rolled away and Miller got in a deflection shot from astern. He saw his tracers going into the Zekes belly, and the plane blew up.

Cordray then made his run on his second Zeke with Miller on his wing, and the pair rejoined the bombers and headed back to base.

Ellsworth, Hedrick's wingman, lost Hedrick on his first pass. He shot at a Zeke, missed, and climbed back to 20,000 ft. He saw another Zeke into a climb, gunned up into him and got a long burst into his engine. The Zeke fell off smoking and tumbled down.

Ellsworth then headed for the rally point, joined up on a Marine, and escorted the TBFs back to base. Lt(jg) Jackson and Ens. Malone, the third section of the high cover, went down on the first attack. Four Zekes went past and one pulled up in front of Jackson. Jackson got a long burst into the cockpit, the Zeke caught fire. Jackson rolled over to join up with Cordray, but saw a Zeke firing at Malone's tail. As Jackson came down the Zeke broke off and dove away. The pair then went to the rally point and began weaving with the bombers. As Malone's plane was badly hit and Jackson was low on gas, they left the formation half way back to base, and came directly home.

Divenney, Gutenkunst, Cordray, March and Killefer destroyed two Zekes each; Hedrick, Miller, Meek and Jackson destroyed one Zeke each; Mims shared a Zeke with a Marine pilot and got one probable Zeke; Miller, Gilbert and Ellsworth probably destroyed one Zeke each.

Three F4Us were damaged by fire from Zekes. One F4U was caught in a slip stream on landing and nosed over. The pilot was uninjured. No bombers were lost to enemy aircraft.

One negative combat air patrol over base was flown.

FOUR EACH FOR KEPFORD AND BURRISS

29 January

20 F4Us were assigned as cover for the SBDs in a joint SBD-TBF strike on Tobera Airfield, New Britain. Four of the planes were forced to return early, leaving 16 with the bombers.

Lt. Cdr. R.R. Hedrick	Lt. S.R. Beacham
Ens. J.O. Ellsworth	Ens. M.M. Kurlander
Lt(jg) G.F. Bowers	Lt. O.I. Chenoweth
Ens. G.M. Keller	Ens. J.C. Dixon
Lt. C.D. Gile	Lt(jg) D.G. Cunningham
Ens. J.M. Smith	Lt(jg) I.C. Kepford
Lt(jg) E. May	Lt(jg) H.M. Burriss
Ens. W.P. Popp	Ens. F.A. Jagger

The bombers went in at about 14,000 ft. The F4Us had one layer at 15,000 ft. another at 16,000 ft., and 2 F4U's (all that remained of a projected 4 plane Roving High Cover) at 30,000 ft.

The approach was made over Cape St. George, north of Duke of York Island, and into the target over Londip Plantation. The retirement was made over Kabanga Bay.

As the formation was coming in, the high cover Lts(jg) Burriss and Kepford) spotted 12 Zekes below them at about 24,000 ft. over Cape Gazelle. They climbed and dove on the enemy. Working as pairs, with just one and then the other, protecting the others tail they accounted for 4 Zekes apiece, the whole action lasting about 10 minutes. Their runs were mostly high sides and overheads, with sharp chandelles between passes. The Japs were apparently caught completely by surprise and it is certain that their intended attack on the bombers was broken up.

"One other occasion, and this sight I'll never forget." Said Roger Hedrick. "Was down on low cover this time, but had sent one divi-

John Malcolm Smith who later made ace with VF-84. Courtesy Therese Smith.

sion ahead under Ike Kepford, who ended up our leading ace, to go in roving patrol again.

I was leading our 5 that time and I looked up and I saw 2 planes, just mammoth torches straight dive coming down side-by-side, almost as if they were in formation. I'll be darned if a minute or 2 later here came 2 more followed by 2 more again all torching both of them each time and finally a final 2 came down for a total of 8 planes.

"This was a marvellous innovation, a fighter sweep which we called Roving High Cover probably the greatest tactic that Tom, in my mind was able to pull off while we were out there".

As it was the low and medium cover was intercepted by about only 15 Zekes. The Japs attacked after the bombers finished their runs. None succeeded in getting at the bombers and the fighters shot down 2 Zekes and got 2 probables.

Lt. Gile, flight leader of the low cover, turned back several attacks, but became separated from his division. As he was heading after the bombers, he looked back and saw a dogfight going on 10 miles southeast of Kabanga Bay. He chandelled from 1,000 ft. to 5,000 ft. in a 180° turn and entering the melee, drove a Zeke off an F4U's tail. The Zeke headed for home at 200 ft., Gile pulled up

behind him and at close range shot off his tail. Gile then followed the bombers and joined up.

Lt(jg) May, the leader of Gile's second section, was engaged in the above mentioned dogfight. He and his wingman made several passes, finally becoming separated. May got on the tail of a Zeke at 50 ft., fired a long burst, and the plane crashed into the water in flames.

Ens. Smith, Gile's wingman was also involved in the melee over Kabanga Bay. His plane was hit, but not seriously, and as he was scissoring with Gile he spotted a Zeke on an F4U's tail. He executed a 360° turn, making a pass at the Zeke during his turn. He was unable to pull through, did a wingover, and came back on the Zeke's tail. He chased the Zeke for about a minute firing most of the time. As his windshield was smeared with oil he could not estimate the exact damage inflicted but he saw pieces fly from the Zeke and as he broke off the Zeke had flopped on his back and was diving from 1,000 ft. Smith joined up with another F4U, picked up the bombers, and came home.

Lt. Chenoweth and Ens. Dixon followed the last division of SBDs down in their dive and levelled out at 4,000 ft. as they retired. As they were crossing over the coastline they saw a lone Zeke

Tom Blackburn with Jack Hospers Chance Vought Service Rep. Ondongo, November 1943. Courtesy U.S. Navy photo. Robert L. Lawson Collection.

"Hap" Bowers gun drawn. Courtesy U.S. Naval Historical Center / M.W. "Butch" Davenport Collection.

trying to sneak up under the SBDs. They made a section run on this Zeke as he tried to pull around into them. Chenoweth fired first and saw his bullets hit. Dixon was firing by the time Chenoweth had stopped, and put a second burst into him. The Zeke passed them on an almost opposite course.

He was smoking and his left wing was dropping as he went into a cloud. He was then diving at a 45° angle.

Light A/A was meagre and inaccurate. Three phosphorous bombs (believed shot up from the ground) were seen.

Weather: slight haze with scattered cumulus clouds at 3,000 ft.

Twenty-seven Zekes were encountered. Burriss and Kepford shot down four Zekes each; Gile and May shot down one Zeke each; Smith, Chenoweth and Dixon scored one probable each.

"Ike" Kepford received his second Navy Cross for his actions on this mission. One of the F4U's was damaged by fire from a Zeke. No bombers were lost to enemy action.

One negative combat air patrol over base (4 sorties) was flown.

30 January
24 F4Us were assigned as part of the cover of a B-25 strike on a supply dump in the Rabaul area, near Lakunai. One was unable to take off and 3 were forced by engine or plane trouble to return early, leaving 20 F4Us with the bombers.

Lt. Cdr. J.T. Blackburn	Lt(jg) I.C. Kepford
Lt(jg) D.H. Gutenkunst	Lt. Cdr. R.R. Hedrick
Lt(jg) R. Mims	Ens. J.O. Ellsworth
Lt(jg) T. Killefer	Lt(jg) G.F. Bowers
Ens. W.P. Meek	Ens. G.M. Keller
Lt(jg) D.C. Freeman	Lt(jg) P. Cordray
Ens. P.E. Divenney	Lt(jg) J. Miller
Lt(jg) E. May	Lt(jg) D.T. Malone
Ens. J.M. Smith	

The B-25s approached at 10-12,000 ft., with the fighters stacked to 25,000 ft. The formation approached over New Ireland at East Cape, proceeded on a direct course to Duke of York Island then went to Rabaul Peninsula then to the target area. The retirement was made out Blanche Bay to Duke of York Island, then northwards, crossing New Ireland with the narrow neck between Makudukudu and Solowakee Bay, and then down the east coast.

Heavy A/A coming from the Rabaul rim was accurate and most intense. Some phosphorus bombs were seen.

The weather over the target was good. There was a thin layer of clouds at 25,000 ft. with broken clouds 2-5,000 ft. Visibility unlimited over the target. There were heavy cumulus formations from 3,000 ft. to 15,000 ft. over Duke of York Island and in the vicinity of Tobera.

The interception started as the bombers finished their runs, and continued out over Blanche Bay, with some contacts occurring as far south as Cape St. George. Average altitude of the interception was 20,000 ft. One group of at least 20 Zekes seemed to come from the direction of Watom Island. These appeared to be waiting for the bombers to start their runs.

Lt. Cdr. Hedrick, leading the flight assigned as high cover, spotted 20 Zekes at about 30,000 ft. north of the target. The bombers

"Butch" Davenport, Skull and Crossbones ace with 6.25 kills stands in front of his plane #9 "Lonesome Polecat". Courtesy U.S. Naval Historical Center / M.W. "Butch" Davenport Collection.

had just made their runs when 4 Zekes closed on Hedrick's division. The divisions dove away. During the dive Ens. Ellsworth, Hedrick's wingman, picked up a Zeke in the dive and at 12,000 ft. set him afire with a burst from dead astern. Hedrick and Ellsworth pulled up after another Zeke who looped and came head-on still on his back. The Zeke dove, with Hedrick following, and as the Jap pulled up Hedrick hit him from 7 o'clock, slightly above, at very close range. The Zeke did not burn but dove steeply into the water.

As Hedrick's division (Mims, Keller, the number 4 man) withdrew down the channel with the bombers 20 Zekes stayed above and behind them. They made occasional runs but did not press home their attacks.

Ens. Keller, lost his section leader Lt(jg) Bowers, at the beginning of the attack. Both had split-S'd away from several Zekes and Keller blacked out, and came to at 11,000 ft. directly over Simpson Harbor. He dove to evade 3 Zekes and ducked into a cloud. Coming out he made a head-on run at a Zeke and saw it smoke heavily. He was jumped by 5 Zekes and again sought cloud cover. As he could find no F4Us on which to join up, he came back alone at 2,000 ft.

"Ike" Kepford and his F4U-1A. Note the flaps burned by exploding ammunition cans. Piva Yoke, January 31, 1944. Courtesy U.S. Navy photo. Robert L. Lawson Collection.

In the split-S in which Keller got lost, Lt(jg) Bowers picked up a Zeke below him at about 20,000 ft. He made an overhead run, hit the Zeke, saw him smoke and fall off. Bowers recovered, and weaved down to about 4,000 ft. He made a run on another Zeke but was himself hit by 20mm. and 7.7s and broke away. He joined up on Hedrick and Ellsworth during the retirement.

"Hap" Bowers remembers this action over Rabaul:

"While flying cover over Rabaul - I was still looking for my first kill and found a Zero alone. My golden opportunity had arrived. I got eager and opened too soon with 6 guns. The Jap rolled over and I followed—still shooting. He had time to check me out and commenced an upside down climb. That's the last thing I ever expected and got the hell out of there. I still don't know if the guns would work upside down or not. I figured the weight of the stack of ammo would not allow the feeding operation to work. I'll probably never know. I didn't ever appreciate hanging from a seat belt anyhow. Should have nailed him!"

"I'd been flying every day through most of the whole Bougainville invasion, and never seen a Jap plane. Everybody else was getting one or two here and there. I was getting pretty edgy. We were then relieved and went back south and reorganized, rested in Australia for a while and came back and were based on Bougainville.

"We were hitting Rabaul which was their stronghold there. There we knew we would get into a fight every day, there were no ifs or buts about it. We were escorting the bombers in to attack them instead of the other way round.

"We heard all the stories, Japs will never press a head-on attack, they can't ever see you when you're coming in from behind, it was real easy.

"I just couldn't wait to get in there and bang a couple down. We were flying cover over the bombers and the group I was in was the highest cover, which was roughly 10,000 feet higher than the bombers.

"We had Japs higher than us, so they picked us on the high cover and were bearing in on a head-on attack. They came shooting all the way in. I thought they are not supposed to do this. Then they had the high cover pretty much broken up by then.

"We were spread out all over and the Japs were attacking each one of us. The Japs just picked on the top cover and we were getting the whole thing. Sometime after that my wife said, 'How was your first day in combat, were you scared.' I said 'no.' I guess I was too dumb. I sure as hell was scared the second time though!"

"From there on in it was pretty easy. It was only the high cover that really caught it. Shortly after that we put in Roving High Cover. 8 planes way over in advance to chase them off, and from there on high cover was pretty good too. The ones on Roving High Cover had nothing to do except attack the Japs. That was the gravy train—where you got them all.

"Jap pilots were supposed not to be very good, but there were a few good ones."

The second division of Hedrick's flight (Lts(jg) Cordray, Miller, Malone and Ens. Smith) made contact with the Zekes at about 16,000 ft. In the ensuing melee each had a Zeke on his tail. Miller took the Zeke on Malone's tail, and firing from dead astern saw it smoke and fall off. Smith, firing at the Jap on Cordray's tail, saw his burst go into the Zeke's nose. The division reformed and came back to form over the bombers.

Hedrick and Ellsworth destroyed one Zeke each; Miller, Smith, Keller and Bowers probably destroyed one Zeke each.

One F4U was damaged by fire from a Zeke.

No bombers were lost to enemy aircraft.

A BAD DAY FOR THE JOLLY ROGERS

Four divisions (16 F4Us) were assigned as part of the TBF cover in a joint SBD-TBF strike on shipping in Simpson Harbor, New Britain. The bombers were at 12,000 ft., with the fighters stacked in 4 layers. Low cover was at 13-14,000 ft., medium at 16,000 ft., high at 20-22,000 ft., and roving high cover (4 planes) at 26,000 ft.

Lt. O.I. Chenoweth	Lt. Cdr. J.T. Blackburn
Ens. J.C. Dixon	Lt(jg) D.H. Gutenkunst
Lt(jg) D.G. Cunningham	Lt. M.W. Davenport
Lt(jg) H.J. Bitzegaio	Ens. E.E. Beeler
Lt(jg) I.C. Kepford	Lt. S.R. Beacham
Lt(jg) M. Schanuel	Ens. M.M. Kurlander
Lt(jg) T.F. Kropf	Lt(jg) E. May
	Ens. W.P. Popp

The bombers went in over the southern end of New Ireland, assed southeast of Duke of York Island, and went in directly to impson Harbor. The retirement was out Blanche Bay and down he channel.

The roving high cover made contact with the enemy before hey had a chance to intercept the formation. About 20 Zekes were ighted and attacked at 20,000 ft. over the harbor, and what was pparently another group of about 12 fighters attacked the cover fter the TBFs pushed over. The Japs were fairly aggressive, but id not get near the bombers, and broke off their attacks when they ad rallied east of Cape Gazelle.

Heavy A/A from warships and land batteries was moderate and naccurate.

Lt. Cdr. Blackburn, leading the roving high cover, spotted 20 Zekes joining up over Simpson Harbor at 20,000 ft., as the bombrs were starting their runs. He came down on the second Zeke of he top pair in a beam run ending astern, and the Zeke exploded. Blackburn broke away and sighted 2 Zekes to the south starting uns on 2 F4Us from 20,000 ft. Blackburn made a low side run on he second Zeke, hit it, and the Zeke went down in a diving spiral vith Blackburn on his tail. The plane caught fire and the pilot bailed ut. His shoulder straps must have burned through, as the parachute seat swung free. Blackburn recovered from his run and folowed the bombers down the channel at 8,000 ft. There were many aps from 2,000 ft. to 12,000 ft. (the cloud ceiling) over Cape Gazelle.

Blackburn made a high side run on a Zeke, hit him, and the Zeke spun. As Blackburn and his wingman then swung back after the bombers they were attacked by 10 or 12 Japs. As he was climbing after a Zeke a Hamp got on his tail, but Blackburn took evasive action and eluded him. Blackburn pulled out over the SBDs and saw 2 Zekes at 5,000 ft. The leading Zeke broke away when Blackburn attacked but he made a beam run on the second, scored hits, and left him smoking in a glide. He rejoined the SBDs and saw a Zeke heading for them at 7,000 ft., 2 miles astern. Blackburn swung back and got a full deflection shot from below. He saw a flash of flame at the cockpit and stopped firing. The flame died out and Blackburn fired again. As he turned back towards the bombers the Zeke was in a 30° dive at 1,000 ft.

Blackburn then joined up on Gutenkunst over the SBDs.

Lt. Davenport, leading the second section of Blackburn's division, went down after Blackburn in the initial attack. He started a run on a Zeke from 9 o'clock and swung in astern. His first burst missed, and he closed the range and hit. The Zeke caught fire as he split-S'd out. Davenport's next 2 passes were unsuccessful, and as he saw his wingman heading away he followed. A Zeke got on the wingman's tail and Davenport dived from 3,000 ft. above and fired. The Zeke half rolled, Davenport rolled with him still firing, and the Zeke went down in flames.

Davenport then joined up on his wingman and 2 other F4Us and went back over the bombers.

Mel Kurlander (center) and groundcrew. Courtesy Mel Kurlander.

Ray Beacham sitting in his Corsair. Courtesy Harry Bridges.

Tom Blackburn in front of the squadron scoreboard at Bougainville early in 1944. Courtesy U.S. Navy photo. Robert L. Lawson Collection.

"Ike" Kepford's plane after crash landing. Courtesy U.S. Navy photo. Robert L. Lawson Collection.

Lt. Chenoweth's division came in at about 24,000 ft. and made contact with 4 Zekes slightly below them. All 4 dove out before the F4Us could get at them. The division scissored down to 12,000 ft. over the bombers where 5 or 6 more Zekes were sighted. Chenoweth and his wingman, Ens. Dixon, made a head-on section run as one Zeke turned into them. The Zeke exploded. Chenoweth then turned behind another Zeke and opened fire at 200 yards. He began to smoke heavily and went into a dive. The pilot bailed out; but as his chute was on fire he plummeted down.

Lt. "Oc" Chenoweth remembers this Jap Zero who tried to mix it up with his Corsair. After a burst from his guns wrecked the Zero, Lt. Chenoweth watched the Jap bail out but didn't worry about him because his chute caught on fire from his flaming plane. "I know what came of him," Lt. Chenoweth said grimly.

Chenoweth turned left to pick up Dixon and as he did, a Zeke pulled up dead ahead of him. The Zeke was very slow, Chenoweth got a 5-second burst, and the Zeke exploded. Dixon was nowhere in sight, and Chenoweth, after one unsuccessful pass at a Zeke, pulled out and took station behind the SBDs.

Lt(jg) Kepford was attacked by 10-12 Zekes who dove from 25,000 ft. to his level (15,000 ft.). They came down in pairs, making good approaches. One Zeke made a run on an F4U and Kepford made a beam run from 7 o'clock and set the Zeke afire.

The sky was full of Japs and Kepford had to weave radically as he went down after the bombers. A Tony split-S'd and made a low side run on him from 12 o'clock.

Kepford was badly hit in the right wing but he kept firing with his left wing guns and the Tony caught fire. The ammunition cases in Kepford's right wing had exploded and his wing caught on fire. He was joined by Schanuel, leader of his second section, and the pair returned to base. Kepford could not get his right wheel down and made a one wheel landing. The plane was washed out, but Kepford was unhurt.

Lts(jg) Schanuel and Kropf, Kepford's second section, spotted a group of Zekes at 25,000 ft. 10 miles southeast of Simpson Harbor. The section climbed to 26,000 ft. and, using cloud cover, tried to sneak up on the Zekes. They were spotted by 3 Zekes who turned into them. Schanuel got a 30° deflection shot at one and saw him disintegrate. Schanuel rolled over and dove through the cloud layer to escape the remaining Zekes. He circled at the base of the clouds waiting for Kropf to join up, but he did not appear. At this time the bombers were directly beneath Schanuel but not under attack. He saw a Zeke in a run on one F4U, fired but over shot. The F4U had been badly hit, and Schanuel joined up with him and started back to base, joining Kepford en route. Kropf was apparently shot down in the preceding action.

Lt. Beacham and Ens. Kurlander, the first section in a division of low cover, were jumped by 4-6 Zekes at 13,000 ft.. The Zekes came down through the overcast and the F4Us dove away (Kepford shot the Zeke on Beacham's tail).

The pair headed off after a Zeke, but another turned in and riddled Beacham's plane with 20mm. Beacham went down to 5,000 ft. and headed for home with Kurlander on his wing. Beacham's hydraulic system was out and there were 6 inches of gasoline in his cockpit from the broken line. He did not dare land on the Torokina strip, so radioed Dane Base that he would land in the water. A crash boat stood by, and Beacham, although it was dark and he had one wheel down, made a good water landing. Despite the fact that his shoulder straps were buckled right he suffered a broken nose. He was groggy, but got out of the plane and was picked up by the crash boat.

Mel Kurlander has vivid memories of this mission:

"After escorting bombers to Rabaul, Ray Beacham and myself found a Zeke and went after him. Both of us were firing at him when he dropped his landing gear and flaps. Ray went flying past the plane, I dropped my landing gear and flaps and stayed on firing—Poor Ray, he was in the firing line of both of us!

"At any rate, the pilot raised his gear and flaps and started into a loop. I did the same—I couldn't have been more than 25 yards behind him, still firing, but at the same time keeping an eye on Ray. He was right over the deck coming out of Rabaul Harbor, flaps down wheels down, a ruptured duck flying at about 85 knots. Hydraulic system shot out. I didn't follow the Zeke all the way down but went down to cover Ray as he was a sitting duck.

"I'm crisscrossing over Ray to protect him and he can only go 65 knots and was going to take a long time to get home. We couldn't find anyone else to help. So I weaved over him to cover him. On the way out of the harbor on the way home, I spotted a barge with personnel aboard, called the position to "Big Hog", and went after the barge, strafed and claimed it.

"We got back to Empress Augusta Bay and called in for a may day for Ray. He put the plane down in a beautiful water landing and the PT boat picked him up shortly after.

"He wound up with a broken nose. I didn't see Ray until 40 years after at a reunion in Norfolk and at that time I told Ray that I might have shot him instead of the Jap. It all turned out Ok in the end. I know one thing for sure, if we hadn't stayed together he wouldn't have got home".

Ray Beacham describes this mission:

"On a mission over Bougainville while fighting the Japanese, my plane's hydraulic system was injured.

"They ripped up some other parts too, but that one thing was enough. There was six inches of gasoline in the cockpit with me. I couldn't land at our base because the metal on the landing field would ignite the gas and start a fire. The only thing to do was make a crash landing in the ocean. The next thing I remember was finding myself swimming in the ocean.

"I don't recall landing or getting out of the cockpit. I had already radioed what I was going to do, so about 15 minutes later I heard the crash boat coming through the night. I had been concentrating on keeping myself afloat with the parachute strung on my back."

On the way home Kurlander had strafed a Jap barge in St. George's Channel.

When the F4Us arrived over the base they found that the fighter strip had been closed because of a crash on the runway. It was dark, and the traffic circle was terribly congested. Coming in to land Lt(jg) Gutenkunst and a Marine collided in mid-air and both were killed. Ens. Popp landed on the bomber strip, a tire blew, and he nosed over, destroying the plane but suffering no injuries.

Tom Blackburn describes the mission:

"Late in the afternoon there had been an erroneous report that a Jap carrier was coming in to Rabaul. The strike command and fighter command launched everything they could get their hands on. Gutenkunst and I came in at high altitude and had to do some very effective fighting. When we came back to Bougainville it was dark and there were a lot of airplanes that had been shot up in this action. Our own strip was closed because of several wrecks being pulled off the runway, so all the dive bombers and torpedo planes and fighters were trying to land at the bomber strip.

"It was utter chaos. I landed without incident and as I was rolling out I looked back in my mirrors actually to be sure it was clear behind me, so I could turn off and I saw this fireball down at the end of the runway.

Another view of "Ike" Kepford's crashed plane. Courtesy U.S. Navy photo. Robert L. Lawson Collection.

"Gutenkunst was making a regular turning approach into the field and a Marine, Major Johnson, who had been badly shot up, was wounded and had no hydraulics and no radio, was making a straight in approach.

"They collided right over the end of the strip and both of them were killed.

"I was extremely close to Gutenkunst and he and I had been through quite a lot together, both playing on the beach and combat action, and I regarded him as a younger brother whom I was very fond. I was really crushed when he got killed in this freak accident. I was having a hard time emotionally with these losses".

Twenty or thirty Zekes intercepted. Blackburn destroyed two Zekes and probably destroyed three Zekes; Kepford destroyed one Tony and one Zeke; Davenport destroyed two Zekes; Chenoweth destroyed two Zekes and shared a third with Dixon; Schanuel destroyed one Zeke.

Popp and Kepford ground looped on landing. The planes were destroyed, the pilots were uninjured. Both planes had been damaged by Zekes.

No bombers were lost to enemy aircraft.

Wilbert Peter Popp describes his part in the mission.

"We had this late strike at Simpson Harbor. Earlier the Army Air Corps observed what they thought was a Jap aircraft carrier in Simpson Harbor. My regular plane, No. 28, was in repair getting a new engine, so I flew No. 9 normally flown by 'Butch' Davenport our engineering officer. This plane had an engine which had no rough spots ie. flying between 1800-2100 rpms which was a characteristic in most of the Corsairs. Somehow Butch and George Mauhar, the leading chief, had worked out the normal vibration. The whole mission was a fiasco. The aircraft carrier turned out to be a garbage scow. Lt(jg) Tom Kropf never returned and was presumed shot down. Ray Beacham took some hits in his gas tank, and because of gas vapors in the cockpit, chose to do a water landing in Empress Augusta Bay, right off the strip. The plane was lost, Ray was saved. Lt(jg) Doug Gutenkunst was killed in a mid-air collision during landing, with a Marine pilot, right off the runway. Ike Kepford had taken a hit by a Jap Tony which he shot down, resulting in his right wing tank being blown up, causing his right wheel

Damage to one of "Ike" Kepford's planes. Courtesy U.S. Navy photo. Robert L. Lawson Collection.

to come down and could not retract. He tried to land ahead of us, even though the tower had waved him off, because of a Marine Corsair having made a belly-up landing, also.

"However, Ike had no alternative but to try an emergency one-wheel landing. Then our normal strip was completely fouled up and unusable. Earl May, my section leader, then took a wave off and circled to make a landing at Bomber One, a parallel strip to the right of our normal strip. Bougainville had 4 parallel strips with adjoining taxiways. It was night. I took my interval and put my wheels and flaps down for my final. Unbeknownst to me I had taken some hits in the lower part of my aircraft and one of my tires was blown. On landing, that caused me to cartwheel down the runway, eventually flipping over and the plane ended up on its back, propped between 2 piles of Marston Matting stored next to the runway for emergency purposes. When the dust settled I pulled my seat belt, resulting in my fall of about 5 or 6 feet, landing on my head. My only injury was a scratched knee when I scraped the side of the cockpit as I exited the plane. Ironically the only injury during my mishap was to a Navy enlisted man in a jeep alongside of the run-

In this photo you can clearly see the extent of the damage to Kepford's F4U. Courtesy U.S. Navy photo. Robert L. Lawson Collection.

way. My out of control airplane was heading towards his jeep and trying to evade it he put it in reverse and the jeep flipped on its back, resulting in him having a broken arm".

Walter Schub has clear memories of this day:

"We received reports of cruisers and a big strike to Rabaul was set up to go after a carrier. The weather was real bad, with thunderstorms. I was on the ground and they asked for some people to check it out to see what it looked like. Me and Tom Killefer went up over Rabaul. I saw nothing down there except a rusty old tanker and some miscellaneous stuff. I was yelling my head off back to them down there and they got the information by radio, and I said. 'There's nothing up there. Not a thing! Not a thing!'

Then an hour later they took off with all these planes. We lost Gutenkunst and had a real bad day. The flight (whole mission not VF-17) lost 8-10 people. Wasted all these people and planes on that mission".

31 January
Sixteen F4U-1s were assigned as low and medium cover on the TBFs in a joint SBD-TBF strike on shipping in Keravia Harbor, New Britain.

Lt. Cdr. J.T. Blackburn	Lt. H.A. March
Lt. L.T. McQuiston	Lt(jg) C.W. Gilbert
Lt(jg) F. J. Streig	Lt(jg) H.M. Burriss
Lt(jg) R. Mims	Ens. F.A. Jagger
Lt(jg) T. Killefer	Lt. W.J. Schub
Ens. W.P. Meek	Ens. W. C. Wharton
Lt(jg) D.C. Freeman	Lt(jg) W.L. Landreth
Ens. P.E. Divenney	Ens. C.H. Dunn

The bombers saw no targets in the assigned area and bombed Tobera Airfield instead. They made their approach over Cape St. George, New Ireland, up St. George's Channel to Duke of York Island, turned south, and went into Tobera over Londip Plantation. They made a right turn into the target and retired over Kabanga Bay.

On this strike the Japanese abandoned their customary waiting tactics and attacked the bombers before they reached the target. They began their runs from about 24,000 ft. (the F4Us were at 14-15,000 ft.), and were most aggressive, continuing their attacks while the formation had left the rally point over Kabanga Bay. No TBFs were hit by the Zekes or by the phosphorus bombs dropped by the Japanese VF, but at least one SBD was hit.

Heavy and light A/A from around the airfield was meagre and inaccurate. The heavy A/A ceased as the bombers began their push-over.

Lt(jg) Burriss and Ens. Jagger, a section in the medium cover, were hit by Zekes about 4 miles southeast of the target. The F4Us were then at 14,000 ft. and dove away. As they were over Kabanga Bay, another Zeke made a run on Burriss, who was smoking heavily and preparing to make a water landing. Jagger turned in and drove the Zeke away, but in doing so lost sight of Burriss. He believes that Burriss made a successful water landing. When last seen, he had his plane well under control.

Andy Jagger relates his part in the mission:

"I flew wing on Burriss and we were both attacked after returning from escorting bombers into Rabaul. We turned away, heading for home, he and I were jumped. I tried to get the plane that was shooting at him, but at the same time another Jap plane was shooting at me.

"I was shot up so badly that I was losing control of the airplane, and I saw Burriss hit the water, and at that point I didn't see the rest of our guys, but I was able to see the TBFs that we had escorted.

"The damage to my plane was perhaps the worst that I had in my entire combat experience. What I did was, and I think it saved my neck, I joined up and actually flew under, part of the TBF formation going home, because I knew that if we were attacked they had tail gunners, so I would be protected by them".

The following tactical observations were reported after this tragic mission.

Up to the action described, the pattern of Japanese defense had been consistently the same. Their fighters are apparently all scrambled when the striking force was about 50 miles distant from the target. The fighters try to take position 3,000 ft. above the top

Ray Beacham on left in front of the squadron scoreboard Bougainville February 1944. The other pilot is believed to be Don Innis. Courtesy U.S. Navy photo. Robert L. Lawson Collection.

Tom Blackburn's "Big Hog" on Bougainville 1944. Courtesy U.S. Navy photo. Robert L. Lawson Collection.

Popp, Smith, Jackson and Kurlander Bougainville 1944. Courtesy Lennard Edmisten.

cover, which is usually at about 19,000 ft. on the approach to the target. The Japs usually made no attempt to attack the bombers before they made their runs. The fighters (particularly the high cover) were their objective during the bombing runs, and it was not until the bombers were either at the rally point or proceeding to it that they were attacked. On the retirement, Jap fighters hung behind on the flanks of the formation and attempted to pick off stragglers, but they usually turned back after the formation passed Cape St. George.

The action described marked a change in Japanese tactics, and the Jap fighters would now be instructed to attack the bombers before they can make their runs.

The quality of Japanese interceptions had been spotty. On occasion the fighters have been extremely aggressive, but in other cases they have failed to press home their attacks. While the Japs were certainly capable pilots, their reputation for suicidal recklessness is exaggerated. As a matter of fact, the F4U pilots show more determination and more recklessness than the Japs.

Japanese fighter tactics have also been spotty, the Japs can certainly work as pairs and in divisions, but even in an engagement in which disciplined formation flying has been observed, other Jap fighters have attacked singly from no discernible formation. The nearest approach to a formation, for this type of attack, has sometimes been a loose figure eight with the Japs in column. It is the belief of pilots in the area that Jap gunnery has improved, and that there has been a falling off in their aerobatic ability.

It was recommended that the tactics in escort missions be revised. High cover should always be high, ie., above the Jap fighters. This type of cover (designated as "roving high cover") should be provided, even if the low and medium cover must be reduced in order to provide it. One division of F4Us placed high enough to slice through the Jap fighters would be enough to disorganize them and consequently make the mission easier for the bombers and their close escort.

Twenty or thirty Japanese fighters intercepted. They were reported as being more aggressive than usual. Burriss' plane was hit and he was forced to make a water landing a few miles east of Kabanga Point, New Britain. He was reported missing in action.

7

Second Tour
February 1944

1 February

On this date VF-17 was composed of 47 officers and 92 enlisted men and had a compliment of 24 F4U-1 aircraft.

Eight pilots made a negative, 2-hour search in St George's Channel for pilots reported down in the water.

A negative, 2-hour patrol (4 sorties) was flown over Camel Base (3DD's).

2 February

All operations cancelled because of weather.

3 February

The B-24s arrived late at the rendezvous (over Torokina at 17,000 ft.) and in loose formation. 18 F4U's (2 were unable to take off) made rendezvous with them and were on course. The B-24's were at 22,000 ft. on the approach with the fighters stacked in four layers from 23,000 ft. to 30,000 ft., 16 P-38s being top cover.

Lt. M.W. Davenport	Lt. C.D. Gile
Ens. H.B. Richardson	Ens. J.M. Smith
Lt. O.I. Chenoweth	Lt(jg) I.C. Kepford
Ens. J.C. Dixon	Ens. D.R. McQueen
Lt(jg) D.G. Cunningham	Lt(jg) M. Schanuel
Ens. L.A. Fitzgerald	Ens. E.E. Beeler

The approach was made over New Ireland just south of Berpop, north of Duke of York Island, over Cape Tawui to Ataliklikun Bay. The bombers turned left as though to attack Keravat and then made a right turn and headed north for almost 30 miles. A ship (tentatively identified as a DD) was in that vicinity and the bombers may have decided to examine it before attacking their assigned target. They made another right turn and crossed the target from north to south.

VF-17 personnel are briefed in the ready tent by Intelligence Officer Lt. B. D. Henning (at right) before a raid on Rabaul, in February 1944. In center, seated is VF-17 commanding officer Lt. Cdr. Tom Blackburn. The squadron was then based on Bougainville. Courtesy National Archives.

Two VF-17 pilots catch up on their mail, in their quarters tent on Bougainville, February 1944. They are (L-R) Lt. Merl W. Davenport, and Ens. Don McQueen. Courtesy National Archives.

20 Zekes were sighted climbing at 10,000 ft. over Simpson Harbor, and 6-8 more were seen at the same altitude, where the formation was midway between Duke of York Island and Cape Tawui on the initial approach. The Zekes made 2 attacks as the B-24s passed over Cape Tawui for the second time. 3 Zekes were in the first attack and 4 in the second; both attacks were identical.

The Zekes approached the formation on an opposite course, on their backs, and when almost over the bombers, made overhead runs on the B-24s. No passes were made at the fighters. Lt(jg) Kepford got a full deflection shot at the #2 Zeke in the second attack. The Zeke was seen to go down in flames. Although a group of Zekes was seen over Talili Bay during the retirement down St. George's Channel, no further attacks were made on the formation.

Many bomb hits were observed in the revetment area south of the airfield.

Heavy A/A from the Lakunai area was accurate and meagre to moderate in intensity.

The following was reported after this mission.

Two tactical errors must be scored against the mission :

1. The bombers, by taking so fantastically circuitous a route into the target, gave the Zekes, originally surprised, a chance to climb to an altitude from which they could attack.

2. The high cover should have gone in slightly ahead of the leading bombers. If this had been done the Zekes would themselves have been intercepted before they began their runs. With all fighters immediately over the bombers it is almost impossible to stop overhead runs of this type made by these Zekes.

About twenty-eight enemy aircraft were in the air but only seven were seen to attack the formation. Kepford destroyed one Zeke, and Chenoweth probably destroyed one Zeke. No bombers were lost to enemy aircraft.

DISASTER FOR DIVENNEY

4 February
20 F4Us were assigned as low and medium cover on a B-24 strike on Tobera Airfield, New Britain. The fighters made rendezvous with the bombers at 17,000 ft. over Torokina, and proceeded to the target.

Lt. Cdr. J.T. Blackburn Lt(jg) G.F. Bowers
Lt. L.T. McQuiston Ens. G.M. Keller
Lt(jg) R. Mims Lt(jg) P. Cordray

Ens. J.O. Ellsworth Lt(jg) J. Miller
Lt(jg) T. Killefer Lt(jg) R.H. Jackson
Ens. W.P. Meek Lt(jg) D.T. Malone
Lt(jg) D.C. Freeman Lt. C.D. Gile
Ens. P.E. Divenney Ens. J.M. Smith
Lt. Cdr. R.R. Hedrick Lt(jg) E. May
Ens. M.W. Cole Ens. W.P. Popp

"Chico" Freeman at Bougainville early in 1944. Courtesy U.S. Navy photo. Robert L. Lawson Collection.

Earl May VF-17 ace with 8 victories to his credit. Courtesy National Archives.

A VF-17 pilot catches up on his sleep in his quarters on Bougainville, in February 1944. Note flight gear hanging by cots. Courtesy National Archives.

Three VF-17 officers chatting in front of the unit's scoreboard, at Piva airstrip, Bougainville, February 1944. Men are (L-R) Lt. Basil Duke Henning, Lt. Merl W. Davenport, Lt(jg) R. L. Mills. Courtesy National Archives.

The B-24s made their approach at 20,000 ft., and the fighters being stacked from 20,000 ft. to 26,000 ft. The approach was made over Kabanga Bay. Since Tobera was covered by clouds the bombers selected Vunakanau as their secondary target.

After dropping their bombs they continued past Vunakanau, to a point about 3 miles east of Keravat Airfield, where they made a left turn. They retired over the mouth the Warangai River, having dropped to about 15,000 ft.

Heavy A/A from Vunakanau area was intense and accurate at the fighters' altitude.

About 30 Jap fighters (including 10 Tonys and 3 Tojos) were seen climbing (probably from Tobera and/or Rapopo) as the formation crossed the coast on the approach. No attempt to attack the bombers was made until the retirement was well underway. One F4U, however, was attacked during the approach. The pilot, Ens. Divenney, apparently mistook the handle of his emergency landing gear release Co2 bottle for the handle of his wing purging bottle because his wheels went down as he was crossing the coast. Divenney, although instructed by radio to get under the bombers, stayed up at 23,000 ft. until he, and his section leader, saw 5 or 6 Zekes, 4,000 ft. above them. They dove for a cloud layer at 17,000 ft., but when emerging 2 or 3 minutes later, saw the Zekes still above. They again dove for a cloud layer at 15,000 ft. and at this point the section leader, Lt(jg) Freeman, lost Divenney. Shortly after (the time cannot be accurately estimated) the second section of another division, Lt(jg) May and Ens. Popp, having seen Divenney's plight, turned back to protect him. They scissored above him (Divenney was taking what evasive action he could) but although they destroyed one Zeke in a section run the F4Us larger radius of

turn prevented them from keeping the Zekes off Divenney's tail. He was badly hit, and spun down smoking.

Wilbert Peter Popp remembers the shooting down of Lt. Divenney."

"We were escorting Marine B-24s over Vunakanau Field over Rabaul. Divenney was flying wing on "Chico" Freeman, I was flying wing on Earl May. We were at about 20,000 feet. That model of Corsair had wing tanks in addition to main tanks.

The Naval Corsair also had 2 Co2 systems. One was to blow the wheels and flaps down in the event of failure of the hydraulic system, the other one to cover the wing tank, to prevent explosions in the wing, if hit by enemy incendiary bullets. We took off on main tanks, switched to wing tanks and, when safely airborne, back to main tank when approaching main target area. Simultaneously, on switching to main we would purge the main tanks with the Co2. There were 2 separate bottles, wing tank bottle handle was yellow, the wheels and flaps was red. Unfortunately they were side-by-side, a grievous mistake by the aircraft designer. If you blew wheels down the only way to retract would be after you were back on the deck, have the aircraft manually hoisted and have the mechanic bleed the lines. Obviously this option was not available while airborne.

"Divenney unfortunately pushed the wrong handle and blew his wheels down. Immediately on seeing this mishap, Blackburn yelled to Divenney to firewall the plane and get under the B-24s so that they could protect him. Divenney panicked and didn't react, Blackburn then gave orders for the rest of us to stay with the bombers and forget Divenney. "Chico" Freeman his section leader chose to ignore the skipper's orders and turn back to cover Divenney, as did my section leader, Earl May.

"I had no choice but to stay with May and "Chico" to protect Divenney as best we could. It was just then, a matter of weaving over Divenney, and kicking the rudder and shoot. I estimated there were 10-20 Zeros. I was able to nail one by a gut shot up the tail, my first combat kill, as was verified by May and Freeman, who saw the plane literally blow apart right in front of me. After what felt like hours, as I was flying inverted at the time, passed over Divenney and observed close hand his plane was on fire and Divenney was fatally wounded. I then saw tracers coming by me and looking around I counted four or five Zeros bearing down. I could not see May or Freeman. Rather than do a split-S I dumped over the top and went straight down. I dove from 20,000 feet to less than approximately 5,000 feet. I think I was still in a high blower, I tried to recover from the dive, but because of my speed, my plane began to tuck. I was very close to the speed of compressibility. By the use of my tabs little by little, I began to recover. My next concern was that I would go into a high speed stall.

"I recovered at about 3,000 feet. I looked around, no Zeros, I then noticed the B-24s approximately 10 miles ahead at about 10,000 feet. I maintained my speed and flew into their formation and let them protect me. I next had problems keeping my knees from uncontrollable tremors. Finally, at about the Treasuries, I bid the B-24s adieu and flew to Bougainville.

Lt. Cdr. Tom Blackburn commanding officer of Fighting Squadron 17 receives the Distinguished Flying Cross from Major General Ralph J. Mitchell. U.S.M.C., in a ceremony on Bougainville, in February 1944. Behind them is the VF-17 scoreboard showing 130 Japanese planes claimed shot down by the squadron at that time. Courtesy National Archives.

"When I landed and reported in, "Chico" and Earl, having seen me dive, reported me being lost. I walked into the ready tent and as I arrived Blackburn was berating May and Freeman for violating his orders, resulting in, they assumed, my being shot down and the loss of Divenney. Upon spotting me both "Chico" and Earl joyously welcomed me. However, this did not placate Blackburn, in fact it made him madder and he continued to give May and "Chico" hell for violating his orders and leaving the B-24s. Blackburn was very proud that he never lost a bomber we were protecting to enemy aircraft".

The first attack over the bombers occurred as they were retiring over the coast. Six Zekes, about 500 ft. above and to the rear, began a series of high side runs. Lt(jg) Cordray's division made a complete turn back into them and they broke off. But when Cordray went back toward the bombers, 2 Zekes made runs, getting on the tails of Lt(jg) Jackson and Lt(jg) Malone, Cordray's lagging section. Malone was hit, his plane began to smoke, and he bailed out about 8,000 ft., reaching the water safely. No more attacks were sustained.

The following tactical comments were reported after this mission.

Three errors were made by the fighters:

1. Divenney, when his wheels went down, should have immediately taken position beneath the bombers. Even with his wheels down he had the 160 knots necessary to do this.

2. May and Popp should not have left their station over the bombers and turned back to help Divenney. Fighters flying cover on bombers should never allow themselves to be diverted from their assignment.

3. Cordray's division maneuvered incorrectly to repulse the threatened stern attack on the retiring bombers.

The following information was reported after this mission.

*The latest model of the F4U-1 seen by the squadron has the purging bottle and the emergency landing gear release bottle placed side-by-side in the cockpit. As both bottles have the same kind of handle a mistake, such as Divenney made, is understandable.

The squadron was informed that a Marine squadron had previously reported the dangers inherent in the similarities of shape and position of the two bottles. It is unfortunate that no action was taken on suggestions made in aircraft action reports.

The squadron installed a locking pin in the handle of the emergency landing gear release bottle which prevented its being opened until the pin was removed.

This should prevent involuntary release of the landing gear. Sketches of this device will be sent to interested commands as soon as possible.

About thirty Japanese fighters were in the air. Despite the efforts of Freeman, May and Popp to protect Divenney from eight Zekes, he was shot down. Popp destroyed one of the Zekes.

No enemy fighters attacked the bombers, but, on the retirement six Zekes attacked the last division and shot down Malone's plane. He was seen to bail out at 8,000 feet and apparently reached the water (Kabanga Bay) safely.

Malone had a history of lagging behind in his division. He paid the ultimate price for doing this once too often as he was not seen again.

No bombers were lost to enemy aircraft. Heavy A/A was accurate and intense.

Ens. E.E. Beeler was detached.

5 February
Twelve F4Us were assigned as part of the SBD cover on a joint SBD-TBF strike on Lakunai Airfield, New Britain.

Lt. H.A. March	Lt(jg) W.L. Landreth
Lt(jg) C.W. Gilbert	Ens. C.H. Dunn
Lt(jg) H.J. Bitzegaio	Lt. M.W. Davenport
Ens. F.A. Jagger	Ens. J.O. Ellsworth
Lt. W.J. Schub	Ens. H.B. Richardson
Ens. W.C. Wharton	Ens. M.M. Kurlander

The approach was made over the tip of New Ireland, Duke of York Island, to the Mother on Crater Peninsula, where a left turn was made into the target. The retirement was made straight down St. George's Channel.

On the approach the SBDs flew at 12,000 ft., with the fighters, as low cover, at 13,000 ft.

As the formation was between Duke of York Island and Crater Peninsula about 12 Zekes were sighted at about 15,000 ft over the Mother. Five of these Zekes made overhead runs on the SBDs just before their pushover. Lt. Davenport, leading a division of the low cover, was able, by depressing his plane's nose, to catch the second Zeke with a 40° deflection shot. The Zeke burned and crashed. None of the attacking Zekes scored hits on the SBDs.

On the retirement the SBDs made an excellent running rendezvous. As they were passing Cape Gazelle, 6-8 Zekes were sighted over Tobera at about 6,000 ft. (these planes had probably just taken off from Tobera). A pair attempted low side runs on Lt. Schub's division of F4U-1s. Lt(jg) Landreth, the leader of the second section of that division, dove for one of the Zekes and got a good burst into the Zeke's engine from high above. The Zeke went down in flames.

"Country" Landreth describes his first air victory:

"As I recall, we were at high altitude over the bombers. They would go in, drop their bombs, and we would cover their bombing run and their retreat. The danger was for the bombers to be overtaken by Japanese fighters as they were going out of the target area to their rendezvous point. We were following their rear.

"I was leading the second section in Wally Schub's division, with Clyde Dunn flying on my wing. In the turn, as you're leaving, it's a little difficult to keep from dragging behind, so I was a little behind and covering the bombers' withdrawal. Wally was out toward the bombers and I was catching up with him. He was turning, sort of, toward me a little bit. I don't think he saw—he's always claimed that he did—a Zero coming in on him, beneath him, coming up from below. I remember hollering at him, 'Wally, quick, turn toward me! Turn more!' I had to get him to bring this guy around. And he did. He tightened it up a little bit, and as he did that, well, then the Zero tried to turn—and that put him right where I

wanted him. So I had to pull up on him, and with the long nose of the Corsair, you've got to pull up for lead on a deflection shot, so the target was clear out of sight under the nose. I squeezed off a good solid burst, eased the pressure on my stick, and here came this ball of flame out from under my nose! I guess that first burst had just nailed him. Then I pulled up and gave him another squirt just for good luck. It was a 60-degree, or better, deflection shot. I was coming in on top of him, and he was in a bank, and I was matching his turn.

"That moment of elation was when I knew I got my first victory. It was astonishing to experience after all that dead time—all that dry run time I'd had when everybody else in the squadron was shooting down airplanes but me. I really did have a soft spot about that business of not being able to catch up with the victories of the other pilots".

In the same attack, Schub, the division leader, spotted another Zeke diving on his formation. As the Jap turned away, Schub fired into his belly from the 8 o'clock position. This Zeke was seen to catch fire and crash into the water.

No further attacks were made on the formation.

Heavy A/A from the Lakunai area and from Matupi Island was moderate and accurate as to the fighter's altitude. Heavy A/A from the Rapopo area was meagre and accurate.

About twenty Zekes attempted interception. Davenport, Landreth, and Schub destroyed one Zeke each. Dunn's plane was slightly damaged by anti-aircraft fire.

No bombers were lost to enemy aircraft.

The following pilots flew Dumbo escort:
Lt. L.T. McQuiston
Lt. Cdr. J.T. Blackburn
Lt(jg) D.C. Freeman
Ens. W.P. Meek

Blackburn sighted a pilot in a life raft bearing 200° forty miles from Cape Manpan, Buka Island. The Dumbo picked up the pilot without incident.

Another shot of Tom Blackburn being presented the D.F.C. by Major General Ralph Mitchell. Courtesy National Archives.

BIG DAY FOR BLACKBURN AND MIMS

6 February

Sixteen F4Us, of which fourteen completed the mission, were assigned to fly high, medium and low cover on one of three squadrons of B-25s striking Lakunai Airfield. An additional four F4Us flew a roving high cover.

Lt. Cdr. J.T. Blackburn	Lt(jg) E. May
Lt. L.T. McQuiston	Ens. W.P. Popp
Lt. W. J. Schub	Lt(jg) I.C. Kepford
Ens. W.C. Wharton	Ens. D.R. McQueen
Lt(jg) W.L. Landreth	Lt(jg) M. Schanuel
Ens. C.H. Dunn	Lt(jg) E.C. Peterson
Lt. C.D. Gile	Lt. O.I. Chenoweth
Ens. J.M. Smith	Ens. J.C. Dixon
Lt(jg) R. Mims	Ens. J.O. Ellsworth
Lt(jg) H.J. Bitzegaio	

The bombers went in at about 12,000 ft., with the immediate cover stacked at 13-14,000 ft. and 15-16,000 ft.

The roving high cover went in at about 25,000 ft. The bombers approached the target south of Duke of York Island, north of Gredner Island and turned right over the target, retiring across New Ireland on the Kambura River - East Cape line.

About 40 Zekes, Hamps, and at least one Tojo were sighted. About 14-16 were over Tobera, the next being over Rapopo. The roving high cover (4 F4Us led by Lt. Cdr. Blackburn) contacted the fighters over Tobera shortly before the bombing attack began.

The action which was violent, rapid and confused proceeded from Tobera to Lakunai to Duke of York. Most of the Japs were kept up at altitude by the roving high cover, as only a few got down to the conventional cover. During the entire action the F4Us on roving high cover worked together as a division, only separating on the actual firing runs, which were made in pairs. All attacks were made with altitude advantage; if Japs were seen above in position to attack, the planes dove away from them. While there was evidence that some of the Jap fighters were well disciplined and could work in four plane divisions, at no time during the action did they have the initiative. The results were gratifying:

About forty enemy aircraft were encountered. Blackburn destroyed three Zekes, one Hamp and probably destroyed two Zekes; Mims destroyed two Zekes, one Tojo, and probably destroyed two Zekes; Bitzegaio destroyed one Hamp; Schub destroyed one Zeke. The action, as stated above, was rapid and confused, lasting 15 or 20 minutes and consisted of a series of runs and recoveries, with little time between combats.

The account of Blackburn's actions reveals the nature of the combat. He (with his division) made the first attack on 4 of 6 Zekes who were over Rapopo headed for the strike at 22,000 ft. He dove at 45° from 25,000 ft., fired from the 5 o'clock position, and the Zeke exploded. He recovered in a right chandelle to 23,000 ft. and saw a group of Japs heading northwest after the bombers. Blackburn reformed his division and followed. Over Lakunai at 20,000 ft. the division jumped several Zekes who were climbing and heading south. Blackburn made a high side run from the left and saw the

Zeke burn. Before he completed his recovery he made a pass at another Zeke and followed him down in a diving spin for about 4,000 ft. (his wingman saw the plane burn).

Blackburn recovered to the left in a tight climbing spiral to 2,000 ft.

He picked up a group of Zekes and Hamps and pursued them to the north. He got in some bursts, and his wingman burned one Zeke (Although it was reported that Blackburn's wingman, Lt. McQuiston burned one Zeke, no mention of it appears in the war diary or official lists!).

Blackburn again reformed his division, and the F4Us headed northeast after the bombers. They were attacked by a single Zeke, without results, and shortly after saw 4 Japs climbing over Rabaul and heading towards them. Blackburn, unwilling to be sucked out of the main fight, kept on his course and pulled away from them.

As the division was above the clouds over Duke of York Island, they jumped 8 or 10 Zekes who were climbing for altitude. Blackburn caught one unaware, saw him smoke and pieces fly off. His section leader Lt(jg) Mims, had dropped back, and the other F4Us headed after him. The reformed division was pursued by four Japs (Zekes or Hamps) but climbed away from them at 160 knots. When they had gained altitude the F4Us turned back. Two of the Japs had disappeared, and the other pair dove away in opposite directions. Blackburn followed one in a radical dive, but recovered in a right chandelle. He saw the Zeke turn sharply to the right and climb vertically, rolling at the top and pushing his nose to the level position—virtually a stalled out Immelman (this maneuver was obviously intended to suck the F4Us into a disadvantageous position). Blackburn fired at long range and saw his tracers go into the Jap, but could observe no damage.

Squadron commanding officer, Lt. Cdr. Tom Blackburn, after his return from a successful raid on Rabaul, in mid February 1944. The squadron was then based on Bougainville. Courtesy National Archives.

Squadron commanding officer, Lt. Cdr. Tom Blackburn, stands before the unit's scoreboard, at Piva airstrip, Bougainville, in February 1944. Note Skull and Crossbones emblem with F4U Corsair silhouettes flanking. Courtesy National Archives.

He joined up with his division, but sent his second section home because of oxygen shortage. He and his wingman saw the B-24s (a later strike) retiring from the target. P-38s were chasing Zekes off the right flank, and Blackburn headed for that melee. En route he picked up a lone Hamp. The Jap pilot apparently had secured, lit a cigarette, and cocked his feet on the dashboard. Blackburn crawled up his tail and set him afire. He and his wingman then headed home.

Tom Blackburn remembers this engagement:

"Toward the latter part of the aerial opposition phase over Rabaul we tailed in some 30-35 mixed Zeros and Hamps and Bobby was leading the second section. He and I worked as a team and attacked these Japs from opposite sides in succession and each of us got 4 flamers out of it.

"The final one I got this Lieutenant whose name I have forgotten, and I were stooging around looking for trouble and here was a lone Jap apparently secured for the day and put his feet up on the dashboard and lit up a cigarette, because he was flying along at about 125 knots with his canopy open, completely oblivious to what was going on and I shot him from about 100 yards. Very close when I shot and the guy who was flying my wing had metallic chunks from the Jap plane bounced off of his wings.

"We got home and I was very pleased with the whole operation which had gone well and we knocked down some 10 Jap planes and hadn't damaged any of ours. I was feeling very up. I turned to this Lieutenant and said well wasn't that a great hop and he says. Skipper I would like to be detached from Fighting 17 today. I think you guys are all crazy!' I said, 'Ok go pack your bag, Jack!'"

Harold Bitzegaio recalls his part in this mission.

"We did some things that probably were standard operating but we developed the Statue of Liberty play and then we did some ambushes that were sort of unique. The skipper asked for volunteers on a deal that he had figured out. He was going to catch the Japs as they came back so he and Bobby Mims and I was Tail-end Charlie and we shot down 7 airplanes. The skipper got four and Bobby got 3 and I got one if I remember right.

"But that was quite exciting to start at 30,000 feet and fight your way to the ground. That was the time Mims unplugged his oxygen mask and passed out and the skipper and I were trying to get his attention and we thought maybe he was hurt. But finally we got down to 8 or 9,000 feet and Mims woke up and joined up and we came back".

Those Zekes who managed to break away from the roving high cover attacked the high cover over the bombers on the turn into the target. This was a favorite spot for the Japs to launch their attacks, as they were in a position to pick off those fighters who swung wide on the turn. This is what happened on this occasion.

As the B-25s made their turn, the second section of Lt. Schub's division (flying at about 15,000 ft. in the high cover) passed from the inside of the turn too far to the outside, and as the bombers straightened out the section was sucked behind. Two or three Zekes at 20,000 ft. at the 6 o'clock position attacked as the second section (Lt(jg) Landreth and Ens. Dunn) turned to their right to cut towards the inside of the bombers. Almost immediately the first section (Lt.

"Country" Landreth, "Fatso" Ellsworth, "Butch" Davenport, "Windy" Hill at Bougainville 1944. Courtesy U.S. Naval Historical Center / M.W. "Butch" Davenport Collection.

Schub and Ens. Wharton) were also attacked by 2 or 3 Zekes, who had obviously coordinated their runs with those of the first attackers.

"Country" Landreth remembers:

"When we were escorting the bombers in and they were making their attacks. There is a period where you have to reverse course and that turn around was kinda tactically difficult. The Japs were very smart about waiting for that time when you had to make this big turn, and those around the outside of the turn were very vulnerable to being picked off by the Jap fighters.

"I remember one occasion when I just about didn't get home because I was on that turn and I happened to glance up into the sun. Here's a vertically diving Zero who had me right in his sights. I jerked on the stick tried to bring my guns up to bear on him first and realized that if I got my guns to bear, his engine and mine were going to become one.

"So, as it happened I placed the stick forward just a little bit and we passed each other vertically. Me going up and him going down. I don't think that more than a few feet separated the 2 airplanes".

Schub's second section turned right 135° into the attack and arrived in time to meet the second Zeke coming down on Landreth's section. Schub got a good burst into him, and he went down in flames. Schub and his wingman then had to nose over and pull through a half loop to evade the Zekes attacking them.

Both sections then joined and scissored over the bombers.

The following is quoted from Schub's account of the action:

"Zekes' runs were in between a high side and overhead attack and were run in very rapid succession. At least four Zekes got in runs before mine and Landreth's sections got back into scissor position.

"Zekes appeared to be coming down power off or with a low power setting and attacked from our five o'clock position. Runs seemed to be expertly planned and conducted."

Walter Schub the division leader stated.

"One of the most gratifying incidents was after landing at Bougainville subsequent to a Rabaul mission, a Marine pilot came busting into our gathering area and yelling 'who was flying number 37.' In unison several pilots said "Wally Schub." His story was that I neatly jumped on a Zero and shot him off his tail like right now. He was most adamant that there was no doubt I had saved his life. I felt pretty good; wish I had more observing gratified saved pilots when I took snap shots at Zeros going through the formation".

Walter Schub describes what it was like to be hit on a mission.

"I was shot up about a good six times. One of the worst was a 20mm hit which went across and slightly forward of my canopy. I mean slightly!

It took out a 4 foot by 2 foot of my left aileron. I don't know if the Zero went through the formation behind his shot—but I swear I saw a big red meatball fill up my windshield as the shell took a piece out of my wing with a bang. Yes I made it home and with a landing speed of 150 knots".

Two F4Us were slightly damaged by enemy aircraft. Heavy A/A was moderate and accurate. No bombers were lost to enemy aircraft.

7 February

Twenty four F4Us were assigned as partial cover on 24 TBFs in a joint SBD-TBF strike on Vunakanau Airfield. These F4Us were to be split evenly between medium, high and roving cover, the last named to go in slightly before the formation.

Lt. Cdr. J.T. Blackburn	Lt(jg) P. Cordray
Lt(jg) E. May	Lt(jg) J. Miller
Lt(jg) T. Killefer	Lt(jg) R.H. Jackson
Ens. W.P. Meek	Lt(jg) E.C. Peterson
Lt(jg) D.C Freeman	Lt. W.J. Schub
Ens. R.H. Hill	Ens. W.C. Wharton
Lt. Cdr. R.R. Hedrick	Lt(jg) W.L. Landreth
Ens. M.W. Cole	Ens. C.H. Dunn

Eight F6Fs provided low cover and 8 P-40s flew close cover. During the retirement, when the Jap fighters had left off their attacks, it was planned to have the medium cover break off from the bombers, round the southern tip of New Ireland, climb and cross over to the Rabaul area in the hope of catching the Jap fighters as they straggled back up the channel. This ambitious but sound project was marred by an abnormal number of F4Us which returned, and

Whit Wharton and Wally Schub, Bougainville 1944. Courtesy U.S. Navy photo. Robert L. Lawson Collection.

VF-17 pilots do own barbering at quarters on Bougainville. L-R. Lt. Basil Duke Henning of Louisville, KY, Lt(jg) Earle Peterson (standing) of Coronado, Calif., Lt. Don Innis of Nevada, Mo, and Lt. Harry March of Washington, D.C. Courtesy National Archives.

by the unusual persistence of the Japs in continuing their attacks. Eight F4Us were unable to reach the target area, necessitating a reshuffling of the cover. The roving high cover came down and joined the regular high cover, making 10 planes in all, and the medium cover was reduced to 6 planes. This group, scheduled to make the sweep around New Ireland after the strike, was forced to remain with the bombers about ten minutes longer than had been expected, as the Japs followed the F4Us far down St. George's Channel. As a result of all these unfortunate circumstances the expected clambake did not materialize. The basic mission however, was successful: No bombers or fighters were lost and VF17 pilots accounted for 3 kills and 3 probables.

The bombers approached the target over the Warangoi River, as Vunakanau appeared closed in, Tobera, the secondary target, was selected; the bombers turning beyond the target and making their runs from west to east. The bombers pushed over at 12,000 ft. with the fighters stacked above in 4 layers to 16,000 ft.

The Jap fighters (estimated as 30-40 Zekes, Hamps and Tonys) were over the target area at about 20,000 ft. As was their custom, they attacked the high and medium cover on the turn into the target.

Lt(jg) Peterson, flying number 4 position in a division of high cover was scissoring with his section leader over the bombers as they began to drop down for their runs.

A Zeke (one of about 6 or 8 making passes at the fighters), made a run on Lt(jg) Jackson, Peterson's section leader, and both F4Us turned and fired at it. Peterson's run was from 5 o'clock 30° below. He saw hits on the cockpit and right wing root and the plane caught fire. Peterson himself was immediately attacked from astern (he was on his back at the time) and hit by 7.7s and one 20mm.

shell which exploded below his cockpit, breaking the glass and wounding him with shrapnel.

Peterson rolled out, recovered and looked for his division. He could not find them and headed for the rally point over Kabanga.

He saw nothing but Zekes, so skirting those, he headed for home alone at 5,000 ft.; one Zeke made an overhead run, pulling up in front of his nose. Peterson fired but could see no results and shortly after passing New Ireland he was joined by Marine F4Us.

Lt. Schub's division at about 16,000 feet was also attacked, as the bombers were turning into the target. Schub saw the Zekes but continued his weave, thus turning away from them, expecting that the pair with which he was scissoring could cover him. This pair, however, had been sucked back, and Schub's plane was hit in the left aileron.

Walter Schub describes this mission.

"I got shot up a little bit with a piece of wing being shot off. I was low on fuel and the reason for in going up our F4U Corsair had 180 gallons in the main tank which was protected by anti-fire protection and auxiliary tanks which had 25 gallons came to 230 gallons. We would use up auxiliary tanks when going into Rabaul.

"On this occasion I could get no suction in one of the auxiliary tanks so I had to go into my main tank which meant on the way back, if I didn't sometime get suction on that 25 gallon tank I was going to be running a bit short on fuel, after about 15-20 minutes combat time, which uses a lot of fuel over Rabaul.

"On the trip back home I could see I wasn't going to make it home unless I could get suction on this tank. I let the 3 others go so that they could make home base so I was by myself.

"So I just got down low on the water to sea level for better fuel economy. I had to go a little bit slower that's why I let the others go home, and this went on for half an hour from Rabaul on the way back to Bougainville.

"I kept trying this tank all the time and no soap until the engine started spluttering. At this time I'm 100-150 feet above the water and in one last desperate attempt to switch tanks—it finally came on. So with that fuel I was able to make a safe landing and kiss the old soil again".

His number four man, Ens. Dunn, got a snap shot at the Zeke and saw pieces fly from its fuselage. Lt(jg) Landreth, the leader of the second section, made a high side run on a Zeke (perhaps the same one that shot Schub) and saw the right side of the fuselage, aft of the cockpit, explode and the Zeke go down burning.

Lt(jg) Freeman, leader of the section in the medium cover, also came under the attack of Zekes at the turn into the target. He was not hit and got in a beam run on a Zeke, closing to forty yards. He saw the enemy plane fly through his tracers and a piece fly off as he passed.

All pilots commented on the aggressiveness of the Zekes during this attack. It will be noted, however, that no runs were made on the TBFs.

The cover returned down St. George's Channel with Zekes nipping and feinting at their flanks. The Zekes did not break off until Cape St. George, the farthest point south they had ever (in the experience of this squadron) reached. When Lt. Cdr. Blackburn saw

"Chico" Freeman sitting on wing of #34. Courtesy U.S. Naval Historical Center / M.W. "Butch" Davenport Collection.

"Country" Landreth and Carl Gilbert in front of squadron scoreboard Bougainville 1944. Courtesy U.S. Navy photo. Robert L. Lawson Collection.

that the bombers were clear he radioed that the Statue of Liberty play (the sweep back around New Ireland) had begun. His section was joined by Freeman's and Landreth's and the six F4Us proceeded up the east coast of New Ireland, climbing the while, to a point south of Cape Sena, where they cut across the island and down to Kabanga Bay. At this point they were at about 20,000 feet.

Tom Blackburn explains the Statue of Liberty Play

"The point being that the attention is being focused in one direction and the action takes place somewhere else.

"When we were finished with a bombing raid over Rabaul we were committed to cover the bombers until they were clear of the normal range of activity of the Jap fighters which was about 20 miles south of the main harbor.

"The Japs would then peel off and go back into land. So we thought that we could take our bombers out then drop down to right down on the water, use an island to the east as visual cover, stay behind it, fly on up to the north, cross over and come back in to the Jap airfields from the opposite direction from which we normally came and from which we had just departed.

"The theory was that they would be still looking to the south and we would come in from the north. It was designed to be a one-

shot thing to make a fast pass through to watch the Jap fighters in the landing circle and on the ground, and shoot down what we could and dust off the rest. Then haul ass out, hopefully before they recovered from the surprise. It wasn't something you did every day. We tried it several times and it was not only exciting but pretty effective".

Only eight Zekes were sighted at this time. One was over Lakunai at 17,000 feet, four were astern of the B-24 formation (a later strike on Vunakanau) at about 20,000 ft., and 3 more over the Warangoi River at 18,000 ft. Blackburn led the F4Us down on the 3 Zekes in a long glide, each section picking a Zeke, but the Japs dove away. The action then developed into a series of chases after single Japs, with the F4Us operating in pairs. Landreth was the only one to get a sure kill. He and his wingman caught a Hamp at 9,000 ft. over Cape Gazelle, Landreth got on his tail and set him afire. Dunn, his wingman, scored 2 probable Zekes shortly afterwards. Both were stern runs at about 10,000 feet, and both Zekes smoked heavily before disappearing in the clouds.

"Country" Landreth recalls this mission:

"I got one airplane before the bombers had done their job, and when we came back I got another airplane. Same flight, but after we had finished the bombing run and come back, I got a second airplane that day. But here's the deal; I could have gotten several more!

"Before we took off that day, I had a standard practice of having my plane captain count the bullets—the 50 caliber bullets—that came out of my guns as I charged them with the hydraulic chargers. I wanted to know not only that my guns were loaded, and had a round in the chamber, but I wanted to know if my hydraulic chargers were working—all six of them.

"So on this particular flight I had arranged with my plane captain to signal me when he was ready for me to charge my guns. I charged them—and nothing happened. At most, one or two of them charged out of the six. So I motioned to the kid that I was trying again. The hydraulic gun chargers were not working properly.

"The protocol was, if your guns are not working, and your chargers are not working, you miss the flight. Now this was going to be my opportunity—remember the "dry-run-kid"—and I knew this special deal was laid on. They're not leaving me behind. Not Uncle Bill. Not this time. I had a feeling this would be the day.

"So I called him up to the cockpit and I said, "Get your butt out there on those guns and manually load and charge all six guns, and leave them that way, so they're ready to fire." He did that and I took off.

"My wingman, Clyde Dunn, followed me around all during the flight. After the bombers had gone, the skipper and a couple of other people stayed up and flew high cover while the rest of us went down and attacked the Zeros going home.

"I ran up on probably half-a-dozen airplanes with my Corsair. I followed a Zero through about three split-S that day. I never did get him, because when he saw my guns fire, he did a split-S, right underneath me. I'd turn over and pull, but you couldn't pull that Corsair through like a Zero. I'm pulling 4 Gs, and my airplane is shaking and stalling, and I'm firing, and the guns are throwing the ammunition all over the sky—and I'm not touching him. I had no means by which I could catch that guy. He finally just flew away unharmed.

"Meanwhile my guns are quitting, one by one. With all the Gs, and all the sometimes-negative Gs, I was finding airplanes, I was

Squadron VF-17 is briefed in Ready Room at Bougainville before raid on Rabaul. Seated at center by door is squadron commander, Lt. Cdr. Tom Blackburn. Courtesy National Archives.

fighting them, I was getting them dead to rights, I'd press the trigger—and I'd get two guns! I was so disconcerted by that time, I'm gonna' fix this. I hit the hydraulic gun charger so I could get my guns back. I wound up with one gun. My left outside gun was all I wound up with, and I was in the middle of the best dogfight I ever had in my life!

"Over Lakunai Airfield, Rabaul, I came up on the tail of one Zero, after I'd already shot down one, and I'm telling you, he was just a dead duck. He was either so lackadaisical about paying attention, or he was so scared he was frozen, because he was going straight back to the base like that. I flew right behind him with Clyde Dunn on my wing, and I started shooting. Every time I'd squeeze the trigger the gun recoil would kick the airplane off line because it's the way outboard gun, and none on the other side. So I said, okay, then I'll fire the gun and then I'll push the right rudder and I'll seesaw back and forth and I'll cut him in two. Never touched him!

"I started out a different system then—I'm still trying to get this guy. So I said, I'll just aim to the right of him, and then as the gun kicked me across it'll get him. Didn't touch him! He's straight and level. No problem. I'm right up behind him. Couldn't get a bullet on him!

All this time Clyde Dunn is following me through all these machinations and all these movements and so on".

Lt(jg) Freeman caught a Hamp at 3,000 feet (he was at 5,000 feet) five miles east of Vunakanau. The Hamp took violent evasive action but Freeman's high side run put him dead astern. His first burst had the Hamp smoke, and the Jap entered a cloud with Freeman close behind. He got in another burst in the cloud but the Hamp disappeared. Ens. Hill, Freeman's wingman waiting above the cloud to rejoin Freeman did not see the Hamp appear. It is possible he was destroyed.

"Chico" Freeman leading a section of F4U-1A's. Courtesy U.S. Navy photo. Robert L. Lawson Collection.

Lt. Cdr. Blackburn and his wingman Lt(jg) May, had a bad day. They got at least 2 good runs apiece, but what with gun stoppages and the elusive character of the Japanese, no kills were made.

Heavy A/A did not open up until half the bombers had passed the target indicating surprise. It was then moderate to meagre, and inaccurate. Several phosphorus bombs were seen.

The mission was reported as follows:

This whole action was most disappointing as the tactical plan was sound. If the roving high cover could have gone in slightly ahead of the strike the Jap fighters would have been sufficiently occupied to prevent their making so determined an attack on the strike cover. Likewise, if the Statue of Liberty play around New Ireland could have started earlier, the fighters could have caught the Japs returning from their pursuit down the channel.

Thirty or forty enemy fighters were encountered. Landreth destroyed one Zeke and one Hamp; Peterson destroyed one Zeke; Dunn probably destroyed two Zekes, and damaged a third Zeke; Freeman probably destroyed two Zekes. Two F4Us were slightly damaged by enemy aircraft. Peterson was wounded by 20mm shrapnel from a Zeke. Heavy A/A was moderate and inaccurate. No bombers were lost to enemy aircraft.

8 February
All operations cancelled because of bad weather.

9 February
Twenty two F4Us from the squadron were assigned low, medium, high and roving high cover (2 planes in the last group) for the TBFs in a joint SBD-TBF strike on Vanakanau Airfield.

Lt(jg) P. Cordray	Lt(jg) D.C. Freeman
Lt(jg) J. Miller	Ens. R.H. Hill
Lt(jg) G.F. Bowers	Lt. M.W. Davenport
Ens. G.M. Keller	Ens. H.B. Richardson
Lt. C.D. Gile	Ens. J.O. Ellsworth
Ens. J.M. Smith	Ens. M.M. Kurlander
Lt(jg) E. May	Lt. O.I. Chenoweth
Ens. W.P. Popp	Ens. J.C. Dixon
Lt(jg) T. Killefer	Lt(jg) D.G. Cunningham
Ens. W.P. Meek	Ens. L.A. Fitzgerald
Lt(jg) M. Schanuel	Ens. M.W. Cole

The formation approached the target from the southeast over the Warangoi River and retired by the same route. The TBFs flew at 12,000 ft. on their approach with the fighters stacked from that level to about 18,000 ft., and the 2 planes on roving high cover at 25,000 ft.

About 25 Zekes were in the area. Six made diving overhead runs on the formation just before it turned into the target; the remaining Zekes stayed in loose formation on the flanks at 12-20,000 ft. until the run was started, at which time they made feinting passes, and broke away out of range.

Twelve Zekes followed from 4,000 ft. to 900 ft. during the run, attacking the bombers and close cover from 6 o'clock and pulling up into low clouds. The attacks continued until the formation had rallied and headed home.

VF-17 pilots celebrate achievements in a Rabaul raid at the mess hut on Bougainville. Courtesy National Archives.

Lt(jg) Schanuel and Ens. Cole, the roving high cover, were at 26,000 ft. when they spotted 12-13 Zekes and Hamps at 15,000 ft. 10 miles N.E. of Vunakanau.

They made an overhead run as a section and saw their tracers hitting a Hamp's left wing. The F4Us recovered and took station over the bombers who were retiring to the rally point.

Lt. Chenoweth's division, at high cover, rounded a cloud over the target, dropping from 18,000 ft. to 8,000 ft., and waited for the TBF's to come across Kabanga Bay on the way to the rally point. The main body passed and the F4U division circled, waiting for stragglers. Chenoweth observed 3 or 4 Zekes at 3-4,000 ft. about 1.5 miles behind the bombers. The Zekes were in a dive, apparently getting into position for stern runs from below. Chenoweth pushed over and fired on the leading Zeke from 2,000 ft. to 300 ft., scoring many hits. Chenoweth overran and pulled away to the left. The Zeke pulled away to the left and Lt(jg) Cunningham, the second section leader, got another burst into him. The Zeke went into a flat spin and crashed. The third Zeke then fired on Chenoweth's # 4 man and he broke away.

The division reformed and Chenoweth turned into another Zeke low on the water making a beam run on the TBFs. The Zeke turned away, and Chenoweth and his wingman chased him. This proved to be a mistake; they were jumped by Zekes and only by violent evasive action were they able to escape without injury.

After the bombers pushed over, Lt(jg) May took his section down through a tunnel-like hole in the clouds and saw a Zeke ahead at 5,000 ft. and climbing out of range. May took a long shot and lobbed a few tracers over the Zeke. He broke his climb and started to split-S and started a 20° climb. The Jap's indecision enabled May to close; he tried a long burst from dead astern, and saw the Zeke explode.

Harold J. Bitzegaio and plane captain at Bougainville. Courtesy U.S. Navy photo. Robert L. Lawson Collection.

"Andy" Jagger Bougainville, 1944. Courtesy U.S. Navy photo. Robert L. Lawson Collection.

May then took his section back over the bombers.

Heavy A/A was moderate to meagre and inaccurate.

About twenty-five enemy fighters were encountered. Chenoweth and May each destroyed one Zeke, and Schanuel damaged one Hamp. Three F4Us were damaged by enemy aircraft. No bombers were lost to enemy aircraft.

Lt. L.T. McQuiston was detached.

10 February

A negative 2 hour combat air patrol over base (4 sorties) was flown. Sixteen F4Us were assigned as low, medium and high cover over one of 2 squadrons of B-25s striking Vunakanau Airfield.

Lt. O.I. Chenoweth	Lt. W.J. Schub
Ens. J.C. Dixon	Ens. W.C. Wharton
Lt(jg) D.G. Cunningham	Lt(jg) W.L. Landreth
Lt. H.A. March	Ens. C.H. Dunn
Lt(jg) C.W. Gilbert	Lt(jg) G.F. Bowers
Lt(jg) H.J. Bitzegaio	Lt(jg) J. Miller
Ens. F.A. Jagger	Lt(jg) R.H. Jackson
Ens. M.W. Cole	

The bombers flew at 12,000 ft. with the fighters stacked to 18,000 ft. The approach was made over Adler Bay to the Governmental Experimental Farm (east of Keravat) where a right turn was made into the target. The bombers made their runs from N.N.W. to S.S.E. and retired in 2 groups, one over Cape Gazelle, the other over Warangoi River.

About 15-20 Zekes (in 3 groups) were sighted at 20,000 ft. north of the target.

These Zekes made single runs on the fighter cover but were not aggressive. When the F4Us turned towards them the Zekes would slow roll and turn away.

On the retirement, Lt(jg) Bitzegaio and Ens. Jagger, spotted a Zeke diving from about 18,000 ft. They pulled up and each fired a long burst, from full to half deflection, and saw pieces fly from the plane from the spinner to the tail. The Zeke dove in a 70° dive on his back, streaming gas from the left wing. Scored as a probable.

The gunners of the #1 and #2 planes of the second section of B-25s were seen to shoot down a Zeke, while he was making a high side run.

Heavy A/A was moderate to intense, accurate as to altitude, but inaccurate as to deflection.

After the retirement was well underway 6 F4Us from the cover joined from the cover on a simultaneous B-24 strike, and went off on a Betty search.

An F4U-1A of VF-17 taxiing out at Bougainville, February 1944. Courtesy U.S. Navy photo. Robert L. Lawson Collection.

About fifteen or twenty enemy fighters attempted interception. Jagger and Bitzegaio probably destroyed one Zeke. No bombers were lost to enemy aircraft.

Four F4Us were assigned as low cover and 3 F4Us as roving high cover on a B-24 strike on Tobera Airfield.

Lt. Cdr. J.T. Blackburn   Lt. M.W. Davenport
Ens. R.H. Hill   Ens. H.B. Richardson
Lt(jg) F.J. Streig   Ens. J.O. Ellsworth
Lt(jg) R. Mims

The B-24s flew at about 17,000 ft., with the low cover 1,000 ft. above them. The 3 F4U's on roving high cover were at 27-30,000 ft.

The approach was made over Adler Bay and north to the target. Because of clouds the B-24's could not get in on their first run. They turned right, went down and came in on the target from the southeast. The retirement was made over the Warangoi River.

The low cover spotted 20-30 Zekes in the area (the P-38s on medium and high cover reported many more) but made no contacts. The 3 F4Us on roving high cover, however, intercepted 6-8

Group of VF-17 pilots in front of scoreboard. Back L-R. Bill Meek, "Windy" Hill, "Butch" Davenport, Mel Kurlander, "Fatso" Ellsworth. Front L-R. "Hap" Bowers, Ray Beacham, Harold Richardson. Front L-R. "Chico" Freeman, Don Innis. Courtesy U.S. Naval Historical Center / M.W. "Butch" Davenport Collection.

Zekes. The Zekes were at about 24,000 ft. diving in column on the bombers as they were turning out to sea after their initial run. Lt. Davenport led his 3 planes down on the Zekes. He got on the tail of one at about 20,000 ft. saw his bullets go into the cockpit and fuselage, and the Zeke spun down in flames. Ens. Ellsworth, the #3 man in the F4U formation got on another Zeke in an identical run and fired until the Zeke exploded. The 3 F4Us continued in their dives and joined up with the low cover. Zekes made spasmodic attacks during the bombing runs but turned away when the fighters feinted. Immediately after the bombs had been dropped most of the Japs broke off and climbed in loose formation over Vunakanau. This maneuver indicated that they anticipated a delayed fighter sweep such as the one attempted on 7 February.

Heavy A/A was moderate and accurate at the fighters level. Phosphorus bombs were dropped by Zekes. Two bomb-carrying Zekes were seen to make vertical dives which carried them beneath the formation. The bombs released at about 17,000 ft. exploded 500 ft. above the bombers.

When the retirement was well underway and no more Zekes were to be seen, Lt. Cdr. Blackburn's section cut wide, to the south and rendezvoused in Wide Bay with 6 F4Us from the cover on a B-25 strike. It was hoped that Jap bombers had been scrambled from fields in the Rabaul area and sent to the vicinity of Open Bay to wait for the all-clear. Blackburn's flight crossed from their rendezvous to Open Bay, keeping low on the mountains to avoid radar detection. As they emerged over Open Bay no Jap planes were in sight but they spotted a 120 ft. wooden auxiliary schooner (100 tons) anchored a few hundred yards off Pondo Point. All 8 F4Us made good strafing runs and as they retired saw that the schooner was smoking very heavily. It was almost certainly left sinking.

The flight then cut back across the island to Wide Bay and returned to base.

Twenty or thirty enemy fighters were encountered. Davenport and Ellsworth destroyed one Zeke each. Following the strike Blackburn and Hill joined Chenoweth, Dixon, Bowers, Miller, Jackson, and Cole (from the B-25 cover) over Jacquinet Bay and proceeded to Open Bay to search for enemy bombers which might have been flown off the Rabaul fields. No bombers were found but the flight strafed and left sinking a 120 feet auxiliary schooner off Pondo Point.

11 February
Four pilots flew cover on B-24s striking Tobera Airfield. Six or eight enemy fighters were sighted but no contacts were made. Heavy A/A was meagre and accurate. No bombers were lost to enemy aircraft.

Eleven pilots escorted TBFs in a joint SBD-TBF strike on Tobera Airfield. Fifteen or twenty enemy aircraft attempted interception but pilots from the squadron made no contacts. Heavy A/A was meagre and inaccurate. No bombers were lost to enemy aircraft.

Four pilots escorted a Dumbo to a point bearing 200° 25 miles from Buka Passage where a B-25 crew (6 men) were picked up from their raft.

A negative, 2-hour patrol over base (4 sorties) was flown.

Back row. L-R. *May, Jackson, Einar, Smith, Meek, Mills, Kincaid, Henning.* Front row. L-R. *Schub, Cordray, Kepford, Kurlander, Hedrick, Killefer, Hill. Bougainville February 1944.* Courtesy Hal and Barbara Jackson.

12 February
Twenty-two pilots escorted B-25s in a strike on Tobera Airfield. No enemy aircraft were sighted. Heavy A/A was meagre and inaccurate.

13 February
Sixteen F4Us were assigned as high and medium cover on the SBDs in a joint SBD-TBF strike on Vanakanau Airfield, New Britain.

Lt. Cdr. R.R. Hedrick	Ens. H.B. Richardson
Ens. M.W. Cole	Ens. J.O. Ellsworth
Lt(jg) G.F. Bowers	Ens. M.M. Kurlander
Ens. G.M. Keller	Lt. O.I. Chenoweth
Lt(jg) P. Cordray	Ens. J.C. Dixon
Lt(jg) J. Miller	Lt(jg) D.G. Cunningham
Lt(jg) R.H. Jackson	Ens. L.A. Fitzgerald
Lt. M.W. Davenport	

The formation approached the target south of the Warangoi River, made a right turn into the target, and retired down the river. The SBDs pushed over from 12,000 ft. and the high and medium cover dropped down as they made their dives.

About 40 Zekes grouped in small bunches were sighted northwest of the target area.

As the fighters were covering the retiring bombers, one of the F4U's was hit by one of the 12 Zekes making runs on the formation. Lt(jg) Cunningham turned into the Zeke and got a good burst, but as the Jap broke off, could not estimate the damage inflicted.

Dan Cunningham had good reason to remember one mission.

"I had a plane that, we would go up in our 2 built-in wing tanks, the gas in that would run out and we'd switch it over to the other one, and just about the time that we usually see the enemy it would poop out and switch it over to the main tank and we would put the Co2 in the 2 wing tanks so they wouldn't blow up in case they're hit.

"Well every time I would get to where I switched it over to the main tank it wouldn't catch and I would have a windmill there and drop back and drop back. It scared the shit out of me because if you drop back too far they would slice through you like rats after cheese because you've got nothing to protect you. I was a sitting duck. It happened about 4 or 5 times and I said to the skipper I don't know whether I'm getting yellow or what but I said I get scared as shit when that plane won't catch and I start dropping back and waiting for those bastards to make runs on me. He said. 'There's nothing wrong with that, I'd be scared as hell too. We've got to get you an airplane that doesn't do that'. I said. I would appreciate that, and the skipper said we'd get it fixed. It was just too nerve-wracking".

None of the SBDs was attacked.

Heavy A/A was moderate and accurate. Two phosphorus bombs were observed.

One was seen dropped by a Zeke over the pushover point, the other was observed over the rally point.

About forty enemy fighters intercepted. Cunningham damaged one Zeke. Dixon's plane was hit by fire from a Zeke which blew up the ammunition cans in his starboard wing. Heavy A/A was moderate and accurate. No bombers were lost to enemy aircraft.

Eight F4Us were assigned as close cover on a squadron of B-24s striking Lakunai Airfield New Britain. The bombers went in at 20,000 ft., with the F4Us slightly above that altitude.

The Japs attempted no interception, but heavy A/A fire from the Lakunai area and Matupi Island was most intense and very accurate at 20-21,000 ft.

One F4U was hit by a piece of shrapnel, which started a bad oil leak, but the damaged plane returned to base safely.

Walter Schub remembers helping his wingman back to base

"My wingman, Whit Wharton and I were over Rabaul and he was hit by A/A.

His plane was streaming the heavy black smoke which indicated his oil cooler had taken the hit. We were a good 2-3 hours from home. In response to his heated question as to what he should do—I directed him to get down to one of the B-24s which we were escorting and to snuggle up to the waist gun station and stay there for all the trip home; but whatever you do don't pull your throttle back too far until you're ready to touch down. He made it home!"

"Whit was my student at N.A.S. Jacksonville, Cecil Field in 1942. My wingman in VF-17 and my section leader in VF-10, 1945 carrier Intrepid CV-10 to the end of W.W.II."

Bomb coverage was described as excellent.

Ensigns J.E Diteman, R.M. Einar and H. Matthews reported for duty.

14 February
A negative, 2-hour patrol (4 sorties) over Task Force 39 was flown.

Seventeen pilots escorted B-25s in a strike on Vunakanau Airfield. Ten enemy aircraft were sighted but the weak interception produced no contacts. Heavy A/A was meager and inaccurate.

15 February
Four negative, 2-hour patrols over Green Island landing forces (30 sorties) were flown.

Three negative, 2-hour patrols over Task Force 39 (12 sorties) were flown.

Four pilots escorted two TBFs in a negative search for pilots reported down in the water.

Ens. L.R. Kincaid reported for duty.

16 February
Four negative, 2-hour patrols (16 sorties) were flown over Task Force 39.

One negative, 2-hour patrol (4 sorties) was flown over Task Unit 31.4.3.

One negative, 2-hour patrol (8 sorties) was flown over Green Island.

Thirteen pilots escorted B-24's in a strike on Vunakanau Airfield. No enemy aircraft were sighted. Heavy A/A was meagre and inaccurate.

Roger Hedrick's plane running up on line.

John Malcolm Smith, "Beads" Popp, Duke Henning, Mel Kurlander, at Bougainville. Courtesy U.S. Navy photo. Robert L. Lawson Collection.

L-R. Les Kincaid, Mel Kurlander, Jim Dixon, John Malcolm Smith, "Beads" Popp, Roger Hedrick, Unknown, Oc Chenoweth, Harold Richardson. Bougainville 1944. Courtesy U.S. Navy photo. Robert L. Lawson Collection.

"Ike" Kepford taxies out of revetment for strike on Rabaul. Delayed in getting away he was unable to overtake VF-17 and when near Rabaul turned back. He had his own little Jap party instead. Courtesy U.S. Navy photo. Robert L. Lawson Collection.

AN UNFORTUNATE LOSS

17 February
Twenty F4Us were assigned as high and medium cover on the SBDs in a joint SBD-TBF strike on shipping in Simpson Harbor.

Lt. Cdr. J.T. Blackburn	Ens. C.H. Dunn
Ens. H. Matthews	Ens. J.M. Smith
Lt(jg) G.F. Bowers	Lt(jg) E. May
Lt(jg) F.J. Streig	Ens. G.M. Keller
Ens. W.P. Popp	Lt(jg) R. Mims
Lt(jg) P. Cordray	Lt(jg) T. Killefer
Lt(jg) J. Miller	Ens. W.P. Meek
Lt(jg) D.C. Freeman	Ens. R.M. Einar
Ens. R.H. Hill	Lt. C.D. Gile
Lt(jg) R.H. Jackson	

One was forced to return because of an hydraulic leak; the rest made rendezvous with the bombers and proceeded to the target at about 14,000 ft. to 16,000 ft. The approach was made over Cape St. George, Gredner Island (where the bombers let down under the overcast), with a left turn into Keravia Bay and Simpson Harbor.

About 30-40 Japanese fighters (Zekes, Hamps, Oscars, and at least 15 Tonys) intercepted the formation just before it reached the target. The Japs made their runs out of the broken clouds at 12,000 ft., making it extremely difficult for the fighters to counter their attacks. The enemy was extremely aggressive and while no bombers were hit several of the division were broken up.

Ens. Dunn, a section leader in the high cover, was seen by his wingman to shoot down a Zeke during the initial attack. Shortly after, while still approaching the target, 4 Tonys came down on his wingman's (Ens. Keller) tail. Keller radioed Dunn to scissor with him, but Dunn apparently did not receive the message, for even after Keller had fired his guns under Dunn's wing he continued straight ahead.

Keller was forced to dive away and take evasive action. At that time no enemy planes were on Dunn's tail, but he was presumably shot down subsequently as he is missing.

"Country" Landreth was Clyde Dunn's usual section leader, and remembers this sad day.

"My wingman lost his life because, a unit flying together and coming back together was violated. Here's the way a man gets killed, loses his life: overeagerness to get into the fray in a situation that was not the way it should have been.

"The next day (after the February 7 flight) a pilot that had come up and flown one hop, and caught a 20mm, turned in his wings. The skipper sent him down.

"Clyde Dunn heard about it, and went and volunteered to go on that flight. I heard about his volunteering and I said, 'Clyde, you're my wingman. You belong in this division. If they need extra pilots, we'll all four take the hop. I'll talk to Wally and I know that he'll go. The people that leave together, fight together, come back together. Don't go with a bunch of strangers you haven't been flying with. You don't know if they'll protect you or not, and you don't know how they're going to fly or what they're going to do.'

"This is the way you survive. You get so you can read that guy's mind. You know when he dips his left wing what you're supposed to do. You go with some other folks, all right, you might survive, but you might not. Clyde went with them, against my wishes, against my pleading - I didn't just ask him, I pleaded with him. I said, 'Clyde, tell them the whole division will go if they need planes.' He went, and didn't come back . . .

"He was so eager to go, he wanted so badly to get into the fray, that he was willing to take the chance that he took. Much to my regret. Clyde was one of the finest gentlemen we had in the squadron. But, there it is. You're thinking is what gets you sometimes. You think yourself into a hole. That's the way you lose your life"!

Wilbert Peter Popp was a close friend of Clyde Dunn's and was devastated by his loss.

"As stated Clyde and I were first cadets at pre-flight, then all the way through training and then to VF-17. Our flight on February 17th was to be escorting B-24s on a strike to Simpson Harbor. Clyde's flight had the day off and were not supposed to fly that day. Clyde had drawn the night duty where you had to stay at the ready tent at the airfield. Normally the duty officer was relieved of his duty when the day flight turned up. However, Clyde, hung around and listened to the daily briefing. One of our pilots, who shall remain nameless, had been recovering from somewhat minor superficial wounds, a week or so prior to this day. He kept missing flights due to this so-called injury. The skipper then turned to this gentleman and asked him if he was ready to fly and he said no. The skipper then turned to Clyde and told Clyde to get into the airplane and replace this other pilot, resulting in Clyde flying in a strange division. He normally was wingman on "Country" Landreth. Nobody saw Clyde being shot down that day.

"On my return into Bougainville I asked about Clyde. He had not returned. I went out to the end of the runway and waited with Clyde's plane captain for Clyde to return. On return to the flight line the first person I saw was the malingering pilot who Clyde had replaced. I'm afraid I lost it. Here my memory is somewhat blank.

"Evidently I went after the malingerer, pulled my knife and one of the other pilots intervened and wrestled me to the ground. A few days later Blackburn, after conferring with our flight surgeon, Doctor Lyle Herrmann, shipped the pilot back to the States. The irony of the whole affair was that when the pilot was back in the States he was considered a hero and was designated to speak before a squadron still in the States on how we were doing in VF-17. Furthermore, he had been a replacement pilot we had picked up in Espiritu Santo in January 1944 and only been in combat one month with less than 5 flights in combat."

Ens. Smith, flying wing on a division leader in the high cover spotted 12-14 Zekes climbing over Blanche Bay and arriving at a position astern of the bombers. The division turned back into them and made several section runs at about 12,000 ft.

Smith lost his section leader after a chandelle, and almost immediately saw a Zeke at his altitude approaching from his port, as though he were trying to join up. Smith made a beam run, fired a long burst and the Zeke spun down in flames. Smith recovered, and looked for someone to join up on. He saw no F4Us, dove to 8,000 ft. (the bombers had pushed over) and made a beam run on another Zeke who rolled over and dove away, obviously damaged. Smith then climbed and headed towards the rally point off Cape Gazelle. Over Ralunana Point he spotted an Oscar slightly below him. He made a stern run, closed to about 1,000 ft. and fired into the Oscar's tail. The Jap spun down with gas streaming from his wing roots. Smith again climbed and started to the rally point to join up. A Zeke got on his tail, boresighted him, and fired into his wings. Smith dove away, eluding the Jap, and eventually joined up.

Wilbert Peter Popp recalls his mistake of trying to loop with a Zeke (Almost a fatal mishap).

"We were in a 4 plane division at about 8,000 feet over Rabaul. I was Tail-end Charlie. Tim Gile was division leader, John Malcolm Smith was his number 2 (Gile's wingman), Earl May number 3, (my section leader) and I was number 4. A single Zero made a dive on us and continued by looping in front of the division.

"Gile pulled up, took a shot, broke off, followed by Smith, took a shot, broke off, followed by May, took a shot, broke off. By

Dan Cunningham on Bougainville 1944. Courtesy U.S. Navy photo. Robert L. Lawson Collection.

Pilot Lt(jg) Dan Cunningham (L) explains details of VF-17's successful raid on Rabaul to Lt. Duke Henning Air Intelligence officer. In Center are Lt(jg) E. Peterson and Ens. M.W. Cole. Courtesy National Archives.

that time I was almost on my back, but I had the Zeke in my sights. I took a couple of shots at him, then I almost stalled out at the top of the loop. By the time I recovered I was losing air speed and had lost my altitude, giving me very little operational chances. I had no area in which I could dive, all I could do was kick the rudder and shoot, kick the rudder and shoot.

"Fortunately at that time a lone Marine Corsair flown by a Major Wilbur plus John Smith, who had seen my predicament came post haste to give me assistance. We formed a 3 man Thach weave and finally were able to extricate me from my mess. I believe I smoked a Zeke, however, neither I nor the other 2 were able to confirm it. I never even got a probable."

Heavy A/A was reported as meagre and inaccurate but Lt(jg) Miller's plane was hit when he was at 10,000 ft. over the target. About 5 feet of his right wing was blown off and he spun down to 5,000 feet where he bailed out.

Wilbert Peter Popp again describes this day:

"That day had been a particular bad day for me. One of the guys in my division Lt. James Miller was shot down by anti-aircraft fire. I watched him come down in a parachute. We strafed the ground. Troops were trying to shoot him while he was dangling in his parachute. We saw him land safely on the runway off the field adjoining Simpson Harbor. He waved at us. He never got out. As was the case of all of our pilots who were captured by the Japanese. We can only assume that he was summarily executed.

"As a footnote the only time downed pilots ever escaped would be when they could make their way to the jungle watchers and have the Australian and New Zealand coast watchers pick them up and radio to the Americans to send in a Dumbo (PBY) to make the rescue."

After the bombers were safely on their way home 6 F4Us left the formation for a delayed fighter sweep around New Ireland and into the target (the Statue of Liberty play). They came in over Kabanga Bay above the overcast, saw no planes, let down into Blanche Bay and found no Japs to tangle with, although some were seen climbing from Tobera. The flight then returned to base.

One F4U was forced to return early with an hydraulic leak. Several pilots reported gun stoppages. It is believed that these were due to the extremely heavy rains preceding the operation.

Forty or fifty enemy fighters intercepted. Dunn destroyed one Zeke; Smith destroyed one Zeke, probably destroyed one Oscar, and damaged one Zeke. No bombers were lost to enemy aircraft.

Fourteen pilots participated in a fighter sweep over Rabaul. No contacts were made.

Two negative, 2-hour patrols (12 sorties) were flown over Green Island.

One negative, 2-hour patrol (4 sorties) was flown over Task Force 38.

18 February

Sixteen F4Us from the squadron were assigned as low and medium cover on the first of 2 squadrons of B-24s striking Vunakanau Airfield. An additional 8 F4Us were assigned as independent roving high cover.

Lt. H.A. March	Lt. W.J. Schub
Lt(jg) C.W. Gilbert	Ens. W.C. Wharton
Lt(jg) H.J. Bitzegaio	Lt(jg) W.L. Landreth
Ens. F.A. Jagger	Ens. M.W. Cole
Lt. O.I. Chenoweth	Lt. Cdr. R.R. Hedrick
Ens. J.C. Dixon	Lt(jg) P. Cordray
Lt(jg) D.G. Cunningham	Lt(jg) G.F. Bowers
Ens. L.A. Fitzgerald	Ens. G.M. Keller
Lt. M.W. Davenport	Lt. C.D. Gile
Ens. H.B. Richardson	Ens. J.M. Smith
Ens. J.O. Ellsworth	Lt(jg) E. May
Ens. M.M. Kurlander	Ens. W.P. Popp

Heavy A/A from the target area was intense but burst above and below the bombers who made their runs at 20,000 ft.

There was practically no interception of the strike itself. Only about 12 Jap fighters were sighted, and 2 who attempted runs on the formation pulled away when the fighters turned into them.

The roving high cover, however, had lots of business. The 2 divisions on roving high cover reached the target half an hour before the bombers. They approached from the south over Wide Bay at 32,000 ft. and made a wide circle of the area with Lt. Cdr. Hedrick's division at 29,000 ft. and Lt. Gile's division at 26,000 ft.

When Gile was over Blanche Bay he spotted 8 Zekes at about his altitude in a climbing turn. The Zekes were in two beautifully formed 4-plane divisions. The Zekes and F4U's continued climbing, each formation seeking altitude advantage. Gile got to 30,000 ft. first and his division made section runs on the Zekes, who dove out.

The action then developed into a running fight. Gile and his wingman, Ens. Smith, made 3 unsuccessful passes followed by

Earl May and groundcrew in front of his plane #27. Number 27 was his regular assigned plane, however on several occasions he flew number 8 usually on special missions like the bombing raid on 26 February 1944. Courtesy Del May.

chandelles, but over Keravat they caught a Zeke at about 25,000 ft. The Zeke split-S'd, but the F4Us were able to make a division run from 5 o'clock. The Zeke caught fire and spun down. This plane credited to Lt. Gile. Two Zekes appeared on Smith's tail and the section made a 180° turn and went into a flat dive. The Zekes turned back and Gile chandelled after them. Smith, thinking Gile's maneuver was part of a scissors, crossed beneath Gile and turned back on opposite course. He could not find Gile and started a climb over Cape Gazelle. He saw a Zeke approaching in a slight left turn on an opposite course. Both the Zeke and the F4U thought the other was friendly and started to join up. Luckily Smith corrected his error first by spotting the Zeke's tail at about 1,800 ft. He gave him 70 mills lead from one o'clock; held his fire until the range had closed to 800 ft., then gave the Jap a long burst. The Zeke never varied his turn. Smith chandelled and saw the Zeke smoking and spinning down. He followed, fired again, and pulled away when the Zeke began to burn (Smith calculated that this was 15 seconds after his initial burst).

Just after Gile and Smith were separated a Zeke got on Gile's tail. He put his F4U into a 30° dive from 20,000 ft. to 10,000 ft. and shook the Jap just before crossing Cape Gazelle. Gile then joined up with Smith and proceeded back to base.

Lts(jg) Cordray and May were flying second section in Gile's division. As Gile attacked, they also went down in a pair in beam high side runs. May missed but Cordray sent a Zeke spinning down, smoking and out of control. The pair then headed towards Vunakanau and got in a running fight with 8 Zekes. As they made a section run, 3 Zekes jumped Cordray, who dove below a layer of clouds at 16,000 ft.

May called him to zoom up through the cloud so that he (May) could shoot the Zekes off his tail. Cordray did not hear, and continued his dive. Uncomfortable at being alone, May headed east. He

(Right) Lt(jg) Ira Kepford in the cockpit of his F4U-1A Corsair fighter on the day Fighting Squadron 17 raided Rabaul on 19 February 1944. Courtesy National Archives.

came up behind a Zeke. The Zeke slow rolled and May shot him all the way round until he burned at the wing roots and went down. As May crossed the coast of New Britain over Put Put at 11,000 ft., he spotted another Zeke and crawled up his tail unobserved. This Zeke also slow rolled when May fired but May again followed him through and saw him go down in flames.

May then joined up with the cover on the retiring B-25s and went home. Cordray, having finally eluded the 3 Zekes by diving to the deck, did the same.

Lt. Cdr. Hedrick made his first contact in the fight begun by Gile's division south of Vunakanau. He and his wingman dove from 29,000 ft. and he caught a Zeke in a stern run at 18,000 ft. The Zeke burned. He recovered, spotted another Zeke below him and made another stern run. The Zeke dove but Hedrick kept on his tail until he exploded at 12,000 ft. Hedrick's wingman lost him in this run so Hedrick headed back towards Cape Gazelle. As he was circling he saw 8 Zekes climbing in a loose column at 1500 ft., a few miles east of Tobera. Hedrick dove and caught the lead Zeke in a stern run. The Zeke burned, and Hedrick, seeing no more Zekes on his recovery, joined up on the B-25s.

The following tactical comments were reported after this mission.

The action demonstrated the effectiveness of a roving high cover. In effect, the cover is a fighter sweep which, when properly executed, eliminates much of the fighter opposition to the bombers. Four conditions must be met to give roving high cover maximum effectiveness:

1. The cover should stay with the strike planes as long as possible in order to prevent radar detection.

2. The cover should precede the strike into the target.

3. The cover should have altitude advantage.

4. Planes must be kept in divisions as long as possible; any tendency to scatter or engage in individual dogfights should be suppressed.

About thirty enemy aircraft were encountered. Hedrick destroyed three Zekes; May destroyed two Zekes; Smith destroyed one Zeke; Gile destroyed one Zeke; Cordray probably destroyed one Zeke. No bombers were lost to enemy aircraft.

Eight pilots escorted SBDs in a strike on the radar station on Cape St. George. No contacts. No A/A.

One negative, 2-hour patrol (4 sorties) was flown over Task Force 38.

CUNNINGHAM'S BIG DAY
KEPFORD'S ORDEAL

19 February

Twenty-four F4Us were assigned as high cover on the TBFs and as high and medium cover on the SBDs in a strike on Lakunai Airfield. An additional 4 were assigned as roving high cover. Because of engine troubles and other eventualities, only 24 F4Us arrived over the target.

Lt. Cdr. J.T. Blackburn	Lt(jg) G.F. Bowers
Lt. S.R. Beacham	Ens. G.M. Keller
Lt(jg) R. Mims	Lt(jg) P. Cordray
Ens. H. Matthews	Ens. J.E. Diteman
Lt(jg) T. Killefer	Lt(jg) R.H. Jackson
Ens. W.P. Meek	Ens. R.M. Einar
Lt(jg) D.C. Freeman	Lt. C.D. Gile
Ens. R.H. Hill	Ens. J.M. Smith
Lt. Cdr. R.R. Hedrick	Lt(jg) E. May
Ens. M.W. Cole	Ens. W.P. Popp
Lt(jg) I.C. Kepford	Lt(jg) M. Schanuel
Ens. M.M. Kurlander	Lt. O.I. Chenoweth
Lt(jg) D.G. Cunningham	Ens. H.B. Richardson

February 19th was a big day for Dan Cunningham and he remembers this mission on "Roving High Cover".

"We took off ahead of the strike, flew to about 32,000 feet, had no duty at all to keep covering the bombers and our only job was that when they'd start reporting bogeys at 12 o'clock-2 o'clock was to go over and split them up and if they didn't break up on the first pass you'd make another pass. No body who got the hop got less than 2 or more than 4.

"This was one of the things that added to my admiration of the skipper, he could have taken that hop every blessed hop, to say he wanted to see how our weaves were working over the bombers and would have been up there and could have come home with many more planes. But instead of that he made sure that every guy in the squadron got the hop at least once.

"I was far enough down the ladder that on February 19th. That's the last day we saw enemy aerial opposition and there were 2 extra planes and they were assigned to 'Oc' Chenoweth and myself.

"We went up there and we were sitting up there waiting and Oc' sees a Jap down below and goes diving after him, and over-ran him, and with that the Jap pulled right straight up and I was hanging above to protect him. This Jap pulled up so I just cut the circle and he was gone.

"When I looked back there was 'Oc' diving after another one. He did the same darned thing. The Jap pulled right straight up and dove down, cut the circle and he was gone. Then when I came around to find 'Oc' he was down on the water chasing a Zeke. They were zigging and zagging and I thought he's all right so far and with that I see a Jap up over here starting to peel off and go get him. So I just peeled off and went right up his tail and he was gone. When he was gone I didn't know what had happened to 'Oc' and by this time the strike had already dropped their bombs and were heading out. I said I'd better join up and start the climb to catch up with them

going away and every time we were weaving there was always one or two of the Japs sitting over here and as you'd weave they'd start to turn in and if you'd weave too wide they'd slice through you.

"This guy was just sitting out there floating and I'm climbing, climbing, climbing and the first thing you know I got to where I was above him and I just went down on him and really blew him to pieces. I pulled back as hard as I could and I still went through shrapnel, pieces of the plane and then, on the way home, the skipper called for what he devised the Statue of Liberty play.

"After we had got the bombers close enough to home; far enough away from the target, we would turn back and catch them on the landing circuit. The guy who I joined up on, he gave me the signal, how much gas. I had about 50 gallons, I had to lean way back to make it back. So he called back and he said, 'we can't go on the end to round play' and came on back to base.

"I think I used 525 rounds. We carried, I think 2400, so they were all four short bursts. See they had no armor plate or nothing, they just blew sky high every time you hit them. It was a big day. I was lucky in that it was the last day we had enemy aerial opposition. Had I been a day later I'd have been sitting there with 3 instead of 7.

"I think what I just told you emphasizes what a great guy he was. He could have taken that hop, every hop we had, and said I want to see how you guys are performing and be up there watching and just shoot the daylights out of them, and being the great shot he was, I think, conservativel,y he would have been one of our leading aces. But to show you the kind of man he was he made sure everybody got it. I just had all the admiration and respect in the world for him".

Lt. Chenoweth and Lt(jg) Cunningham, were the only F4Us on roving high cover to complete the mission. They arrived over the target area about 20 minutes before the bombers. They came in

"Ike" Kepford returns from his eventful mission of 19 February, 1944. Piva Yoke. Courtesy U.S. Navy photo. Robert L. Lawson Collection.

Lt. Oc Chenoweth (L) Lt(jg) Earle Peterson (C) with Lt. Basil Duke Henning after a Rabaul strike in February 1944. Courtesy U.S. Navy photo. Robert L. Lawson Collection.

at 30,000 ft. and circled, letting down to 24,000 ft., when they saw 6-8 Jap fighters over St. George's Channel at 18,000 ft. Chenoweth made a run with Cunningham on his wing. Chenoweth followed the Zeke down to 12,000 ft. (Cunningham stayed at 18,000 ft. as cover) and saw him crash on Cape Gazelle. He then climbed and rejoined Cunningham. The section made a second run, Chenoweth overshot, and as the Zeke pulled up he was an easy target for Cunningham who burned him. The section recovered and headed westward over Blanche Bay where they spotted Zekes below them on the same course. A section run was made and Cunningham again caught the Zeke as he pulled up and set him afire. In both cases the Zekes were slow and Cunningham used only about 75 mills lead.

In the recovery from the run the F4Us were separated and Chenoweth spotted a lone Zeke, made a stern run but as only one gun was firing the Jap got away.

Chenoweth turned away, got his guns working, and headed for a group of Zekes at 10,000 feet milling over our bombers between Duke of York Island and Rabaul. He made a stern run, the Zeke caught fire, and the pilot bailed out at 4,000 ft.

Chenoweth went back to Cape Gazelle and saw some Japs low on the water attempting to sneak in on the retiring bombers. He turned into a pair (believed to be Tojos) and the wingman rolled away and into the water. Chenoweth then joined the cover on the SBDs.

Lt. "Oc" Chenoweth once got a Jap without firing a gun. He took after the Zero, fought it down to the water level over Rabaul and kept on top—the strategic position for a fighter plane—until the Jap was forced to try more fancy maneuvers than he could man-

age. After doing some "split-S" turns in an effort to escape the Corsair, the Zero turned on his back and fell directly into the ocean.

When Cunningham lost Chenoweth he was over Simpson Harbor at 5,000 ft. He headed for Blanche Bay at full throttle. Spotting an F4U he turned north to join up, but the F4U also turned north in pursuit of a Zeke. Cunningham spotted another Zeke coming down astern. He turned hard into him but the Zeke pulled through and started after the other F4U. Cunningham closed on the Zeke and sent him down flaming. He recovered at 3,000 ft. and headed for Cape Gazelle to join the bombers. Cunningham then joined up with the bomber cover.

The strike itself was not overly molested on the approach, with only a few Zekes making feints at the formation. On the retirement, however, the spam hit the fan, the principle attack being made on the 6 F4Us on the TBF high cover. Lt(jg) Schanuel and Ens. Richardson, all that were left of the second division, spotted 7 Zekes 3,000 ft. above them (19,000 ft.) on the port quarter. The F4U's turned into the Japs and tried to pull them into them but were cut off when the Zekes sliced down.

One got on Richardson's tail and he dove to 3,000 ft., the Zeke abandoning the pursuit half way down. Schanuel joined Richardson and as the latter's wheel doors and tail wheel had been shot up, the pair proceeded to base.

The first division of the high cover, led by Lt. Gile, had to fight its way through about 20 Zekes and possible Tojos to get to the rally point off Cape Gazelle. Ens. Smith scored first. At 14,000 ft. he caught a plane which he believed to be a Tojo and in a stern quarter shot, set it afire. Almost immediately after this pass, the section made a similar run on a Zeke and Lt. Gile got in a long burst. The Zeke caught fire, spun down, and was seen to crash. By this time the Japs had withdrawn and Gile and Smith continued their weave over the TBFs.

Gile's second section, Lt(jg) May and Ens. Popp, went into action almost simultaneously with the first section. May dove on a Zeke in a head on run, and the Zeke exploded. May and Popp recovered at 3,000 ft. and headed towards Cape Gazelle. Zekes were all over the sky but May and Popp repulsed all attacks by scissoring. May shot down 2 Zekes and Popp one, all runs being from astern, with the section well joined up.

Lt(jg) Kepford led the second division of the high cover on the TBFs. His wingman had engine trouble off Buka Passage and was forced to return to base.

Kepford continued on as far as Cape St. George where, finding that the fighter cover was adequate, he also decided to turn back, as he did not want to go over Rabaul without a wingman. He began an easy turn to the right and saw something low on the water off Cape Siar. He went down to investigate and found a Rufe at about 1,000 ft. flying north. He dove on it and in a stern run set it afire. At this moment, he saw 20 Jap fighters coming down out of a cloud at 16,000 ft. over New Ireland. Four came down on him in a loose column, and the leader made a stern run, but Kepford popped his flaps and the Zeke overran him. As the Zeke pulled up, Kepford got in a good burst and sent it down in flames. He was then at 1,000 ft. and making 200 knots.

. Oscar Chenoweth (L) gives his version of VF-17 attack to Lt. Basil uke Henning, Air Intelligence Officer at Piva Airstrip, Bougainville.Lt(jg) arle Peterson (C) listens in. Courtesy National Archives.

Three Japs now had Kepford boxed. The two on his right pre- ented his turning east to Green Island, and one was on his left, so at his only course was to head north.

This he did, putting his plane in a slight dive, shoving his throttle orward, and using his water injection (Kepford had one of the few 4U's with this device, which was designed to increase speed for a ort time). He had 2750 rpm and 62 inches manifold pressure and as jinking in a very gentle left turn (about half needle width).

The Japs (Kepford thought the two on his right were Tojos) ere still just within range so Kepford stopped jinking and tried a entle climb. He figured that he was pulling away at the rate of ly 40 knots. Consequently, he nosed over the hills on New Ire-

land (in the Namatanai area) and headed for the deck. Just as he crossed the western shore, his water injection gave out. The engine missed, Kepford pulled back the throttle and pushed it forward again. The water injection caught for a few seconds and the engine missed again. At this point Kepford noticed that he was making 355 knots indicated. As he was at sea level this means that his true speed was 365 mph.

Kepford kept a course of 300° for about 15 or 20 minutes. When he had 100 gallons left he decided that he would have to head south. He made a violent turn to the left (his speed was 270 knots indicated) and the Zeke on his left in trying to turn inside him, dug his left wing in the water and crashed. The Tojos were sucked wide on the turn and gave up the chase so Kepford crossed New Britain at Open Bay.

After his turn, Kepford throttled back to 2600 rpm and 48 inches. He kept this setting for 10 minutes then went to 2150 and 27 inches with his mixture in automatic lean (he had been in rich until this point) until he sighted land. He throttled back to 1300 rpm and landed with 40 gallons in his tank. He had been airborne for 4 hours and 10 minutes.

Kepford believed that his water injection lasted for only about 4 minutes.

Afterwards he said that the engine smelled hot (he could smell the alcohol) but that it ran smoothly. The plane was flown the next day and was apparently in good shape.

About fifty enemy aircraft intercepted. Chenoweth destroyed two Zekes and one Tojo; Cunningham destroyed four Zekes; May destroyed three Zekes; Popp destroyed one Zeke; Gile destroyed one Zeke; Smith destroyed one Zeke. One F4U was slightly damaged by fire from a Zeke. Heavy A/A was meagre and inaccurate.

No bombers were lost to enemy aircraft. At Cape St. George on the approach, Kepford, his wingman having turned back because of engine trouble, also decided to turn back. He saw a Rufe low on the water off Cape Siar, went down and destroyed it, but was himself attacked by twenty enemy fighters. He destroyed one but was forced to run north as he was boxed in by one Zeke and two Tojos. He passed over New Ireland and at a point well north of Watom Island made a violent left turn. The Zeke pursuing him crashed into the water while attempting to turn inside Kepford, who was then able to outrun the two Tojos.

A negative, 2-hour patrol (4 sorties) was flown over base.

Lt(jg) E.C. Peterson, Jr. was detached.

This mission was the last time the squadron encountered any Japanese planes as they had withdrawn all their planes from Rabaul.

FIGHTER BOMBERS

) February
rom this day on Japanese aerial opposition was nonexistent.

VF-17 still flew the routine missions such as patrols and es- orts but were looking for alternative ideas.

The skies were now safe to try out something that VF-17 had eveloped, an improvised bomb rack. Tom Blackburn received the o ahead to put this idea into practice.

VF-17 had limited success with bombs, but as developed in later squadrons the Corsair was an excellent fighter bomber. VF-17 pioneered this work, by the end of the war many squadrons were flying Corsairs as fighter bombers.

Twelve pilots escorted B-25s in a strike on Lakunai Airfield. No enemy aircraft were sighted. Heavy A/A was moderate and inaccurate.

Four pilots escorted a Dumbo which picked up a B-25 crew off Cape St. George and a single pilot off Cape Pallisier.

A negative, 2-hour patrol (8 sorties) was flown over Green Island.

A negative, 2-hour patrol (8 sorties) was flown over shipping south of Green Island.

21 February
Eleven pilots escorted TBFs in a strike on Lakunai Airfield. No enemy aircraft were sighted. Heavy A/A was meagre and inaccurate.

Four negative, 2-hour patrols (31 sorties) were flown over Green Island.

22 February
Twenty-three pilots escorted SBD's and TBF's in a strike on Lakunai Airfield. No enemy aircraft were sighted. Heavy A/A was meagre and inaccurate.

A negative, 2-hour patrol (4 sorties) was flown over base.

Four pilots escorted a Dumbo which picked up an SBD crew 40 miles N.W. of Cape Torokina.

Pilot Lt. Oscar Chenoweth describes his activities to Air Intelligence Officer, Lt. Duke Henning, after returning from a raid on Rabaul. Courtesy National Archives.

"Ike" Kepford's F4U-1A parked on Bougainville, 19 February, 1944. Courtesy U.S. Navy photo. Robert L. Lawson Collection.

23 February

Eight pilots were assigned to cover TBFs in a strike on Vunakanau Airfield. The bombers turned back because of bad weather and the F4Us scouted the area south of St. George's Channel with negative results.

Sixteen pilots escorted B-25s in a strike on Vunakanau Airfield. No enemy aircraft were sighted. Heavy A/A was intense and inaccurate.

24 February

Twenty-five pilots escorted B-25s in a strike on Lakunai Airfield. No enemy aircraft were encountered. Heavy A/A was meagre and inaccurate.

Four pilots scouted the Rabaul area to spot shipping for a projected destroyer raid.

A negative, 2-hour patrol (4 sorties) was flown over four destroyers west of Empress Augusta Bay.

A negative, 2-hour patrol (4 sorties) was flown over base.

25 February

Three negative, 2-hour patrols (15 sorties) were flown over Green Islands.

Hedrick, Smith, Matthews, Meek, Herrmann, Gile, Ellsworth, at Bougainville, February 1944. Courtesy Lennard Edmisten.

Three negative Dumbo escorts (12 sorties) were flown.

One negative, 2-hour patrol (4 sorties) were flown over a Task Force of nine destroyers.

26 February

Sixteen pilots escorted B-24s in a strike on the Vunapepe supply dump. No enemy aircraft were encountered. Heavy A/A was moderate and accurate.

A negative, 2-hour patrol (8 sorties) was flown over Green Islands (This report as referred to in Tom Blackburn's book is probably the bogus one to cover up the bombing raid on a Japanese whorehouse at Rabaul!).

A negative, 2-hour patrol (4 sorties) was flown over base.

27 February

Fifteen pilots escorted B-24s in a strike on the Vunapepe supply dump. No enemy aircraft were encountered. Heavy A/A was moderate and accurate.

A negative 2 hour patrol (8 sorties) was flown over Green Islands.

28 February

Sixteen F4Us were sent on a fighter sweep over the Rabaul area preceding the bombing strikes. The sweep was negative, no enemy aircraft being encountered.

After the bombers had retired 8 F4Us (4 of them equipped with 500lb. general purpose bombs with 4-5 seconds delay fuses) searched the coastal area from Cape Lambert to Open Bay for shipping or suitable bombing targets were found and the pilots carrying bombs made practice runs on a beached hulk and a deserted building.

Lt. O.I. Chenoweth	Lt. C.D. Gile
Ens. J.C. Dixon	Ens. J.M. Smith
Lt(jg) D.G. Cunningham	Lt(jg) E. May
Ens. L.A. Fitzgerald	Ens. W.P. Popp

Lt(jg) May and Ens. Popp whose planes did not carry bombs spotted a 30 foot motor launch just as it was disappearing into a small cove north of Pondo Plantation. They made 2 runs from the seaward and set the boat afire. Immediately afterwards they made one run on a similar launch docked at Pondo Plantation.

During the course of this run they were fired upon by a light A/A weapon from the plantation. They made a run on the gun position and probably silenced it.

Popp's plane was slightly damaged by links and empty casings from May's plane.

At the conclusion of a negative, 2-hour patrol over Green Island 6 of the 8 F4Us on patrol proceeded to Ambitle Island.

Lt. Cdr. R.R. Hedrick	Ens. G.M. Keller
Ens. M.W. Cole	Lt(jg) P. Cordray
Lt(jg) G.F. Bowers	Ens. J.E. Diteman

Earl May in plane number 8 after the February 26 1944 bombing raid on a Japanese officers club (House of Flowers). Courtesy Del May.

All 6 made strafing runs, the targets being one 50 foot landing barge drawn up on the beach on the south end of Babase Island, one similar barge and a 50 foot sloop on the east side of Ambitle Island, and a camouflaged barge in a small inlet south of Balanum Bay. Three Japs were seen to jump out of the last target as the fighters began their run. All targets were well hit, but only the last barge, on which 2 runs were made, was seen to smoke.

No A/A fire was encountered.

All runs were made from very low altitudes.

A negative, 2-hour patrol (8 sorties) was flown over Green Islands.

29 February

Eight pilots were assigned as cover on a B-24 strike on Rabaul city. Because of bad weather the bombers turned back. The following pilots proceeded to Namutanai Airfield:

Lt. O.I. Chenoweth   Lt(jg) D.G. Cunningham
Ens. J.C. Dixon   Ens. L.A. Fitzgerald

Two pilots dropped 500 lb. bombs with no results and all four made strafing runs on buildings near the airfield getting good hits. One F4U was slightly damaged by light A/A fire.

Eight pilots escorted a Dumbo to the Namatanai area to search for a pilot reported in the water with negative results. Heavy A/A from Borpop was meagre and inaccurate. Light A/A from Nabuto Bay was intense and accurate. One F4U was slightly damaged.

Two barge hunts (8 sorties) were made around Bougainville.

Group of VF-17 pilots in front on F4U-1A. Courtesy U.S. Naval Historical Center / M.W. "Butch" Davenport Collection.

Squadron commanding officer, Lt. Cdr. Tom Blackburn (left), discusses a raid on Rabaul with another officer, after returning to his unit's base on Bougainville, February 1944. Courtesy National Archives.

8

End of Second Tour
March 1944

1 March
On this date VF-17 was composed of 44 officers and 94 enlisted men and had a compliment of 36 F4U-1 aircraft.

A negative, 2-hour patrol (3 sorties) was flown over a destroyer task force south of St. George's Channel.

Four negative, 2-hour patrols (31 sorties) were flown over Green Islands.

2 March
Eight pilots escorted SBDs in a strike against shore installations around Keravia Bay. No enemy aircraft were encountered. Heavy A/A was moderate and inaccurate.

Four pilots escorted one negative Dumbo mission.

Eight F4Us were assigned to a barge hunt from Cape St. George to Kalili Bay on the west coast of New Ireland.

Lt. Cdr. J.T. Blackburn	Lt(jg) T. Killefer
Lt. S.R. Beacham	Ens. W.P. Meek
Lt(jg) R. Mims	Lt(jg) D.C. Freeman
Ens. H. Matthews	Ens. R.H. Hill

Tom Killefer, March 1944. Courtesy U.S. Navy photo. Robert L. Lawson Collection.

Just north of the Jalu river Lt. Beacham spotted a 60 foot barge camouflaged with palm fronds. As he made his run he received machine gun fire from the barge. Lt. Killefer, leader of the second division, made 3 runs on the barge. It was left burning.

Lt. Killefer made 2 runs on a 50 foot sailing vessel anchored just off Bulbuk. It was filled with what appeared to be wooden boxes, and was left smoking. Lt. Killefer then dropped his bomb on a building (100 ft x 300 ft, with a large smoke stack and 3 exterior boilers) believed to be a saki distillery near Kaboman. The bomb hit the ground, skipped into the building and exploded, blowing out one wall.

The flight then proceeded to the mouth of the Warangoi River, New Britain. Five F4Us made single bombing runs on a wooden bridge, 100 yards long and 20 ft. high, spanning the river. Ens. Hill scored a direct hit, his bomb skipping under the bridge and exploding, knocking out 30 feet of the center section. He released his bomb at a range of 200 or 300 yards, altitude 150 feet, speed 220k.(ind.). Two bombs were near misses which tore up the road. The fifth bomb exploded on the northern end of the bridge, doing considerable damage. All runs were made from south to north at a very slight angle to the longitudinal axis of the bridge. Most runs were made at an altitude of about 40 feet.

At the conclusion of the bombing attack the flight strafed buildings at Rugen Bay.

All planes were equipped with 500 lb. G.P. bombs fitted with 4-5 second delay tail fuses.

Two negative, 2-hour patrols (15 sorties) were flown over Green Islands.

3 March
A negative, 1-hour patrol (4 sorties) was flown over base.

Four pilots escorted TBFs in a strike on Lakunai Airfield. No enemy aircraft were encountered. No A/A fire was encountered.

Ten pilots escorted B-25s in a strike on Rabaul. No enemy aircraft were encountered. No A/A fire was encountered.

Eight F4Us searched the coast of New Ireland from Labur Bay to Cape St. George for barges or other suitable targets.

Lt. Cdr. R.R. Hedrick	Lt(jg) P. Cordray
Ens. M.W. Cole	Ens. J.E. Diteman
Lt(jg) G.F. Bowers	Lt(jg) R.H. Jackson
Ens. G.M. Keller	Ens.R.M. Einar

The search was conducted at altitudes from 5,000 feet to 100 feet.

Two 35 foot barges camouflaged with palm fronds were spotted on the beach at Nakudukudu Bay. All eight F4Us made two passes, the runs being made singly and from various directions. Two barges were well hit and a small explosion was seen in one of them. One division then strafed a small motor whaleboat on the beach 4 miles south of the first target. Another camouflaged barge was found on the shore near Mt. Konogalang. Each plane made a pass. The barge was set afire. Heavy black smoke gave evidence of a cargo of oil. Four planes then strafed a small motor whaleboat on the beach 2 miles south of the barge.

Three bombs were dropped in a plantation at the mouth of the Kanduru River. The target was a 40 ft. observation tower. One bomb was a dud, the other two exploded behind the target.

Two more bombs were dropped in a plantation at Kaboman. Both were over but a strafing run was also made which set one large building smoking.

Bombs were released at altitudes ranging from 30 feet to 200 feet. Speeds were between 220 and 300 knots (indicated) with the most efficient speed calculated to be about 250 knots.

4 March

A negative, 2-hour patrol (7 sorties) was flown over Green Islands.

Six pilots participated in a negative barge hunt.

Thirteen pilots escorted B-25s in a strike on Rabaul. There was no interception and heavy A/A was meagre and inaccurate.

Don Innis beside sign on Bougainville 1944. Courtesy U.S. Naval Historical Center / M.W. "Butch" Davenport Collection.

Mechanics swarm over Lt(jg) Tom Killefer's plane which made an emergency landing on the strip at Nissan Island, Green Island group, which had not been officially opened. Indeed before all machinery was off the strip. March 1944. Courtesy U.S. Navy photo. Robert L. Lawson Collection.

5 March
Two negative patrols (8 sorties) were flown over Green Islands. Lt. Killefer had to make an emergency landing on the Green Islands strip because of engine trouble and remained there until 7 march.

Six pilots participated in a negative barge hunt.

One negative, 2-hour patrol (4 sorties) was flown over base.

6 March
A negative, 2-hour patrol (8 sorties) was flown over Green Islands.

Fourteen F4Us were assigned to a barge hunt on the coasts of New Ireland and New Britain.

Lt. M.W. Davenport	Ens. L.A. Fitzgerald
Ens. H.B. Richardson	Lt. H.A. March
Ens. J.O. Ellsworth	Ens. R.H. Hill
Ens. M.M. Kurlander	Lt. W.J. Schub

Lt. O.I. Chenoweth	Ens. W.C. Wharton
Ens. J.C. Dixon	Lt(jg) W.L. Landreth
Lt(jg) D.G. Cunningham	Ens. F.A. Jagger

Of the fourteen only one division of four found targets.

This division found 6 barges (type A) beached in Massava Bay. Each plane made 4 runs and the barges were left smoking. A 125 foot barge (with pointed bow and stern) was found camouflaged with palm fronds in a cove on the southern end of Watom Island. Three pilots strafed this barge, leaving it smoking.

Light A/A fire was received from the west side of the cove.

Chenoweth, Dixon, Cunningham and Fitzgerald strafed six barges (type A) on the beach at Massava Bay and a 125 foot barge in a cove on the south end of Watom Island. All craft were left smoking. Light A/A fire was received from Watom Island.

HOMEWARD BOUND

7 March
Eight pilots escorted SBDs in a strike on Lakunai Airfield. There was no interception. Heavy A/A was moderate and inaccurate.

Eight pilots covered three TBFs in a strike on shipping in Simpson Harbor. No enemy aircraft were encountered. Heavy A/A was meagre and inaccurate.

On this date VF-17 were officially relieved by VF-34.

Wilbert Popp recalls leaving the combat area.

"We left Bougainville on March 8, 1944 with an overnight stop at Guadalcanal. I landed at 'Buttons' on 9 March, 1944. We landed at the Marine Corps strip and our planes were then turned over to the Marines under a new squadron under the command of Major Joe Foss U.S.M.C.

"The squadron flew from Espiritu to Pearl with a refueling stay at Johnson Island.

"From Pearl Harbor after a 5 day rest we were transported to San Francisco again on the Prince William. The squadron was then disbanded. After a months leave in Portland, Oregon I reported to VF-84 a newly formed squadron at N.A.S. North Island, San Di-ego. The commander was Roger Hedrick former XO of VF-17. "Besides myself there were about 10 other VF-17 pilots including Ike Kepford, Chico Freeman, Jimmy Dixon, John Malcolm Smith, Whitey Matthews and others".

Eleven (11) enlisted men were detached.

8 March
The following pilots flew F4U's to Guadalcanal :

Ens. J.M. Smith	Lt(jg) R.H. Hill
Lt(jg) F.J. Streig	Lt. O.I. Chenoweth
Lt(jg) T. Killefer	Ens. W.P. Meek
Lt(jg) D.C. Freeman	Lt(jg) R.H. Jackson
Lt. M.W. Davenport	Ens. H.B. Richardson
Ens. J.C. Dixon	Lt. C.D. Gile
Ens. L.A. Fitzgerald	Lt(jg) D.G. Cunningham
Lt(jg) R. Mims	Lt. Cdr. R.R. Hedrick
Lt(jg) J.O. Ellsworth	Lt(jg) P. Cordray
Ens. G.M. Keller	Ens. M.W. Cole
Lt(jg) G.F. Bowers	Ens. J.E. Diteman
Lt(jg) E. May	Ens. W.P. Popp
Lt(jg) I.C. Kepford	Lt(jg) M.M. Kurlander
Lt(jg) M. Schanuel	Lt. H.A. March
Ens. H. Matthews	Lt(jg) H.J. Bitzegaio
Ens. F.A. Jagger	Ens. R.M. Einar
Lt(jg) W.C. Wharton	Lt(jg) W.L. Landreth
Lt. S.R. Beacham	

As the planes were taking off the enemy shelled the Piva Yoke strip. No planes were damaged on take off but Robert Whitley AMM3c, and Hugo Engler ARM1c, were severely wounded by shrapnel and taken to hospital.

It had been originally planned to fly out the enlisted personnel, and remaining officers to Espiritu Santo but enemy shellfire made it impossible for planes to land.

"Country" Landreth was the last VF-17 plane to leave when the tour ended, he recalls this day:

Another view of Tom Killefer's plane at Nissan Island. Courtesy U.S. Navy photo. Robert L. Lawson Collection.

"The day we left we were under 75mm artillery fire and there were a couple of Corsairs burning. As I was taxiing away from my revetment, my plane captain jumped on my wing and reached inside the cockpit and grabbed my first aid kit. He said the plane captain of the revetment next to me had been seriously wounded. I got out of there in pretty rapid order after that.

"We were officially relieved by another fighter squadron on March 7 and were scheduled to depart from Piva Yoke the next morning.

"During our time there we had grown accustomed to sporadic artillery fire from our forces directed towards the Japanese, who were in the mountains surrounding our twenty-eight square mile Bougainville beachhead.

"As I was happily tying my parachute bag of clothes inside the fuselage of my Corsair the next morning, I kept hearing a steadily increasing amount of artillery firing. I thought, 'Our troops are really giving the Japanese hell this morning.'

"Shortly thereafter, as I finished my packing, I looked up and couldn't believe my eyes. It wasn't our guns firing, it was the enemy bombarding the airfield. I could see several aircraft on fire, shells exploding nearby, and people scrambling for cover.

"I thought to myself, 'Wouldn't it be rotten luck to be clobbered the day you are leaving the combat zone?'

"I jumped into my plane, fired the shotgun shell starter, and prayed that my engine would start. As soon as the prop kicked over, I charged out of our parking revetment, heading for the runway. My seat belt, shoulder straps, radio cord, oxygen mask, etc., were not connected. 'Forget engine warm-up and mag checks—let's get the hell out of here!'

As the squadron rendezvoused and departed on the first leg of our long journey across the Pacific, I whispered those beautiful, poignant words which have a tremendous emotional impact on me: I'm going home!"

9 March

The pilots listed above flew from Guadalcanal to Espiritu Santo, where they turned over their planes to C.A.S.U. TEN.

All enlisted personnel (64) and the remaining officers (9) were evacuated to the beach at Torokina as the enemy continued shelling the former camp area.

Lt. Cdr. Blackburn, on orders from ComAirSoPac, was flown from Torokina to Munda by TBF, and from Munda to Guadalcanal by DC-3.

10 March

All enlisted personnel (except Whitley and Engler, who remained in hospital) and the eight (8) remaining officers were flown from Torokina to Guadalcanal.

11-12 March

All enlisted personnel (except Whitley and Engler, who were still in hospital) and eight (8) officers were flown from Guadalcanal to Espiritu Santo.

"Country" Landreth at Bougainville in 1944. Courtesy U.S. Navy photo. Robert L. Lawson Collection.

13-14 March

Eighteen (18) enlisted men were detached.

15 March

Lt. L.F. Herrmann (MC), Lt(jg) R.L. Mills and Ens. L.R. Kincaid were detached.

Flight Surgeon Lt. Lyle Herrmann reported the following account after the squadron's second tour of duty.

Squadron History

Fighting Squadron SEVENTEEN finished their first combat tour at Ondongo 3 December, 1943. They returned to Espiritu with their planes, 4 December, 1943, and left 6 December, 1943 for Sydney for seven (7) days rehabilitation. On 16 December, 1943 the pilots returned from their rehabilitation period at Sydney and were stationed at Bomber #1 at Espiritu and began their preparations for the next tour of duty. Thirteen (13) new pilots were added to the squadron as replacements for the pilots lost and reclassified during the first tour. A number of these men had no fighter training, and all but one had never been in combat before. The middle of January the squadron moved to Fighter #1 and based on M.A.G. #11.

Here the work continued on the planes, and a syllabus of tactical training and night flying for the new pilots was carried out. 24 January the squadron, numbering forty-nine (49) pilots, moved back into the combat area, being based on Piva Yoke strip on Bougainville Island. The squadron took off on their first combat flight of the second tour 26 January, 1944, as bomber escort over Rabaul. For the next six (6) weeks the pilots operated under the following schedule set up by the commanding officer. The squadron was organized tactically into five flights of eight pilots each.

Each day one (1) flight rested and the various types of missions were rotated between flights so as nearly as possible each pilot carried an equal load; flying four days and resting one.

Type of Plane

The F4U-1 was used and during the tour the newer type with the water injection arrived to replace the older types, until, at the end of the tour, some seventeen (17) of this type were in operation in this squadron. Each regular pilot was assigned his own plane, his name was painted on it, and it was his responsibility to see that it was kept in perfect condition. The advantages of this policy are obvious.

Oxygen Equipment

The new Mark-A14, diluter type of oxygen mask was used. Each pilot owned and cared for his own mask. There were no difficulties experienced in this department.

Combat Statistics (see war diary)

MEDICAL REPORT

Sanitation - Satisfactory
Housing - Satisfactory, four pilots to one hut.

Food - Adequate
Dispensary facilities - Adequate
General Health - Good

Espiritu Santo. March 1944. Full squadron of VF-17 - The last they will see of these fine aircraft. VF-17 are headed home after flying in from Bougainville. Courtesy U.S. Naval Historical Center / M.W. "Butch" Davenport Collection.

Each pilot, before arriving in the combat area, was equipped with a first aid kit which was carried in a waterproof pouch as a shoulder holster. Each plane had a tourniquet and a vial of ammonia installed in the cockpit and within easy reach.

Upon arriving at the Piva Yoke strip the medical set-up was as follows. There was a medical tent at the strip equipped with the meager facilities necessary for first aid only. The squadron flight surgeons rotated on the watch here so that each medical officer stood a half day watch about every three days. The A.C.O.R.N. and C.A.S.U. dispensaries were located rather inconveniently for the pilots' sick call so one of the huts adjoining the flight surgeons living quarters in the pilots' camp was used as a dispensary, and recreation center. It was equipped with a Massage table and adequate medical supplies to handle sick call. No regular hours were set for sick call; the pilots knew the medical officers' services were available at any time of the day or night. The physiotherapist (PhM2/c) was present during the afternoons to tend to minor ailments or administer massage for tired and cramped muscles.

Sick call was held at C.A.S.U. #12 dispensary for the enlisted personnel and the pharmacist's mate spent his mornings there.

This program worked out very well.

The flight surgeon divided his time between the above places and the ready hut; always being present to check the pilots in from a hop.

From a strict medical standpoint the past tour has been uneventful. Only a few minor colds or an occasional non-specific diarrhoea kept the pilots from regular duty, and very little time was lost from these causes. On the other hand the results of the daily combat showed rapidly. From the first day until the close of the fourth week, contacts with the enemy were a daily routine and the enemy was always above. The first ten (10) days cost us eight pilots, the majority of whom were seasoned men.

The whole outfit became tense and worried. This tenseness was evident in everything they did. It was very noticeable even in the approach to the field and in the traffic circle. At camp in the evenings the pilots were irritable, looked very tired and slept poorly. Sedation was used in some of these cases, but on the whole was unsatisfactory. Liquor proved to be the only solution. Sedation produced sleep, but the channel of thought remained and dreams robbed them of the rest and relaxation that undisturbed sleep should bring. However, when they gathered around and had a few beers the morbid channel of thought was discarded, they became "happy", sang a few songs and when they turned in they usually slept "like babies". This type of living, while expedient, cannot be continued for ever. After four weeks of this type of stress, and after losing two more pilots in one day, the situation became serious.

It seemed advisable to terminate the tour at that point, however, from that day on nearly all enemy air resistance disappeared, and the situation was relieved. It has been an important psychological factor now that they have continued, for they, while tired, have regained their confidence and this is important if they are to return to combat flying again.

Conclusion

Fighting Squadron Seventeen has just completed its second tour of combat duty.

Seventy-five percent of the pilots that now comprise this group have completed both tours. These pilots as a group average well over two hundred twenty combat hours.

This in itself I believe parallels most squadrons' three average tours. The tour just completed can in no sense be termed average due to the fact that contacts with the enemy were the daily rule and all missions were carried out over enemy territory, the pilot knowing at all times that even engine failure meant death or worse. It is my opinion that the majority of this squadron is not physically or mentally conditioned for a third combat tour without seriously jeopardizing their future as combat pilots.

Miscellaneous Remarks and Suggestions
Rest and Rehabilitation

There seems to be a general misunderstanding in regards to the seven (7) day rehabilitation period in Sydney as to its place in the pilots' program. This seven (7) day period is rehabilitation alone and not rest, as was proven to me by experience with this squadron. It does play a very important part in the program as originally planned. It was intended originally, I believe, to be the "Saturday night", as it were, after the big game; an opportunity for the pilots to forget their experiences, to completely forget flying and its talk and do other things. This purpose it serves well but physical rest it does not promote. This I believe should follow the rehabilitation.

In the case of this squadron they returned from their first combat tour completely "washed out". They were sent to Sydney immediately where they led a very exciting, yet fatiguing seven (7) days.

The trip back was quite tiring in itself, but the first day back they had hurled in their teeth a strenuous night flying syllabus calling for thirty-six (36) planes at 0300 and thirty-six (36) planes at 1900 and these pilots were in no shape to handle it. One might say, "one hour of flying is not too much "for anyone at any time", and so it isn't, but when pilots have been sleeping poorly for a period of

weeks it would be much better for these people to be allowed to get caught up on their sleep, yet carry on their day time duties of getting their planes ready and engines run in.

At that particular time and in their condition our pilots worried more about living through the night take offs and landing than they ever have about a hop over Rabaul, and yet they had night operations every 24 hours of their first tour and never was there a complaint heard. It is true that the condition of the strip played no little part in this dread.

It is obvious that this training is necessary and I am not trying to question it, but from a psychological standpoint and in the interest of the pilot's proper conditioning, I do sincerely recommend that a short period of rest and relaxation be considered following the rehabilitation period.

The Use of Alcoholic Beverages In Combat Areas

In the report of the first combat tour this officer mentioned the importance of the use of liquor, for those who like it, in the combat area. He also mentioned the lack of, and the preference for, beer. On this tour we were able to obtain some one hundred and fifty

Espiritu Santo. March 1944. Full squadron of VF-17 - The last they will see of these fine aircraft. VF-17 are headed home after flying in from Bougainville. Courtesy U.S. Naval Historical Center / M.W. "Butch" Davenport Collection.

Piloted by the Navy's then-leading "Ace", Lt(jg) Ira Kepford, taken over Bougainville in early March 1944, at the end of VF-17's combat tour. Courtesy National Archives.

cases which we brought with us. This proved to be the "life's blood" of the squadron. It was used quite freely. It was on hand for those who wanted it at the ready hut upon return from each mission. One or two bottles of beer taken when the pilot is still tense and strained was just the depression needed to relax him and put his feet back on the ground where he could give a good report and account of what happened and take the sting out of our own losses. In the evenings very little hard liquor was taken, but the beer was liberally used and proved to be by far the best sedative available, producing relaxation and sleep and yet very little hangover.

It is recommended that all squadrons be provided with an adequate supply of beer, whenever it is available, and that they should be put on a priority above that of the rear echelons.

14-20 March
The remaining officers and enlisted men were flown from Espiritu Santo to Pearl Harbor.

23 March
Lt. Cdr. J.T. Blackburn was flown from Pearl Harbor to the West Coast.
All officers and enlisted men went aboard the U.S.S. Prince William.

24 March
At 0700 the U.S.S. Prince William sailed for San Francisco, California.

30 March
All officers and enlisted men disembarked at N.A.S., Alameda, California.

10 April
Fighting Squadron 17 decommissioned.

FINAL THOUGHTS

"Country Landreth recalls flying in his division.

"I never got a bullet in my airplane. I'm gonna give you a sales talk now. Wally Schub, his wingman, and I and my wingman, went through all the combat—and remember, now, there's sixty or seventy Zeros sitting over the target waiting for us when we got there—we went through all the scraps, chasing airplanes away from the bombers—that was our job, and we never lost a bomber to air combat—and with all that falderal and chasing planes away, and covering each other, and keeping ourselves from getting killed, none of us got a bullet in our airplane in that division.

And we came back from each mission as a unit—which is not so of a great many of our people. When we returned from a mission, we were four planes in formation".

One of Tom Blackburn's strongest recollections was the teamwork of the people involved wanting to work as a unit and pull together rather than as individuals.

"One of the things one has to look out for in the fighter business is the tendency for people to want to take center stage and forget about who is supporting and it's much more effective if the squadron or division or section of 2 aircraft as a minimum, worked as a team rather than have one person as the star".

EPILOGUE

At the end of its two successful tours VF-17 was the top scoring squadron, Navy or Marine, in the Solomons. They were credited with 152 confirmed victories, 13 of the squadron were aces, with Ike Kepford the top Navy ace at that time.

No bombers were lost to enemy air attack and no shipping was lost that VF-17 covered. They delivered an extremely successful Roving High Cover tactic, many design modifications were developed and the squadron proved the F4U in carrier operations under fire. Although it was felt some of the pilots were under-decorated, they did receive many awards, including the Navy Unit Commendation, for covering the Marine landings at Empress Augusta Bay.

Much recognition has come in later years such as being honored guests by the E.A.A. and by various books and articles. But whatever way you look at it VF-17 ranks among the best of their day and records will show they played a vital part in the Pacific War.

THE JOLLY ROGERS INSIGNIA
1. Skull and Crossbones/Jolly Rogers

1 January 1943	Established	VF17
5 November 1946	Redesignated	VF-5B
28 July 1948	Redesignated	VF-61
15 April 1959	Decommissioned	

2. Vagabonds/Jolly Rogers
1 July 1955   Established as VA-86
Redesignated to VF-84 During ceremony (Switching with VF-84 which Became VA-86).

15 April 1959 VF-61 Jolly Rogers decommissioned.
Many personnel integrated into VF-84 after F8U transition with VF-174 (58-59).

VF-84 adopted Jolly Rogers insignia and nickname.

At the VF-17 reunion in 1994 the first Jolly Rogers met with their descendents who flew F-14 Tomcats at N.A.S. Oceana. For this event they flew one of their Tomcats (complete with insignia) in formation with 11 F4U Corsairs.

When VF-84 was decommissioned in 1995 it looked like the end of the Jolly Rogers. However, VF-103 adopted the famous insignia and are currently flying F-14 Tomcats on the U.S.S. Enterprise.

Notes:
VF-17 were decommissioned on 10 April, 1944.

On 18 April, 1944, the squadron was reformed having transitioned to F6F Hellcats, under the command of Lt. Cdr. Marshall U. Beebe. To my knowledge none of the original squadron were with the newly formed VF-17.

After extensive training the squadron reported to the U.S.S. Hornet (CV-12) on 1 February, 1945.

The squadron served with distinction in combat action in the Iwo Jima campaign and later in strikes against Tokyo and Okinawa.

The VF-17 Hellcat squadron, along with VBF-17 helped destroy 254.5 enemy planes in their tour of duty.

'Ike" Kepford leading a division of VF-17 Corsairs near Bougainville, March 1944: 29-Kepford, 8-Hal Jackson, 3-Jim Streig, 28-Wilbert Peter Popp. Courtesy U.S. Navy photo. Robert L. Lawson Collection.

9

The Men of VF-17

Original Pilots
ROBERT SIDNEY "ANDY" ANDERSON

Robert S. "Andy" Anderson was born August 23, 1917 in Claremore, Oklahoma, where he attended school through high school. After a year out of school he entered the University of Arkansas for 3.5 years as an engineering major. His war effort was building planes until he enlisted the day after "Pearl Harbor". He met Joy Williams in St. Louis and they were married and had 3 children—a girl named Sidney, and 2 boys, Scott and Ross.

He had a carefree childhood going out with his friends to the lake and fishing or up on the water works where they had a net and you could play some tennis. He loved the out of doors and tried to instill that in his children. If he was your friend he was faithful to the end.

In 1941 "Andy" was in his senior year at the University of Arkansas as a Mechanical Engineering major. As summer approached he decided to go live in St. Louis, Missouri, where his brother lived and go to work for Curtiss-Wright Aircraft as a help toward the war effort.

He did not enroll when September rolled around and stayed in St. Louis doing what he thought necessary. Then—"Pearl Harbor" and he was one of the first to enlist the next day. He enlisted as a Naval Cadet hoping to be a fighter pilot—which was everyone's wish who went into aviation. There were many barriers to hurdle before getting your wings—there was basic training which did away with a lot of 'would-be' pilots. From there you went to another phase where you could be 'washed out' and then another. Every step was like facing the firing squad.

"Andy" got his wings in Corpus Christi, Texas, and then was sent to Miami, Florida, to train as a fighter pilot. He had made it all the way! It was in Miami that those who were training found out where they would go next and "Andy" was ordered to Norfolk, Virginia, to report to squadron VF-17, which was to be stationed aboard the aircraft carrier, "Bunker Hill".

After he was shot down in the Pacific he was returned to the Naval Hospital at Alameda, California, and then to the Ahwanee Hotel in Yosemite National Park, California, to recuperate.

It was dawn on 17 November, 1943, while attached to VF-17, that the squadron was engaged in a dog-fight with the Japanese.

Robert "Andy" Anderson on the doorstep of his first home after being married. Taken in Miami, Florida in the fall of 1942. Courtesy Joy Anderson Schroeder.

Robert "Andy" Anderson in 1945. Courtesy Joy Anderson Schroeder.

Joy and "Andy" Anderson. Courtesy Joy Anderson Schroeder.

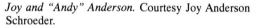

Mr and Mrs Robert Sidney Anderson in 1942. Courtesy Joy Anderson Schroeder.

Lt(jg) Anderson did not see the Jap that crept up on his back and shot at him.

His wingman, Jack Chasnoff was the first to contact "Andy" telling him to bail out that his plane was on fire! "Andy", knowing that each plane had cost the government over $135,000 figured he better try to save it and would ride it down but as he got low over the water it was evident that he had to bail out so he slow-rolled it over and left the plane at about 400 feet off the water.

He was so low by that time that as his 'chute' opened, he hit the water at the same time, causing him to jack-knife, breaking his back in three places, breaking three ribs and an ankle.

He got into his life raft and waved at the squadron and knew that they had seen him and would return for him as soon as possible; so he cut loose his parachute.

After the dog-fight the squadron refueled and did go out to rescue him but the Pacific is a mighty big ocean, and though he could hear them droning all day long and he waved at them, they could not see him. The sun shone so hot he got 3rd degree burns even in his hair as he had nothing to cover up with. At night it got so cold he almost froze. Three times he climbed out of his raft as he could see an island and tried to swim but his injuries were too much for him to make any progress. The "Skipper" told the men they would be able to go out at dawn and see if they could find "Andy" one more time.

As it turned out when they were airborne over the water there was a light and they figured it must be "Andy" and so they hovered until daylight and there he was—eureka!

A PBY was called in to secure the rescue and when he was brought back on a stretcher they all said they would never have

Robert "Andy" Anderson, sportsman. Courtesy Joy Anderson Schroeder.

Robert "Andy" Anderson, Businessman 1946. Courtesy Joy Anderson Schroeder.

found him if he hadn't had a flashlight and were stunned to find that he had no flashlight or any way to signal them. He was so sorry to leave this group of men that he had lived with for so long, but on to the hospital.

BRADFORD WARREN BAKER

Bradford Warren Baker was born on 3 July, 1918 in Los Angeles, California. He was educated at Eastern Washington College of Education, University of Idaho.

He became an Aviation Cadet on 1 July, 1942 and reported to N.A.S. Jacksonville for training. He accepted an appointment as an Ensign on 1 January, 1943, and was designated a Naval Aviator on 5 January, 1943.

He then went to N.A.S. Melbourne for training reporting on 10 March, 1943.

After Melbourne he reported to Carrier Qualification Training Unit, Norfolk, Virginia, and then to VF-17 on 12 May, 1943.

After recuperation he was ordered to the Naval Aviation Supply Depot, Philadelphia, PA, for one year. He could not believe it would take him a year so he put in for another fighter squadron immediately! At the end of the year he was given his desire and was sent to Cape Cod, Massachusetts, to a new squadron (VBF-74) with the same skipper he had at VF-17—he was so happy; on 14 August, 1945, the Japanese surrendered and the war was over.

He moved back to St. Louis, Missouri, where he attended Aircraft and Engine School and while there was able to buy out a parts company and became a businessman until he retired in 1968 at age 50. He had by-pass surgery in 1971 and for many years suffered from Paget's Disease (a painful bone disease) and died one year after attending his first reunion in Illinois in 1984. He died on his 43rd wedding anniversary during his second by-pass surgery on May 14, 1985.

Decorations:
Purple Heart
Air Medal
Navy Unit Commendation
"Andy" Anderson shot down one Japanese plane and 2 damaged in his brief combat tour with VF-17.

Medals :
World War II Victory Medal
American Campaign Medal
Navy Unit Commendation
Asiatic-Pacific Area Campaign Medal (1 bronze star)
Purple Heart
Air Medal
Died :
Missing in action 17 November, 1943. Failed to return from patrol duty following action over Empress Augusta Bay.

He is credited with one confirmed Zeke on 11 November, 1943.

(Back Row) L-R *Earl May, Thad Bell, "Duke" Henning, Tom Killefer, Walter Schub.* (Front Row) *"Timmy" Gile, Tom Blackburn, Brad Baker, Hal Jackson. Brad Baker third from left, front row.* Courtesy U.S. Naval Historical Center / M.W. "Butch" Davenport Collection.

SHELTON "RAY" BEACHAM

The original native aviator from Kitty Hawk, N.C.; the Wright brothers were residents of Dayton, Ohio.

Shelton Ray Beacham was born on 28 September, 1918 in Norfolk, Virginia. He was educated at Kitty Hawk High School, Kitty Hawk, N.C., Eastern High School, Washington D.C., and Wilson Teachers College, Washington D.C.

He reported for duty at N.A.S. Anacostia, D.C., on November 15, 1939 until December 15, 1939 for aviation training. He then reported to N.A.S. Pensacola, FL, on February 26, 1940 until August 26, 1940 for aviation training.

He was designated a Naval Aviator on 11 January, 1940, and on 10 December, 1940 reported to Instructors school, Pensacola. He instructed cadets in Jacksonville VN-11A in 1941-42, with Wally Schub, who would also later serve with VF-17.

On 1st April, 1944 the following account was released to the press.

Lieutenant Shelton R. Beacham, 1617 "B" Street S.E. Washington, D.C., wears the Air Medal for his exploits with the famous "Skull and Crossbones" Fighter Squadron in the Pacific.

The squadron covered the initial landings on Bougainville in November 1943.

Lt. Beacham was awarded the medal for his part in two air actions in this area and has just returned to the States for leave. In the first air engagement Beacham shot down a Zero, even though his plane was damaged by cannon fire.

The second action was a low altitude dog fight over Empress Augusta Bay when Beacham's four plane division had a perfect score. They engaged six Jap Zeros, shot them all down. Beacham had another Jap plane added to his total.

Lt. Beacham also wears the purple Heart for wounds incurred when returning from a raid on Rabaul. The air group was attacked by 75 Zeros, and Beacham's plane was damaged. He was able to

Lt. Shelton "Ray" Beacham, Bougainville 1944. Courtesy National Archives.

bring it back to Bougainville, but was forced to crash land in the water.

He finished the two tours with VF-17 credited with 2 confirmed victories. After VF-17 he spent the next year and a half as Executive Officer of three squadrons in sequence; VOF-3, VF-89, and VBF-152. After the war he underwent six months C.I.C. Officers' training at St. Simons Island, GA, in 1946. Upon graduation joined staff of C.I.C. Officers' school and later helped move it to N.A.S. Glenview, IL. In October 1948 became staff C.I.C. Officer of Carrier Division Fifteen at San Diego. Participated in advanced A.S.W.(Hunter-Killer) operations for 18 months. Left ComCarDiv Fifteen in June 1950 for General Line School at Newport, R.I., but Korean police action caused the cancellation of General Line School, so after a two month tour of duty as All-Weather Air Controller at Fleet Training Center, NorVa, was transferred to N.A.S., NorVa in September 1950. Spent 9 months as Assistant Operations Officer at N.A.S. Norfolk before becoming Inspection Group Officer in the Overhaul and Repair Department, N.A.S. Norfolk.

Ray Beacham died on 11 January, 1997 after a long illness.
Decorations:
Distinguished Flying Cross
4 Air Medals
Purple Heart
Navy Unit Commendation
Asiatic-Pacific Campaign Medal with 3 stars
American Defense Service Medal

Close up of "Ray" Beacham's medals on display at Dare County Regional Airport Museum. Courtesy Harry Bridges.

THADDEUS RICHARD "JUGGY" BELL

Thaddeus Richard Bell was born on 8 June, 1918 in Montreal, Canada. He was educated at Stanford University where he received an A.B. Degree.

On 1 February, 1941 he became an Aviation Cadet. On 10 February, 1941 he reported to N.A.S. Pensacola for training then to Miami on July 4, 1941. On 16 July he accepted an appointment as an Ensign, and on 23 July he was designated a Naval Aviator.

On 2 September, 1941 he reported to N.A.S. Jacksonville, and was appointed Lt(jg) on 1 October, 1942. On 4 February, 1943 he reported to Carrier Qualification Training Unit and then to VF-17. On 1 October, 1943 he was appointed Lieutenant.

Medals :
Air Medal
Purple Heart
Navy Unit Commendation
American Defense Service Medal
Asiatic-Pacific Area Campaign Medal with (2) bronze stars
World War II Victory Medal
Died :
Missing in action 27 January, 1944. Failed to return from a combat mission over Rabaul Airfield, New Britain.

The following account was released in January 1944.

Lieutenant Thaddeus Richard Bell, U.S.N.R., 26 year old son of Edward H. Bell, care of American Can Company, 111 Sutter St., San Francisco, and previously declared missing in action, has been awarded the Air Medal with a citation for "outstanding airmanship and gallant devotion to duty", Twelfth Naval District Headquarters announced today.

Lieutenant Bell, a member of a Naval fighting squadron operating against the Japanese in the Solomon Islands' area until this

L-R (Back Row) *Paul Cordray, "Ike" Kepford, Thad Bell, "Butch" Davenport.* (Front Row) *Hal Jackson, "Chico" Freeman. Thad Bell back row third from left.* Courtesy U.S. Navy photo. Robert L. Lawson Collection.

year, was flying cover with his squadron when attacked by more than one hundred Jap aircraft threatening the security of American surface forces.

Fighting against tremendous odds, Lieutenant Bell held tenaciously to his targets, flying through the intense anti-aircraft fire of our own ships to press home his attack, the citation reveals. He succeeded in shooting down two Jap bombers out of a formation of thirty during the action.

The citation was signed for the president by Secretary of the Navy, James Forrestal.

He is credited with 2 confirmed and one damaged Japanese plane.

JOHN T. "TOM" BLACKBURN

Tom Blackburn was born in Annapolis, Maryland, on 24 June, 1912. Blackburn kept his family tradition going and graduated in 1933 from the same U S Naval Academy as his father, uncle and brother.

After obligatory duty in surface vessels, he was accepted for flight training and finished the course in 1937. He flew with various carrier squadrons over the next four years, becoming commanding officer of VF-29 in 1942.

In January 1943 Blackburn was given orders to form a new Fighter Squadron, VF 17.

The squadron would fly the tricky and new Chance Vought Corsair. Blackburn had until September 1943 to have the squadron ready for combat.

The squadron worked hard to make the unforgiving F4U a suitable carrier airplane despite numerous technical problems that had to be overcome. The pilots loved the Corsair and after extensive training grew accustomed to the new high performance fighter.

They were called Hogs as one pilot said. "On the ground they were about as cooperative as a hog on ice".

In training Blackburn stressed the importance of teamwork and gunnery, and by the time the Bunker Hill was ready he had molded together an effective fighting squadron.

Tom Blackburn, Bougainville 1944. Courtesy National Archives.

VF 17 shipped out on the Bunker Hill in September 1943, but en route to Pearl Harbor the squadron received new orders. They were to be transferred from their carrier home to a land base in the Solomon Islands.

After two tours VF-17 became the top scoring Navy squadron and broke records in the Pacific theater.

In his post-war career Tom Blackburn was Commander Air Group 74 on the U.S.S. Midway, the carrier he would later command. Other flying duty included command of the Heavy Attack squadron 5 and Heavy Attack Wing 1. Captain Blackburn retired in 1962 to grow grapes in California's Napa Valley.

He died on 21 March 1994 at age 81, and is Interred in the Arlington National Cemetery.

Decorations
2 Navy Crosses
2 DFCs
3 Air Medals.

He shot down 11 confirmed, 5 probable, and 3 damaged Japanese planes.

Vice-Admiral James Stockdale put it this way. "If ever a man was tailor-made to be an across the board role model and leader of men flying and fighting from ships at sea, it was Tommy Blackburn".

"Hap" Bowers, Bougainville 1944. Courtesy National Archives.

GEORGE FRANKLIN "HAP" BOWERS

"Hap" Bowers was born on 15 September, 1918 and was educated at the University of Wisconsin (B.S. Engineering, class of 1940). He was assigned to VF-17 after he completed his training and arrived on 4 January, 1943.

He completed two tours of duty with VF-17 and scored one probable victory.

His other assignments included N.A.S. Miami, N.A.A.S. Green Cove Springs, Fighting Squadron 74, Fighting Squadron 58A, and Fighting Squadron 724.

Decorations
D.F.C.
Navy Unit Commendation
World War II Victory Medal
American Campaign Medal
Asiatic-Pacific Campaign Medal

"Hap" Bowers at the 1994 VF-17 reunion in Oshkosh. Courtesy Donna Bushman EAA.

HOWARD McCLAIN "TEETH" BURRISS

"Teeth" Burriss was born on 28 March, 1921, in Washington, D.C., and grew up in Granville, Ohio. He was educated at Denison University.

He joined the Navy in 1942, winning his wings at N.A.S. Jacksonville in April 1942.

From there he reported to VF-17.

He died on 31 January, 1944, missing in action in aerial combat, after a strike on Tobera, New Britain.

Decorations:

Silver Star

DFC

Purple Heart

Air Medal.

Asiatic-Pacific Area Campaign Medal with 2 bronze stars.

World War II Victory Medal.

He is credited with 7.5 confirmed victories.

JACK M. CHASNOFF

Jack Chasnoff was born in St. Louis, Missouri, on 23 July, 1921. He describes how he became a Naval Aviator with VF-17.

"In December of 1941, I was in my senior year at the University of Chicago. I was 20 years of age, and with a clarity of vision which I have not been able to match in my later years, I had recog-

Jack Chasnoff at Ondongo, November 1943. Courtesy U.S. Navy photo. Robert L. Lawson Collection.

Skull and Crossbones ace "Teeth" Burriss who scored 7.5 Japanese planes whilst flying with VF-17. Courtesy U.S. Naval Historical Center / M.W. "Butch" Davenport Collection.

nized the inevitability of our involvement in World War II. The movies depicted the trench warfare, and the aerial warfare of World War I, had convinced me that flying was the only viable choice for me, so I had taken advantage of the Civilian Pilot Training Program, which the government had instituted a couple of years before. The program provided free ground school and flight training and led to a private pilot's license.

"After the Japanese attack on Pearl Harbor, I went home for the Christmas holidays and told my parents that I intended to leave the University and join the Navy. From the Navy's point of view, however, I was seriously underweight, tipping the scales at 115 lbs. It took me almost two months of physical training and heavy calorie intake before I could meet the Navy's minimum weight of 125 lbs. by eating bananas and drinking water before reporting to be weighed. I began my Navy career in February of 1942 with primary flight training at the Naval Air Station at St. Louis airport. From there my class was sent to Corpus Christi Naval Air Station for basic training, after which I was selected for advanced training in fighters, which had been my choice.

"I completed my training and was commissioned an Ensign in October of 1942, and was assigned to operational training in Miami, Florida. Alice and I took advantage of my travel time to marry in St. Louis before reporting to Opa Locka Naval Air Station in Miami. After completion of that training and of carrier qualification landings in Chesapeake Bay, I was assigned to VF-17, which was commissioned on January 1, 1943, at the Naval Air Station at Norfolk, Virginia.

"After leaving VF-17 in January of 1944, I became a flight instructor in operational training at Melbourne, Florida, and then applied for a transfer to fighter director school.

"Upon completion of that training, I was assigned as fighter director to a new Essex class aircraft carrier, the Boxer, then under construction at the Portsmouth Navy Yard.

"In the interim, in December 1944, Alice had returned to St. Louis and had given birth to our daughter, Judith Ann.

LEMUEL D. COOKE

Lem Cooke was born on 7 October, 1916, in Hernando, Mississippi. On 9 July, 1935, he was appointed Midshipman in the U.S. Navy Naval Academy.

On 1 June, 1939, he accepted appointment as an Ensign at the U.S. Naval Academy Annapolis, Maryland.

On 24 June, 1939, he reported to the U.S.S. Ranger, and on 2 October, 1941, reported to N.A.S. Pensacola, Florida.

On 1 November, 1941, he was appointed Lt(jg), and on 22 February, 1942, designated a Naval Aviator. He reported to the aviation unit of the U.S.S. South Dakota on 21 April, 1942, and accepted temporary appointment as Lieutenant on 15 June, 1942.

On 28 February, 1943, he reported to Patrol Squadron 211 and on 5 March, 1943 reported to VF-17. When he finished his tour with VF-17 he reported to Fighting Squadron 38 as Commanding Officer on 28 January, 1944.

On 15 April, 1944, he reported to Naval Operational Training, N.A.S. Jacksonville and on 23 June, 1944, assigned permanent duty at Naval Auxiliary Air Station, Green Cove Springs, Florida.

He reported to N.A.S. Miami, Florida, on 6 January, 1945, and then on 22 May, 1945, reported to Bombing Fighting Squadron 74.

He assumed command of Bombing Fighting Squadron 74 on 24 May, 1945 and reported to Staff of Commander Air Atlantic on 23 September, 1946.

On 1 October, 1947, he accepted appointment as Lieutenant Commander to rank from 15 March, 1944.

On 27 April, 1949, he reported to Aircraft Development Squadron Three in N.A.S. Atlantic City, New Jersey.

On 31 August, 1949, he accepted appointment as commander, temporary to rank from 1 July, 1949.

Medals :
Distinguished Flying Cross
Gold Star in lieu of second Distinguished Flying Cross
Air Medal
Gold Star in lieu of second Air Medal
Gold Star in lieu of third Air Medal

"In the following months and until August 1945, I was with the Boxer, going on her shakedown cruise to Guantanamo Bay, Cuba, refitting in Norfolk, and eventually going to sea, taking her through the Panama Canal and up the west coast to San Francisco. While we were making final preparations there to join the Pacific fleet, the war against Japan ended, and within a few days, I was detached and sent back to St. Louis for a month before being discharged in September. I entered law school, completed it in two calendar years by attending classes on a year-round basis, passed the bar examination late in 1947, and began to practice law early in 1948".

Decorations :
Air Medal with Gold Star in lieu of a second one
Distinguished Flying Cross
Navy Unit Commendation
World War II Victory Medal
Asiatic-Pacific Campaign Medal with 1 star
American Campaign Medal

Lem Cooke at Ondongo, November 1943. Courtesy Lennard Edmisten.

Gold Star in lieu of fourth Air Medal
Gold Star in lieu of fifth Air Medal
Gold Star in lieu of sixth Air Medal
Gold Star in lieu of seventh Air Medal
Gold Star in lieu of eighth Air Medal
Letter of Commendation with Ribbon
Navy Unit Commendation (U.S.S. South Dakota)
Navy Unit Commendation (VF-17)
American Defense Service Medal with "Fleet" clasp
American Campaign Medal
Asiatic-Pacific Campaign Medal
World War II Victory Medal
Lem Cooke died on 17 May, 1950, in Atlantic City, New Jersey, when the jet fighter he was flying crashed.

PAUL CORDRAY

Paul Cordray was born on 4 September, 1919, in Grand Prairie, Texas. He was educated at Winnetha Trade School, Sunset High School, and East Texas Teacher College.

He joined the Navy in 1942 and graduated from N.A.S. Corpus Christi, Texas, in August 1942. He was assigned to VF-17 at N.A.S. Norfolk.

"Paul and Earl (May) went out wolfing together. I flew on Paul a lot and he was a hell of a nice guy and a good pilot". Said Dan Cunningham. He completed two tours of duty with VF-17 and scored 6 confirmed, one probable, and 3 damaged.

He returned to the States in May 1944 and was assigned to VBF 10 flying F4U-1Ds from the U.S.S. Intrepid. During his next combat tour he was credited with one more victory when he destroyed a Zeke on 16 April, 1945, near Kikai Airfield, Japan.

Whilst in the Naval service Paul Cordray had the following assignments: N.A.S. Dallas, TX, N.A.S. Miami, TX, N.A.S. Greencove Springs, FL, N.A.S. Memphis, TN, and Composite Squadron 3 (VC-3).

Paul Cordray left the Navy after the war and passed away on 20 October, 1963.

Decorations
DFC with 3 gold stars
Air Medal with 5 gold stars.
World War II Victory Medal
Asiatic-Pacific Campaign Medal
Navy Unit Commendation

VF-17 ace Paul Cordray who scored 6 Japanese planes, at Bougainville 1944. Courtesy National Archives.

DANIEL GERALD CUNNINGHAM

Dan Cunningham was born on 3 July, 1919, in Chicago, Illinois. He graduated from Loyola University in 1940 with a BSC in Economics. Cunningham joined the Navy shortly after, and entered flight training. He received his wings at N.A.S. Corpus Christi, Texas, with follow on fighter training at N.A.S. Miami, Florida.

In February 1943, Lt(jg) Cunningham joined VF-17. The squadron was the first Navy unit to be assigned the new F4U-1 Corsair, and the short, stocky Cunningham needed two extra parachute cushions and one parachute behind his back to function in the big gull-winged fighter's huge cockpit.

He completed two tours of duty with VF-17 and scored seven confirmed victories and 1.5 damaged.

He shot down four Zekes on a single mission on 19 February, 1944.

Cunningham returned to combat in early 1945 with VBF-10 aboard the Intrepid but did not add to his score again.

After the war, Cunningham became a successful life insurance and real estate salesman. He later bought a seat on the Chicago Mercantile Exchange, trading commodities.

Dan Cunningham ace with seven victories at Bougainville 1944. Courtesy National Archives.

Decorations
Navy Cross
DFC
3 Air Medals
Navy Unit Commendation Medal.
Asiatic-Pacific Campaign Medal
World War II Victory Medal

MERL WILLIAM "BUTCH" DAVENPORT

"Butch" Davenport was born on 14 March, 1918, in Sterling, Michigan. He was educated at Wayne University for 3 years.

He completed the Navy pilot training program early in 1942 and then joined VF-17.

He completed both tours of duty with VF-17 and served as Engineering Officer. He is credited with 6.25 Japanese planes.

In his Naval career Davenport had the following assignments: N.A.S. Pensacola, U.S.S. Saipan, N.A.S. Corpus Christi, N.A.S. Patuxent River, Office of ComNavEu., London, England.

He also served at N.A.S. Thosse Ile, and N.A.S. Atlantic City.

He returned to civilian life after World War II.

"Country" Landreth has fond memories of "Butch".

"As a Test Pilot "Butch" made the record of the fastest climb to 10,000ft in an F8F (prop aircraft) I think it was 96 seconds from a standing start. He did that out of Wright Patterson. He held the record for some time.

"Butch" has gone now. He came by here in California flying his own airplane, in 1989. He stayed overnight and it was a wonderful visit. We didn't know it at the time as he was still in good shape and was out jogging before the sun came up while he was here.

"Later it dawned on us that he was going around saying goodbye to all the guys in the squadron he could find, because he subsequently died of cancer. Even though he had a daughter in the experimental cancer clinic up in Washington State (University of Washington).

"He tracked down every possible lead for a cure to treating his cancer including his daughter's studies. So without saying so I think he was going round and having a last visit with everybody". He died in Dexter, Michigan, on 19 September, 1989.

Decorations;
D.F.C.
American Campaign Medal
American Defense Service Medal
World War II Victory Medal

CLYDE HOWARD DUNN

Clyde Dunn was born on 17 December, 1922, in Pawnee Station, Kansas. He was educated at Fort Scott Junior College, Fort Scott, Kansas.

He accepted appointment on 1 June, 1943 as an Ensign, and on 9 June, 1943, was designated a Naval Aviator. He reported to Corpus Christi for training and on 15 June reported to Melbourne, Florida, for further training. On 9 August he reported to Carrier Qualification Unit, Glenview, Illinois, then further ordered to N.A.S. Norfolk.

Dan Cunningham at Oshkosh for the VF-17 reunion in July/August 1994. Courtesy Donna Bushman EAA.

"Butch" Davenport Engineering Officer and ace with 6.25 Japanese planes to his credit. Courtesy National Archives.

On 1 September he reported to Carrier Air Force Unit 21, and then reported to VF-17 on 6 September, 1943.

Medals :
American Area Campaign Medal
World War II Victory Medal
Navy Unit Commendation
Asiatic-Pacific Area Campaign Medal-Two (2) bronze stars
Purple Heart
Air Medal

He was listed as missing in action on 17 February, 1944, in the vicinity of Rabaul, New Britain, when his plane failed to return from an attack against enemy shipping.

JOHN ORRIN "FATSO" ELLSWORTH

John Ellsworth was born on 22 September, 1923, in Kingston, New York. He became an Aviation Cadet on 1 July, 1942 and reported to N.A.S. Jacksonville for training. He accepted an appointment as an Ensign on 16 January, 1943. He was designated a Naval Aviator on February 2, 1943. He was detached from N.A.S. Jacksonville and then reported to N.A.S. Melbourne for training.

On 20 April, 1943 he reported to Carrier Qualification Training Unit Norfolk, Virginia, and reported on May 12 to VF-17.

He was appointed Lt(jg) on 1 March, 1944, and detached from VF-17 on 2 April, 1944.

He completed two tours of duty with VF-17 and scored two confirmed and one probable victory.

After a short leave he reported, on May 9, to Headquarters Squadron Fleet Air Wing. He died in a plane crash on 4 June, 1944, near Weeksville, North Carolina.

DORIS CLYDE "CHICO" FREEMAN

"Chico" Freeman was born on 18 April, 1920, in Los Angeles, California. He was educated at Ventura Junior College and Oceanside Junior College.

Joining the Navy after the Pearl Harbor attack, "Chico" won his wings at N.A.S. Jacksonville and became carrier-qualified on the paddle wheel carrier Wolverine.

He reported to VF-17 on 11 March, 1943 and completed two tours of duty and scored two confirmed and two probable victories.

Returning to the States in April 1944, Freeman helped form VF-84 under Roger Hedrick. Flying from the U.S.S. Bunker Hill, he downed a Tony on 17 February, and in April added three more to become an ace. His last victories occurred on 11 May, 1945, when he downed two Nates. He had just landed his F4U and was in the VF-84 ready room when a kamikaze hit the Bunker Hill and exploded killing Freeman and many of his squadron mates.

His final score was 9 confirmed and 2 probables.

Decorations

D.F.C. with 2 gold stars

Purple Heart

Air Medal with 4 gold stars

Asiatic-Pacific Area Campaign Medal.

The following account was released to the press shortly after Freeman's return home from VF-17's tour of duty.

"Two Japanese planes were shot down and two more probably destroyed when they approached "Los Angeles City Limits.""

"The enemy was in the Solomon Islands when the action occurred, however, and the "City Limits" was a Navy fighter plane piloted by Lt(jg) Doris Clyde Freeman, 24, U.S.N.R., of 5141 Sunlight Place, Los Angeles.

"Operating in the Solomon Islands and Bismarck Archipelago, Lieutenant Freeman flew the "Los Angeles City Limits" on 83 combat missions, strafing enemy positions and escorting American bombers.

"Over Empress Augusta Bay, Bougainville, two Japanese pilots got too close to the 'City Limits' and were shot down. The Navy flyer was awarded the Air Medal for this brilliant action. Last February 7 Lieutenant Freeman probably destroyed one of many

John "Fatso" Ellsworth at Bougainville 1944. Courtesy National Archives.

"Chico" Freeman who later made ace with VF-84, at Bougainville 1944. Courtesy National Archives.

enemy fighters which attempted to intercept a formation of bombers he was escorting over Vunakanau airfield, Rabaul.

"In a delayed sweep, after the bombers had attacked and retired, Lieutenant Freeman severely damaged another Zero as it was making a run on a member of his flight.

"For these achievements, a Gold Star in lieu of a second Air Medal was recently awarded the Navy flyer by Rear Adm. William K. Harrill, U.S.N., Commander, Fleet Air, West Coast, in ceremonies at the San Diego Naval Air Station, where he is now on duty."

CARL WILSON GILBERT

Carl Gilbert was born and raised in St. Louis, Missouri. He completed two tours of duty with VF-17 in the Solomon Islands and scored one confirmed and one probable victory.

Carl Gilbert at Bougainville 1944. Courtesy National Archives.

CLEMENT DEXTER "TIMMY" GILE

"Timmy" Gile was born on 30 January, 1918, in New York City, New York. Lt. Gile graduated from Yale (American History BA), class of 1939, where he stroked the varsity crew in his senior year.

After completing the Navy flight training program he completed a tour of instructor duty before joining VF-17. He completed two tours of duty with VF-17 and scored 8 confirmed Japanese planes and .5 damaged.

Clement Gile returned to civilian life following World War II and ended up a Vice President with Morgan Stanley.

He died in November 1978.

Decorations

Silver Star

D.F.C.

The following press statement was released shortly after VF-17 and Gile returned to the States:

"Lieutenant Clement D. Gile of Pittsburgh, PA, one of the aces of the famous "Skull and Crossbones" Fighter Squadron, is back in the United States after action-crammed months in the Pacific in which he shot down seven Jap Zeros and one Torpedo Bomber.

"Lt. Gile got the Jap Torpedo Bomber just off the bow of an aircraft carrier he was covering while the carrier planes were bombing enemy installations on Bougainville. Lt. Gile spotted the Jap plane in a torpedo run on the carrier, hit him on the first pass at about 1,000 yards from carrier. However, the plane continued its run, was brought down by Gile just as it was passing the bow of the carrier. The Jap plane blew up immediately without ever having launched its torpedo. Lt. Gile refuses credit for saving the carrier, but it is likely that his initial attack on the Jap at 1,000 yards threw him off so that he was unable to release his torpedo.

"Lt. Gile had a field day in bringing down Jap Zeros on November 17, 1943, when he made three passes on a Japanese force headed back to Rabaul, got a Zero each time.

"Lt. Gile bagged his four other Zeros while escorting U.S. bombers in their daily attacks on Rabaul in January and February of this year. Lt. Gile is a Yale graduate (American History BA), class of 1939, where he stroked the varsity crew in his senior year."

"Timmy" Gile VF-17 ace with 8 Japanese planes. Courtesy National Archives.

Doug Gutenkunst's grave on Bougainville. Courtesy U.S. Navy photo. Robert L. Lawson Collection.

DOUGLAS HUGO CHARLES GUTENKUNST

Doug Gutenkunst was born on 17 January, 1919, in Owen Sound, Canada. He was educated at Brown University (A.B. Degree).

He became an Aviation Cadet on 7 April, 1942, and reported to N.A.S. Corpus Christi for training. He accepted an appointment as an Ensign on 1 October, 1942 and designated a Naval Aviator on 8 October, 1942. On 15 October, 1942, he reported to N.A.S. Miami for training. He reported to Carrier Qualification Training Unit on November 22 and then to VF-17. He was appointed Lt(jg) on 1 October, 1943.

He scored 4 confirmed Japanese planes and one damaged before his tragic accident. He died on 30 January, 1944 one mile south of Piva Yoke strip Bougainville B.S.I., as pilot of an F4U that crashed following mid-air collision with a Marine pilot.

Decorations
D.F.C.

The following press release was made in July 1944:

"The Distinguished Flying Cross has been awarded posthumously to Lt(jg) Douglas H.C. Gutenkunst, pilot of a Navy fighter plane, for 'heroism and extraordinary achievement' during two tours of duty in the Solomons Islands area.

"Lt. Gutenkunst, son of Mrs. Gertrude Gutenkunst, of 3418 N. Summit, Milwaukee, Wisconsin, was commended first for his accomplishments from October 27 to December 1, 1943. During that time, the citation accompanying the award reported, he 'ably assisted his section leader in downing three hostile planes and, operating repeatedly in the face of heavy anti-aircraft fire, participated in numerous strafing missions against Japanese shipping and shore installations on Bougainville.'

"On his second tour of duty," the citation continued, "he relentlessly engaged enemy aircraft in combat on numerous occasions, escorted a group of scout bombers in a strike on Lakunai Airfield, shooting down two hostile craft, and while accompanying a squadron of torpedo bombers in fierce attack on Tobera Airfield, destroyed two more enemy planes."

JAMES ALEX HALFORD

Jim Halford was born in Taurusa, California, on February 7, 1919. He attended the Junior College, Visalia, California, and Fresno State College, Fresno, California. On January 14, 1941, he entered the U.S. Naval Reserve in Oakland, California, and had preliminary flight training at the Naval Reserve Aviation Base there. He was appointed Aviation Cadet April 31, 1941, and had flight training at the Naval Air Station, Corpus Christi, Texas. He was commissioned Ensign, U.S.N.R., December 24, 1941, and was ordered to active duty in a fighting squadron attached to a carrier.

He was awarded the Distinguished Flying Cross with the citation: "For heroic achievement in aerial flight as a pilot of a Fighting Squadron in action against enemy Japanese forces in the Battle of Midway, June 4-6, 1942. While engaged in combat patrol, Ensign Halford, at great personal risk, made a determined attack against enemy aircraft approaching the U.S.S. Yorktown and assisted in the destruction of at least one enemy airplane. On June 6, 1942, he delivered an effective strafing attack against two enemy Japanese heavy cruisers and two destroyers, inflicting heavy damage on those enemy vessels. His skill as an airman, his courageous perseverance and devotion to duty were in keeping with the highest traditions of the United States Naval Service."

He completed one combat tour with VF-17 but did not add to his 3.5 kills.

He has not been heard of by the squadron since VF17 was decommissioned in April 1944.

ROGER RICHARDS HEDRICK

Roger Richards Hedrick was born in Pasadena, California, on September 2, 1914, son of Perry Lee and Mabel Richards Hedrick. He attended Los Angeles Junior College, from which he graduated with the degree of Associate in Arts, and entered the Naval service as an Aviation Cadet, U.S. Naval Reserve, on October 26, 1936, after brief enlisted service that summer. He was designated a Naval Aviator on September 10, 1937, and commissioned Ensign, U.S.N.R., on August 3, 1939. Through subsequent promotion he attained the rank of Captain, to date from July 1, 1956, having transferred to the U.S. Navy in the rank of Lieutenant (junior grade) on March 21, 1941. Upon retirement on November 1, 1958, he was advanced to the rank of Rear Admiral on the basis of combat citations.

After flight training (Class 95-c) at the Naval Air Station, Pensacola, Florida, he was ordered to Fighting Squadron 4, based on the U.S.S. Ranger. Spending three and one-half years as a fighter pilot, he next served from May, 1941, until January, 1943, at the Naval Air Station Miami, Florida. This solid background, enhanced by a reputation as an exceptional aerial marksman brought Hedrick to VF-17. Then served as Executive Officer of Fighting Squadron 17, the first Naval squadron in combat in F4U (Corsairs).

His squadron was land based in the Solomon Islands and operated from Ondongo, New Georgia, and Bougainville, and he took part in the Bismarck Archipelago operation and the Treasury Island-Bougainville operation, with nine confirmed air victories during the period ending in May 1944, when he returned to the United States.

Lt. Cdr. Roger Hedrick, VF-17 Executive Officer and ace with nine Japanese planes. He later went on to score another three planes as commanding officer of VF-84. Courtesy National Archives.

Fighting Squadron 17 was awarded the Navy Unit Commendation for operations at Treasury Island, Bougainville, Rabaul and Green Islands, and he was personally awarded the D.F.C. and a Gold Star in lieu of the second D.F.C.

In May 1944 he was assigned duty as Commanding Officer of Fighting Squadron 84. He led that squadron in the Iwo Jima operation and first carrier strikes on Tokyo, getting three more Jap fighters for a total of 12 confirmed victories. He participated in the Okinawa Gunto operation until the U.S.S. Bunker Hill was hit by two kamikazes on May 11, 1945. That aircraft carrier was awarded the Presidential Unit Citation for heroic service (and that of her Air Groups-17, 8, 4 and 84) during the period November 11, 1943 through May 11, 1945. He was personally awarded the Silver Star Medal, Gold Stars in lieu of the third and fourth D.F.C.s, and the Air Medal and two Gold Stars in lieu of the second and third Air Medal. The Air Medals were for meritorious achievement in aerial flight during operations against the Japanese (five strikes each) during the periods February 16 to March 23, 1945; March 24 to 30, 1945; and March 31, to April 13, 1945; and the fourth Distinguished Flying Cross was for completing twenty strikes on hostile shipping, airfields and installations during the overall period of February 16 to May 5, 1945.

In July 1945 he assumed command of Experimental Fighting Squadron 200, and from October of that year until May 1946 had command, successively, of Fighter Squadron 200 of Composite Air Group, Operational Development Force, and of the Composite Air Group, Operational Development Group. He was a student at the Naval School, General Line, Newport, Rhode Island, the next year,

Roger Hedrick in 1946. Courtesy National Archives.

Roger Hedrick in 1954. Courtesy Roger Hedrick.

and in June 1947 reported to the Naval Air Station Jacksonville, Florida, for duty as Officer in Charge of the Instructors Aviation Training Unit. From November 1948 to July 1949 he had similar duty at the Naval Air Station, Corpus Christi, Texas.

Completing the course at the Naval War College, Newport, Rhode Island, in June 1950, he became Executive Officer of the Fleet All Weather Training Unit, Pacific, at Barbers Point, T.H., training night attack and night fighter pilots for the Korean hostilities. On September 19, 1952, he reported to the Naval Air Station, Whidbey Island, Washington, as Executive Officer. When detached in June 1954 he had brief instruction at the Naval Schools Command, U.S. Naval Station, Treasure Island, San Francisco, California, and the same month reported on board the U.S.S. Boxer (CVA-21). He served as Executive Officer of that carrier until September 1955, after which he was Commanding Officer of Air Development Squadron 4, the F7U-3M Cutlass squadron which first deployed the Sparrow 111 air-to-air missile, until July 1957.

In August 1957 he reported for a tour of duty in the Bureau of Ordnance, Navy Department, Washington D.C., where he served as Deputy Director, Plans and Programs Division for development of the Polaris ballistic missile submarine weapons system, until October 1958, when he was relieved of all active duty for retirement on November 1, 1958.

In addition to the Silver Star Medal, Distinguished Flying Cross with three Gold Stars, Air Medal with two Gold Stars, Presidential Unit Citation Ribbon and Navy Unit Commendation Ribbon, Rear Admiral Hedrick has the American Defense Service Medal with star; the American Campaign Medal; Asiatic-Pacific Campaign Medal with four operation stars; World War II Victory Medal; and the National Defense Medal.

Mills Schanuel said this about Roger Hedrick.

"I flew on Roger Hedrick's wing during the life of VF-17. This is true—from the day the squadron was commissioned in Norfolk to its decommissioning in San Francisco, Hedrick was the 'nuts-and-bolts' engineer who made things work. In addition, he was a superb flyer. Never, no matter how hairy the combat situation, did I ever see him rattled or confused. Watching him carefully position his plane for a kill is something I will never forget. I feel that Roger Hedrick's contribution to the success of the squadron has not been fully appreciated".

Roger Hedrick at the VF-17 reunion in Oshkosh July/August 1994. Courtesy Donna Bushman EAA.

ROBERT HUGH "WINDY" HILL

Robert H. Hill, U.S.N.R. (Ret.), was born on 21 May, 1920, in Beaufort, North Carolina, graduated from the University of North Carolina in June 1940, and was selected for the first class of the V-7 Midshipman School in New York City. He graduated and was commissioned an Ensign in November 1940, and was assigned to the four-stack destroyer U.S.S. Upshur (DD-144). In July 1941 he was transferred to the U.S.S. Texas (BB-35), remaining aboard until he resigned his commission in February 1942 to enter Naval Aviation Cadet Flight Training at N.A.S. Atlanta, Georgia.

He was re-commissioned an Ensign and received his Navy Wings of Gold at N.A.S. Jacksonville, Florida, in January 1943. After being assigned to VF-17 (the first Navy carrier-based F4U Corsair squadron) he served aboard the U.S.S. Bunker Hill (CV-17) and was land based at New Georgia and Bougainville, Solomon Islands, in 1943/44, where he is credited with one confirmed victory.

In 1945 he was a member of VBF-10 operating in the Okinawa and Japan areas aboard the U.S.S. Intrepid (CV-11) and, immediately following World War II, operated over China and Korea.

During 1949, as a Corsair pilot in VF-23, he flew from the U.S.S. Coral Sea with the Sixth Fleet. In 1952 he returned to the Sixth Fleet with VF-22 flying F2H Banshees aboard the U.S.S. Tarawa (CV-40). Later, while stationed at N.A.S. Pensacola, Florida, he qualified as a helicopter pilot. In his last active duty assignment, he was in charge of running the Navy's Survival, Escape, and Evasion School at N.A.S. North Island, California. His awards include the Distinguished Flying Cross with two Gold Stars, an Air Medal with seven Stars, the Purple Heart, and the Navy Unit Commendation.

After leaving the Naval service in 1958, he was employed by the Lockheed-Georgia Company as a military sales representative, retiring in 1975. He then worked in county government for DeKalb County, Georgia (metro Atlanta area), until his retirement in 1985. He now enjoys taking frequent adventure trips to the far corners of the world.

CDR Hill and his wife Evelyn live in Atlanta, Georgia. They have one daughter, Mrs. Cynthia Lee, and one granddaughter, Jennifer.

ROBERT ROY HOGAN

Bob Hogan was born on 10 February, 1920, in Atlanta, Georgia. He was educated at the University of Denver, Colorado.

Bob Hogan entered his flight training at N.A.S. Corpus Christi, and completed his training at N.A.S. Miami. He served one combat tour with VF-17 and is credited with .25 of a Betty bomber on 6 November, 1943. He is also credited with shooting down a Zeke on 11 November, 1943.

Decorations:
Air Medal
Asiatic-Pacific Campaign Medal
World War II Victory Medal
Purple Heart

He was listed as missing in action after a strike on Lakunai Airfield, New Britain, on 26 January, 1944.

Robert "Windy" Hill, Bougainville 1944. Courtesy National Archives.

DONALD ALLAN "STINKY" INNIS

Don Innis was born on November 14, 1915, in Nevada, Missouri. He was educated at the University of Missouri.

He became an Aviation Cadet on 1 February, 1941. He reported for training to N.A.S. Pensacola in February 1941 then N.A.S. Miami in August for further training.

He accepted an appointment as an Ensign on 16 July, 1941, and was designated a Naval Aviator on September 8, 1941. He reported to Advanced Carrier Training Group N.A.S. Norfolk, Virginia on 24 October, 1941.

He reported on 3 January, 1942 to a Fighting Squadron. On 2 September, 1942 he transferred with the Fighting Squadron to the South Pacific, where he was credited with the shooting down of a Zero.

He was appointed Lt(jg) on 1 October, 1942, and reported to VF-17 on 6 April, 1943. He was appointed Lt. on 1 October, 1943.

Innis was detached on 3 April, 1944, from VF-17, and after a short leave, reported to N.A.S. San Diego for duty involving flying in Aircraft Ordnance Development Unit.

Medals :
American Defense Service Medal
Asiatic-Pacific Campaign Medal
Purple Heart

Innis died on 20 June, 1944, in a plane crash in the Salton Sea, California.

Robert Hal Jackson in 1943. Courtesy Hal and Barbara Jackson.

Don "Stinky" Innis (left) and "Butch" Davenport at Bougainville 1944. Courtesy U.S. Navy photo. Robert L. Lawson Collection.

Robert Hal Jackson at the 1993 VF-17 reunion in Denton, Texas. Courtesy Hal and Barbara Jackson.

ROBERT "HAL" JACKSON

Hal Jackson was born on 29, November, 1920. Hal joined the squadron on January 1, 1943 when it was commissioned in Norfolk, Va. and served with it in the Pacific on two tours of duty until it was decommissioned in April 1944.

It was Hal Jackson who came up with the idea of storing cases of beer in ammunition cans in the wings of the F4U's, thus being able to transport the squadron beer from Espiritu Santo to Bougainville at the start of their second tour.

He is credited with shooting down 4.25 Japanese planes; 2.25 with VF-17. His other assignments included N.A.A.S. Green Cove Springs and VF-83A.

Decorations:
2 D.F.C.'s
8 Air Medals
Silver Star
(Received in VBF-10 for role in sinking battleship Yamato, April 7, 1945)
World War II Victory Medal
Asiatic-Pacific Campaign Medal with 4 stars
American Campaign Medal
Navy Unit Commendation

FRANK ANDREW "ANDY" JAGGER

In Tom Blackburn's book I am quoted as "gump." "The nickname really annoyed me. No one ever called me that. Another mistake is I am quoted as Frederick instead of Frank." Said Jagger.

FAMOUS PICTURE

I was in No 4 position in "Dirty Eddie" March's flight as Tail end Charlie. I was talking to "Dirty Eddie" in the famous picture. I am telling him about the experience of shooting down the first airplane flying with "Butch". In 1990 the following was reported in the press about Jagger's famous picture.

Jagger's Triumph Goes to Washington

Forty-seven years ago, Andy Jagger of Southampton was a young fighter pilot in the U.S. Navy flying against the Japanese in the South Pacific. After knocking down a Japanese Zero fighter in a mission over Rabaul, the elated Navy ensign returned to his base on Bougainville. A Navy photographer happened to be there and he captured Mr. Jagger's emotions seconds after he climbed out of his F4U Corsair.

Now the Smithsonian Institution has accepted the well known and often-reproduced photograph of Mr. Jagger for inclusion in its "Carrier Warfare in the Pacific" exhibition in the National Air and Space Museum.

"I was just a little insignificant, unimportant ensign. I just can't believe how the photo keeps showing up over the years," said the 72-year-old Mr. Jagger, who is now retired and living in Virginia Beach, Virginia, with his wife Betty.

"Andy" Jagger at Bougainville 1944. Courtesy National Archives.

By Navy estimate, the February 19, 1943 photograph of Mr. Jagger has been reprinted more often than any image of any other Naval aviator. It has appeared in nationwide magazines and newspapers, four books on World War II, and even two video cassettes. The more recent of the videos, named after Mr. Jagger's squadron and called "Fighting 17-The Jolly Rogers" was released earlier this year.

Famous Picture. Ensign "Andy" Jagger of Southampton, NY, describes kill made over Rabaul to Lt. H.A. March of Washington, D.C., in February 1944. Courtesy National Archives.

The Jagger family is an institution in Southampton. Mr. Jagger's ancestors came here in 1650, just 10 years after the town was settled, and some of his relatives still reside in the community. There is a street in the village named after the Jaggers.

Andy Jagger, more properly known as Frank Andrew Jagger, was born on 29 June, 1918 and raised in Southampton and was graduated from Southampton High School in 1936. He left to attend the University of Michigan, although he continued to call Southampton his home. He worked briefly for the Grumman Corporation before enlisting in the U.S. Navy in late 1941, shortly before Pearl Harbor. After World War II, he returned to his job at Grumman's Bethpage facility, living in Bethpage until his retirement in 1973.

During a telephone interview Monday, Mr. Jagger said that when he first enlisted, he had high hopes of flying a Grumman fighter built on Long Island. But fate was against him and he found himself flying Corsairs.

The Southampton native flew a total of 50 combat missions during World War II, shooting down four Japanese aircraft in intense fighting over the Solomon Islands. He was awarded seven Air Medals and a Distinguished Flying Cross; the Flying Cross was awarded after Mr. Jagger and three other Navy pilots took on six Japanese Zeros and shot all six enemy planes down with no losses.

Mr. Jagger recalled that when he first saw the war photo, he couldn't believe that it was really him because he had never seen the photographer. The former pilot said officials at the Smithsonian grew interested in the photo after learning that it had been displayed at the Pensacola, Florida, Naval Aviation Museum. Although the photograph was taken by an official Navy Photographer, Fenno Jacobs, the Smithsonian called Mr. Jagger and asked him for permission to include it in the carrier warfare exhibit. He agreed, and the photo went on display in Washington this fall.

Mr. Jagger said that if there was something that made the photo special, it was probably the emotion he showed. "The emotion is not just the emotion of victory but the emotion of survival," he said.

One out of every four pilots in Mr. Jagger's squadron never made it home.

DURING AND SINCE WORLD WAR TWO, THIS PICTURE HAS APPEARED IN:
Magazines: "Colliers", July 7, 1944, and "Coronet" September 1945
All Major Newspapers: "This Week" (Sunday Supplement) Sunday, April 8, 1945
Books: "U.S. Camera Annual for 1945",
"F4U Corsair at War" Abrams, 1981
"Steichen at War", Phillips, 1981
"History of the U.S. Navy", Morris, 1984
"The Jolly Rogers", Blackburn, 1989
Video Cassettes: "VF-17 Remembered", RDR Video Productions, 1984
"Fighting 17-The Jolly Rogers", Kenwood Productions, 1990

By Navy estimate, has been reprinted more often than any other photo of a Naval aviator.

This is the original Navy "Caption" when the picture was first published in 1944.

Elation reaches a high pitch as Ensign Andy Jagger, of Southampton, N.Y., describes his kill to Lt. H.A. March, of Washington D.C. Both belong to the VF-17 fighter plane squadron, commanded by Lt. Cdr. J.T. Blackburn, which operated with much success from Bougainville. Jagger shot down a Jap plane over Rabaul shortly before this picture was taken on February 19. His kill added one more rising sun to the flag in the picture on the opposite page. Each small flag surrounding the appropriate death's head on the scoreboard signifies a Jap plane knocked down by a member of Fighting Squadron 17. When this high-scoring fighter plane squadron of the U.S. Navy completed its tour of duty early in 1944, 154 Jap planes had been shot down.

Known as "Blackburn's Irregulars," the squadron was composed of a bunch of self-assertive individuals, boys who were the bane of every training-field commander's existence. Transferred to Skipper Blackburn's command, he condoned their love of buzzing the field, dogfighting, whipped them into perhaps the finest fighting squadron of the Navy, with 13 aces among their number.

In its two tours of duty (the first was on New Georgia), the squadron flew 7,192 combat hours, averaging over 200 for each of its 24 pilots, for the record bag of 154 planes in 76 days of combat flying. No ship or bomber, moreover, for which the squadron provided aerial protection, was ever hit by the enemy: On the February 19 raid, the "Irregulars" met up with 50 to 75 Jap planes, got 16 of them without loss.

Not since have the Japs dared send a plane from Rabaul against our squadrons. This photo is now on display at the Navy SEA-AIR GALLERY exhibit of the National Air and Space Museum.

JOHN HENRY KEITH

Johnny Keith was born on 30 October, 1921 in Bourbon County, Kansas. He was educated at Fort Scott Junior College.

He entered flight training at N.A.S. Corpus Christi, and completed his training at N.A.S. Miami. Johnny Keith reported to VF-17 early in 1943. He was the first pilot missing in action from the squadron, when he was hit by anti-aircraft fire over Kulitunai Harbor, Shortland Island. As a result of this damage he was forced to make a water landing about 15 miles S.E. of Faisi Island. He was seen to get out of his plane, but was not seen with his raft. Searches for Keith over the next 2 days were negative.
Decorations:
Navy Unit Commendation
Asiatic-Pacific Campaign Medal
World War II Victory Medal
Purple Heart

LOUIS M. KELLEY

Lou Kelley joined the squadron early in 1943 and completed the first combat tour with VF-17. Kelley was detached from the squadron on 13 January, 1944.

IRA CASSIUS "IKE" KEPFORD

Ira Cassius Kepford was born in Harvey, Illinois, on May 29, 1919, son of George Raymond and Emma McLaughlin Kepford. His family moved to Muskegon, Michigan, shortly after he was born. An all-around athlete at Muskegon High School from 1935 to 1937, he capped his prep career by being named an All-State back in his senior year. He enrolled at Northwestern University in 1938 to study for a dentistry career.

Kepford was a key figure in a star backfield at Northwestern. He enlisted in the U.S. Naval Reserve on August 18, 1941, and was honorably discharged on April 29, 1942, to accept appointment as Aviation Cadet, U.S.N.R. After flight training at the Naval Air Stations, Corpus Christi, Texas, and Miami, Florida, he became a Naval Aviator on November 5, 1942, and was commissioned Ensign, U.S.N.R., with date of rank October 16, 1942. He was promoted to Lieutenant on May 1, 1945, and was transferred to the Retired List of the U.S. Naval Reserve on June 1, 1956, and advanced to the rank of Lieutenant Commander on the basis of combat citations.

Detached from Naval Air Station, Miami, Florida, in December 1942, he served with Fighting Squadron 17 in the Pacific War Area until March 1944. That squadron won the Navy Unit Commendation and he was personally awarded the Navy Cross, a Gold Star in lieu of the second Navy Cross, the Silver Star Medal and the Distinguished Flying Cross.

From March until June he was attached to the Fleet Air, Alameda, Command, and the last six months of that year served with Fighting Squadron 84. In December 1944 he was transferred to the staff of Commander Fleet Air, West Coast, and remained in that assignment throughout the remaining period of hostilities. After the Japanese surrender, and a period of terminal leave, he was released from all active duty on November 7, 1945.

In addition to the Navy Cross with Gold Star, the Silver Star Medal, the Distinguished Flying Cross and the ribbon for the Navy Unit Commendation to Fighting Squadron Seventeen, Lieutenant Commander Kepford has the American Defense Service Medal; the American Campaign Medal; Asiatic-Pacific Campaign Medal; and the World War II Victory Medal.

A student at Northwestern University, Evanston, Illinois, where he was a football star at the time of his enlistment in August 1941,

VF-17's top ace "Ike" Kepford at Bougainville 1944. Courtesy National Archives.

he returned to Chicago after becoming the U.S. Navy's leading ace scoring a record 16 confirmed Japanese planes destroyed during World War II. In January 1956 he was Vice-President, Marketing and Advertising, Liggett-Rexall Drug Company. He left the Ligget-Rexall post in the late sixties to dabble in investments in New Jersey and Connecticut. He retired in the early seventies and returned to Harbor Springs, Michigan, where he remained until his death in 1987. He was survived by his wife Kraeg, a daughter Tracy, and son Tim. To his family, his classmates, and many admirers in the Muskegon area, Ike remains the classic prototype of an American hero—a title earned in two distinctly different fields of endeavor.

TOM KILLEFER

Tom Killefer was born in Los Angeles, California, on 7 January, 1917. Before VF-17, he flew Corsairs in VF-18 under 'Jumping' Joe Clifton-the first Navy Corsair squadron and then on the jeep carrier Bogue flying F4Fs (Wildcats) on convoy anti-submarine duty in the North Atlantic to Murmansk.

After VF-17 his other assignments included running a school for Instructors of fighter tactics in Jacksonville, FL, to the R.A.F. Central Flying School in England, and VBF-74 on the Midway, with Tom Blackburn as Commander Air Group.

Then finished Law school at Harvard, on to Oxford for two years where, on U.S.N.R. duty, he got to fly R.A.F. Spitfire 21's, with the counter rotating propellers and Griffon Engine. Since then

Tom Killefer at Bougainville 1944. Courtesy National Archives.

his only flying has been on jet fighters as a Director of Northrop Corporation.

He is credited with 4 kills with VF-17. He died in 1997.

JOHN MILTON KLEINMAN

John Kleinman was born on October 3, 1919, in Kissimmee, Florida. He became an Aviation Cadet on 1 May, 1941, and reported to N.A.S. Pensacola for training and then for further training on 13 October, 1941 to N.A.S. Miami.

On November 6, 1941, he was designated a Naval Aviator, and was appointed an Ensign on 8 October, 1941. He reported on 2 January, 1942, to Advanced Carrier Training Group and on 26 February, 1942, to a Fighting Squadron. He was appointed Lt(jg) on 1 October, 1942.

He reported on 1 January, 1943, to N.A.S. Norfolk for active duty involving flying in connection with the fitting out of Fighting Squadron 17 when commissioned. When he reported to VF-17 he was already a combat veteran with one confirmed and one probable victory.

He was appointed on October 1, 1943, to Lieutenant and detached from VF-17 on December 17, 1943, after their first tour of duty. He is credited with one Kate torpedo bomber shot down and one damaged whilst flying with VF-17.

He reported on 27 December, 1943, to Fleet Air Coast. Kleinman then reported to N.A.S. Jacksonville and then shortly after N.A.S. Melbourne reporting on January 30, 1944.

Medals

American Defense Service Medal

Asiatic-Pacific Area Campaign Medal

Purple Heart

Here is the press release for Kleinman's Distinguished Flying Cross.

"For heroism and extraordinary achievement as pilot of a fighter plane during action against enemy Japanese forces in the Solomon Islands Campaign on August 24, 1942. Intercepting a division of enemy bombers as they peeled off in a determined dive for our surface units, Lt(jg) Kleinman, grimly trailing them down with persistent fire, shot two into the sea before they could release their bombs. By his relentless fighting spirit and aggressive courage he saved one of our aircraft carriers from possible bomb hits and contributed greatly toward demoralization of the entire Japanese offensive. His unyielding devotion to duty, maintained with complete disregard for his personal safety, was in keeping with the highest traditions of the United States Naval Service."

Kleinman died on 18 February, 1944, while flying a plane that crashed after take-off for a gunnery flight 2 miles southwest of Naval Auxiliary Air Station, Melbourne, Florida.

THOMAS FREDERICK KROPF

Tom Kropf was born on January 26, 1919, in Wamego Kansas. He was educated at Kansas State College and graduated with a Degree in Mechanical Engineering.

He became an Aviation Cadet on 4 May, 1942, and on May 14 reported to N.A.S. Corpus Christi for training. He was appointed

an Ensign on 16 October, 1942, and designated a Naval Aviator on November 5, 1942.

On 12 November, 1942, he reported to N.A.S. Miami then on to N.A.S. Jacksonville for training. He reported to Carrier Qualification Training Unit, Norfolk, Virginia, then VF-17 on March 8, 1943. He was appointed Lt(jg) on January 1, 1944.

Medals :

Navy Unit Commendation Ribbon

Purple Heart

World War II Victory Medal

Asiatic-Pacific Campaign Medal with (2) bronze stars

He was reported missing in action on 30 January, 1944, when he failed to return from an attack on enemy shipping in Rabaul Harbor.

MELVIN "KURLY" KURLANDER

Mel Kurlander was born in St. Louis, Missouri on 16 March, 1921. He was educated for 3.5 years at the University of Illinois.

He joined the Navy in December 1941 and retired a permanent Lieutenant in January 1946.

The following press report details citations awarded to Mel Kurlander.

Mel "Kurly" Kurlander at Bougainville 1944. Courtesy National Archives.

AREA NAVAL RESERVE OFFICER IS AWARDED PERMANENT CITATIONS

M.M. Kurlander, naval reserve lieutenant of 1127 North Shore Av., has been awarded permanent citations for the Navy Air Medal, Distinguished Flying Cross, and Gold Stars in lieu of additional Air Medals.

The presentation was held before a reserve battalion in the naval training center at the foot of Randolph St. The citations were awarded by Cdr. C. M. Terry, assistant inspector-instructor of the center. Kurlander earned the citations while assigned to a Navy fighter squadron. He participated in 72 air strikes during the campaigns against Bougainville, Rabaul and Green Island.

Mel Kurlander at Oshkosh for the VF-17 reunion in July/August 1994. Courtesy Donna Bushman EAA.

WILLIAM LEE "COUNTRY" LANDRETH

"Country" Landreth was the youngest original pilot in VF-17 and is credited with three air combat victories before being captured by the Japanese in March 1945 and serving six months as a prisoner of war until repatriation.

"Country" spent another 24 years in the Navy in various assignments, including Commanding Officer of VS-37, a carrier-based anti-submarine squadron. From VS-37 he went on staff to Commander Carrier Division 17, then to the Naval Research Lab, then became the Pt. Mugu Liaison Officer to Vandenberg Air Force Base.

He was the founding director of a degree-granting program at Naval Air Station Pt. Mugu, California, and helped to start degree-granting programs on two other military bases.

Bill Landreth is authorized to wear the following ribbons and medals: Distinguished Flying Cross with Gold Star; Air Medal with 4 Gold Stars; Purple Heart; Navy Unit Commendation; Prisoner of War Medal (finally authorized in 1991!); and numerous theatre ribbons. He received a Bachelor Degree at the age of 47 from Chapman College in Orange, California, just before retiring as a Commander in 1969.

William "Country" Landreth at Bougainville 1944. Courtesy National Archives.

L-R. *Ginger and Bill Landreth and Thelma and Earl May taken in late 1944 after the VF-17 tour and just before Bill and Earl left for the Pacific with VBF-10 aboard the carrier Intrepid. Bill and Earl were good friends and each stood up as best man for the others wedding during this period. A few months later Bill was forced down over Honshu, Japan and was a prisoner of war for the duration.* Courtesy Del May.

After retiring, Bill spent five years in the educational field and received his Master of Arts Degree in Education in 1975, and a Master of Science Degree in Counseling in 1976, both from Cal-Lutheran University in Thousand Oaks, California. Presently living in Camarillo, California, with his wife, Ginger, they celebrated their 50th wedding anniversary on 4 July, 1994. Bill has been self-employed in a specialized form of insurance for financial institutions over the last 20 years.

DONALD THOMAS MALONE

Don Malone was born on 16 April, 1920, in Eureka, California. He was educated at Humboldt State College, and Fresno State College.

He became an Aviation Cadet on 1 June, 1942, and reported to N.A.S. Corpus Christi for training. He was appointed an Ensign on 1 December, 1942, and on December 17, 1942, designated a Naval Aviator. He reported on 24 December, 1942, to N.A.S. Miami for training and on 5 February, 1943, to N.A.S. Jacksonville for further training. On April 11 he reported to Carrier Qualification Training Unit, Norfolk, Virginia, and from there reported to VF-17.

He was appointed Lt(jg) on 1 January, 1944.

Medals :
Asiatic-Pacific Area Campaign Medal
World War II Victory Medal
Air Medal
Navy Unit Commendation
Purple Heart

He was reported missing in action on 4 February, 1944. Shot down by a Japanese Zeke on retirement from an attack against Tobera Airfield near Rabaul.

HARRY ANDREW "DIRTY EDDIE" MARCH, JR.

Harry March was born on 4 February, 1919, in East Liverpool, Ohio. He was educated at the University of North Carolina where he graduated with a B.A. Degree in Physical Education class of 1940.

He qualified for the Olympic team 1940 (400m hurdles) and was named on the All American Track Team 1940.

He became an Aviation cadet on 1 March, 1941, and was designated a Naval Aviator on 23 September, 1941. He was appointed an Ensign U.S.N.R. on 18 August, 1941, and reported on 29 November, 1941, to Fighting Squadron Six on the U.S.S. Enterprise. He is credited with two confirmed Japanese planes with Fighting Squadron Six.

He reported on 31 December, 1942, to Fighting Squadron 24 on the U.S.S. Belleau Wood, and on 6 October, 1943, to Fighting Squadron 17. He reported to N.A.S. Jacksonville on 4 May, 1944 and shortly after to N.A.A.S. Green Cove Springs on 6 May, 1944.

On 16 May, 1945 he reported to N.A.S. Norfolk and on 21 May, 1945 reported to Bombing Fighting Squadron 74 at Camp Edwards Massachusetts. He was appointed Lieutenant Commander U.S.N.R. in October 1945.

Medals
Air Medal
Gold Star in lieu of Second Air Medal
Presidential Unit Citation - U.S.S. Enterprise

*William "Country" Landreth at San Diego in 1991.*Courtesy William Landreth.

Skull and Crossbones ace Harry "Dirty Eddie" March, 5 Japanese planes, at Bougainville 1944. Courtesy National Archives.

Presidential Unit Citation - First Marine Division Re-inforced
Asiatic- Pacific Area Campaign Medal with one bronze star
American Defense Service Medal
World War II Victory Medal
Harry March died on 2 March, 1946, at Watts Hospital, Durham, N.C., of primary Pneumonia.

Earl May in Early 1942 as a member of the "Flying Badgers" in primary training at Glenview, Illinois. Hap Bowers was believed to have been in this group also. Courtesy Del May.

Earl May, a brand new Ensign from Corpus Christi with his proud brother Del, in October 1942. Courtesy Del May.

William Meek at Bougainville 1944. Courtesy National Archives.

EARL MAY JR.

Earl May was born on 1 June, 1920, in Milwaukee, Wisconsin. May joined the Navy on February 22, 1941, for flight training. He was designated a Naval Aviator, and commissioned an Ensign on October 1, 1942. He joined VF-17 and served land-based, in the Solomons from October 1943 to April 1944, where he is credited with eight confirmed Japanese planes shot down.

"Earl used to wax his plane and he said it could be the difference between getting back and not getting back". Remembers Dan Cunningham. He received a Silver Star, and a D.F.C. He was promoted to Lt. on January 1, 1945.

He joined VBF-10, and served on the Intrepid in March and April 1945. He received a D.F.C., and two strike/flight A.M.s (for ten combat missions).

Medals :

Silver Star

Distinguished Flying Cross

Gold Star in lieu of the second Distinguished Flying Cross

Air Medal

Gold Star in lieu of the second Air Medal

Navy Unit Commendation

Asiatic Pacific Campaign Medal

American Campaign Medal

World War II Victory Medal

Navy Occupation Service Medal "Asia" clasp

Philippine Liberation Ribbon with two bronze stars

Earl May remained in the Navy after World War II and his last assignment was at the Navy Air Test Center at Patuxent, MD. Earl May died on 22 October, 1951, in a flying accident 1.5 miles S.E. of Cedarville, New Jersey, on a routine test flight.

WILLIAM PRESTON MEEK

William Meek was born on 9 June, 1921, in Long Beach, California. On August 10, 1942, he became an Aviation Cadet. He was appointed an Ensign on 16 April, 1943, and designated a Naval Aviator on 28 April, 1943. He reported to N.A.S. Corpus Christi and then N.A.S. Jacksonville for training. He reported to the Atlantic Fleet then joined Fighting Squadron 17 on August 29, 1943. After completing two combat tours with VF17 he was detached on April 2, 1944.

He reported to VF-84 on May 4, 1944, and was appointed Lt(jg) on July 1, 1944.

Medals

Asiatic-Pacific Area Campaign Medal

Air Medal

William Meek died on 23 July, 1944, in a plane crash. The following as an account of his Air Medal citation.

"Posthumous award of the Navy Air Medal to the late Lt(jg) William P. Meek, U.S.N.R., of Covina, was disclosed by the Navy this week (Nov. 1 1944).

"Lieutenant Meek, son of the late George Meek who for many years was postmaster here, was awarded the Air Medal for bravery in action while piloting a Navy fighter plane as escort for a bombing strike against Tobera Airfield in New Britain, January 28.

"The citation which accompanied the posthumous medal award was signed for the president by James Forrestal, Secretary of the Navy. Detailing Lieutenant Meek's record of heroic air combat, the citation said in part:

"As pilot, attached to a fighter squadron during action against enemy Japanese forces in the Solomon Islands and Bismarck Archipelago areas from October 27, 1943, to March 8, 1944, Lieutenant Meek is cited for meritorious achievement."

"Intercepted by an overwhelming force of hostile fighters while acting as escort for a bombing strike against Tobera January 28, he fought gallantly despite great odds, pressing home his attack vigorously and shooting down one Japanese Zero."

"His splendid airmanship and outstanding devotion to duty throughout this engagement and during numerous other combat missions in this vitally strategic area were in keeping with the highest traditions of the United States Naval Service."

CHARLES ALFRED "CHUCK" PILLSBURY

Chuck Pillsbury was born on 4 April, 1917, in Minneapolis, Minnesota. He was educated at St. Paul's School, Concord, N.H., and Yale University (B.A. Degree) Class of 1939. He became an Avia-

Wilbert Peter "Beads" Popp at Bougainville 1944. Courtesy National Archives.

WILBERT PETER "BEADS" POPP

"Beads" Popp was born 15 November, 1921, in Fresno, California. His family moved to Portland, Oregon, when he was 2.5 weeks old. He spent 8 years in Grammar school and 4 years at Jefferson High school. He graduated in January 1941. He went to Junior College for 1.5 years studying Electrical Engineering, while there he worked in service stations, etc. In May 1942 he enlisted in the Navy as

tion Cadet on 2 December, 1940, and reported on 9 December to N.A.S. Pensacola for training. On 21 May, 1941, he was designated a Naval Aviator.

On 31 May, 1941, he was appointed an Ensign, and on 2 September, 1941, he reported to N.A.S. Corpus Christi. On 15 June, 1942, he was appointed Lt(jg) and reported on 10 August, 1942, to N.A.S. New York for duty with the Aircraft Delivery Unit. He reported on 8 October, 1942, to Naval Proving Grounds, Dahlgren, Virginia, and on December 31, 1942, reported to Norfolk Virginia and VF-17. He was appointed Lieutenant on 1 March, 1943.

Medals :
American Defense Service Medal
World War II Victory Medal
American Area Campaign Medal
Navy Unit Commendation
Asiatic -Pacific Area Campaign Medal (1) bronze star
Purple Heart
Air Medal

Chuck Pillsbury died on 21 November, 1943 when he failed to return following an attack on enemy positions on the southeast end of Bougainville.

Seaman 2nd class. War interrupted his education and after the war he went to the University of Washington from November 1945 to June 1947, graduating with a BA Business Administration.

Beads was the nickname given to Bill Popp by Tom Blackburn. It came when Tom Blackburn noticed beads of perspiration running down Popp's nose. Peter is his middle name for which he was better known in the Navy.

On July 21, 1942, he became an Aviation Cadet. He then went to St. Marys for pre-flight aged 20 for 13 weeks at Moraga, California, near Oakland. After pre-flight he went to Los Alamedos, N.A.S. California, near Long Beach, where he went into the primary flight training program. This program lasted until January 1943. From there he reported to Corpus Christi, Texas to finish flight training and receive his wings.

Popp received his wings as an Ensign on June 9, 1943. From Corpus Christi he went to Melbourne, Florida, for operational flight training in the Grumman F4F Wildcat, his first combat type of aircraft. This program lasted until the early September 1943. After 3 weeks leave en route to his next duty station he reported to Norfolk Virginia under C.A.S.U. 21, assigned to his first fighter squadron VF-17.

He completed two tours of combat with VF-17 and was credited with 2 confirmed enemy planes shot down.

VF-17 were relieved on March 7, 1944 and returned to the States. After a month leave he was reassigned to VF-84 at San Diego under the command of Lt. Cdr. Roger Hedrick, who had been the exec. in VF-17. There were about twelve pilots from VF-17 who became the nuclei of VF-84 including Ike Kepford, Chico Freeman, John Malcolm Smith, Jimmy Dixon, Whitey Matthews.

Admiral Marc Mitscher was in command of this task force and from Pearl Harbor they went to the first Navy carrier raids over Tokyo on February 16 & 17, 1945. They then took part in the invasions of Iwo Jima and Okinawa, and also took part in the sinking of the last Japanese super battleship, the Yamato, on April 7, 1945. During this period of time he was credited with one more kill a Japanese Kate torpedo bomber.

The Bunker Hill was kamikazed on May 11, 1945. Many pilots in the ready room and in planes preparing to take off, were killed, including "Chico" Freeman. They returned to the States via Espiritu Santo-Pearl and Bremerton and was assigned shore duty at Los Alamitos assigned to the base at Thermal Calif., June to September 1945 as a type instructor in Corsairs for pilots preparing to go to the fleet.

Popp was separated from active duty in October 2, 1945. From Thermal Island Naval Air Base he returned to Portland. When he returned to civilian life he enrolled at the University of Washington. While attending there he got into the reserve flight status with the weekend warriors San Point N.A.S. Seattle, Washington, and later in a reserve squadron Santa Morgan. Eventually Popp retired as a Lt. Cdr. with 25 total credit years active and reserve duty.

After the war he completed his education at the University of Washington in Seattle, graduating in June 1947 with a BA degree and an insurance major. He then became an agent in the life insurance business, and is still somewhat active. He was married in May 11, 1950, and has three grown married daughters and five grandchildren, three girls and two boys.

Decorations
3 D.F.C.s
7 Air Medals
VF-17 Navy Unit Commendation
VF-84 Presidential Unit Citation
2 Asiatic-Pacific Campaign Medals
World War II Victory Medal

Bill Popp at Oshkosh for the VF-17 reunion in July/August 1994. Courtesy Donna Bushman EAA.

MILLS SCHANUEL

Mills Schanuel was born on 13 March, 1918. Schanuel went into the U.S. Navy from a position of staff writer for a St. Louis, MO, newspaper, the Post Dispatch.

He completed two combat tours with VF-17 and shot down 3 Japanese Zeros and damaged one Val and one Hamp. His other assignments included Fighting Squadron 95, Air Force Atlantic Fleet, Air Wing Five, and N.A.S. Corpus Christi.

He was married in 1947 and now has four grown children. One lady lawyer, one lady musician, one male engineer, and one male security consultant. He spent his early years traveling, in America and abroad, building up his business, with the main office in Chicago. Later, he raised cattle in northwestern Illinois.

Decorations:
Air Medal with Gold Star
World War II Victory Medal
American Campaign Medal
Asiatic-Pacific Campaign Medal with Bronze Star

Mills Schanuel at Bougainville 1944. Courtesy National Archives.

Mills Schanuel in San Francisco 13 June 1964. Courtesy Mills Schanuel.

Walter Schub at Bougainville 1944. Courtesy National Archives.

WALTER JOHN SCHUB

Walter Schub was born on 17 July, 1919, in East Cambridge, Mass. He was educated at Long Beach State (Jr. Cert.) and High school from 1936-37. He attended the University College California, Long Beach from 1938-1940 and the De La Salle Academy-Prep (high school) in Newport, Rhode Island. He then went to Naval Line School (U.S. Naval Academy curriculum level).

He Instructed in Jacksonville VN-11A 1941-42 with another future VF-17 pilot Ray Beacham. He served with VF-17 in two combat tours and is credited with shooting down 2.25 Japanese planes and one probable. He then reported for duty with VF-10 U.S.S. Intrepid in the Okinawa campaign of 1944-1945.

His other service included being commanding officer of VF-33 from 1953-1954, U.S.S. Midway CV-41, and Air Operations Officer on the U.S.S. Saratoga CV-60. He was Executive Officer at N.A.S. Jacksonville in 1961-1963 and Acting C.O. at Jacksonville in the 1962 Cuban missile crisis.

He is credited in air-to-air combat with a total of 4.25 kills, adding to the 2.25 with VF-17 by downing 2 kamikazes before the U.S.S. Intrepid was disabled. His log book records 400 Pilot hours and 150 carrier landings.

Decorations
Command at Sea Medal
5 D.F.C.s
12 Air Medals
Navy Unit Commendation

Walter Schub in 1961. Courtesy Walter Schub.

FREDERICK JAMES "BIG JIM" STREIG

Jim Streig was born on 24 April, 1921, in Sacramento, California. He was educated at Hollister High School, Salinas Junior College and the University of California.

Jim Streig joined the Navy on January 9, 1942, for flight training. He was designated a Naval Aviator, and commissioned an Ensign on October 1, 1942. He joined VF-17 in 1943, and served two land-based tours in the Solomons from October 1943 to March 1944. He was promoted to Lt(jg) with effect from January 1, 1944. He was promoted to Cdr. on July 1, 1956, and retired from the Navy in July '1969.

Decorations:
D.F.C. with 2 gold stars
Air Medal with 1 silver and 1 gold star
Navy Unit Commendation
American Campaign Medal
Asiatic-Pacific Campaign Medal with 3 stars
World War II Victory Medal
"Big Jim" Streig died on 31 August, 1995, after a long illness.

"Big Jim" Streig at Bougainville 1944. Courtesy National Archives.

WHITFIELD CARLISLE WHARTON, JR.

Whit Wharton served in the Navy from 1942 to June 1947. He was appointed an Ensign in 1942, and Lt(jg) in 1944. He was promoted to Lt. in 1945 and finished his Naval career in 1947.

Whit was Wally Schub's student in Jacksonville when primary training in 1942. He flew wing on Wally Schub in VF-17 and in Wally Schub's 2nd section in VF-10 on the U.S.S. Intrepid. About 70% of Whit's flying (all of his combat) was with Wally Schub.

Whit Wharton graduated from the University of Florida in June 1956.

"Whit thought VF-17 was the very best and had a wonderful reunion in May 1983 shortly before he died of a heart attack in September 1983. Whit said it was like old times. They all got along so well together." His wife Joyce recalled.

Decorations
D.F.C.
3 Air Medals

In his service with VF-10 Wharton shot down two Japanese dive-bombers as detailed below.

WHARTON DOWNS 2 JAP BOMBERS

2 June 1945
Greenwood Navy Fighter Pilot Scores in Air Battles Off Okinawa

Lieutenant (junior grade) Whitfield Carlisle Wharton, U.S.N.R., of 122 West Cambridge Street, Greenwood, Navy fighter pilot based aboard a big Essex-class aircraft carrier operating in the Western Pacific, recently shot down two Japanese dive bombers during a furious air battle northwest of Okinawa.

Lieutenant Wharton knocked down the two Japs during a scrap in which 12 Chance-Vought Corsairs destroyed 22 of a flight of about 30 enemy craft. Two American planes went down during the fight, but both pilots were rescued. The Jap flight, which included a number of kamikaze suiciders, was headed to attack our sea and

Whit Wharton at Bougainville in 1944. Courtesy National Archives.

ground forces at Okinawa when it was intercepted by the 12-plane combat air patrol of carrier-based Navy and Marine Corsairs.

In the ensuing fight, Lieutenant Wharton sent two Val dive-bombers spinning in flames into the Pacific. These Jap planes were among 74 shot down during two weeks off Okinawa by the Navy pilots on Lieutenant Wharton's carrier. In addition, the Marine fliers aboard shot down another 10 enemy planes.

As a member of Vice-Admiral Marc A. Mitscher's famed Task Force 58, these fliers participated in all but annihilating the Jap fleet task force which tried to relieve Okinawa, in neutralizing raids on Kyushu, and in leading air-ground support and protecting our forces at Okinawa.

By their wholesale destruction of Jap airplanes, including the Kamikaze suiciders, and by their sinkings of enemy warships and merchant ships, these Navy fliers greatly hastened the end of the enemy's sea and air power.

Whit Wharton and buddies after serving with VF-17. Courtesy Joyce Wharton.

NON FLYING OFFICERS

G F. HALL

Ensign G.F. Hall served with VF-17 as Assistant Operations Officer from early 1943 until he was detached on 17 January 1944.

BASIL DUKE HENNING

Basil Duke Henning was born in Louisville, Kentucky, in 1910. He was the grandson of a famous Confederate General-Basil Duke, and great-nephew of General John Hunt Morgan of Morgan's Raiders. He was Colgate Professor of History at Yale University from 1932, and Yale Graduate school in 1935 (Phillips Andover prep school).

He was in the Navy service from the start of W.W. II in U.S.A. and was Operations and Air Combat Information Officer with VF-17. He then served with Air Group 10 and finished the war, as a Lt. Cdr.

He volunteered when the U.S. declared war, and went to aviation intelligence school at Quonset, R.I. as he was too old for combat flying. He taught English History which brought him to London every summer and for 10 years after his retirement. He was Master of Saybrook College at Yale for 29 years, the longest tenure at the University.

Published for the History of Parliament Trust by Seeker and Warburg in 1983 London, his 3 volumes on the House of Commons 1660-1690.

The following press report was in released in 1984.

Basil Duke Henning at Bougainville in 1944. Courtesy National Archives.

Commons award for Basil Henning

The House of Commons is about to pay an unprecedented tribute to a citizen of the United States: Professor Basil Henning, of Yale. In recognition of more than 20 years' labor on the history of Parliament in the 17th century, he will receive a silver-gilt medallion at his home in New Haven, Connecticut.

The size of the great seal of England, it bears an engraving of the Houses of Parliament and the legend, "God Save Queen Elizabeth." The designer is Philip Nathan, who was also responsible for the royal wedding crown piece.

Such medallions are awarded sparingly at the discretion of the Speaker to distinguished persons connected with Parliament. Speaker George Thomas gave one to Lord Denning and another to the Prince and Princess of Wales.

Basil Henning's well-merited testimonial was initiated by the present Speaker Bernard Weatherill, and Robert Rhodes James, MP for Cambridge and chairman of the History of Parliament Trust.

Basil Duke Henning died in 1990.

Basil Duke Henning Air Combat Intelligence Officer relaxing at the beach. Courtesy U.S. Naval Historical Center / M.W. "Butch" Davenport Collection.

LYLE F. HERRMANN

Lyle Herrmann served with VF-17 as Flight Surgeon. He reported for duty on 25 October, 1943 and was detached on 15 March, 1944.

ROGER L. MILLS

Lt(jg) R.L. Mills reported for duty with VF-17 as Squadron Duty Officer on 3 January, 1944 and was detached on 15 March, 1944.

Lyle Herrmann VF-17 Flight Surgeon at Bougainville 1944. Courtesy National Archives.

Lt(jg) R.L. Mills squadron duty officer at Bougainville 1944. Courtesy National Archives.

LESTER R. KINCAID

Ensign Lester R. Kincaid reported for duty with VF-17 as Assistant Gunnery Officer on 15 February, 1944 and was detached on 15 March, 1944.

Lester Kincaid Assistant Gunnery Officer at Bougainville 1944. Courtesy National Archives.

CIVILIAN PERSONNEL

A number of Chance Vought personnel contributed to the success of VF-17 among them Test Pilot Boone Guyton, Russ Clark, Jack Hospers and Service Representative Ray DeLeva.

RAYMOND PATRICK DeLEVA

Raymond Patrick DeLeva, was a veteran of 44 years in aviation, 40 years at Vought, and 35 years in Vought Field Service. Born in 1908 in Paterson, New Jersey, Ray grew up in Queens, Long Island, where he attended Jamaica High School. In 1929 he hired on at Curtiss Aero and Motor Company, Garden City, Long Island, as a mechanic in final assembly. Occupied also as a field mechanic at nearby Roosevelt Field, he got his first aviation experience working on a wide variety of aircraft, including both Air Force and Navy types and special aircraft, some designed for Lieutenant Jimmy Doolittle.

In 1931, when Curtiss merged their Garden City operation with their Buffalo division, Ray joined a construction company for a couple of years before getting back into aviation, this time as a mechanic at Chance Vought Aircraft Corporation—at that time affiliated with United Aircraft and located at Hartford, Connecticut. After a period of more-or-less steady work as a mechanic and machinist for Vought, highlighted by his marriage in 1934 and by work on the early SU-3 and the SB2U-1, and -3 scout bombers, Ray was recruited in 1938 by Jack Hospers, the head at that time of Vought's tiny (5 person) field service department. Accepting the offer, he took his first assignment to N.A.S. Anacostia, D.C. (at that time the Navy Flight Test Center), where he worked in support of the Marine SB2U-3 monoplane sea/land scout bomber—a versatile aircraft which later was to play a role in the successful defense of Midway Island in 1942.

On completing this assignment, Ray was reassigned to support the STBU-1 torpedo bomber in flight tests and carrier suitability trials at Anacostia and catapult and arresting gear tests at N.A.M.C. Philadelphia. In 1941, Ray got an exciting new assignment. He was detailed to work in the testing of the F4U Corsair and in the development of the first night fighter F4U squadron (later designated VFN-75), which used an early version of the then highly secret radar and became the first night fighter F4U outfit to be deployed into the South Pacific combat areas. In addition, Ray was involved in the field servicing of the OS2U-1, -2, and -3 scout and observation plane used both on land and off battleships and carriers.

Later Ray was assigned as Senior Rep. at N.A.T.C. Patuxent River, Maryland, which had just opened as the new Navy Flight Test Center, replacing Anacostia. Then after brief work with Cdr. Tom Blackburn's famous VF-17 "Skull and Crossbones" squadron at Norfolk, VA, Ray went, in 1943, to the West Coast to work in support of VMF-115 and VMF-451 at M.C.A.S. Santa Barbara and of testing activity at N.O.T.C. Inyokern (now China Lake).

VMF-451 and VMF-115 (then skippered by Major Joe Foss, already a famous war ace since his feats in early Solomon Islands actions) were just transitioning to the F4U at this time. After 9 months in Santa Barbara, Ray was directed to proceed to the South Pacific war zone, in October of 1943. Following temporary assignment to various training bases on Oahu, he went to ComFairSoPac

Ray DeLeva (L) and "Butch" Davenport in front of "Big Hog". Courtesy U.S. Navy photo. Robert L. Lawson Collection.

at Espiritu Santo in the New Hebrides, covering F4Us for both Navy and Marine squadrons in air groups at Efate, Noumea, and Espiritu Santo in the New Hebrides and Guadalcanal, the Russell Islands, Bougainville, and the Green Islands in the Solomons, teaming up with Tom Blackburn and VF-17 again.

In these areas he covered M.A.G.s 11, 12, 15, and 25, each of which handled at least 4 squadrons of 14 planes each. These included the famous squadrons led by "Pappy" Boyington, Joe Foss, Tom Blackburn, and many others who became famous. After 9 months of combat action, in which he was exposed repeatedly to bombing, ground attacks, and bugs, Ray again returned to the U.S., in 1944, where he spent some time lecturing to new F4U squadron officers and maintenance personnel on the problems he'd encountered supporting the Corsair under combat conditions.

On his return to the East Coast, Ray was assigned to VF-11, N.A.S. Atlantic City; but just before the scheduled departure with this squadron to combat areas, he was reassigned as Senior Rep. at Pax. River again. On completion of that assignment he was made Senior Rep. on Vought's first jet-the XF6U-1 "Pirate". Flight testing took place at Muroc Dry Lake, California (now Edwards A.F.B.). With three of these experimental Pirates, he spent almost a year in the desert. Then he was recalled and assigned as Assistant Supervisor of the Field Service Technical Group, just before Chance Vought moved from Connecticut to Dallas, Texas.

Ray DeLeva at the VF-17 reunion in Denton, Texas in 1993. Courtesy Milly DeLeva.

As assistant supervisor of this group (which then consisted of a maximum of 10 people), Ray was helping support about 100 reps. in the field at the time on the F4U-4, -5, -7, and the F6U, F7U, and F8U aircraft. Soon he was promoted to supervisor of the Field Service Technical Group; and he held this position for the next 15 years, working in the Dallas-based office until 1965.

In 1965, Ray requested a change from management to working with airplanes in the field again. In January of that year, he was assigned to N.A.S. Dallas as Senior Rep. on the F-8 Crusaders assigned to the Navy and Marine Reserves at that base. With this assignment he was also responsible for support of other groups and activities at N.A.S. Miramar, Calif.; Point Mugu, Calif.; New Orleans; Cecil Field, Florida; N.A.S. Olathe, Kansas; Guantanamo, Cuba; Atlanta, Ga.; N.A.S. Roosevelt Roads, Republic of the Phillippines; and aboard U.S.S. John F. Kennedy.

Nearly two-thirds of Ray's life had been spent in connection with Vought Aircraft. After nearly 40 years of service to Vought, he retired on 1 August 1973, taking with him many pleasant memories of what he referred to as "this great company and the great personnel connected with it."

Ray DeLeva died on July 9, 1995 after a brief illness. Roger Hedrick had this to say about Ray DeLeva.

"The members of Fighting 17 all clearly remember how much Ray's expertise, advice and undaunted spirit helped overcome the many difficult problems encountered while operating planes from front line air strips at Ondongo, New Georgia and Empress Augusta Bay, Bougainville in the Solomon Islands. Ray contributed thereby in a very large measure to the success the squadron achieved in the war against the Japanese".

BOONE GUYTON

Boone Guyton, the famous test pilot for Chance Vought was a close friend of Tom Blackburn and had this to say about him and his association with VF-17. "Our association began in 1938 when Lt(jg) Blackburn arrived at our dive bombing squadron VB-5 in San Diego Naval Air Station, for duty. He had been in the Navy for two years after graduating from the Naval Academy at Annapolis, MD. I was an Aviation Cadet at the time, one of the first class of this new breed for the U.S. Navy, and had been in the squadron for two years.

From his day of arrival, we became firm friends, flew in the same three-plane section, made several war gaming cruises on our carrier, the U.S.S. Lexington, and engaged in social activities about the Naval Air Station together. He was, at the time married and I was, by Naval decree, a bachelor.

Despite Tom's being an academy graduate, and I, as a short time (four year tour of duty) cadet, there was no rank barrier between us. Tom was that way. Many regular officers carried a resentment of sorts toward cadets, as college intruders without the correct portfolio for a true Naval Officer. Tom cared nothing about displaying his rank over cadets. He associated freely with us and enjoyed our company at all times.

The chemistry between us was always good, and our friendship lasted-for the next fifty-three years. I should add, that as Tom later acknowledged, after his retirement from the Navy as Captain, he was out of touch with many of us for some twenty years. He became a patron of the drinking class, and spent much time off the beaten path, raising grapes for a winery in California. When he finally married—to a lovely Navy widow who brought him around properly—our old relationship returned and we visited each other and kept in contact. His later years were spent in Jacksonville Florida, while I continued to reside in Connecticut.

During our two years of active duty together in the squadron, Tom and I enjoyed cavorting, and competing in the air when we could measure off against each other. This occurred in simulated dog fighting, or simply using our training flights when occasion arose to roust about the countryside in southern California, land at times in oddball fields and enjoy life.

Tom was a dogged, persevering fighter pilot, always boring in and never quitting. Several times as our one-on-one mock combat continued, we would end up in a tail chasing dog fight, until with a tired arm or dizziness from high "G" turns I would pull out and wave-"enough!" Tom never once did. From contacts with his war time squadron mates, he performed that way in combat. He was a stern but fair disciplinarian, demanding regulation from subordinates if they became sloppy in attitude or execution. This was as I knew him during the pre W.W. II days. Despite contacts at our Vought-Sikorsky plant and my assistance visits with his squadron on the Corsair, as they prepared for deployment, I was not in combat with them.

I like to think it was my continual urging, in later years, that convinced Tom to write his fine book "The Jolly Rogers." You will note his foreword in mine, "Whistling Death," that Tom acknowledged about our relationship. Tom Blackburn was an exemplary military person from a family of Naval officers. I need not comment on his war record. It was one of the finest in the Navy's war in the Pacific. There remains great camaraderie in the squadron as yet, with reunions continuing despite reduced participants due to the attrition of aging."

Boone Guyton has passed away since he sent this information.

REPLACEMENT PILOTS

K.P. BABKIRK
Ens. K.P. Babkirk reported to VF-17 on 21 December, 1943. He was detached from VF-17 on 8 January, 1944.

EDWARD E. BEELER
Ens. E.E. Beeler reported to VF-17 on 11 January, 1944. He was detached from VF-17 on 4 February, 1944.

HAROLD JAMES "BITZ" BITZEGAIO
Harold J. Bitzegaio was born on 29 January, 1921, in Coalmont (in S.W. Clay County), Indiana. He began flying in the Civilian Pilot Training Program in the spring and summer of 1940 and received his private pilots license on 2 September, 1940. He enlisted in the Navy in September, 1941 and reported for duty in the NavCad program on 15 January, 1942 and was designated a Naval Aviator in October 1942, at Pensacola, Florida.

Lt(jg) H. J. Bitzegaio reported to VF-17 on 10 December, 1943. He served with VF-17 until they were relieved by VF-34 on 7 March, 1944. He finished his tour with 2 confirmed Japanese planes and 2.5 probables. After the war he became an Attorney at law, and later Judge, Vigo Superior Court from 1958-1980.

Harold Bitzegaio at Bougainville in 1944. Courtesy National Archives.

OSCAR IVAN CHENOWETH JR.
Oscar Ivan Chenoweth, Jr., was born on 16 July, 1917, in Salem, Oregon. He moved later to McMinnville, Oregon, and graduated from high school there in 1935. Enrolling later at Oregon State University, he left college studies to join the Navy in October 1940.

After receiving his wings and commission as an Ensign in 1941, he spent nearly a year as an Instructor in the training command. In mid-1943, however, he was sent to the Pacific Theater and was

Harold Bitzegaio at the 1994 reunion in Oshkosh July/August. Courtesy Donna Bushman EAA.

"Oc" Chenoweth at Bougainville in 1944. Courtesy National Archives.

assigned to VF-38 flying F6F-3 Hellcats out of Segi Strip on Munda. He scored one victory, a Zeke shot down five miles northwest of Ballale Island on September 1943, prior to completion of his first combat tour three months later.

Returning to the combat theater in January 1944, Lt. Chenoweth was assigned to VF-17, where he went on to score a further 7.5 confirmed victories and 2 probables. Chenoweth returned to the U.S. in June 1944, and commanded a dive bomber squadron. He was later in the second class of test pilots to graduate from the Naval Air Test Center at Patuxent River, Maryland. He left the service as a commander in 1954 to go to work for Chance Vought aircraft in military sales.

In 1968, "Oc" Chenoweth became a manufacturing representative for a food service company and moved to Orlando, Florida. Shortly after, on 19 May, 1968, he died of a heart attack.

Decorations

Silver Star

D.F.C.

Air Medal with 2 gold stars.

M. W. COLE

Ens. M.W. (Ward) Cole reported to VF-17 on 11 January, 1944. He served with VF-17 until they were relieved by VF-34 on 7 March, 1944.

JAMES EVANS DITEMAN

"Jack" Diteman was born on 21 November, 1921. He was educated at Shattuck Military School, and Montana State College.

He served at N.A.S. Corpus Christi, N.A.S. Jacksonville and then reported to VF-17 on 13 February, 1944. He served with VF-17 until they were relieved by VF-34 on 7 March, 1944. He later served with VF-84 on the U.S.S. Bunker Hill.

"Ward" Cole at Bougainville in 1944. Courtesy National Archives.

"Ward" Cole at the 1994 VF-17 reunion in Oshkosh. Courtesy Donna Bushman EAA.

Jack Diteman at Bougainville in 1944. Courtesy National Archives.

PERCY EUGENE DIVENNEY

Percy Divenney was born on January 1, 1924, in Cherryville, North Carolina. He was educated at Lenoir Rhyne College.

He became an Aviation Cadet on 7 August, 1942. He then on 16 June, 1943, accepted an appointment as an Ensign. He was designated a Naval Aviator on 2 July, 1943. He trained at Pensacola then Jacksonville and on to Carrier Qualification Training Unit, Glenview, Illinois. He reported to Fighting Squadron 21 on 12 November, 1943, and on December 7, to Carrier Aircraft Service Unit 5. He reported on 11 January, 1944, to VF-17, and scored 2 confirmed Japanese planes.

Medals :
World War II Victory Medal
American Area Campaign Medal
Navy Unit Commendation
Asiatic-Pacific Area Campaign Medal (1) bronze star
Purple Heart
Air Medal

He was listed as missing in action on 4 February, 1944; shot down by a Japanese Zeke during an attack against Tobera Airfield.

JAMES CASS DIXON

Jim Dixon was born on 29 December, 1922, in Parsons, Kansas, and attended Parsons Junior College for 1.5 years prior to joining the Navy. His assignments included N.A.S. Livermore, N.A.S. Corpus Christi, N.A.S. Jacksonville and N.A.S. Glenview.

He served with VF-17 at Bougainville for 4 months and is credited with one plane and one probable. After a short leave he served as Assistant Communications Officer with VF-84.

He relates his time with VF-17.

"My stay with VF-17 was very short (less than three months). I joined the squadron for their second tour of duty, as a replacement pilot on their return from R & R in Australia. My accomplishments with VF-17 were very few, but I did fly many missions to Rabaul as a wingman for many of the squadron's experienced pilots. I shared one plane with "Oc" Chenoweth over Rabaul.

VF-17 returned to the States and I became part of VF-84 with VF-17 executive officer Roger Hedrick as our skipper."

"We headed straight for Japan with the Task Force and made the first carrier raids on Tokyo. From Tokyo we headed for the invasion of Iwo Jima. After Iwo Jima we participated in the Okinawa campaign and I was shot down over Southern Kyushu and was taken prisoner of war. I later wound up in the same prison camp as "Country" Landreth in Japan near Yokahama.

"After the war I was a feed salesman for Ralston Purina Co. for 12 years. In 1958 I left Purina and purchased a large grain elevator and started to move into the commercial laying hen business. In 1966 we purchased a shell egg processing plant from Ralston Purina and continued to expand the laying hens. Today my son Chris is still operating this business".

Decorations:
Prisoner of War Medal
World War II Victory Medal
Asiatic-Pacific Campaign Medal
American Campaign Medal
Air Medal with 8 stars
D.F.C.
Purple Heart
Presidential Unit Citation

ROBERT EINAR

Ens. R. M. Einar reported to VF-17 on 13 February, 1944. He served with VF-17 until they were relieved by VF-34 on 7 March, 1944.

Jim Dixon at Bougainville in 1944. Courtesy National Archives.

Robert Einar at Bougainville in 1944. Courtesy National Archives.

JAMES WARREN FARLEY

James Farley was born on 13 October, 1919, in Horton, Kansas. He was educated at Ambrose College, Davenport, Iowa.

On 2 February, 1942, he became an Aviation Cadet. On February 5, 1942, he went to Corpus Christi for training. On July 13 he accepted an appointment as an Ensign. On July 25, 1942, he was designated a Naval Aviator. On 17 September he reported to NAS Miami, and on 27 October, 1942, to Carrier Qualification Training Unit N.A.S. Glenview. On 30 November, 1942, he reported to Escort Scouting Squadron Twenty.

On March 1, 1943, Escort Scouting Squadron Twenty was changed to Composite Squadron Twenty. On March 5, 1943, he reported to Fighting Squadron 3, and on 29 March, 1943, reported to Composite Squadron Thirty One.

On 1 July, 1943, he was appointed Lt(jg). On 13 July, 1943, he reported to Composite Squadron 16. On September 11, 1943, he reported to Fighting Squadron 11, and on November 21, 1943, reported to Fighting Squadron 10. He finally reported to VF-17 on 10 December, 1943.

Medals :

Purple Heart

Navy Unit Commendation

Asiatic-Pacific Area Campaign Medal with (2) bronze stars

American Defense Medal

World War II Victory Medal

He was listed missing in action on 26 January, 1944, after crash landing in the sea during an attack on Lakunai Airfield, New Britain.

LOUIS A. FITZGERALD

Ens. L.A. Fitzgerald reported to VF-17 on 22 December, 1943. He served with VF-17 until they were relieved by VF-34 on 7 March, 1944.

GEORGE M. "DUMBO" KELLER, JR.

Ens. G.M. Keller, Jr. reported to VF-17 on 11 January, 1944. He served with VF-17 until they were relieved by VF-34 on 7 March, 1944. He is credited with one probable victory.

George Keller's claim to fame in the squadron was how he obtained the nickname "Dumbo". He was given the high priority assignment to ferry a new TBF from Guadalcanal and utilize the huge storage space for loading large quantities of booze for the squadron. Unfortunately for him he flew over an A/A barrage which put paid to the squadron's large beer and whisky arrival. As you can imagine he was not the most popular person after this incident!

HARVEY MATTHEWS

Harvey Matthews was born on 22 August, 1921. He was educated at Texarkana Junior College, and the University of Arkansas.

Lou Fitzgerald at Bougainville in 1944. Courtesy National Archives.

George "Dumbo" Keller at Bougainville in 1944. Courtesy National Archives.

Ens. H. Matthews at Bougainville in 1944. Courtesy National Archives.

Ens. H. Matthews reported to VF-17 on 13 February, 1944. He served with VF-17 until they were relieved by VF-34 on 7 March, 1944. His other assignments included VF-3, N.A.S. Jacksonville, N.A.S. Atlanta, VF-84 and ComFairWestCoast.

Decorations:
American Campaign Medal
Asiatic-Pacific Campaign Medal with 4 stars
3 Air Medals
World War II Victory Medal
2 D.F.C.s
Presidential Unit Citation

JAMES MILLER

James Miller was born on 7 August, 1921, in Kansas City, Kansas. He was educated at Kansas City, Kansas, Junior College. He was President of the Athletic club, and was interested in football, basketball and track.

On 19 March, 1942, he became an Aviation Cadet. After Training at N.A.S. Pensacola, he accepted an appointment as an Ensign on 5 August. He joined Scouting Squadron 20 in October 1942. Scouting Squadron 20 was later changed to Composite Squadron

Bobby Mims, Skull and Crossbones ace with six planes at Bougainville in 1944. Courtesy National Archives.

ROBERT MIMS

Bobby Mims was born on 20 March, 1920, in Dallas, Texas, and educated at the Southern Methodist University. He completed the Navy flight training program at N.A.S. Corpus Christi and received a commission as an Ensign on 1 October, 1942. He was subsequently assigned to VF-17 in December, 1943.

Lt(jg) Mims had his introduction to aerial combat on 27 January, 1944, when he was greeted over the big Japanese Naval base at Rabaul, New Britain, by a pack of enemy fighters. He shot down one Zeke, another fighter he couldn't identify and shared credit for another Zeke. The next day the air was full of hostile aircraft over Tobera Airfield and he shared credit for shooting down a Zeke and probably got another. Then on 6 February his division was back

20. On March 5, 1943, he reported to Fighting Squadron 3. On March 29 he joined Composite Squadron 31.

On July 1, 1943, he was appointed Lt(jg). On 13 July he reported to Composite Squadron 16. Composite Squadron 16 was changed to Fighting Squadron 33, and on 26 September he reported to Fighting Squadron 11.

On November 12, he reported to Fighting Squadron 10. On November 30 he was detached from Fighting Squadron 10 and ordered to Fleet Air South Pacific, and reported December 5, 1943. On December 8, 1943, he reported to Fighting Squadron 17. He is credited with 2 confirmed and 2 probable victories.

Medals
Asiatic-Pacific Area Campaign Medal (1) bronze star.
World War Victory Medal
Navy Unit Commendation Ribbon
Distinguished Flying Cross
Purple Heart

He was listed as missing in action on 17 February, 1944, having been seen to parachute from his plane, when it was damaged by anti-aircraft fire during an attack against enemy shipping in the vicinity of Rabaul.

over Rabaul to pound the enemy again. This time he shot down a Tojo, two Zekes and probably got two other Zekes. This concluded his scoring, and he finished the tour with a total of 6 confirmed, and 3 probable Japanese planes. His other assignments included U.S.S. Hancock, N.A.S. Atlantic City and New London.

Decorations:
D.F.C.
3rd Fleet Unit Citation
American Campaign Medal
World War II Victory Medal
Asiatic-Pacific Campaign Medal with 5 stars

DONALD ROY McQUEEN

Ens. D.R. McQueen reported to VF-17 on 10 January, 1944. He served with VF-17 until they were relieved by VF-34 on 7 March, 1944. He is credited with one Japanese plane.

Don McQueen at Bougainville in 1944. Courtesy National Archives.

Earle Peterson at Bougainville in February 1944. Courtesy National Archives.

Harold Richardson at Bougainville in 1944. Courtesy National Archives.

LOUIS T. McQUISTON
Lt. L.T. McQuiston reported to VF-17 on 18 January, 1944. He was detached from VF-17 on 9 February, 1944.

EARLE CARPENTER PETERSON, JR.
Lt(jg) E.C. Peterson, Jr. reported to VF-17 on 22 January, 1944. He shot down a Zeke on 7 February, 1944, and was detached from VF-17 on 19 February, 1944.

HAROLD B. RICHARDSON
Ens. H.B. Richardson reported to VF-17 on 3 January, 1944. He served with VF-17 until they were relieved by VF-34 on 7 March, 1944.

C.L. SMITH
Lt(jg) C.L. Smith reported to VF-17 on 10 December, 1943. He was detached from VF-17 on 19 January, 1944.

JOHN MALCOLM SMITH
John Malcolm Smith was born April 2, 1922, in Owatonna. He attended Owatonna schools and was a 1939 graduate of Owatonna High School. He attended St. Mary's College in Winona before World War II intervened.

Lt(jg) Smith served for 4 months with VF-17 at Bougainville. He shot down 3 confirmed enemy planes, 3 probables and one damaged and was awarded the D.F.C. He later served with VF-84 as Assistant Engineering Officer and scored a further 7 victories taking his total to 10 confirmed.

John left the service at end W.W. II attending college and became a successful attorney. In 1950, he received his law degree from Creighton University Law School. He was admitted to the Nebraska and Minnesota bars in 1950.

John Malcolm Smith at Bougainville in 1944. Courtesy National Archives.

He married Therese Frances Martin on July 29, 1950, in Emmetsburg, Iowa. They had seven children.

He remained in the Naval Reserve as a pilot and was recalled to active duty during the Korean war where he served as a legal officer until end of 1954 when he opened a law practice in Owatonna, Minnesota.

From 1954 Smith practiced as an attorney in Owatonna. In 1957, he was winner of the Noel Davis Trophy awarded annually by the Navy Department for the most efficient aviation division of the U.S. Naval Reserve. Smith headed the unit based at Minneapolis. He was honored in 1965 as Boss of the Year in Owatonna.

He spent 30 years in reserves, had been a wing commander, and held the rank of Captain at the time of his retirement. He died on June 9, 1981 of a heart attack.

Roger Hedrick who was his commanding officer in VF-84 said.

"John was an outstanding fighter pilot and had 10 confirmed victories. He was a modest man and dearly loved flying".

J.R. TRAVERS
Ens. J.R. Travers reported to VF-17 on 21 December, 1943. He was detached from VF-17 on 8 January, 1944.

THE MEN ON THE GROUND

When VF-17 arrived in the Solomon Islands it was generally thought that the Marines looked after their planes. George Mauhar Leading Crew Chief explains:

"When we first got there we relieved a Marine squadron. Their aircraft were gone, but the groundcrew were still there, and they helped us get indoctrinated, not on the airplanes, we had our own mechanics who were superior to what the Marines had, as far as I'm concerned. The Marines and VF-17 plane captains worked together but they were only there for about a week. Then they went. From then on we were on our own.

We had a group called A.C.O.R.N. that were a kind of support. They weren't aircraft mechanics, but welders, craftsmen, etc. We did all our own maintenance. That's where Blackburn made a mistake in his book. The Marines helped us for a week or so. They were just awaiting orders to leave".

Among the VF-17 groundcrew was Lennard Edmisten and he relates his story:

"I was living in Green River, Wyoming, working on the railroad as a machinist apprentice when the war broke out. In May of 1942 I enlisted in the Navy. December of that year, I finished the Navy Aviation Machinist School in January and was sent to Norfolk, VA. assigned to VF-17. When you finished school you got your Third Class Petty Officer rating.

"Butch" Davenport and Crew Chief George Mauhar in front of a Corsair. Courtesy U.S. Navy photo. Robert L. Lawson Collection.

"I was plane captain on the first F4U we got in the squadron and Charlie Goyette was on the other one. Those planes had what was called a "shotgun" starter. It would give the engine a couple of revolutions and usually wouldn't start in the cold Norfolk weather. The engine had a "up draft" carburetor on it and every miss-start would dump raw gas into the air intake ducts. This would sometimes catch fire and blaze up both sides of the engine. If you could get a start, the flames would get sucked back into the engine and no harm done. If no start, you grabbed a CO_2 bottle, put out the fire and dropped the air ducts to see how bad you burnt the gaskets.

"One morning I was out on the line by myself when I started up the plane to get it warmed up for the pilot. I had a "stack fire," hopped out of the cockpit and grabbed a CO_2 bottle only to find it empty. I had to run to the hangar to get a full bottle and put out the fire. Someone must have seen the flames, panicked and called the fire department. By the time all these big fire trucks got to my plane, the fire was long out and I was busy repairing a burnt out gasket.

"The next day the leading chief and I were called into the office of the Group Commander. He asked me about my instructions on how

Lennard "Red" Edmisten AMM1c. Courtesy Lennard Edmisten.

to start one of their two new planes. I told him no one showed me anything—I had to learn on my own. The officer started chewing out the chief and he told him that "Red" and Charlie were the only people that could even get them started.

"Couple of months later a draft came out to send some mechanics to the Vought Aircraft plant in Stratford, Conn. I never knew if it was my F4U fire or not but my name was on the list to go up to the factory for several weeks training on the F4U. As I recall, I was the only person from our squadron to make the trip. Was wonderful liberty up there in Connecticut but didn't learn too much about starting planes! About this time they changed to an inertia starter anyway."

The F4U was a hard plane to work on in a lot of ways because of size and location of many of the components but it was a good one.

"Even with the many maintenance problems, we took great pride in keeping them in good running order and have as many as possible in flight condition at all times."

We qualified on our shakedown cruise on the U.S.S. Bunker Hill, CV-17. In September we headed for the Pacific by going through the Panama Canal. It was here that I took my test for Second Class Petty Officer and passed.

"When we arrived in Pearl Harbor—someone had decided to remove the Corsairs off the Bunker Hill in favor of F6Fs. A lot of stories about this; but I believe the one was true about making the aircraft compatible on all the carriers operating together. If your plane had trouble and was forced to land on another carrier—it only made sense to have parts and personnel to work on your downed aircraft."

Then it was decided that VF-17 were to become land based. All the pilots and support officers left the carrier Bunker Hill with the planes. Both the squadron and carrier wanted to keep the experienced enlisted personnel. It was finally agreed to divide us into two groups-ship based and land-based. My best friend and shipmate stayed aboard the Bunker Hill while I continued my tour of duty on Islands in the South Pacific."

Everett Lanman was one of the groundcrew who stayed on the Bunker Hill.

"When the Bunker Hill came back from Boston to pick us up, we were then headed for the Pacific. Arriving at Pearl Harbor they took off VF-17 and ferried them on the converted carrier Pee Willie to the Island I believe somewhere near Munda. I stayed with the U.S.S. Bunker Hill and several of us did to work on the F6Fs which had the same type of engine, the R-2800 Pratt and Whitney. We became plank owners of the ship and got into every action from Rabaul to Okinawa where two Jap suicide planes knocked us out of action, something we will never forget."

"I feel very proud to have been a part of VF-17 and to me they earned the title as top squadron in the Pacific. Believe me it was sure good to see them at Rabaul. Even though we stayed and were attached to the ship we had a place in our heart for VF-17".

On September 27, 1943 all of VF-17 planes pilots and crew were off loaded at Ford Island. Fourteen enlisted personnel stayed at Ford Island, among them was George Mauhar.

Lennard Edmisten continues his story:

"The rest of the enlisted personnel were sent to Kaneohe on the other side of the island to get a F6F squadron ready to go back aboard the Bunker Hill. These "white-hats" consisted of mechanics, metal smiths, ordnance men and a few seamen.

"On October 5 thirty more of us went back to Ford Island and rejoined VF-17. I don't know how they picked who would stay with the squadron and who would go back aboard ship. A lot of good friendships were broken up at this time. My friend and ship mate Harry "Hap" Harlow was assigned to the ship and I went to the squadron. Later we picked up twenty-three more enlisted personnel to give us a total of sixty-seven but not enough to operate a large squadron.

"I haven't read anything about the VF-17 squadron taking these men with them. Even Blackburn in his book "The Jolly Rogers" gives the Marines credit for maintaining their planes but didn't mention us sailors who had been with him from the start."

"We boarded the Prince William in Pearl Harbor and headed for the South Pacific. The "Pee Willie" was a small jeep carrier and not anything like our new Essex class carrier CV-17. It was so crowded and hot below deck that many got permission to sleep on the flight deck. I got my cot under a wing of an SBD, Douglas Dauntless dive bomber. I had hoped to stay dry under there when we hit rain storms but that wing leaked like crazy! I lost my birthday when we crossed the International Dateline on October 23rd. I always claim I'm a year younger but no one will believe that!

"We spent a couple of days in Espiritu Santo while the pilots ferried the planes up north. We flew by DC-3 to Guadalcanal and then on to Munda. We waited all afternoon for a L.S.T. to take us around to the Island of Ondongo. We were just off shore in pitch black when a lone Jap plane came over. I don't know if he even dropped a bomb but every ship and shore gun started firing at him. What a noisy, scary welcome that was!

"Ondongo was mostly made up of hard coral which made good roads and runways. The airfields our planes operated from were either coral or volcanic dust which caused major problems with our aircraft. I was assigned to work on nothing but hydraulic leaks to keep as many planes in the air as possible. Because we didn't have a full compliment of ground personnel we initially had Marines working with us on our planes.

"Unserviceable planes were immediately cannibalized for spare parts. We even had a tank outfit that was near to us and we used to borrow parts off of them to try to keep our planes flying all the time. So many hydraulic problems that the skipper put me and Charlie Goyette as hydraulic mechanics, because of the lava dust and everything got into the 'O' rings and cut those out".

The following is an example of the checks performed by the groundcrew on the F4Us. This was issued in December 1943.

**WORK TO BE DONE ON VF-17 PLANES-
TYPE F4U-1 ENGINES:**

1. Check harness for weak or burned out leads.
2. Check entire ignition system, mags., etc.
3. Check push rod housings for oil leaks.
4. Check all quick disconnects, oil return lines, diverter valves and oil coolers for oil leaks.
5. Inspect all drains for metal filings.
6. Check superchargers (visual) for wearing away of blower vanes.
7. Check and clean out entire duct system; blow out sand etc., check for duct leaks.
8. Check emergency fuel pumps-grease or replace as necessary (those have seen considerable use).
9. Check engine instruments replacing bad ones; fuel gauges, cylinder head, temperature gauges.

STRUCTURAL:

1. Check all planes throughout for structural failures or near failures.
2. Raise wings and check hinge pins, locking pins and linkages for fractures, operation and greasing.
3. Check control cables for fraying, binding, stretching, etc.
4. Check tab control cables and tab gears for slipping and wear and loose cables.
5. Smooth out any skin fractures and replace puffy filling around blast tube openings where necessary.
6. Touch up all paint work where necessary.

LIVING CONDITIONS

Lennard Edmisten describes the living conditions:

"Our camp ground was in a coconut grove and we were told they belonged to Palmolive. We weren't supposed to cut any trees down as the military would have to pay for them. I thought that was rather funny! Our tents were in a soggy hole that water ran through every time it rained. The Marines had pitched our tents and I am quite sure they knew how wet it could be. We finally got ditches dug to run the water outside the tents. We had six men to a tent and they were supposed to hold eight. It was so hot and muggy that we stretched the side out to let more air in. This also gave us more area to move around in.

"The floors were dirt and mud depending on the weather. We were always on the lookout for boards to make a little platform to get in and out of our bunks. We also got some old packing crates to make crude lockers for our gear. We found a piece of plywood for a table and some ammo cans for stools. We had cots to sleep on with mosquito netting over them. And could you believe we were issued double down arctic sleeping bags? Anyway they served as a mattress. The showers were about a block away and consisted of a wooden platform with a dozen or so shower heads. No walls, no roof, no hot water and setting in a lake to run off soapy water. Lucky they also issued us rubber boots that came about knee high. Most of us used them for shower shoes to get on and off the shower platform. Couldn't find any other use for the boots.

"We were issued green pants and shirts—I think they were for the Seabees. Most of us cut the legs from the pants making shorts and sleeves and long tail from the shirts. Sun helmets were mostly used to shed rain and sun. When you met a stranger, the first thing you asked was what branch of the service he was in. Couldn't tell Navy personnel from Marines, Army or Seabees. Most of us grew beards—pilots and enlisted personnel. There was little saluting and everyone used first name or nicknames.

"At that time they had their own planes. They took a lot of pride in their aircraft and they would clean it and wax it, do a lot of maintenance."

Being as how we were working on the planes and had conversations almost every day with the pilots you lost that kind of of-

Living conditions. Courtesy Lennard Edmisten.

These shacks serve as quarters for VF-17 pilots at Bougainville. Courtesy National Archives.

These shacks serve as quarters for VF-17 pilots at Bougainville. Courtesy National Archives.

ficer-enlisted man thing. We were a lot more friendly—first name basis—a little bit more personal."

"We ate in the Marine chow hall and their food wasn't all that good. Most servicemen complain about the spam they ate overseas. I don't remember ever eating it—our island got all the Vienna sausages. We had them boiled, fried, stewed in tomatoes and even served to us in the can. We gave them the nickname "Ondongo Round Steak." I don't know what the batter was made out of but it wouldn't even melt when we washed our mess kits in barrels of boiling hot water.

"A lot of us worked at night on the planes. From late afternoon when the first hop came back on until early morning. We kept at it as long as we thought we could have another plane in flying condition for the next day. All the work was done outside in revetments near the fighter strip. Quite often we would have a single Jap plane come over at very high altitude. I never seen them drop any bombs and never seen any get shot down by our A/A guns. They made us shut down all lights until an all clear sounded.

"We usually went into large bunkers and had our night meal. Usually K rations. One night a driver on a Seabee truck joined us in our bunker. When he saw our chow—he offered us some coffee and sandwiches that were left over from his delivery to some guys working on the flight strip. When he found out we could get him plexiglass and aluminium from our crashed planes he started making a regular food delivery. The material we gave him was highly prized by the troops to make jewelry and knife handles.

"One night on Bougainville a Jap plane got back of some nearby mountains and then came roaring over our parked planes at a couple of hundred feet and laid a string of small bombs on us. I had a plane on wing jacks and was pumping the landing gear into the up position. I was afraid he would knock the plane off the jacks and we would have an F4U sitting on its belly. Only one of his bombs hit near our

"Butch" Davenport's two plane captains in front of #9 their responsibility. Two fine young men but I always suspected that the one on the right was only 15 years old. Said "Butch" Davenport. Courtesy U.S. Naval Historical Center / M.W. "Butch" Davenport Collection.

planes blowing a few small holes in the tail section. We called the Jap pilots Washing Machine Charlie, Piss-call Bill from Bougainville or Piss-call Paul from Rabaul. Depended on where we thought he came from".

Harold Bitzegaio remembers one night:

"Every night when Washing Machine Charlie came round "Big Jim" would never get up.

So this night they dropped a magnesium bomb which exploded right over our tent area and he made a silhouette through the tent. He went through the side".

"Big Jim" Streig recalls this particular night:

"Hap Bowers was on the other side of the tent and we had a fan on the table between us. This Washing Machine Charlie—never had his engines in sync—he dropped a string of bombs over the hospital and right toward us. All I could see was bombs everywhere. I cleared the table I didn't hit the fan, Hap Bowers was just getting out of bed, I knocked him under the bunk went through a 2 x 4 and ended up in the foxhole on my back and not a stitch of clothes on. "Hap, about 5 minutes later, started moaning and groaning. 'What happened!'

Bougainville tents-We city Navy types were really roughing it. Said "Butch Davenport. Courtesy U.S. Naval Historical Center / M.W. "Butch" Davenport Collection.

Roger Hedrick outside Bougainville tents. Courtesy U.S. Naval Historical Center / M.W. "Butch" Davenport Collection.

I sure knocked him."

"Red" Edmisten continues:

"We moved up to Bougainville in January 1944 at Empress Augusta Bay. The Marines and Army took just enough territory so three airfields could be built and left the rest of the island to the Japanese. We could hear the ground fire as the troops kept the Japs at bay. On one road on the mountains we could sometimes see a Jap truck.

"We were near an active volcano and could see the smoke and glow at night. We often got some pretty good earthquakes. The soil was a very fine volcanic dust that got into the planes and started a lot of hydraulic problems. Charlie Goyette was put on working on hydraulic problems on day shift and I took care of them at night.

"The pilots were so eager to fly that they hated to have their planes grounded. I remember "Chico" Freeman had a bad hydraulic leak in a manifold in the cockpit of his plane and every time I wanted to down it so I could repair it he would say "Red—just give me a handful of rags so I can keep my instruments wiped clean." The plane finally came in for a maintenance check and I got that mess cleaned up.

"We started hearing 'scuttlebutt' in March that the Japs were bringing every gun they had on the island to make one big push against us. Sure enough—one morning I was sitting in the chow hall having a late breakfast. They had a second feeding for men who worked late at night. We were used to hearing our artillery firing over our heads at the Jap positions but these were heading in the opposite direction. That mess hall cleared out real fast! We went back to our tent area and everyone was in their foxholes or nearby. We just had to wait around because we had no transportation or officers to tell us where to go. We took a lot of shells in our area because we were near a tank outfit and the Japs were trying to hit them.

"We were issued helmets, which I used to wash clothes in, but no weapons of any kind. I was pretty sure the Japs wouldn't break through our perimeter. In the mean time the day shift down at the field got all the planes away without getting hit and then joined us with what officers were left. Someone decided we should head for the beach in case we would leave that way. We couldn't dig foxholes in the soft sand, no food or water. So we went to a second, more secure, camp before finally returning to our own area when

"Big Jim" Streig, Bougainville March 1944, 5.5 kills. Courtesy Jim Streig.

the shelling let up. We had two enlisted men wounded in the legs so were lucky that way. They got a DC-3 in on the second or third day and flew us out and finally home.

"I made First Class Petty Officer while in the South Pacific and when I got back States-side was sent to Chicago, IL, to a Navy school to specialize in hydraulics. My rate then was AMMH1/C. That was for Aviation Machinist Mate Hydraulics First Class. Between WW II and the Korean War the rate was changed to Aviation Metalsmith Hydraulic 1/c - AMH1/c".

"Hap" Harlow was one of the groundcrew who stayed on the Bunker Hill after VF-17 were detached at Pearl Harbor.

"Their feeling was different than many pilot-mechanic relationships in other squadrons that I was attached to. VF-17 were the tops in their field".

"At the time of the famous November 11 mission, I was working on the flight deck as a plane captain." He recalled.

FOOD

The tough self-reliant pilots had definite thoughts about their chow.

"Food was terrible, it was K rations powdered eggs, spam 3 times a day." Said "Country" Landreth.

"2 pieces of bread and 2 thick slices of spam. I took one bite and I thought I was biting into a lard can. I said these aren't sandwiches we can't have that." Recalls Dan Cunningham.

Groundcrew at Ondongo, November 1943. Maintenance crews of VF-17. These very few, dedicated young men, literally made VF-17's accomplishments possible. Courtesy Lennard Edmisten.

Groundcrew at Ondongo, November 1943. Courtesy Lennard Edmisten.

Ray DeLeva on left with a company rep. in front of "Big Hog". Courtesy U.S. Navy photo. Robert L. Lawson Collection.

Groundcrew at Ondongo, November 1943. Courtesy Lennard Edmisten.

"To have to eat green looking eggs and spam left something to be desired." Said "Windy" Hill.

"Reconstituted this that or the other and our good old standby spam. It was horrible." Remembers Roger Hedrick.

"It was absolutely dreadful we damn near starved." Recalled Tom Blackburn.

George Mauhar has clear memories of what the food was like.

"A lot of dehydrated food—butter you had to roll bread around it so it didn't stick to your mouth. Dehydrated eggs and potatoes. Potatoes were ok if you fried them. A lot of spam, sausages—small canned sausages. Once in a while fresh meat from Australia, goat meat or mutton.

"I admired the Seabees, they knew how to live and work. I got acquainted with one of their chiefs and they had an ice making machine. I ate with the Seabees. We had what you call a listrus bag. A big canvas bag that you put water into and then something like iodine. You were thirsty all the time and your stomach distended due to this. Once in a while we'd get beer. Pilots would fly and get some occasionally. The beer was put where the gun heaters had been taken out. Then the pilots would fly and cool beer!"

"Country" Landreth has a lasting memory of the living conditions.

"Powdered eggs. Have you ever had any powdered eggs? They look like something you don't want to eat until you taste them—then you're sure you don't want to eat them! Powdered milk, and spam. I guess the potatoes were real. We had Quonset huts, with cadet-type upper and lower bunks. When it rained they were not quite waterproof and we called it "Mud-Plaza" at Ondongo.

"That's the main place we saw "Washing Machine Charlie." One lone airplane—bzzzz, bzzzz, bzzzz, bzzzz—he would come over every night regular as clockwork and drop bombs randomly. He never did any damage that I know of, but was very distracting when you tried to sleep...They'd throw the searchlights on him, shoot at him, but as far as I know never put a hole in him. This was before our night fighters were available".

Harold Bitzegaio recalls.

"The thing that I remember most about, aside from the combat was our living conditions. We lived in tents and each of us had a foxhole dug right outside the door".

Groundcrew at Bougainville, February 1944. George Mauhar first L-R. Courtesy U.S. Navy photo. Robert L. Lawson Collection.

"In the steaming, bug-infested Solomon Islands during World War II, the war in your tent could be almost as bad as the one outside." Ray DeLeva, Vought Aeronautics Company field representative, recalls.

"It's sure easier," he recalls, "than in the early '40's when the military forces were recapturing, one by one, islands occupied by the Japanese after Pearl Harbor". The bright spot of the hour in those days was the Vought bent-wing Corsair, and it took experts like DeLeva at the frontlines to make sure as many of the Corsairs

Battle damage to an F4U-1A of the Skull and Crossbones squadron. Courtesy U.S. Navy photo. Robert L. Lawson Collection.

Yeoman Harry V. Meeteer keeps the squadron's flight logs, at Bougainville base, February 1944. Courtesy National Archives.

as possible stayed in the air. "Those were the days." DeLeva says. "When a Vought field representative's duties were just a bit trying!

The Japs were bad enough on Bougainville, but he found the scorpions, snakes, centipedes, lizards, ants and mosquitoes even worse. "On many a night I'd wake up with a foot-long lizard crawling cross my chest. I'd brush him off fast with one hand and then try to get back to sleep."

Sleep was almost a luxury for DeLeva and the other maintenance personnel, who worked day and night between Japanese air attacks to keep the Corsairs flying.

The Japanese were making an all-out attempt to re-take the allied airfield near Empress Augusta Bay and for most of this period, DeLeva was "fortified" in a tent a scant 2,000 yards from the front lines where the enemy had pushed to the very edge of the airfield.

"We had bombing raids almost every night by Japanese twin-engined airplanes operating from Rabaul," DeLeva recalls. "Sometimes there would be three or four raids in one night; at such times it would just be a case of jumping back and forth between your cot and your foxhole."

George Mauhar, leading crew chief with VF-17 tells his story.

"I was born in Pennsylvania, a little suburb called East Brady, in May 1918. My folks were from Croatia, met and married in America. They couldn't speak English. I had 2 older sisters one older brother, and 2 younger brothers. The family bought a dairy farm in Wisconsin, sight unseen. Black River Falls was the nearest town. At 5-6 years old I was milking cows and helping the family run the farm."

I was educated in a one room country school (6 years) then town school in Black River. All grades together. I didn't speak En-

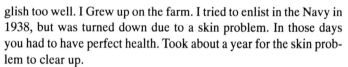

Groundcrew with "Butch" Davenport on an F4U-1A of VF-17. Courtesy U.S. Navy photo. Robert L. Lawson Collection.

"Ike" Kepford's wrecked plane at Bougainville 1944. Courtesy U.S. Navy photo. Robert L. Lawson Collection.

glish too well. I Grew up on the farm. I tried to enlist in the Navy in 1938, but was turned down due to a skin problem. In those days you had to have perfect health. Took about a year for the skin problem to clear up.

"In 1940 one of my friends Bill Adams got talking about going in the Navy. Recruiters came to town and we signed up. I got accepted to go to Chicago for another test. They rejected him. I said. 'I'm not going if you're not'. He said. 'Go ahead'. He talked me into it. Took oath in Chicago. It was my first time on a train going to Chicago.

"40 people in all, medical, interview and oath. Then they took us to Great Lakes training station. First thing you did was to get your hair cut. Took it off down to bare skin. Then took a shower. Then we picked up clothes still naked, dressed, and had an evening meal. In the chow line, you were not allowed to talk. We then marched out to barracks. We slept in hammocks 4 feet high, lots of people fell out!

"Training 6 weeks, then 10 days off. Reported back after Xmas. I later served on U.S.S. Ranger (carrier). Clothes had to be rolled, then packed into a sea bag. Ditty bag for shaving gear and personal stuff. We slept on the mess deck. They asked for volunteers every day. I didn't volunteer for anything. I learned the lesson in boot

camp not to volunteer. Any truck drivers, yes, pushed wheelbarrows all day! No more volunteering.

"Eventually there were only 5-7 people left who were told, 'we're going to make aviators out of you' and we were transferred to a squadron. I got into VF-4 with F-3s with the bi-wings. I was always interested in engines so I got to go to school. It lasted about 3 months. Came back to U.S.S. Ranger and went to the Caribbean. First liberty Ponce, Puerto Rico. Rum and coke, 10 cents, Cuba libra. They used to say for a dollar you could get screwed, stewed and tattooed! Liberty was cheap.

"The Ranger went back to Norfolk, and then on to the Invasion of Africa. I then received orders to report to VF-17. This squadron had a new type of engine with the Corsairs. I was sent to indoctrination school in Hartford, Connecticut, for a 2-3 week course. By that time I was first class (AMM1c).

"Blackburn believed in having fun, but he was strict. He had a bunch of pilots he really rode hard on. They were all high spirited dare-devils. On the shakedown cruise the Corsairs were a little rough to land. We nearly cracked up over half of them. By the time we got to Hawaii I was in charge of the engine section. Not all of the groundcrew would go with the squadron, but I knew the skipper pretty well and he assured me I would stay with him, as I believed in hard work".

George Mauhar recalls an interesting experience.

"The ship was leaving at 0800 from Norfolk. I woke up a few minutes before 0800 after a last night of liberty, and the ship was sailing out of the harbor. They always left a motor launch for stragglers. There was 10-15 of us, some were officers. They dropped the Jacobs ladder and got aboard. I was put on report. I had to see the skipper, Blackburn.

He said. 'What's your excuse?' I looked him right in the eye and said. 'I don't have any. If I gave you an excuse it would be a lie, I overslept'. He said, as he looked me in the eye. 'You better not do that again or I'll bust you!' 'Yes sir!' I was a good boy after that. But I didn't believe in things like that, we just had a bit too much to drink".

George Mauhar continues his story:

"The planes were stacked on the Pee Willie, along with Army troops also. I slept on the hangar deck, as we had no quarters. They hoisted the planes aboard and off again, then they were put on to a big raft to go to the airfield at Espiritu Santo.

"The first night on Ondongo we were told be prepared for an air raid. It was dark when we arrived. By that time Japs were bombing. They didn't hit us luckily. Next day we went to the airfield and got tents. Everybody was told to dig a foxhole. 'Doc' Condon, Morfield and Kern and me were all pals and shared the tent. We dug a foxhole right off the tent. Everyone slept on mosquito netting. Rugged conditions and rain all the time. If you took a shower your feet were muddy when you got back. We had this Yeoman. He was an older guy, as he already had grey hair. He said. 'I'm not going to dig any foxhole'. So that night we had an air raid. Guess who was in our foxhole. Old Meeteer. We picked him up bodily and threw him out. He dug a foxhole after that!

Ordnancemen service .50 cal. machine guns in the wing of one of VF-17's F4U-1A Corsair fighters, at Bougainville, in February 1944. Note cut-off toes in one man's boots. Courtesy National Archives.

Groundcrew at Ondongo, November 1943. L-R. Front Row. J.A. "Johnny" Craig, Lennard R. "Red" Edmisten, T.B. Fisher, E.W. Gober, E.W. Flynn. L-R. Back Row. E.R. McLean, D.D. McLaughlin, T.S. "Tommy" Pitts, G.C. Duke. Courtesy Lennard Edmisten.

"We had a lot of oil leaks. It was a great airplane but very difficult to keep in flying condition, especially around the rocker box covers. The first Corsairs had cowl flaps all around and the rocker box (we called them clam shells) had a gasket on and they would warp and leak. Oil would come back and cover the windshield. They were constantly pulling those rocker boxes off and repairing them. They would last for a while, then they would warp again. These cowl flaps had hydraulic lines and individual cylinders that operate the flaps. These would leak and oil would pour onto the windshield. Later on they modified them, after VF-17, to correct this fault.

"To keep track of 36 aircraft I had a black book and a status board with lines on it. Bureau numbers, sequence numbers, engines, airframe, radio, electric, ordnance were all kept track of this way.

"We had a rep called Ray DeLeva, who took this information and relayed it back to the factory. He knew this aircraft and was a prince. He was willing to work with the crews.

"We had some incidents. I don't care how good you are, when you're working on something sometimes there are mistakes. We had problems with oil coolers. On landing they would vibrate and cause leaks, by the hose cracking. We repaired one and sent it up for a test flight and you could see the smoke pouring out. He made his turn and came back just about dead stick and landed ok just as the engine seized up, due to no oil. I had a couple of mechanics check it out. I suspected what was wrong. To prevent the oil running out and draining the tank they would plug the hose. When he put it back on he forgot to take the plug out and it caused the hose to burst. We had to replace the engine after that.

Squadron groundcrewmen await the return of their planes from an attack on Rabaul, February 1944. VF-17 was then based on Bougainville. Note tape over muzzles of F4U-1A's .50 cal. machine guns. Courtesy National Archives.

Ground crewmen ride the wings of VF-17 F4U-1A Corsair fighters, as they taxi into take off position for a raid on Rabaul, February 1944. VF-17 was then operating out of Bougainville. Courtesy National Archives.

"After battle damage we would check the skin over. If there was no structural damage, just a hole through the skin we put gunnery tape over it. It would last for 2 or 3 flights and then you would put some more on. If it was structural damage then we had to do a repair on it.

"We had a couple of good metalsmiths who could make a quick repair, especially if the bullet went through the forward part of the cockpit, the fuel tank. If the bullet went through there you had to pull the tank out. A lot of times the self-sealer in the tank would get to the strainer and you would have to change the carburetor or engine. You did visual inspections on the planes but every 30 hours you had to do a more specific check on various things. We had quite a few extensive repairs. This A.C.O.R.N. outfit had some good metalworkers and they could do all sorts of repairs.

Getting broken studs out, etc. For parts we robbed Peter to pay Paul, mixed parts from other planes, lots of swapping".

The following memo was issued in January 1944.

OPERATIONS MEMORANDUM

1. All aircraft assigned to air activities on Bougainville will be given standard periodic checks. These checks will be commenced upon return of the first major mission each day and every effort will be made for completion prior to daylight the following day.

Not more than ten percent of the planes assigned a unit will be out of commission for this purpose at any one time during daylight hours. During hours of darkness, up to fifty percent may be out for check, depending on the tactical situation.

2. Newly assigned planes will be combat checked immediately upon delivery by the ferry pilot and prior to their first combat mission.

3. Field Commanders and Squadron Commanders are responsible that this procedure is carried out. **These checks are absolutely essential for successful combat operations.**

George Mauhar continues:

"One incident after first tour when pilots left for Espiritu Santo a guy named Lampe, a painter, who painted all the Japanese flags on. He had a little tent and he would close the flap on this tent and inhale all the paint fumes. He would get high, and get as happy as if he'd been drinking. I had to get on to him to keep the tent ventilated!

"We had no liberty in Australia, too busy getting planes back in shape. We had a club and by that time I made chief. At the C.P.O. club you could get beer. A bit more civilized there. When the pilots came back they had to break in some new airplanes and pilots.

The skipper got some beer and was going to have a beer party. So ice was scarce. I said to the skipper. 'I don't know how we are going to cool this beer'. I had a little ice but not enough. He said why don't you use the Co2. Those Corsairs were prone to catching fire with the up-draft carburetor. If they back-fired the whole damn thing would catch fire. I said. 'What are we going to do tomorrow when you want to fly'.

He said. 'We'll worry about that tomorrow'. So we took all the Co2 bottles and a bunch of canvas and we laid all the beer in a big trough and used the Co2 and covered it and had cold beer. The next day we had to be real careful not to start a fire. I told them if a fire starts throw dirt on to it. If a guy was careless and over primed it they were awful about catching fire.

"More parts were available when we went to Bougainville, but we still had the same maintenance problems as Ondongo. Once in a while a plane would come in from Australia to pick up casualties and had nurses aboard. Everyone knew about it a couple of days before and would rush down to see them. A round eyed gal. They would bring us liquor. I have paid as much as $50 for a fifth of bourbon, but it was worth it. You couldn't spend money anyhow.

"One of our guys used to make jungle juice. There was this big food dump where they kept all the canned food. Lampe made friends with this great big old black guy. Only authorized people could go in there. He bribed this guy with a drink and he would get all this canned fruit. He would put it all together and let it ferment after he put a little sugar in it. It then turned into what we called jungle juice. We would get quite a bang out of it! There wasn't much to do except work 24 hours a day.

"The incident that I remember is when the Japs start shelling us. There was a Navy squadron supposed to be coming in to relieve us for us to go home. Things had cooled off for a while. Our job was to maintain the aircraft 24 hours a day. We had 2 crews one night and one day. We had one revetment at night which did all the work because they had lights. A little generator. My working hours were 24 hours. I would catch a little sleep in a cot made up as I was working. We had 2 crews working 12 hour shifts.

"I would always get wakened to sort out various problems here and there. At one revetment which was working on 3 planes, we were sitting on this wall smoking a cigarette discussing some prob-

Two VF-17 personnel relax, prior to take off from Piva airstrip Bougainville, for a raid on Rabaul, February 1944. Plane is a F4U-1A Corsair. Note smoking volcano in the distance, and pierced steel mat on the airfield's runway. Courtesy National Archives.

lem when all of a sudden this Jap came over and dropped a bomb. It hit 30 feet from where we were, I think it was an armor piercing bomb as it threw sand and dirt everywhere. After that one morning we were getting about ready to leave. The Japs started shelling, early in the morning. I was driving back and forth trying to make sure all the planes were started and ready to go, with shells whistling around. Suddenly a great big explosion in front of me. I just put this thing in reverse and made a 180 and went the other way. This one guy got hit by shrapnel and it cut his leg and he was bleeding like a stuck hog. We put a tourniquet on it to stop the bleeding. We carefully put him into the jeep and took him to the first aid station. I heard later on that he was ok.

"Everyone was issued a rifle as we were the second line of defense, the Army was the first line. They called up some Marines who sent the Japs back again. We stayed that night then the next day we flew out to Espiritu Santo".

Just before leaving the combat area to go home George Mauhar remembers this incident:

"When the planes left we couldn't leave until the following day. Lampe was kinda dippy, but a real nice guy. He said. 'I know a place where they took some P-40 belly tanks and made canoes out of them'. He talked to Kern and said. 'Let's go over to this island over the bay where they had a big battle a few weeks before'. They said to me.

'Let's go over and get a lot of souvenirs'. I said. 'No'. But they finally talked me into it. We got into these tanks and went over there. We tied up these canoes and had to walk quite a way to this battle field. It was getting dark. They picked up a few things. I

Groundcrew at Ondongo, November 1943. Courtesy Lennard Edmisten.

Groundcrew at Ondongo, New Georgia, November 1943. Courtesy Lennard Edmisten.

George Mauhar at Oshkosh for the VF-17 reunion July/August 1994. Courtesy Donna Bushman EAA.

didn't get anything. Coming back we couldn't see our canoes, because the tide had come in.

"Anyhow we eventually found them, tied to this tree. By that time it was dark and you couldn't see the lights from our airfield. I guess it was about a mile across the bay. I said. 'You guys follow me', and we headed for the lights. By that time the tide had gone out. We started paddling. I couldn't hear the others paddling as we got about half way, so I turned round and the canoe capsized. So here I'm in the middle of the bay with my heavy boondockers on, flight suit, and I tried to flip the canoe over. Finally after trying to right it, it sunk. By this time Kern and Lampe came up. I took my shoes off and slipped off my flight suit and started to swim for the lights. I was a pretty good swimmer. Well after a while, there was a tug boat going by. I told Kern to see if he could get its attention. We didn't make contact with it, and I was starting to get tired, and the tide was carrying us way off. Lampe said. 'Are you ok'. He said. 'Let me swim'. So he took all his clothes off and he jumped in, held the canoe steady and I managed to get back in. Fortunately we kept our boondockers and coveralls. He swam the rest of the way and we finally got way out from where we were supposed to be, about 5 miles from the airfield. So we got our clothes on and left the souvenirs and followed the water line.

"It was dark and jungle. We were tired, cold, thirsty and hungry and it was about midnight to one o'clock. I saw a light, a Marine outpost, who said. 'Halt!' Then shots were fired. We said. 'Hey! don't shoot we're Americans, we're lost!' They were kinda leery because the Japanese pulled stunts like that all the time. We finally got in. They fed us and they had a jeep. I could see us getting stranded on Ondongo, but they took us back and we got back at about 5am. We ran to our tents got our gear together had a quick meal, got to the airfield and went to Espiritu Santo. On board I said to Kern and Lampe. 'Never again am I going to listen to you!'

"We wore cut-off dungarees, which were really indecent. Shirts with cut-off sleeves. We were all black (tanned). We had to take Atabrine to stop malaria. One a day. A lot of guys threw them away. In the mess line they put food on and at the end of the line you opened your mouth and they threw this pill in. Your skin turned yellow. One a day, 2 on Sunday. I never got sick. I weighed usually 180lbs but I came home at 145lbs". Said George Mauhar.

When asked what he missed most while overseas Mauhar said. "The thing I missed most while overseas was a jug of cold beer and a home cooked meal."

George Mauhar went on to join VF-84 on the Bunker Hill, at the request of Roger Hedrick. He took Cantrell (Ordnance) and Kern (Electrician) with him. George Cantrell was on duty on the Bunker Hill the day of the fateful kamikaze attack on May 11, 1945. He received the Purple Heart for his wounds but this was not formally presented until 1987!

Mauhar was also on the Bunker Hill when it was hit by Kamikaze attack.

"When the Bunker Hill got hit I was on the flight deck in between the 2 bombs. I got a little wound on my knee and got a Purple Heart. I then went back to the States, then to San Diego for shore duty. I served in the Navy for 22 years, with VF-84 my last fighter squadron. Then went into multi-engined aircraft.

"I served in Guam and finished my service there. I was then shipped back and paid off. I went and got a job in the Civil Service, doing the same thing, supervision and engineering type work, and retired there after 17 years. I retired to Missouri then sold and moved to Coronado.

"I met up again with VF-17 after attending a reunion in Virginia Beach. I lost all track of the enlisted men, I met up with Andy Jagger and then took it from there."

10

Reunions

The squadron first got together again in Virginia Beach some 40 years after they were first commissioned. In connection with the Association of Naval Aviation Convention. "Andy" Jagger arranged it and it worked out very well.

The following is a part of a press report at the time.

"June 3, 1983 was an exciting day at Hangar 500 in Oceana, VA. Seventeen members of VF-17, in town for the annual Association of Naval Aviation Convention, met with their lineal descen-

dents: the Jolly Rogers of VF-84." The sight of a fully restored, Skull and Crossbones emblazoned F4U Corsair circling the field and taxiing into the Jolly Roger flight line was a treat for all hands. Piloted by Dr. Lou Antonacci of St. Louis, MO, the plane's presence misted many an eye as the former fighter pilots took turns climbing aboard.

"The first annual Jolly Rogers reunion came to an end all too soon, with alumni and active duty members crowding the flight

At the 1984 reunion Lou Antonacci flew his Corsair in the original Skull and Crossbones markings with an F-14 Tomcat of the then current Jolly Rogers VF-84 over the Kitty Hawk memorial. Courtesy Andy Jagger.

VF-17 reunion Norfolk, Virginia, 1986. L-R. Mrs Lyle Herrmann, Barbara Jackson, Lyle Herrmann, Hal Jackson, "Ike" Kepford. Courtesy Hal and Barbara Jackson.

L-R. Hal Jackson and "Ike" Kepford at the 1986 reunion. Courtesy Hal and Barbara Jackson.

line to watch Dr. Antonnaci's Corsair depart". Since the first reunion at Virginia Beach the Jolly Rogers arrange to have a reunion once every year or two years depending on circumstances.

"Big Jim" Streig sums up attending the reunion in Chicago in 1984.

"For people who have never been through a situation like that, you develop a camaraderie and you are all brothers together. You treat each other as a member of the family and what amazed me, I didn't make the reunion last year. I got here this year, there was a lot of them I haven't seen in 40 years and yet we're just the same friends we were then".

One of the reunions was held in Washington, D.C., at the Navy Yard, where on display is an F4U in the colors of Tom Blackburn. A copy of Andy Jagger's famous picture is also there.

"Country" Landreth organized a San Diego reunion in 1986.

In San Francisco Tom Blackburn arranged a 45th year reunion in October 1988.

VIRGINIA BEACH

The 1992 reunion returned to Virginia Beach in May with "Andy" Jagger once again organizing.

Part of the press release at the time is as follows:

"Thirteen of the Jolly Rogers were in Virginia Beach this week—Andy Jagger and Ward Cole of Virginia Beach are members—to socialize, reminisce and attend the Association of Naval Aviation convention. Only 17 of the 42 original Jolly Rogers are believed to be alive.

"On Friday, the men from the famous squadron met with the Navy's latest Jolly Roger Squadron VF-84, based at Oceana Naval Air Station." Like their predecessors, the Oceana fliers have a skull and crossbones painted on their F-14 Tomcats.

"Jagger, an engineer who helped design the F-14, was particularly eager to inspect the Tomcat. The commanding officer of VF-84, Ron Rahn, showed the hog fliers photos of strafing runs made while the squadron was part of Operation Desert Storm. The old and new Jolly Rogers swapped lots of stories. Jagger said".

L-R. Bill Landreth, Hal Jackson, Rog Hedrick, "Andy" Jagger, Jim Streig. VF-17 reunion San Francisco October 1988. Courtesy Hal and Barbara Jackson.

L-R. Bill Landreth, Bill Popp, Tom Killefer, "Windy" Hill, Lennard Edmisten, Hap Harlow, Rog Hedrick, Tom Blackburn, "Andy" Jagger, Jim Streig. Kneeling *Mel Kurlander, Hal Jackson.* Courtesy Hal and Barbara Jackson.

1993 Reunion Denton, Texas: L-R. Bill Landreth, "Andy" Jagger, Dan Cunningham, Bill Popp, Hal Jackson, Jack Chasnoff, "Windy" Hill, Jim Dixon, George Mauhar, Ray DeLeva. Front. Mel Kurlander, Wally Schub, Harold Bitzegaio. Courtesy Hal and Barbara Jackson.

DENTON

Hal Jackson organized the Fighting Seventeen 50th anniversary reunion in Denton, Texas in May 1993.

The press report included the following:

"The men of the famous Navy fighting unit will celebrate their 50th anniversary in Denton this weekend, bringing along memories of their 76 days of glory over the Pacific.

"Denton attorney Hal Jackson was one of those top guns. He will be host of the reunion at the Radisson Hotel, Thursday, Friday and Saturday.

"Only 17 of the fighter pilots still live and 13 are expected at the reunion, Mr. Jackson said. Most are in their early 70s. Tom Blackburn, who was commander of the unit, is in his 80s and won't be able to make the trip."

Mr. Jackson had four kills while in the unit, but he later was credited with helping sink the Japanese battleship Yamato.

This week the Texas House of Representatives passed a resolution.

"Whereas the boisterous behavior of VF-17 pilots perplexed and infuriated some Navy traditionalists, but through their courage and skill in life-and-death struggles in the South Pacific, Blackburn's Irregulars became exemplars of the Navy flyers who prevailed against a formidable enemy during World War II;... be it resolved that the House of Representatives of the 73rd Texas Legislature hereby commend the gallant men of Navy Fighting Squadron 17...."

E.A.A. OSHKOSH

The first opportunity for me to meet the squadron came at E.A.A. OSHKOSH '94 where they were honored guests of the E.A.A. The E.A.A. had organized many events including:

"The Jolly Rogers—E.A.A. OSHKOSH's salute to the famous aerial groups of World War II continues with recognition of Navy Squadron VF-17, better known as the

George Mauhar at the Jolly Rogers reunion in Denton, Texas, May 1993. Courtesy George and Laurie Mauhar.

1994 reunion Oshkosh. Bill Landreth speaking at the E.A.A. Museum. L-R. Bill Landreth, "Andy" Jagger, Mel Kurlander, Jim Streig, Harold Bitzegaio. Courtesy Lee Cook.

VF-17 reunion Oshkosh 1994 L-R. Roger Hedrick and Ward Cole at Oshkosh. Courtesy Lee Cook.

A Corsair VF-17 remembered at Oshkosh, August 1994. Courtesy Lee Cook.

3 Skull and Crossbones aces. L-R. Roger Hedrick, Dan Cunningham, "Big Jim" Streig at Oshkosh, 1994. Courtesy Lee Cook.

'Jolly Rogers'. Join them for a special program at Theater in the Woods on Thursday, July 28, as members of this famous fighting force recall their heroic exploits in the Pacific Theater".

"Those who made it to Oshkosh encountered a response that both surprised and pleased them. Appreciation for what the Navy pilots did half a century ago is still going strong...as are the pilots. Though none of them are still active fliers, they remain very active people, full of energy and sharp as tacks when it comes to recalling their days in the air war".

"Country" Landreth had this to say about Oshkosh.

"We, the members of Fighting 17 are most sincerely grateful to the officers and members of the Experimental Aircraft Association and all the affiliated organizations for the invitation to gather here in this place and at this time. Many squadron reunions have kept our fighting spirit alive: This surely will be the very most memorable meeting.

"We are shipmates in the deepest sense. There are 14 survivors here.

VF-17 at Oshkosh in 1994. Back Row. Kurlander, Landreth, Cole, Hedrick, Bitzegaio, Jackson, Jagger. Front Row. Cunningham, Streig, Chasnoff, Mauhar, Bowers, Popp, Schub. Courtesy Donna Bushman, E.A.A.

Group photo of VF-17 and their descendants VF-84 at Oshkosh in front of F-14 Tomcat with Skull and Crossbones insignia. Two VF-84 pilots in front. Courtesy Donna Bushman, E.A.A.

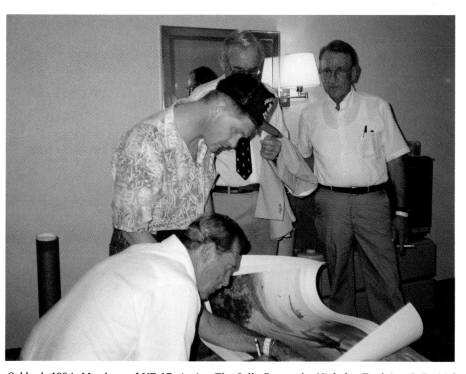

This world famous gathering of aviators, aircraft, and those devoted to aviation is the perfect time and place to do him honor for his leadership in the crucible of combat. To the founder Paul Poberezny, the president, Tom Poberezny, the E.A.A. coordinator, John Ellis III and Carl Swickley, Museum Director:

WE SALUTE YOU!!"

Oshkosh 1994. Members of VF-17 signing The Jolly Rogers by Nicholas Trudgian. L-R. Mel Kurlander (signing), Lee Cook (with cap), George Mauhar (behind Lee Cook), Harold Bitzegaio. Courtesy Hal and Barbara Jackson.

Theater in the Woods presentation to VF-17 by the E.A.A. Jagger, Jackson, Cunningham, Cole, Chasnoff, Bowers, Bitzegaio. Courtesy Donna Bushman, E.A.A.

Theater in the Woods presentation to VF-17 by the E.A.A. Kurlander, Landreth, Mauhar, Popp, Schub, Streig. Courtesy Donna Bushman, E.A.A.

Lee Cook standing next to Corsair "VF-17 Remembered" at Oshkosh, 1994. Courtesy Lee Cook.

A rare photo of a group of Corsairs flying together at Oshkosh, 1994. Courtesy Donna Bushman, E.A.A.

Six Corsairs flying at Oshkosh in 1994. In all eleven Corsairs flew in for the 1994 E.A.A. event. Courtesy Donna Bushman, E.A.A.

ST. LOUIS

Jack Chasnoff arranged the 1996 reunion in Clayton, St. Louis in April which was my second opportunity to meet the squadron. A great deal of hard work from Jack and his wife Alice to put it all together. An excellent reunion with 11 members of the Jolly Rogers attending with their families.

Wally Schub, "Hap" Bowers, "Andy" Jagger, and Lee Cook at St. Louis reunion, 1996. Courtesy Hal and Barbara Jackson.

11

Corsairs in VF-17 Colors and Aviation Art

Corsair in the colors of VF-17 ace Oscar Chenoweth at Oshkosh July/August 1994. Note the missing Skull and Crossbones insignia. Courtesy Lee Cook.

Owned by Evergreen Ventures "Ruthless II" is displayed in the markings of "Skull and Crossbones" ace Lt. Oscar I. "Oc" Chenoweth who finished with 7.5 kills and two probables while flying with VF-17. He was credited with a Zeke prior to reporting to VF-17.

Selection of photos of a Corsair operated by the Old Flying Machine Company which used to fly in the colors of Tom Blackburn's "Big Hog" at Duxford, England. Note only four Japanese flags shown instead of eleven. Unfortunately this Corsair has recently been re-painted in New Zealand markings. Courtesy Lee Cook, Howard Cook, and Bruce Malcolm.

My favorite photo of two Corsairs in VF-17 colors flying in England. Courtesy Howard Cook.

Corsair VF-17 Remembered at Oshkosh, 1994. Courtesy Donna Bushman, EAA.

Another view of Corsair VF-17 Remembered at Oshkosh, 1994. Courtesy Lee Cook.

VF-17 Remembered is owned by Charles Osborne Jr. After a great deal of work it arrived at Oshkosh 1994 still with primer on, the goal being just to get it there in time for the airshow. It has Roger Hedrick's name under the cockpit and a distinctive feature is a list in memory to all the VF-17 pilots that were lost or killed in action.

Corsair VF-17 Remembered at Oshkosh, 1994. Note: Still to be painted. Courtesy Donna Bushman, EAA.

A selection of photos of a Corsair in "Ike" Kepford's markings which flies at the Imperial War Museum Duxford Cambridge England. Note this is the same plane which flew at the 1984 VF-17 reunion. Unfortunately this plane has recently undergone a change of color scheme. Courtesy Lee Cook, Howard Cook, and Bruce Malcolm.

Kepford is owned and operated by the Fighter Collection at the Imperial War Museum, Duxford, England.

Louis Antonacci applied the VF-17 markings before selling it and it eventually found its way to England. At the "Jolly Rogers" reunion in 1984 it was flown by Louis Antonacci alongside an F-14 Tomcat in the present day colors of the "Jolly Rogers". An interest-

ing feature of this plane is the signatures of Tom Blackburn and Ike Kepford in large letters around the cockpit hood. This plane is due for a color scheme change for the 1997 air show season.

Owned by C.C. Air Corporation this FG-1D (*bottom photo*) has been restored by Chuck Wentworth from a pile of parts to a beautiful flying Corsair. It is displayed in the markings of VF-17 ace Lt(jg) Earl May who scored 8 victories whilst flying two tours with the Skull and Crossbones squadron.

Earl May usually flew number 27 but on several occasions flew number 8 on special missions.

FG-1D Corsair in the colors of Skull and Crossbones ace Earl May, 8 kills. Courtesy Warbirds International.

PACIFIC PARADISE by Les Vowles: Ike Kepford No. 29 leading his section shows that "Jim" Streig No 3 still carried the then out-dated red surround to the insignia. This provided the artist with just a touch of extra color. F4U-1's taxiing at Bougainville. Pacific Paradise is available from, Les Vowles, 56 Westwood Glen, Tilehurst, Reading, RG 31 5NW, England.

PACIFIC SUNRISE by Sam Lyons, Jr.: Lt(jg) F.J. "Big Jim" Streig taxiing his F4U-1 on the coral strip at Bougainville. Mr. Lyons is an artist member of the American Society of Aviation Artists (A.S.A.A.) which he served two years as secretary. Pacific Sunrise is available from S & V Enterprises/Lyons Studio, 4600 Kings Crossing Dr., Kennesaw, GA, 30144.

FIGHTING 17 by Jim Laurier: In this painting, artist Jim Laurier has depicted a VF-17 mission on February 7, 1944. After safely escorting U.S. bombers in and out of Rabaul, Commanding Officer Tom Blackburn led several of his Corsairs back to the east side of Rabaul's Simpson Harbor in a low-level strafing run on Lakunai Airfield. At the top of the painting, six Jolly Roger pilots are shown, left to right: "Timmy" Gile, "Country" Landreth, "Tommy" Blackburn, "Rog" Hedrick, "Danny" Cunningham, and "Ike" Kepford. Mr. Laurier is an artist member of the American Society of Aviation Artists (A.S.A.A.). Fighting 17 is available from Jim Laurier, P.O. Box 1118, Keene, NH, 03431.

BIG HOG Chance Vought F4U-1A Corsair by Jerry Crandall: Capt. Tom Blackburn's, BIG HOG F4U Corsair by Jerry Crandall; the scene depicts moments before Blackburn pulled the trigger on the J.A.A.F. Tony from the 68th Fighter Regiment based at Rabaul. Tom waited to fire until he was very close making sure the Tony did not escape. Limited edition collector prints available, each co-autographed by artist Jerry Crandall and Capt. Tom Blackburn U.S.N. (Ret.). Contact publisher Eagle Editions Ltd. at P.O. Box 580 Hamilton MT 59840 or call 1-800-255-1830. Copyright 1988, all rights reserved. Mr. Crandall is an artist member of the American Society of Aviation Artists (A.S.A.A.).

BIG HOG ABOVE BAGANA *by Joseph Szady: On November 1, 1943, 18 Vals escorted by 12 Zeros fly towards U.S. invasion forces landing at Empress Augusta Bay on Bougainville. Eight Corsairs from VF-17 intercept and the Japanese attack breaks up. Above an eerily smouldering Mt. Bagana, Lt. Cdr. Tom Blackburn dives out of the early morning sun and blasts a Zero out of the sky, then flies through the fireball for his first of eleven victories: "What a sensation!". Joseph Szady is a member of the prestigious American Society of Aviation Artists and a 1973 graduate of the University of Notre Dame. Big Hog Above Bagana is available from Joseph Szady, 6900 Prairie Road NE, #918 Alburquerque, NM, 87109.*

12

VF-17 In the News

When Mills Schanuel went into the U.S. Navy he left from a position of staff writer for a St. Louis, MO, newspaper the Post Dispatch. While in service he wrote four articles of approximately 10,000 words each, describing life as a fighter pilot with VF-17. Only one of these was published (December, 1943) in the Post Dispatch; the rest were lost in the Navy archives, victims of Navy censorship. The following articles are what I managed to find.

Post Dispatch
April 8 1944

St. Louisan Tells How His Group Downed 154 Jap Planes in Pacific

Better Teamwork and Equipment Beat Enemy, Says Lt. Mills J. Schanuel,

Who Got Three Zeros.

It was the superior teamwork and equipment of the Navy's land-based Skull and Crossbones fighter squadron which enabled its members to shoot down 154 Japanese planes recently in two campaigns in the South Pacific, Lt(jg) Mills J. Schanuel, a Post Dispatch reporter and a member of the squadron, said today.

Lt. Schanuel, son of Mr. and Mrs. Robert J. Schanuel of 2 Jean Drive, Florissant, is credited with having shot down three Japanese Zero fighting planes and having damaged another and a Japanese bomber. He arrived home yesterday on leave before reporting to an East Coast port, where the members of the squadron will be re-assigned.

The squadron was credited with shooting down 47 Japanese planes while maintaining an air patrol during the American landings at Empress Augusta Bay on Bougainville Island and with destroying 107 more planes while escorting American bombers in assaults on Rabaul

Knew What Each Would Do

"Our squadron had trained so long together that everyone in it knew what everyone else would do in a given situation," Lt. Schanuel said. "We had the advantage of training together for six months at Norfolk before being assigned to a carrier. We trained together on the carrier's shakedown cruise, went into the Pacific together and later were land-based together."

The squadron's first assignment in the Pacific was to escort Army and Navy bombers on missions over Buka Passage, Kara, Southern Bougainville and Kahili.

"We didn't encounter any enemy aircraft during these missions," Lt. Schanuel related, "and members of our squadron kept their aim in trim by hunting out and shooting up small Japanese barges.

"When our forces landed at Empress Augusta Bay early last November, it was a different story. The enemy would frequently send fighters and bombers from Rabaul to harass our shipping. Our squadron was maintaining a constant air patrol and, because of our superior detection equipment, we could spot their bombers about 50 miles out and get out there to scatter them and break up their attack. This went on for about five weeks and during this time members of our squadron shot down 47 planes."

He Downs Two

Lt. Schanuel got two Japanese planes, both Zeros, during this time.

"One day we spotted a group of Jap fighter planes about 50 miles out," he related. "They saw us and formed a big Lufbury circle. We had the altitude advantage and selected our targets. I picked out one of four fighter planes which was attempting to get into the circle and opened fire on him.

"It was my first plane and as he started down, I kept after him. Pretty soon chunks of his plane started coming past me. Then it caught fire and fell apart.

"Even after his ship had disintegrated, I found I was still firing my guns. When I landed, I learned I had burned out the barrels in three of them."

He got his second Zero in the same area a few days later. "On this occasion," Lt. Schanuel said, "the Japs saw us coming and turned away. We went after them and overtook them. I got one of them."

The squadron was sent to Sydney, Australia, for a rest, and then returned to the Solomon Islands to escort the bombing missions to Rabaul.

"Every day during this period," Lt. Schanuel said, "the Army, Navy and Marine Corps would send up bombers from another island. We would meet them over the sea and escort them to Rabaul.

Japanese Always Waiting

"Invariably the Jap fighter squadrons would be waiting for us over New Ireland. I saw my first big dog fight there. It was like something in a movie. Planes were zooming around and many were going down in flames. I saw a Marine plane go down with a Zero on his tail and turned my guns on the Zero, but missed. I followed the Marine down to ascertain and radio his position.

"Going back up, I saw another Corsair in a spin with his wing burning like a pile of straw. I radioed for him to bail out but he refused and stayed with his plane.

Miraculously, the fire went out, but all the way home his ammunition kept exploding, tearing holes in that wing. When we arrived at the landing strip his wheels wouldn't lower and he had to make a belly landing. The next morning that $100,000 plane was thrown in the junk heap.

"It is a most amazing thing to see how much punishment a plane can take and still get home. Our fighter planes showed they could take it as well as our bombers."

Friend Killed in Fight

On one of the Rabaul missions, Lt. Schanuel got his third Zero, but lost a close friend.

"As we flew near the target area, a group of Zeros tried to get at our bombers. I went after one as they came around and shot it down. Ens. Tom Kropf, my wingman, went after another. He never came back. He's still missing."

Lt. Schanuel, 25 years old, has been awarded the Air Medal for his work in the Pacific. He was graduated from the University of Missouri in June 1941, and was employed as a reporter by the Post-Dispatch until his enlistment in December 1941. He received preliminary flight training at Lambert-St. Louis Field and advanced training at Miami, Fla. He was commissioned in November, 1942, at Corpus Christi, Tex.

A Post-Dispatch Reporter at War
Flyer Schanuel Tells of Fight In Which 15 U.S. Pilots Routed 100 Jap Planes and Saved Ships

Americans Downed or Damaged 25 of Enemy Craft Trying to Pierce Defenses and Sink Carriers in Task Force After Rabaul Was Pulverized.

By Lt(jg) Mills J. Schanuel

A Post-Dispatch reporter, now a Naval fighter pilot, who has downed at least two Japanese Zeros in the Southwest Pacific.

February 27 1944

Lt. Duke Henning, who came to us as intelligence officer from Yale University, stood beside a large map of Bougainville and pointed to an island just east of the Shortlands.

"That's Ballale," he said.

We leaned forward to scrutinize the heart-shaped island with its single landing strip.

Henning shifted his finger to Southern Bougainville. "Down here are the strips of Kahili and Kara. And up here, north and south of the passage, are the strips at Buka and Bonis. All these strips are cut off from supplies and inoperative-as airfields, but the Japs there still have nothing to do but take potshots at our planes."

I had the opportunity the day before to observe how Army and Navy bombers kept the field at Buka Passage, for instance, so churned up that nothing short of a helicopter could have landed there.

Rendezvous With Bombers.

We had rendezvoused with the bombers over Baga Island just west of Vella Lavella, proceeded up the coast of Bougainville and then circled wide to come in over Buka from the west. Above us were Army fighters providing high cover, while below, looking extremely businesslike, were the bombers. To the Japs waiting nervously at their guns on Buka, this swarm of planes moving steadily in toward them must have been an impressive spectacle.

This was my first escort mission into enemy territory, and as I slid back and forth under our flight leader for a better view of the sky, my eyes began to ache from staring into the sun. Where were their fighters? Time and again I thought I had them spotted, but they always turned out to be our own fighters. I finally realized that, on this occasion, the Japs had no air opposition to throw against us.

And then, while the fighters ranged nervously overhead and the bombers, flying in close formation, pressed relentlessly on toward their target-the brown stretch of runway north of the Passage-black puffs of anti-aircraft fire blossomed erratically above, below and around them. Sporadic flashes on Sohana, a small island nestling innocently in the southwest mouth of the Passage, were extinguished by an abrupt, spectacular column of smoke as a well-aimed bomb seemed to sweep it clean.

Scattered Fires.

Then a column of explosions marched methodically down the Jap runway and the whole area below was enveloped in a cloud of dust and smoke, but through occasional rifts in this cloud we could catch glimpses of scattered fires started.

Henning moved his finger back to Ballale."This is the spot the front office wants us to work over occasionally-and of course, this little harbor in the Shortlands."

He pointed to Faisi.

Strafing Ballale was a blood-curdling business because frequently we could see enemy anti-aircraft fire neatly bracketing our planes from the beginning to the end, of our runs. Standard practice was to make a low, high-speed attack straight down the runway; but, curiously enough, no matter how fast we went, no matter how violently we kicked the planes around to shake off their fire, we still had the sensation of crawling. It was like a nightmare in which you try to run but barely succeed in lifting your feet.

Zooming low over the barren island, we could catch quick glimpses of the pitted runway below, the pattern of bare trunks that were all that remained of a lush coconut grove, the deep revetments walled with logs and the occasional flash of a hidden gun. Then abruptly, the island would be behind us; a quick glance back was enough to show that Ballale had resumed its disguise of lifelessness and desolation.

The leading Ace of VF-17 was Lt(jg) Ira C. Kepford with 16 kills, shown here flying his raised canopy F4U-1A near Bougainville in the Solomon Islands March 1944. Courtesy U.S. Navy photo. Robert L. Lawson Collection.

Harrowing Stories

It was only natural, therefore, that most of the harrowing stories kicked around in the evenings as we relaxed in our quarters centered about incidents which occurred during strafing attacks.

There was the big Jap transport plane, for instance, which the skipper and his division liquidated just as it was landing at Buka. Crashing clumsily, it exploded and burned a few hundred yards from the scattering troops waiting to meet it.

There was Burriss, who attacked a Jap ship near Chabai Plantation and used as his aiming point a large Jap flag hanging from the stern. "When I stopped firing," he said, "there wasn't enough left of that flag to blow your nose on. At about the same time a bomb from a B-25 exploded on the deck and gave that tub a shove that sent it aquaplaning 300 yards before it sank."

There was Jack Chasnoff, who, while strafing barges in Tonolei Harbor, looked up to see a sniper in the top of a coconut tree firing at him with a machine gun. Jack's voice always rose with indignation when he told of this.

Lt(jg) Earl May playfully sent his 50-caliber shells into the boiler of a small cargo ship and was startled to see the thing blow up-almost in his face.

And then there was Ira (Ike) Kepford, who caught several Japs working on the runway at Ballale and enthusiastically nailed them cold before they could escape into the brush. One of them jumped high, turned lazily in midair and fell to the ground about 20 feet away when Ike opened fire. The others rolled over and over like shot rabbits.

It is easy to see, therefore, why strafing assignments were generally popular.

Preying on Foe.

As the time passed, more and more Jap flags began to appear on our planes and on the propeller blades stuck outside the ready hut-our squadron scoreboard.

Combat narratives recorded by Lt. Duke Henning after each scrap, when wildly-gesticulating pilots crowded around our long-suffering intelligence officer to tell their stories, fitted pretty much the same pattern: enemy fighters and bombers intercepted and smeared in abortive attempts to strike our shipping in Empress Augusta Bay.

And attached to these reports were detailed accounts of the battle which, when I read them, always seemed utterly meaningless—not because they weren't complete, but because words fail miserably to describe the spectacle of an exploding airplane; for instance, the tense moment before the first pass, the surprise we always felt at the sight of those big crimson circles, the time when six of us looked down to see a giant Lufbury circle of Jap fighters form in 30 seconds or (say) the thrill I got once when I saw two Corsairs cleverly box a Jap bomber and destroy him as he squirmed like an eel to escape their fire.

It is equally difficult to give a very comprehensive description of the events of November 11, 1943, when, after a large carrier attack on Rabaul, the Japs sent out from the smoking shambles of their airfields more than a hundred planes to seek out and destroy the United States task force that had hit them. I can only describe the small part I saw of the attack.

Something Big in Air

A few days before, the scuttlebutt experts, whose ears constantly vibrate like insects' antennae, roused themselves from their lethargy and began to pass the word around that "something big was in the air," something outside our daily combat routine. In these rumors the name "Rabaul" figured prominently.

Curious, I consulted the reconnaissance photographs and maps of the area. There she was, the last Jap bastion in the South Pacific, on the north side of New Britain—a sprawling place with a good harbor, five vicious-looking airfields, several not quite extinct volcanoes and acres of installations.

But the puzzling feature of the assault on Rabaul was the distances involved. An attack by planes based in New Guinea seemed out of the question and, since the strip at Torokina was not yet completed, Solomons-based planes could not very well participate. There were carriers, of course, but to bring the flattops into range of Rabaul-based planes would be a risky business.

But I had the answer the next morning when I saw mechanics re-installing the arresting gear on my plane.

The plane captain, Rasmussen, grinned at me. "Looks like you're headed back for the carrier, Mr. Schanuel."

I looked at the hook for a moment and shuddered. "Who told you to put this thing on?" I asked.

"Captain's orders."

"Did he say why?"

"No, sir! He just told all the plane captains to get the hooks back on."

Straight Dope.

When we got the straight dope from the captain, we learned that while carrier-based planes were hitting Rabaul, we were to furnish the combat air patrol for the carriers; and when our gas ran low, the captain explained, we would land aboard to refuel. It was all very simple.

And so it came to pass that early in the morning on November 11 we took off into the predawn murk and headed out to intercept our task force, then a few hundred miles away. At this time of the morning, when the light seems to seep down into the gloom from above, the sky was like a scene from another planet. Towering cloud formations formed vague mountains and valleys, while an almost unbroken layer of clouds below created the illusion of a vast floor that stretched away as far as the eye could reach. Hanging "motionless" in the sky nearby were the long silhouettes of the other planes, their under-cowling weirdly illuminated by the blue torch from the exhaust stacks.

An hour later we spotted the task force pounding along below like shadowy ghost-ships, tracing intricate patterns in the sea as the wakes crossed and re-crossed with the weaving of the vessels.

All morning long we ranged lazily overhead while the carriers launched their planes. Apparently, the Japs never suspected we were in their backyard or they would have thrown everything they had against us before the flattops could attack.

Enemy 'Catches Hell.'

Late in the morning we landed aboard, and while our planes were serviced, had coffee in the ready-room and listened to a play-by-play account of the attack as it was radioed in by our planes. The Japs, we concluded with grim satisfaction, were catching hell.

The enemy certainly knew by then that our carriers were nearby and would be eager for revenge-it looked like a busy afternoon.

And it was. For the Japs cleverly trailed our bombers back to the ships, worming their way in while we frantically hunted them out like a pack of excited dogs.

Some of their planes were intercepted and destroyed; others got in but were smashed by the ships' screen of ack-ack before they could release their bombs. Some, harassed by the fighters, dropped their bombs wildly and withdrew; others wheeled in combat overhead with the Hellcats and Corsairs.

It was Ike Kepford's day. He and Thad Bell were just turning for home when they looked back to see the ships beginning to fire; then, realizing the task force was under attack, they turned back and entered the fight a fraction of a minute after the Jap dive bombers had pushed over into their attack. Bell, following one column of bombers down, nailed two just as they were entering the anti-aircraft screen. But Kepford, who had broken away from Bell at the beginning of the attack, began to run hog-wild.

Weaving in and out of the descending column of Jap bombers', Ike shot down four in as many minutes. This number included a torpedo bomber which he pursued deep into our anti-aircraft screen to destroy.

Meanwhile, Lt. Cdr. Hedrick and I flushed out a Zero which darted for home at high speed-with the two of us but a few hundred yards behind. The Jap sped down a long corridor of clouds, weaving slightly to confuse our aim, and swept out of sight into a cloud. We

Roger Hedrick, Bougainville, February 1944. Courtesy U.S. Navy photo. Robert L. Lawson Collection.

went in after him and immediately burst out into the sunshine again to see the quarry breaking away for a dense cloud-bank ahead. But we were closing on him, for his wing steadily grew in my sight. When he was within range, I opened fire; but Hedrick had beaten me to the draw-the Jap, already smoking and burning, fell away into the water.

Bomber Shot Down.

While this was happening, shortly after the skipper had pursued and destroyed two Jap fighters, Lt. Johnny Kleinman and Burriss, the second section of Lt. Cdr. Blackburn's division, dove down close to the water in search of bombers. Burriss, spotting a bomber almost instantly, broke away from Kleinman and shot it down—almost under the noses of several of our fighters who were already on the Jap's tail.

Burriss then joined up on Lt. Lem Cooke in time to catch a torpedo bomber heading back toward the north, and when, after several runs the Jap failed to explode, Burriss sat on his tail and fired until the bomber fell apart.

Kleinman, meanwhile, had caught and destroyed a Jap torpedo bomber before it could drop its pickle but was wounded by our own anti-aircraft in the attempt. The shell, which exploded in the cockpit, smashed his instrument panel—and Kleinman had to navigate home by the sun.

But the same stories of the day's fighting could be repeated a dozen times with different names. Fifteen pilots of our squadron destroyed or damaged 26 Jap planes in the few minutes of the attack.

Gradually, the warships ceased firing as the sky cleared. The tiny black puffs that hung over the scene of the battle became indistinct wisps of grey, and the destroyers, which had moved in at the first of the attack to protect the carriers, returned to their original positions. Tiny columns of smoke hanging in the center of oil slicks on the water marked the spots where the Jap fighters and bombers had gone in.

And over the whole area there hung a sudden calm: it was as though everyone, when the fight was over, had taken time out for a sigh of relief and to take stock of the situation.

I counted the warships—they were all there.

St. Louis Pilot Writes Parents Of Shooting Down His First Zero
November 27, 1943

Lt(jg) Mills J. Schanuel a Navy fighter pilot and a member of the Post-Dispatch staff on leave with the armed services, shot down his first Japanese Zero recently in air combat in the South Pacific, he informed his parents, Mr. and Mrs. Robert J. Schanuel, 2 Jean Drive, Florissant, in a recent letter.

"I have tangled with Zeros twice so far," Lt. Schanuel wrote, "and have succeeded in shooting down one. I'll give you the details when I get home—and only God knows when that will be."

In the same letter, postmarked November 16, the 24-year-old flyer explained that he could not disclose the location of his squadron, but he gave indication of where he is by saying: "Living conditions here are a little primitive and we receive no mail and we have no assurance that the mail we send will get through. This, I

think, will give you some idea of how isolated we are at this outpost."

Flying from land, he said, more than compensates for the greater personal comfort the aircraft carrier offers, and the only nuisances he could think of at the moment, he said, "are mud and Jap bombers." The bombers, he explained, "interfere with our sleep. After a half hour or so in a foxhole, however, everything quiets down and we go to sleep again."

"In our daily flying," he wrote, "we come in constant contact with the Sons of Nippon. We strafe them in evacuation barges; we shoot up their airfields and our squadron has already an excellent record in Jap planes shot down."

In an earlier letter, Lt. Schanuel said he was sending to his parents a picture "of a group of the roughest, toughest, hottest pilots ever to fly into a barrier, or a slow roll under a bridge." He explained they were the flying personnel of his squadron. The picture, however, was never received.

Lt. Schanuel was graduated from the University of Missouri in 1941. He enlisted as an aviation cadet in the Navy in December, 1941, and received his preliminary training at Lambert-St. Louis Field. From there he was given advanced training at Miami, Fla., and a year ago was commissioned an ensign at Corpus Christi, TX.

LIEUT. SCHANUEL GETS 2ND ZERO IN PACIFIC COMBAT
Dec 13, 1943

Post-Dispatch Man in Navy Squad of Six That Attacked 39 Enemy Planes, Downed 5.

Lt(jg) Mills J. Schanuel of Florissant, who has written his parents that he has shot down two Japanese Zeros and damaged an enemy bomber, was one of six American Navy fighter pilots who swept into formations of 15 Japanese bombers and 24 fighters over Bougainville November 8 and shot down a total of five planes without loss to themselves, delayed Associated Press dispatches disclosed today.

Lt. Schanuel, 25 years old, son of Mr. and Mrs. R.J. Schanuel, 2 Jean Drive, and a member of the Post-Dispatch staff, wrote his parents a month ago that he had shot down his first Zero "when the fellow happened to pass through my sights." A more recent letter told of getting another enemy fighter plane and damaging a bomber.

"I've got two Zeros to my credit now," he wrote, "although I think I've shot at every Japanese plane ever built."

He is a member of the "Skull and Crossbones" gang-the name chosen by his squadron-which has been described by war correspondents as the deadliest land-based Navy fighter group in the South Pacific.

Vern Haugland, Associated Press correspondent, wrote that the squadron was led into battle for the first time October 29. Since then the outfit has shot down 47 Japanese planes, destroyed 21 barges, nine cargo ships and one tug. Also it has silenced a number of anti-aircraft positions on Bougainville and in the Shortlands area of the Solomon Islands.

That first action of the squadron was comparatively tame, considering later battles. It was a barge hunt. Three days later, covering the Marine invasion of Bougainville, Schanuel and his squadron got into its first air combat near Mt. Bagana volcano in Bougainville and shot down six Zeros.

Following the November 8 fight with the bombers and Zeros, the squadron, which Lt. Schanuel has described in letters to his parents as the roughest, hottest and fightingest bunch in the Navy, led a flight of American bombers on a North Bougainville strike, shooting down a Japanese transport and destroying a Zero on the Buka airfield.

Action came fast and thick after that. The group, under command of Lt. Cdr. John Blackburn of Washington, drove off 40 to 50 enemy bombers and 50 to 60 fighters as they attempted to attack an American aircraft carrier off Bougainville after the carrier had launched its planes for an attack on Rabaul, big Japanese naval base.

When Schanuel and his companions ran short of fuel in this action, they landed on the carrier, refueled and went up again. They shot down a total of 18 planes. Only one member of the group has been lost.

A letter received last week by Mr. and Mrs. Schanuel told of a member of the squadron being shot down in flames. The flyer bailed out at the last minute, Lt. Schanuel wrote, "to keep from being strafed by Japs." The Lieutenant continued: "We looked for him but he was nowhere to be found. The next morning, however, some of the boys were out before dawn. They thought they saw a light on the water and circled until daylight. Sure enough, it was our man, floating around in a rubber boat."

ST. LOUIS NAVY FLYER GETS HIS THIRD ZERO

MARCH 17 1944

Lt. Mills J. Schanuel Writes Parents Encounter Was 'Quite Decisive.' Lt(jg) Mills J. Schanuel, a Post-Dispatch reporter on leave as a Navy fighter pilot in the South Pacific, has shot down his third Zero, a Marine Corps correspondent related in a dispatch received here today. Lt. Schanuel described the encounter laconically as "quite decisive" in a letter to his parents, Mr. and Mrs. Robert J. Schanuel, 2 Jean Drive, Florissant. His battle score now is two downed over Bougainville, one over Rabaul.

At the time Lt. Schanuel was knocking the two Japanese planes out of the sky over advancing Marine troops on Bougainville, the dispatch recounted, on the ground covering the action was Tech. Sgt. Theodore C. Link, 5322 Savoy Court, another reporter on leave from the Post-Dispatch. Neither knew of the presence of the other.

Sgt. Link, also a Marine combat correspondent, was one of the first reporters to land at Empress Augusta Bay, hitting the beach with the first wave of troops. Lt. Schanuel was flying with a squadron based in the New Georgia Islands. The fighting was the first action for both.

Early in the assault at Bougainville, Sgt. Link was wounded by seven pieces of shrapnel. Though his wounds were painful, he refused hospitalization and after medical treatment resumed his duties in action, assisting corpsmen with the injured. Keith Palmer, an Australian correspondent and a writer for Newsweek magazine, was

killed in the same battle by a bomb which exploded near Sgt. Link's foxhole.

Lt. Schanuel and Sgt. Link still have not met overseas, but they now know one another's location and plan to have a reunion somewhere in the South Pacific.

By the time the Bougainville air field was completed for occupancy by the Navy fighters, Sgt. Link had moved on to another base. Several weeks ago, however, he returned to Bougainville. By the time Lt. Schanuel learned of his presence there, Sgt. Link had moved again to another island.

Much was written about the "Skull and Crossbones Squadron" in World War II.

I have included some of these reports.

Four Southland Flyers Destroy 16 Jap Planes

Four Southlanders, members of a record-breaking Navy Corsair fighter squadron which has destroyed 154 planes in nine weeks of combat in the South Pacific, have a combined total of 16 Zeros as their contribution. High man among the quartet is Lt. Cdr. Roger R. Hedrick of San Gabriel. He is third ranking ace in the squadron with nine planes. In 30 minutes of action over Rabaul he downed three ships. His wife Barbara and 2-year-old daughter Barbara Lee live with his mother in San Gabriel. He graduated from City College in 1934.

Four Zeros are listed for Lt(jg) Tom Killefer, 27, of Hermosa Beach, son of Wade (Red) Killefer, former minor league baseball manager. A Stanford graduate, former Rhodes scholar and Harvard Law School student, Killefer was in the thick of the heaviest fighting in the Rabaul area.

Lt(jg) Doris Clyde Freeman of 2325 S. Sycamore Ave. shot down two planes last November 26 when six enemy ships attempted a strafing run against marine installations near Rabaul. None of the enemy planes got away, Freeman's fellow pilots getting the remaining four. Freeman operates a plane named Los Angeles City Limits.

He is the son of Mrs. H. Duke Hancock of Los Angeles.

One plane is credited to Ensign William P. Meek, of Covina, who shot down a Zero over St. George Channel between New Britain and New Ireland.

Five Southern Californians are serving in the ground maintenance crew of the crack fighter group which is known as the Skull and Crossbones Squadron.

They are: Aviation Machinist's Mates First Class George H. Lampe, 23, of Venice; William Yager, 20, of Los Angeles; Edgar A. Homewood, 29, of Hollywood; Aviation Machinist's Mates Second Class Paul R. Kagel, 22, of Glendale. and medical attendant for the entire squadron, Pharmacist's Mate Second Class Ellsworth E. Miller, 21, of North Hollywood.

ONE AIR SQUADRON BAGS 47 ZEROS IN MONTH

During its first tour of duty, lasting less than a month, the deadliest land-based Navy fighter squadron in the South Pacific shot down 47 Jap planes, destroyed 21 barges, 9 cargo ships and 1 tug.

They also silenced a number of anti-aircraft positions on Bougainville and in the Solomons, and destroyed three houses.

Led Squadron

Twenty-two pilots in the Corsair squadron known as the "Skull and Crossbones" gang accounted for at least one Japanese plane each. Ensign Bradford Baker of Seattle, the only pilot lost in combat, shot down a Jap bomber before he crashed.

Lt. Cdr. John Blackburn, 31, Washington D.C., led the squadron into action for the first time October 29, on a barge hunt. Three days later, during the Empress Augusta Bay landing of Marines November 1, the squadron got into its first air combat near Bougainville's Mt. Bagana volcano, and shot down six Zeros. Blackburn got two, and Lt. Cdr. Roger Hedrick, Hollywood; Lt. Shelton Beacham, Kittyhawk, N.C.; Lt(jg) Tom Killefer, Hermosa Beach, Cal., and Ensign Frederick J. Streig, Watsonville, Cal., each bagged one.

Hedrick led a six-plane formation into battle with 15 Jap bombers and 24 fighters over Bougainville November 8, and the Navy flyers shot down five, without a loss themselves.

In other air battles Lt. Thad Bell, Los Angeles, got two Jap bombers, and Lt. Doris (Chico) Freeman of Beverly Hills, Cal., got one.

"Ike" Kepford returned to a heroe's welcome and the reports that follow detail some of the recognition he received for his many accomplishments.

Kepford Sends Four Japanese Bombers Crashing Into Sea in Rabaul Battle
Has Biggest Toll of His Squadron When 18 Enemy Warplanes Destroyed

He'd rather block than carry the ball...He liked to throw himself at opponents to clear the way for his ball carriers. That was Ira (Ike) Kepford at Muskegon High School, and later when he was an outstanding football player at Northwestern University.

Thursday of last week Ira showed the same disregard for his personal safety in an engagement over the South Pacific, Associated Press dispatches today relate. All he accomplished was to send four Japanese bombers crashing into the sea.

Ensign Kepford, with a land based unit of the Navy Air Corps, aided his squadron as it shot down 18 enemy planes in helping ward off a Japanese air attack on the United States carrier force which struck Rabaul that day. Eleven of the victims were bombers, seven fighters, and Ensign Kepford took the biggest toll.

"I got the first three before they knew what was happening," Ira said when he returned to his base.

Kepford shaken, Humble after Downing 16th Plane

An advance South Pacific Base, February 23 Lt(jg) Ike Kepford of Muskegon, Mich., has a total of 16 Japanese planes to his credit, but the last three gave him his biggest thrill—and his biggest score.

Nos. 14, 15 and 16 came during a raid on Rabaul February 19. First he picked off a Jap float plane. Then things started happening. Three Zeros jumped the former Muskegon High School and North-

western University athlete at 1,000 feet. He didn't dare go higher so he dropped his flaps to brake his plane. After he caught one Zero off balance another took its place and hemmed him in.

With his gas running low he radioed his base:

"Boxed in by three. Chalk two up for Ike. This looks like the works, boys."

One of the Zeros dived at him but a quick maneuver sent it spinning into the water—that was number three for the day.

Kepford, speeding for home, out-distanced his pursuers and arrived at his base with only a mite of gas left. He sat for a full minute with bowed head after cutting his motor, then remarked: "I am shaken and I am humble."

NAVY PACIFIC ACES PRAISE FOE'S SKILL
Skull and Crossbones Squadron Fliers, Back From War, Deny Japanese Pilot Decline

Recent statements that the Japanese are running short of pilots and that the quality of their airmen is deteriorating were contradicted here today by aces of the Navy's leading fighter group—the famous "Skull and Crossbones" F4U (Corsair) Squadron whose members have set a Pacific record by shooting down 154 Japanese planes in seventy-six days of combat, including sixty missions of escorting bombers in the New Georgia-Bougainville and Rabaul sectors.

If anything, said Lt. Cdr. J.T. (Tommy) Blackburn, 31, of Chevy Chase, MD, the squadron commander, the Japanese pilots have improved since the early days of South Pacific air combat at Guadalcanal. "The Japs used to have some awful jerks," he remarked, "but those we met at Rabaul recently are much better."

Lt(jg) Ira C. (Ike) Kepford of Muskegon, Mich., former Northwestern University halfback, who is the Navy's leading ace with sixteen enemy planes to his credit, commented that the Japanese airmen seemed to "run in streaks."

Some Underestimated Japanese

"Some days they will be very good," he commented, "and other days they will mill around independently of each other with no pattern to their attack at all.'

AMM3c L.W. Jordan adds "Kill" flags to the squadron's scoreboard, bringing the total to 154 Japanese planes destroyed. Photo taken at Bougainville. Note censored squadron number above its Skull and Crossbones emblem. Courtesy U.S. Navy photo. Robert L. Lawson Collection.

Some of our own new pilots, Lieutenant Kepford added, are inclined to underestimate the performance of the Japanese planes, if not the pilots, until they have gone out on a mission. "That was my experience too," he admitted, "but after the first time we actually tangle with the Japs we all 'get religion,' so to speak."

These young aces also exploded the popular supposition that Japanese pilots seldom used parachutes. "A Jap will jump unless he's killed," Commander Blackburn said. "As soon as his plane starts to smoke he's out."

The Skull and Crossbones outfit has completed its combat assignment and is now returning to the States with the record of never having lost a bomber from a group that its fliers escorted. Asked how he accounted for this, Commander Blackburn answered, "That's what we were sent down there for."

Twelve Aces on Roster

This squadron which is also known as "Blackburn's Irregulars," has thirteen aces on its roster. Commander Blackburn, with eleven planes shot down, ranks next to Lieutenant Kepford. The junior ace, Lt. Harry March, former University of North Carolina athlete who won the National Pentathlon Championship in 1940, has five planes.

In addition to destroying 154 Japanese planes and probably shooting down half again as many, the Irregulars have sunk seven Japanese cargo ships and seventeen barges, a record for damage to the enemy by a fighter group. To accomplish this they have flown more sorties and combat hours than any other fighter squadron in all the Pacific area.

Navy Corsair Carrier-Land-Based Squadron Blasted 154 Japs for All-Time Navy Record
Blackburn's "Jolly Rogers" Make Aviation History

The greatest Navy fighter squadron in history—Commander John T. "Tommy" Blackburn's "Skull and Crossbones" gang, returned to this country from the Southwest Pacific last week with a new record of 154 Japanese aircraft shot down in 79 days of combat.

Flying Vought Corsairs, Blackburn's pilots operated both from a carrier and from land bases. They took part in 60 bomber escort missions in the New Georgia, Bougainville and Rabaul areas and never lost a bomber on any of the missions in which they participated.

Besides blasting 154 Jap planes from the skies, the "Jolly Rogers", as they were also called, destroyed two more on the ground and sank five cargo ships and 16 troop and supply barges. Since January 25 they sent 106 enemy planes to a flaming end in the Rabaul sector.

Smashed Navy Records

The Chance Vought Corsair has added a new chapter to its magnificent fighting record in World War II.

Already established by U.S. Marine Corps pilots as one of the world's most formidable fighters, the Corsair in the hands of Lt. Cdr. Tommy Blackburn's "Jolly Rogers" has set a new Navy squadron record: 154 Jap planes downed.

This mark, according to records now available, is the highest ever attained by any fighter squadron-either Navy or Marine.

Lt. Cdr. Tom Blackburn stands in front of squadron VF-17 as General Ralph Mitchell (left foreground) reads citation. F4U planes in background, on Bougainville in the Solomons. Courtesy National Archives.

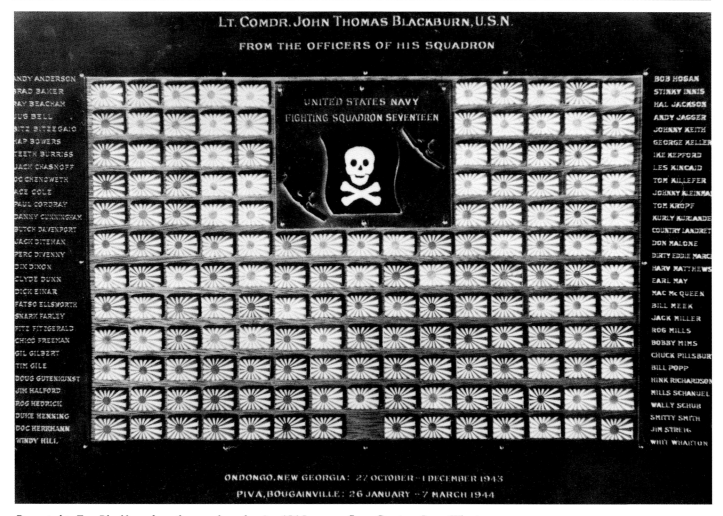

Presented to Tom Blackburn from the squadron showing 154 Japanese flags. Courtesy Joyce Wharton.

They made more sorties and had more combat hours-8,000-than any other squadron. In one five-day period they made what is probably an all-time record by bagging 60 planes. They lost 13 of their own pilots during their 76 days of combat.

Saved a Carrier

In November, during the first carrier strike on the Jap base at Rabaul, the "Jolly Rogers" introduced a new combat tactic-and saved a carrier in the bargain. Flying from land bases, they provided high cover for a carrier while the flattop's planes were many miles away pounding Rabaul. Eighteen Jap torpedo bombers headed for the carrier, but the Corsairs pounced from above, downing 17 in the first pass and the 18th just before it could loose its deadly tin fish.

The squadron had 13 aces-more than any other fighter unit in the Pacific. One of them, Lt(jg) Ira C. "Ike" Kepford, former Northwestern University halfback, is the Navy's leading ace with 16 enemy planes to his credit. Commander Blackburn, with 11 to his credit, and Lt. Cdr. R.R. Hedrick, executive officer, with nine, rank next to Kepford. The squadron's junior ace is Lt. Harry March, former University of North Carolina athlete who won the National Pentathlon championship in 1940, who has five.

NAVY PILOT SAVED BY SPEED GADGET

Lt(jg) Ira C. Kepford of Muskegon, Mich., the Navy's high-scoring fighter pilot, owes his life to a gadget used for needling Navy planes into an extra burst of speed.

The Navy told of the incident today. The device injects, upon the pressing of a switch, a jet of water into the fuel mixture of the engine, producing an effect much like that on an automobile motor running into a blanket of foggy, damp air-a sudden surge of power.

Lt. Kepford was flying in a squadron of Vought Corsairs (F4Us) on a mission over Japanese-held Rabaul on February 19. The 25-year-old pilot had downed an enemy seaplane and a Zero when he found himself only fifty feet above the water with three Zeros closing in. His squadron mates heard him report by radio that he was boxed in and that "this looks like the works, boys".

He opened his throttle wide, flicked the water injection switch-and his plane streaked out of range. He flew over Rabaul at rooftop level, with the enemy planes still trying to catch him. Out over the water again he turned left and one of the Zeros attempted to make the same turn, but caught a wing in the water and cartwheeled into a crash. The other two gave up the chase.

Lt. Kepford is credited with destroying sixteen enemy planes.

Appendix A:
VF-17 Victory Credits (Olynyk)

110143	0745-0800	2 Zeke	Lt. Cdr. John Thomas Blackburn	6-30S, 155-10E
110143	0745-0800	2 Zeke dam.	Lt. Cdr. John Thomas Blackburn	6-30S, 155-10E
110143	0745-0800	Zeke	Lt. Shelton Ray Beacham	6-30S, 155-10E
110143	0745-0800	Zeke	Ens. Frederick James Streig (0.5) Lt(jg) Tom Killefer (0.5)	6-30S, 155-10E
110143	0745-0800	Zeke	Lt(jg) Tom Killefer	6-30S, 155-10E
110143	0745-0800	Zeke dam.	Lt. Thaddeus Richard Bell	6-30S, 155-10E
110143	0745-0800	Val dam.	Lt(jg) Douglas H C Gutenkunst	6-30S, 155-10E
110143	1330	Zeke	Lt. Cdr. Roger Richards Hedrick	6-30S, 155-10E
110143	1330	Zeke dam.	Lt. Clement Dexter Gile (0.5) Lt(jg) Daniel Gerald Cunningham (0.5)	6-30S, 155-10E
110143	1330	Val dam.	Lt(jg) Mills Schanuel	6-30S, 155-10E
110643	1040	Betty	Lt. Merl William Davenport (0.25) Lt. Walter John Schub (0.25) Lt(jg) Robert Hal Jackson (0.25) Ens. Robert Roy Hogan (0.25)	15 m SW of Cape Moltke, Bougainville
110843	0710	Ruth	Lt. Cdr. John Thomas Blackburn Lt. Harry Andrew March, Jr (0.0)	Buka Airfield
110843	1100	3 Zeke dam.	Lt. Cdr. Roger Richards Hedrick	W coast of Bougainville
110843	1100	Zeke	Lt(jg) Mills Schanuel	W coast of Bougainville
110843	1100	Hamp	Lt(jg) Robert Sidney Anderson	W coast of Bougainville
110843	1100	Zeke dam.	Lt(jg) Robert Sidney Anderson	W coast of Bougainville
110843	1100	Zeke	Lt(jg) Daniel Gerald Cunningham	W coast of Bougainville
110843	1100	Zeke dam.	Lt(jg) Daniel Gerald Cunningham (0.0) Lt(jg) Paul Cordray	W coast of Bougainville
111143	1315-1415	Tony	Lt. Cdr. John Thomas Blackburn	Approx. 6-30S, 153-30E
111143	1315-1415	Zeke dam.	Lt. Cdr. John Thomas Blackburn	Approx. 6-30S, 153-30E
111143	1315-1415	Zeke	Lt. Cdr. Roger Richards Hedrick	Approx. 6-30S, 153-30E
111143	1315-1415	Zeke	Lt(jg) Robert Hal Jackson	Approx. 6-30S, 153-30E
111143	1315-1415	Zeke dam.	Lt(jg) Paul Cordray	Approx. 6-30S, 153-30E
111143	1315-1415	Tony	Ens. Frederick James Streig	Approx. 6-30S, 153-30E
111143	1315-1415	Zeke	Ens. Frederick James Streig	Approx. 6-30S, 153-30E
111143	1315-1415	Zeke dam.	Ens. Frederick James Streig	Approx. 6-30S, 153-30E
111143	1315-1415	Hamp dam.	Ens. Frederick James Streig	Approx. 6-30S, 153-30E
111143	1315-1415	Kate	Lt. Clement Dexter Gile	Approx. 6-30S, 153-30E
111143	1315-1415	Zeke dam.	Lt(jg) Jack M Chasnoff (0.5) Lt(jg) Robert Sidney Anderson (0.5)	Approx. 6-30S, 153-30E
111143	1315-1415	Kate	Lt. John Milton Kleinman	Approx. 6-30S, 153-30E
111143	1315-1415	Kate dam.	Lt. John Milton Kleinman	Approx. 6-30S, 153-30E
111143	1315-1415	Val	Lt. Thaddeus Richard Bell	Approx. 6-30S, 153-30E
111143	1315-1415	Val	Lt. Thaddeus Richard Bell	Approx. 6-30S, 153-30E
111143	1315-1415	3 Val	Ens. Ira Cassius Kepford	Approx. 6-30S, 153-30E
111143	1315-1415	Kate	Ens. Ira Cassius Kepford	Approx. 6-30S, 153-30E
111143	1315-1415	Val dam.	Ens. Ira Cassius Kepford	Approx. 6-30S, 153-30E
111143	1315-1415	Zeke	Ens. Robert Roy Hogan	Approx. 6-30S, 153-30E
111143	1315-1415	Zeke	Ens. Bradford Warren Baker	Approx. 6-30S, 153-30E
111143	1315-1415	Kate	Ens. Robert Hugh Hill	Approx. 6-30S, 153-30E
111143	1315-1415	Kate	Lt(jg) Howard McClain Burriss	Approx. 6-30S, 153-30E
111143	1400	0.5 Kate	Lt(jg) Howard McClain Burriss (0.5)	Approx. 6-30S, 153-30E (VF-33 : 154-15E)
111143	1400	Betty	Lt(jg) Howard McClain Burriss	Approx. 6-30S, 153-30E
111743	0800	Kate	Lt(jg) Paul Cordray	Empress Augusta Bay

111743	0800-0815	Zeke	Lt. Cdr. Roger Richards Hedrick	Empress Augusta Bay
111743	0800-0815	2 Zeke	Lt(jg) Jack M Chasnoff	Empress Augusta Bay
111743	0800-0815	Zeke	Lt(jg) Mills Schanuel	Empress Augusta Bay
111743	0800-0815	3 Zeke	Lt. Clement Dexter Gile	Empress Augusta Bay
111743	0815	2 Tony	Lt(jg) Paul Cordray	over Empress Augusta Bay
112143	0535	2 Zeke	Lt. Merl William Davenport	Empress Augusta Bay
112143	0535	Zeke	Lt. Shelton Ray Beacham	Empress Augusta Bay
112143	0535	2 Zeke	Lt(jg) Doris Clyde Freeman	Empress Augusta Bay
112143	0535	Zeke	Ens. Frank Andrew Jagger	Empress Augusta Bay
012644	1215-1230	Zeke	Lt. Cdr. John Thomas Blackburn	Rabaul Area
012644	1215-1230	2 Zeke	Lt(jg) Douglas H C Gutenkunst	Rabaul Area
012644	1215-1230	Zeke	Lt. Cdr. Roger Richards Hedrick	Rabaul Area
012644	1215-1230	Zeke	Lt(jg) J M Miller	Rabaul Area
012644	1215-1230	Zeke	Lt(jg) Paul Cordray	Rabaul Area
012644	1215-1230	Zeke dam.	Lt(jg) Paul Cordray	Rabaul Area
012644	1215-1230	Zeke	Lt(jg) Tom Killefer	Rabaul Area
012644	1215-1230	Zeke	Lt. Clement Dexter Gile	Rabaul Area
012644	1215-1230	Zeke prob.	Lt(jg) William Lee Landreth (0.5) Ens. Clyde Howard Dunn (0.5)	Rabaul Area
012744	0900	2 Zeke	Lt(jg) Daniel Gerald Cunningham	Rabaul Area
012744	0900	2 Zeke	Lt(jg) Frederick James Streig	Rabaul Area
012744	0900	Zeke	Lt(jg) Frederick James Streig (0.5) Lt(jg) Robert Mims (0.5)	Rabaul Area
012744	0900	Zeke	Lt(jg) Robert Mims	Rabaul Area
012744	0900	u/i A/C	Lt(jg) Robert Mims	Rabaul Area
012744	0900	Zeke	Lt. Oscar Ivan Chenoweth , Jr	Rabaul Area
012744	0900	Zeke	Lt(jg) Harold James Bitzegaio	Rabaul Area
012744	0900	2 Hamp prob.	Lt(jg) Harold James Bitzegaio	Rabaul Area
012744	0900	Zeke	Lt(jg) Carl Wilson Gilbert	Rabaul Area
012744	0900	Zeke	Lt(jg) Howard McClain Burriss	Rabaul Area
012744	0900	Zeke	Lt(jg) Earl May	Rabaul Area
012744	0900	2 Zeke	Lt(jg) Ira Cassius Kepford	Rabaul Area
012744	0900	Zeke prob.	Lt(jg) Ira Cassius Kepford	Rabaul Area
012744	0900	Zeke	Ens. Donald Roy McQueen	Rabaul Area
012744	0900	Zeke prob.	Lt. Walter John Schub	Rabaul Area
012744	0900	Zeke	Ens. Frank Andrew Jagger	Rabaul Area
012844	0900	2 Zeke	Lt. Harry Andrew March , Jr	over Tobera A/F
012844	0900	0.5 Zeke	Lt(jg) Robert Mims (0.5)	over Tobera A/F
012844	0900	Zeke prob.	Lt(jg) Robert Mims	over Tobera A/F
012844	0900	2 Zeke	Lt(jg) Douglas H C Gutenkunst	over Tobera A/F
012844	0900	2 Zeke	Ens. Percy Eugene Divenney	over Tobera A/F
012844	0900	2 Zeke	Lt(jg) Tom Killefer	over Tobera A/F
012844	0900	Zeke	Ens. William Preston Meek	over Tobera A/F
012844	0900	Zeke	Lt. Cdr. Roger Richards Hedrick	over Tobera A/F
012844	0900	2 Zeke	Lt(jg) Paul Cordray	over Tobera A/F
012844	0900	Zeke prob.	Lt(jg) J M Miller	over Tobera A/F
012844	0900	Zeke	Lt(jg) J M Miller	over Tobera A/F
012844	0900	Zeke	Lt(jg) Robert Hal Jackson	over Tobera A/F
012844	0900	Zeke prob.	Ens. John Orrin Ellsworth	over Tobera A/F
012844	0900	Zeke prob.	Lt(jg) Carl Wilson Gilbert	over Tobera A/F
012944	1105-1115	4 Zeke	Lt(jg) Ira Cassius Kepford	over Cape Gazelle area
012944	1105-1115	4 Zeke	Lt(jg) Howard McClain Burriss	over Cape Gazelle area
012944	1105-1115	Zeke	Lt. Clement Dexter Gile	over Cape Gazelle area
012944	1105-1115	Zeke	Lt(jg) Earl May	over Cape Gazelle area
012944	1105-1115	Zeke prob.	Ens. John Malcolm Smith	over Cape Gazelle area
012944	1105-1115	Zeke prob.	Lt. Oscar Ivan Chenoweth , Jr	over Cape Gazelle area
012944	1105-1115	Zeke prob.	Ens. James Cass Dixon	over Cape Gazelle area
013044	1120	Zeke	Lt. Cdr. Roger Richards Hedrick	over Rabaul area
013044	1120	Zeke	Ens. John Orrin Ellsworth	over Rabaul area
013044	1120	Zeke prob.	Lt(jg) J M Miller	over Rabaul area
013044	1120	Zeke prob.	Ens. John Malcolm Smith	over Rabaul area
013044	1120	Zeke prob.	Ens. G M Keller , Jr	over Rabaul area

013044	1120	Zeke prob.	Lt(jg) G F Bowers	over Rabaul area
013044	1740	Tony	Lt(jg) Ira Cassius Kepford	over Simpson Harbor
013044	1740	Zeke	Lt(jg) Ira Cassius Kepford	over Simpson Harbor
013044	1740	2 Zeke	Lt. Merl William Davenport	over Simpson Harbor
013044	1740	Zeke	Lt(jg) Mills Schanuel	over Simpson Harbor
013044	1740	2 Zeke	Lt. Oscar Ivan Chenoweth , Jr	over Simpson Harbor
013044	1740	Zeke	Lt. Oscar Ivan Chenoweth , Jr (0.5) Ens. James Cass Dixon (0.5)	over Simpson Harbor
013044	1740	2 Zeke	Lt. Cdr. John Thomas Blackburn	over Simpson Harbor
013044	1740	3 Zeke prob.	Lt. Cdr. John Thomas Blackburn	over Simpson Harbor
020344	1350	Zeke	Lt(jg) Ira Cassius Kepford	Cape Tawui , New Britain
020344	1350	Zeke prob.	Lt. Oscar Ivan Chenoweth , Jr	Cape Tawui , New Britain
020444	1130	Zeke	Lt(jg) Earl May (0.0) Ens. Wilbert Peter Popp	over Tobera area
020544	1100-1105	Zeke	Lt. Merl William Davenport	over Lakunai off Cape Gazelle
020544	1100-1105	Zeke	Lt. Walter John Schub	over Lakunai off Cape Gazelle
020544	1100-1105	Zeke	Lt(jg) William Lee Landreth	over Lakunai off Cape Gazelle
020644	1105	Tojo	Lt(jg) Robert Mims	Rabaul area
020644	1115-1145	Zeke	Lt. Walter John Schub	Rabaul area
020644	1115-1145	Hamp	Lt(jg) Harold James Bitzegaio	Rabaul area
020644	1115-1145	3 Zeke	Lt. Cdr. John Thomas Blackburn	Rabaul area
020644	1115-1145	Hamp	Lt. Cdr. John Thomas Blackburn	Rabaul area
020644	1115-1145	2 Zeke prob.	Lt. Cdr. John Thomas Blackburn	Rabaul area
020644	1115-1145	2 Zeke	Lt(jg) Robert Mims	Rabaul area
020644	1115-1145	2 Zeke prob.	Lt(jg) Robert Mims	Rabaul area
020744	1030-1100	Zeke	Lt(jg) William Lee Landreth	Rabaul area
020744	1030-1100	Hamp	Lt(jg) William Lee Landreth	Rabaul area
020744	1030-1100	Zeke	Lt(jg) Earle Carpenter Peterson , Jr	Rabaul area
020744	1030-1100	Zeke dam.	Ens. Clyde Howard Dunn	Rabaul area
020744	1030-1100	2 Zeke prob.	Ens. Clyde Howard Dunn	Rabaul area
020744	1030-1100	Zeke prob.	Lt(jg) Doris Clyde Freeman	Rabaul area
020744	1030-1100	Hamp prob.	Lt(jg) Doris Clyde Freeman	Rabaul area
020944	1230	Zeke	Lt. Oscar Ivan Chenoweth , Jr	Vunakanau area
020944	1230	Zeke	Lt(jg) Earl May	Vunakanau area
020944	1230	Hamp dam.	Lt(jg) Mills Schanuel	Vunakanau area
021044	1235	Zeke prob.	Lt(jg) Harold James Bitzegaio (0.5) Ens. Frank Andrew Jagger (0.5)	Vunakanau A/F
021044	1245	Zeke	Lt. Merl William Davenport	Tobera area
021044	1245	Zeke	Ens. John Orrin Ellsworth	Tobera area
021344	1050	Zeke dam.	Lt(jg) Daniel Gerald Cunningham	over Vunakanau
021744	0900	Zeke	Ens. Clyde Howard Dunn	over Cape Gazelle
021744	0900	Zeke	Ens. John Malcolm Smith	over Cape Gazelle
021744	0900	Zeke dam.	Ens. John Malcolm Smith	over Cape Gazelle
021744	0900	Oscar prob.	Ens. John Malcolm Smith	over Cape Gazelle
021844	1050-1110	3 Zeke	Lt. Cdr. Roger Richards Hedrick	over Cape Gazelle
021844	1050-1110	Zeke	Lt. Clement Dexter Gile	over Cape Gazelle
021844	1050-1110	2 Zeke	Lt(jg) Earl May	over Cape Gazelle
021844	1050-1110	Zeke	Ens. John Malcolm Smith	over Cape Gazelle
021844	1050-1110	Zeke prob.	Lt(jg) Paul Cordray	over Cape Gazelle
021944	0945	Rufe	Lt(jg) Ira Cassius Kepford	Cape Siar , New Ireland
021944	0945	2 Zeke	Lt(jg) Ira Cassius Kepford	Cape Siar , New Ireland
021944	1010-1025	4 Zeke	Lt(jg) Daniel Gerald Cunningham	Rabaul area
021944	1010-1025	2 Zeke	Lt. Oscar Ivan Chenoweth , Jr	Rabaul area
021944	1010-1025	Tojo	Lt. Oscar Ivan Chenoweth , Jr	Rabaul area
021944	1010-1025	3 Zeke	Lt(jg) Earl May	Rabaul area
021944	1010-1025	Zeke	Ens. Wilbert Peter Popp	Rabaul area
021944	1010-1025	Tojo	Ens. John Malcolm Smith	Rabaul area
021944	1010-1025	Zeke	Lt. Clement Dexter Gile	Rabaul area

VF-17 VICTORY CREDITS (OLYNYK)

	RANK	NAME	CONFIRMED	PROBABLE	DAMAGED
1	Lt(jg)	Ira C. Kepford	16	1	1
2	Lt. Cdr.	John T. Blackburn	11	5	3
3	Lt. Cdr.	Roger R. Hedrick	9		3
4	Lt.	Oscar I. Chenoweth	8.5 (1)	2	
5	Lt.	Clement D. Gile	8		0.5
6	Lt(jg)	Earl May	8		
7	Lt(jg)	Howard M. Burriss	7.5		
8	Lt(jg)	Daniel G. Cunningham	7		1.5
9	Lt.	Merl W. Davenport	6.25		
10	Lt(jg)	Paul Cordray	6	1	3
11	Lt(jg)	Robert Mims	6	3	
12	Lt(jg)	Frederick J. Streig	5.5		2
13	Lt.	Harry A. March , Jr.	5 (2)		
14	Lt(jg)	Tom Killefer	4		
15	Lt(jg)	Doug H.C. Gutenkunst	4		1
16	Lt.	James A. Halford	(3.5)		
17	Lt(jg)	William L. Landreth	3	0.5	
18	Lt(jg)	Mills Schanuel	3		2
19	Lt(jg)	John M. Smith	3	3	1
20	Lt(jg)	Robert H. Jackson	2.25		
21	Lt.	Walter J. Schub	2.25	1	
22	Lt.	Shelton R. Beacham	2		
23	Lt.	Thaddeus R. Bell	2		1
24	Lt(jg)	Harold J. Bitzegaio	2	2.5	
25	Lt(jg)	Jack M. Chasnoff	2		0.5
26	Ens.	Percy E. Divenney	2		
27	Ens.	John O. Ellsworth	2	1	
28	Lt(jg)	Doris C.Freeman	2	2	
29	Ens.	Frank A.Jagger	2	0.5	
30	Lt.	John M. Kleinman	2 (1)	(1)	1
31	Lt(jg)	James Miller	2	2	
32	Ens.	Wilbert P. Popp	2		
33	Ens.	Robert R. Hogan	1.25		
34	Lt(jg)	Robert S. Anderson	1		1.5
35	Ens.	Bradford W. Baker	1		
36	Ens.	Clyde H. Dunn	1	2.5	1
37	Lt(jg)	Carl W. Gilbert	1	1	
38	Ens.	Robert H. Hill	1		
39	Lt.	Donald A. Innis	(1)		
40	Ens.	Donald R. McQueen	1		
41	Ens.	William P. Meek	1		
42	Lt(jg)	Earle C. Peterson , Jr.	1		
43	Ens.	James C. Dixon	0.5	1	
44	Lt(jg)	George F. Bowers		1	
45	Ens.	George M. Keller , Jr.		1	
Totals			**152**	**31**	**23**

Notes

In brackets score of pilots previous kills before reporting to VF-17, not included in totals.

Official lists count 152 confirmed victory credits not 154 as stated in the war diary.

An interesting example of a conflict between citations and squadron records.

Citations for awards to Blackburn and March appear to give them both credit for the Ruth shot down on 8 November, 1943. The VF-17 war diary gives full credit to Blackburn, while the aircraft action report would appear to share the credit. March was therefore given an assist in the victory, as being the accreditation closest to the contemporary reports. The citation for March's first Air Medal gives him credit for one bomber on this date. In the above totals this credit is counted as one for Blackburn.

Streig had two shared victories, one with Killefer, and one with Mims. The aircraft action report indicates the victory with Killefer is shared, while the war diary says that Streig got full credit.

The war diary and official lists have conflicting information on the 8 November, 1943.

The official lists and the aircraft action reports have the same information. However, the war diary has Anderson given full credit for a Zeke instead of damaged. Cordray was also given full credit for a Zeke on this date. Marine Air Intelligence reports on this date have found their way into the VF-17 war diary with conflicting information with two more full victory credits added to the total.

Appendix B:
War Diary

OCTOBER

Enemy airplanes destroyed   None.

Enemy ships destroyed   2 AK
                         5 Landing barges

Note
As ships were destroyed as the result of strafing by entire flights, pilot's names are not given.

Losses
Pilots   None
Airplanes   None

NOVEMBER

Enemy surface vessels destroyed   2 AK, 11 Barges.
(Note: As ships were destroyed as the result of strafing by entire flights, pilots' names are not given.)

Enemy aircraft destroyed in the air: 47

                                         28 Zekes
                                         4 Tonys
                                         1 Hamp
                                         5 Vals
                                         6 Kates
                                         2 Bettys
                                         1 Ruth

Individual scores:

Lt. Cdr. J.T. Blackburn	2 Zekes, 1 Ruth, 1 Tony.
Lt. Cdr. R.R. Hedrick	3 Zekes.
Lt. S.R. Beacham	2 Zekes.
Lt. T.R. Bell	2 Vals.
Lt. M.W. Davenport	2 Zekes.
Lt. C.D. Gile	3 Zekes, 1 Kate.
Lt. J.M. Kleinman	1 Kate.
Lt(jg) R.S. Anderson	1 Zeke, 1 Hamp.
Lt(jg) H.M. Burriss	1 Zeke, 1 Betty.
Lt(jg) J.M. Chasnoff	2 Zekes.
Lt(jg) P. Cordray	1 Zeke, 1 Kate, 2 Tonys.
Lt(jg) D.G. Cunningham	1 Zeke.
Lt(jg) D.C. Freeman	2 Zekes.
Lt(jg) R.H. Jackson	1 Zeke.
Lt(jg) T. Killefer	1 Zeke.
Lt(jg) M. Schanuel	2 Zekes.
Ens. B.W. Baker	1 Kate.
Ens. R. H. Hill	1 Kate.
Ens. R.R. Hogan	1 Zeke, 1 Betty.
Ens. F.A. Jagger	1 Zeke.
Ens. I.C. Kepford	1 Kate, 3 Vals.
Ens. F.J. Streig	2 Zekes, 1 Tony.

Enemy aircraft destroyed on the ground: 2

Lt. L.D. Cooke)	
Ens. W.P. Popp)	1 Betty.
Ens. J.O. Ellsworth	1 Betty.

Own losses: 3 Pilots:

Lt(jg) J.H. Keith	by enemy A/A fire.
Ens. B.W. Baker	by enemy aircraft.
Lt. C.A. Pillsbury	probably by enemy A/A fire.

7 Planes:

2 shot down	by enemy aircraft.
3 shot down	by enemy A/A fire.

2 lost as the result of water landings due to gas shortage after prolonged cover and air combat over Task Force 50.3 on 11 November, 1943.

DECEMBER

No enemy planes or surface craft were destroyed during the month of December.
One F4U-1 was lost after an accident during night flying operations.

JANUARY

Surface vessels destroyed: None.
Enemy aircraft destroyed in the air: 60.5

                                        58.5 Zekes
                                        1 Tony
                                        1 unidentified aircraft

Individual scores:

Lt. Cdr. J.T. Blackburn	3 Zekes
Lt. Cdr. R.R. Hedrick	3 Zekes
Lt. O.I. Chenoweth	3 Zekes
Lt. M.W. Davenport	2 Zekes
Lt. C.D. Gile	2 Zekes
Lt. H.A. March	2 Zekes
Lt(jg) T. Killefer	3 Zekes
Lt(jg) H.J. Bitzegaio	1 Zeke

Lt(jg) R.H. Jackson	1 Zeke		
Lt(jg) J. Miller	2 Zekes		
Lt(jg) P. Cordray	3 Zekes		
Lt(jg) D.G. Cunningham	2 Zekes		
Lt(jg) C.W. Gilbert	1 Zeke		
Lt(jg) H.M. Burriss	5 Zekes		
Lt(jg) D.H. Gutenkunst	4 Zekes		
Lt(jg) R. Mims	2 Zekes, 1 unidentified aircraft		
Lt(jg) E. May	2 Zekes		
Lt(jg) M. Schanuel	1 Zeke		
Lt(jg) I.C. Kepford	7 Zekes, 1 Tony		
Lt(jg) F.J. Streig	2.5 Zekes		
Ens. F.A. Jagger	1 Zeke		
Ens. J.O. Ellsworth	1 Zeke		
Ens. D.R. McQueen	1 Zeke		
Ens. P.E. Divenney	2 Zekes		
Ens. J.C. Dixon	1 Zeke		
Ens. W.P. Meek	1 Zeke		

Losses: 5 pilots missing in action.

Lt. T.R. Bell	shot down by enemy aircraft
Lt(jg) R.R. Hogan	shot down by enemy aircraft
Lt(jg) J.W. Farley	shot down by enemy aircraft
Lt(jg) T.F. Kropf	shot down by enemy aircraft
Lt(jg) H.M. Burriss	shot down by enemy aircraft

1 pilot operational loss.

Lt(jg) D.H. Gutenkunst killed in mid-air collision.

13 planes

5 shot down by enemy aircraft
1 destroyed in mid-air collision
3 destroyed in operational crash landings
4 destroyed in crash landings after serious damage had been inflicted by enemy aircraft

FEBRUARY
Surface vessels destroyed:	1 AK	
	1 Barge	

Enemy aircraft destroyed in the air:	46	
	40 Zekes	
	3 Hamps	
	2 Tojos	
	1 Rufe	

Individual score:

Lt. Cdr. J.T. Blackburn	3 Zekes, 1 Hamp
Lt. Cdr. R.R. Hedrick	3 Zekes
Lt. O.I. Chenoweth	3 Zekes, 1 Tojo
Lt. M.W. Davenport	2 Zekes
Lt. C.D. Gile	2 Zekes
Lt. W.J. Schub	2 Zekes
Lt(jg) E.C. Peterson	1 Zeke
Lt(jg) H.J. Bitzegaio	1 Hamp
Lt(jg) D.G. Cunningham	4 Zekes
Lt(jg) W.L. Landreth	2 Zekes, 1 Hamp
Lt(jg) E. May	6 Zekes
Lt(jg) R. Mims	2 Zekes, 1 Tojo
Lt(jg) I.C. Kepford	3 Zekes, 1 Rufe
Ens. J.O. Ellsworth	1 Zeke
Ens. C.H. Dunn	1 Zeke
Ens. W.P. Popp	2 Zekes
Ens. J.M. Smith	3 Zekes

Losses:

Lt(jg) J. Miller	shot down by enemy A/A fire
Lt(jg) D.T. Malone	shot down by enemy aircraft
Ens. P.E. Divenney	shot down by enemy aircraft
Ens. C.H. Dunn	shot down by enemy aircraft

4 planes

1 shot down by enemy A/A fire
3 shot down by enemy aircraft

MARCH
Surface vessels destroyed:	2 Barges	
Enemy aircraft destroyed:	None	
Losses:	None	

Footnote
The VF-17 War Diary gives two more aircraft credited shot down than the official lists (see notes after VF-17 victory credits).

COMBAT STATISTICS
(from War Diary)

I. First Tour: based at Ondongo, New Georgia, from October through 1 December 1943.

1. Combat hours flown: 4,985.5
2. Combat sorties flown: 1,570
3. Average hours flown by regularly flying pilots: 132
4. Damage inflicted on enemy:
    a. Planes destroyed in the air: 47.5
    b. Planes destroyed on the ground: 2
    c. AK's sunk: 4
    d. Barges sunk: 14
5. Own losses:
    a. Planes lost: 8
        I. 2 shot down by enemy aircraft
        II. 3 shot down by enemy anti-aircraft fire
        III. 2 lost in water landings as the result of gas shortage after prolonged cover and air combat over Task Force 50.3 on 11 November
        IV. 1 lost in operational crash landing
    b. Pilots lost: 3
        I. 1 shot down by enemy aircraft
        II. 2 shot down by enemy anti-aircraft fire

II. Second Tour: based at Piva Yoke, Bougainville, B.S.I. from January through 4 March 1944.

1. Combat hours flown: 3,386.9
2. Combat sorties flown: 1099*
    a. Missions to Rabaul: 671
    b. Dumbo escorts: 50
    c. Combat air patrols: 44
    d. Scouting: 35
    e. Task Force covers: 60
    f. Green Island covers: 201
    g. Barge hunts: 38
3. Average hours flown by regularly flying pilots: 89.8**
4. Damage inflicted on the enemy:
    a. Planes destroyed in the air: 106.5
    b. AK's sunk: 1
    c. Barges sunk: 3

5. Own losses:
    a. Planes lost: 16
        I. Shot down by enemy aircraft: 8
        II. Shot down by enemy anti-aircraft fire: 1
        III. Crash or water landings due to injury in combat: 4
        IV. Operational losses: 3
    b. Pilots lost: 10
        I. Shot down by enemy aircraft: 8
        II. Shot down by enemy anti-aircraft fire: 1
        III. Lost in operational crash: 1

* This figure includes only missions actually completed. If a pilot was forced to return early his flight was not counted as a combat sortie.

** This figure represents the average time flown by 30 pilots. It does not include the time of missing pilots, or those who were grounded for more than a week because of injuries, or of those pilots who arrived after 10 February.

III. Totals for two tours of combat duty (76 days)

1. Combat hours flown: 8,372.4
2. Combat sorties flown: 2,669
3. Average hours flown by regularly flying pilots:
    a. First tour: 132.0
    b. Second tour   89.8
4. Damage inflicted on the enemy:
    a. Planes destroyed in the air: 154
    b. Planes destroyed on the ground: 2
    c. AK's sunk: 5
    d. Barges sunk: 17
5. Own losses:
    a. Planes: 24
        I. Combat losses: 20
        II. Operational losses: 4
    b. Pilots: 13
        I. Combat losses: 12
        II. Operational losses: 1

IV. Individual records of pilots attached to Fighting Squadron Seventeen on 21 February 1944:

	Previous Combat Hours	Days Flown	SECOND TOUR--4 weeks Combat Sorties Completed	Missions to Rabaul	Combat Hours Flown	Planes Shot Down
Lt. Cdr. J.T. Blackburn	168.3	21	26	17	81.8	11
Lt. Cdr. R.R. Hedrick	127.0	13	14	11	49.7	9
Lt. S.R. Beacham	123.0	7	9	7	27.7	2
Lt. O.I. Chenoweth	120.0	16	21	12	72.3	8
Lt. M.W. Davenport	163.0	16	18	12	57.4	6
Lt. C.D. Gile	152.0	16	19	13	59.8	8
Lt. H.A. March, Jr.	322.0	12	15	11	45.3	5
Lt. W.J. Schub	122.9	15	17	12	52.9	2
Lt(jg) T. Killefer	327.1	19	20	15	65.9	4
Lt(jg) H.J. Bitzegaio		16	18	11	49.4	2
Lt(jg) R.H. Jackson	130.0	11	13	10	47.8	2
Lt(jg) G.F. Bowers	148.7	15	16	14	61.0	
Lt(jg) P. Cordray	149.0	13	15	12	46.1	7
Lt(jg) D.G. Cunningham	148.0	16	19	12	64.6	7
Lt(jg) D.C. Freeman	132.0	18	21	14	68.8	2
Lt(jg) C.W. Gilbert	123.0	13	15	9	41.9	1
Lt(jg) W.L. Landreth	126.9	14	17	11	49.3	3
Lt(jg) E. May	143.9	18	21	16	75.4	8
Lt(jg) R. Mims		17	20	13	68.8	6
Lt(jg) M. Schanuel	130.0	10	12	9	38.9	3
Lt(jg) I.C. Kepford	158.0	10	11	10	36.9	16
Lt(jg) F.J. Streig	108.0	14	18	8	48.9	5.5
Ens. R.H. Hill	123.0	12	14	9	43.8	1
Ens. F.A. Jagger	63.8	14	16	12	46.1	2
Ens. W.C. Wharton, Jr.	110.0	17	19	11	49.7	
Ens. J.O. Ellsworth	138.9	16	19	12	66.0	2
Ens. W.P. Meek	112.3	21	22	13	64.7	1
Ens. D.R. McQueen		10	12	6	39.2	1
Ens. W.P. Popp	47.8	14	18	12	58.4	2
Ens. J.M. Smith		18	20	15	63.0	3
Ens. M.W. Cole		11	15	9	48.0	
Ens. J.C. Dixon		14	19	11	65.3	1
Ens. G.M. Keller, Jr.		15	18	10	52.5	
Ens. H.B. Richardson, Jr.		16	17	11	56.1	
Ens. L.A. Fitzgerald		12	15	8	57.3	
Ens. M.M. Kurlander	143.5	17	20	11	60.5	
Ens. R.M. Einar		5	5	4	15.4	
Ens. J.E. Diteman		5	5	11	6.7	
Ens. H. Matthews		6	10	4	36.2	

Appendix C:
Decorations (Navy)

Navy Cross
Instituted : 1919
Criteria : Extraordinary hero-
ism in action against an enemy
of the U.S. or while serving
with friendly foreign forces.
Devices : Gold, silver star.
Notes : Originally issued with
a 1.5" wide ribbon.
Courtesy Medals of America.

Silver Star
Instituted : 1932
Criteria : Gallantry in action
against an armed enemy of the
United States or while serving
with friendly foreign forces.
Devices : Gold, silver star.
Notes : Derived from the 3/16"
silver "Citation Star" pre-
viously worn on Army cam-
paign medals.
Courtesy Medals of America.

Distinguished Flying Cross
Instituted : 1926
Criteria : Heroism or extraor-
dinary achievement while
participating in aerial flight.
Devices : Bronze letter "V" (for
valor), gold, silver star.
Courtesy Medals of America.

Purple Heart
Instituted : 1932
Criteria : Awarded to any
member of the U.S. Armed
Forces killed or wounded in an
armed conflict.
Devices : Gold, silver star.
Notes : Wound Ribbon ap-
peared circa 1917-18 but was
never officially authorized.
Courtesy Medals of America.

Air Medal
Instituted : 1942
Criteria : Heroic actions or
meritorious service while
participating in aerial flight.
Devices : Bronze letter "V" (for
valor), bronze numeral, gold
numeral, bronze star, gold, sil-
ver star.
Courtesy Medals of America.

Prisoner of War Medal
Instituted : 1989
Criteria : Awarded to any
member of the U.S. Armed
Forces taken prisoner during
any armed conflict dating from
World War I.
Devices : Bronze, silver star.
Courtesy Medals of America.

American Defense Service Medal
Instituted : 1941
Dates : 1939-41
Criteria : Naval Service : Any active duty service.
Devices : All Naval Services : bronze letter "A" (not worn with bronze star).
Bars : All Naval Services : "Base", "Fleet."
Courtesy Medals of America.

American Campaign Medal
Instituted : 1942
Dates : 1941-46
Criteria : Service outside the U.S. in the American theater for 30 days, or within the continental U.S. for one year.
Devices : Navy : silver star (obsolete).
Courtesy Medals of America.

Asiatic-Pacific Campaign Medal
Instituted : 1942
Dates : 1941-46
Criteria : Service in the Asiatic-Pacific theater for 30 days or receipt of any combat decoration.
Devices : Navy : bronze Marine Corps device; Navy : silver star (obsolete).
Courtesy Medals of America.

World War II Victory Medal
Instituted : 1945
Dates : 1941-46
Criteria : Awarded for service in the U.S. Armed Forces during the above period.
Devices : None.
Courtesy Medals of America.

Navy Unit Commendation
Instituted : 1944
Criteria : Awarded to units Navy/Marine Corps for outstanding heroism in action or extremely meritorious service.
Devices : Bronze, silver star.
Courtesy Medals of America.

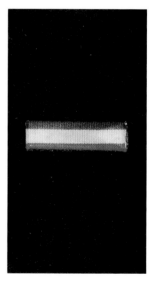

Navy Presidential Unit Citation
Instituted : 1942
Criteria : Awarded to Navy/Marine Corps units for extraordinary heroism in action against an armed enemy.
Devices : Gold globe, gold letter "N", blue star, bronze, silver star.
Courtesy Medals of America.

Appendix D:
Tactical Organization

Radio calls indicated in parentheses
This was issued at Manteo in approximately June 1943.

A Flight		B Flight		C Flight		D Flight	
1 Blackburn	(Tom)	9 Kleinman	(Johnnie)	17 Hedrick	(Rog)	25 Halford	(Lucky)
2 Gutenkunst	(Gute)	10 Gilbert	(Gil)	18 Schanuel	(Mills)	26 Henderson	(Tuffy)
3 Streig	(Jim)	11 Bowers	(Hap)	19 Ferguson	(Fergy)	27 Keith	(John)
4 Mims	(Bobby)	12 Hill	(Windy)	20 Baker	(Brad)	28 Landreth	(Country)
5 Bell	(Jug)	13 Pillsbury	(Chuck)	21 Gile	(Tim)	29 Cooke	(Lem)
6 May	(Earl)	14 Schub	(Wally)	22 Cunningham	(Dan)	30 Burriss	(Teeth)
7 Beacham	(Beach)	15 Hogan	(Bob)	23 Cordray	(Paul)	31 Davenport	(Butch)
8 Anderson	(Andy)	16 Jackson	(Hal)	24 Freeman	(Chico)	32 Kepford	(Ike)

Relief Flight Leaders:
1. Pillsbury
2. Bell
3. Cooke

Relief Division Leaders
In order of preference:
1. Davenport
2. Streig
3. Beacham
4. Ferguson

Relief Section Leaders
In order of preference:
1. Anderson
2. Henderson
3. Jackson
4. Kepford

Relief Pilots-In order of preference:
1. Malone   -   #33 (Maloney)
2. Chasnoff   -   #34 (Jack)
3. Kurlander   -   #35 (Kurly)
4. Kropf   -   #36 (Kropf)
5. Wharton   (Whit)
6. Kelley   (Kelley)
7. Jagger   (Jag)

Shortly after this was issued Ray Ferguson had to leave VF-17 due to eye trouble and "Tuffy" Henderson was killed in a mid-air collision. Bobby Mims is shown on this list but due to a burst appendix in October 1943 had to wait until December 1943 to join up with the squadron.

Appendix E:
Officer and Enlisted Personnel Rosters

FIGHTING SQUADRON SEVENTEEN
ALPHABETICAL ROSTER OF SQUADRON OFFICERS
AS OF 31 OCTOBER 1943

TOTAL 46
PILOTS (43)

ANDERSON, R.S.	Lt(jg)	FREEMAN, D.C.	Lt(jg)	KILLEFER, T.	Lt(jg)
BAKER, B.W.	Ensign	GILBERT, C.W.	Lt(jg	KLEINMAN, J.M.	Lt.
BEACHAM, S.R.	Lt.	GILE, C.D.	Lt.	KROPF, T.F.	Ensign
BELL, T.R.	Lt.	GUTENKUNST, D.H.	Lt(jg)	KURLANDER, M.M.	Ensign
BLACKBURN, J.T.	Lt. Cdr	HALFORD, J.A.	Lt.	LANDRETH,W.L.	Lt(jg)
BOWERS, G.F.	Lt(jg)	HEDRICK,R.R.	Lt. Cdr	MALONE, D.T.	Ensign
BURRISS, H.M.	Lt(jg)	HILL, R.H.	Ensign	MARCH, H.A.	Lt.
CHASNOFF, J.M.	Lt(jg)	HOGAN, R.R.	Ensign	MAY, E.	Lt(jg)
COOKE, L.D.	Lt.	INNIS, D.A.	Lt.	MEEK, W.P.	Ensign
CORDRAY, P.	Lt(jg)	JACKSON, R.H.	Lt(jg)	PILLSBURY, C.A.	Lt.
CUNNINGHAM, D.G.	Lt(jg)	JAGGER, F.A.	Ensign	POPP, W.P.	Ensign
DAVENPORT, M.W.	Lt.	KEITH, J.H.	Lt(jg)	SCHANUEL, M.	Lt(jg)
DUNN, C.H.	Ensign	KELLEY, L.M.	Ensign	SCHUB, W.J.	Lt.
ELLSWORTH, J.O.	Ensign	KEPFORD, I.C.	Ensign	STREIG, F.J.	Ensign
				WHARTON, W.C. Jr.	Ensign

HALL, G.F.	Ensign	Assistant Operations Officer
HENNING, B.D.	Lt(jg)	Operations and Air Combat Information Officer
HERRMANN, L.F.	Lt.	Flight Surgeon

FIGHTING SQUADRON SEVENTEEN
ALPHABETICAL LIST BY RATE OF SQUADRON ENLISTED PERSONNEL

(67 total) AS OF 31 OCT. 1943

ACMM
MURRAY, B.(N)

AMM1c
CONDIT, R.K.
GOBER, E.W.
GOYETTE, C.H. Jr.
MAUHAR, G. (n)
MORFELD, E.R.
ODEM, F.R.
WHITE, M. "A" "B"

AMM2c
BRETZ, K.G.
COX, B.L.
EDMISTEN, L.R.
FEHR, L.F.

AMM3c
BRANDENBURG, F.M.
EMANUEL, A.J.
FISHER, T.B.
FLYNN, E.W.
GAFFORD, J.H.
GILL, H.M.
GROGAN, J.J.
HARE, J.J.
HYDER, B.H. Jr.
JAMISON, W.A.
JORDAN, L.W.
LANDRY, M.R.
McCABE, T.A.
McLAUGHLIN, D.D.
PARKER, W.L.
RASMUSSEN, B. (n)
SIMONEAUX, N.F.
SLETTERRINK, D.G.
GLOVER, D.E.
GREEN, D.C.
GROCHOWSKI, N.R.
HOMEWOOD, E.A.
LAMPE, G.H.
PITTS, T.S.
POLITE, F. (n)
SARNECKI, J.A.
TAYLOR, R.E.
WESTPHAL, E.C.
WHITE, L.E.
YAGER, Wm. (n)
WOOD, A.K.
DUKE, "G" "C"
McLEAN, E.R.

AOM2c
BARAK, L.T.
FOUTTY, C.S.

AOM3c
DINEEN, J.T.
OLAES, R.J.
RANKIN, D.M.

PR2c

Y3c
NEIL, J.L.

S1c
MEETEER, H.U.

AM2c
JACOBS, E.W. Jr.

AEM2c
KERN, C.J.

AOM1c
CANTRELL, G.G.
FURZE, G.F.
McDONOUGH, G.J.

ARM2c
ENGLER, E.O.
ENGLER,H.E.

S2c
BASKIN, C.R.
CRAIG, J.A.
HAMILTON, R.A. Jr.
HOYLE, B.C.
SHORE, M.E.
TURNER, J.R. Jr.
WERT, E.M.
WHITLEY, R.N.

ALPHABETICAL ROSTER OF SQUADRON OFFICERS
AS OF 30 NOVEMBER 1943

TOTAL 42
PILOTS (39)

BEACHAM, S.R.	Lt.	GILBERT, C.W.	Lt(jg)	KLEINMAN, J.M.	Lt.
BELL, T.R.	Lt.	GILE, C.D.	Lt.	KROPF, T.F.	Ensign
BLACKBURN, J.T.	Lt. Cdr	GUTENKUNST, D.H.	Lt(jg)	KURLANDER, M.M.	Ensign
BOWERS, G.F.	Lt(jg)	HALFORD, J.A.	Lt.	LANDRETH,W.L.	Lt(jg)
BURRISS, H.M.	Lt(jg)	HEDRICK,R.R.	Lt. Cdr	MALONE, D.T.	Ensign
CHASNOFF, J.M.	Lt(jg)	HILL, R.H.	Ensign	MARCH, H.A.	Lt.
COOKE, L.D.	Lt.	HOGAN, R.R.	Ensign	MAY, E.	Lt(jg)
CORDRAY, P.	Lt(jg)	INNIS, D.A.	Lt.	MEEK, W.P.	Ensign
CUNNINGHAM, D.G.	Lt(jg)	JACKSON, R.H.	Lt(jg)	POPP, W.P.	Ensign
DAVENPORT, M.W.	Lt.	JAGGER, F.A.	Ensign	SCHANUEL, M.	Lt(jg)
DUNN, C.H.	Ensign	KELLEY, L.M.	Ensign	SCHUB, W.J.	Lt.
ELLSWORTH, J.O.	Ensign	KEPFORD, I.C.	Ensign	STREIG, F.J.	Ensign
FREEMAN, D.C.	Lt(jg)	KILLEFER, T.	Lt(jg)	WHARTON, W.C. Jr.	Ensign

HALL, G.F.	Ensign	Assistant Operations Officer
HENNING, B.D.	Lt(jg)	Operations and Air Combat Information Officer
HERRMANN, L.F.	Lt.	Flight Surgeon

FIGHTING SQUADRON SEVENTEEN
ALPHABETICAL LIST BY RATE OF SQUADRON ENLISTED PERSONNEL

(66 total) As of November 1943

ACMM	AMM3c	AOM2c
MURRAY, B.(n)	BRANDENBURG, F.M.	BARAK, L.T.
	EMANUEL, A.J.	FOUTTY, C.S.
AMM1c	FISHER, T.B.	
GOBER, E.W.	FLYNN, E.W.	AOM3c
GOYETTE, C.H. Jr.	GAFFORD, J.H.	
MAUHAR, G. (n)	GILL, H.M.	DINEEN, J.T.
MORFELD, E.R.	GROGAN, J.J.	OLAES, R.J.
ODEM, F.R.	HARE, J.J.	RANKIN, D.M.
WHITE, M. "A" "B"	HYDER, B.H. Jr.	
	JAMISON, W.A.	PR2c
	JORDAN, L.W.	
	LANDRY, M.R.	NEIL, J.L.
AMM2c	McCABE, T.A.	
	McLAUGHLIN, D.D.	Y3c
BRETZ, K.G.	PARKER, W.L.	
COX, B.L.	RASMUSSEN, B. (n)	MEETEER, H.U.
EDMISTEN, L.R.	SIMONEAUX, N.F.	
FEHR, L.F.	SLETTERRINK, D.G.	S1c
GLOVER, D.E.	WOOD, A.K.	
GREEN, D.C.		DUKE, "G" "C"
GROCHOWSKI, N.R.	AM2c	McLEAN, E.R.
HOMEWOOD, E.A.		
LAMPE, G.H.	JACOBS, E.W.	Jr.S2c
PITTS, T.S.		
POLITE, F. (n)	AEM2c	BASKIN, C.R.
SARNECKI, J.A.		CRAIG, J.A.
TAYLOR, R.E.	KERN, C.J.	HAMILTON, R.A. Jr.
WESTPHAL, E.C.		HOYLE, B.C.
WHITE, L.E.	AOM1c	SHORE, M.E.
YAGER, Wm. (n)		TURNER, J.R. Jr.
	CANTRELL, G.G.	WERT, E.M.
ARM2c	FURZE, G.F.	WHITLEY, R.N.
	McDONOUGH, G.J.	
ENGLER, E.O.		
ENGLER,H.E.		

ALPHABETICAL ROSTER OF SQUADRON OFFICERS
AS OF 31 DECEMBER, 1943

TOTAL 49
PILOTS (46)

BABKIRK, K.P.	Ensign	FITZGERALD, L.A.	Ensign	KURLANDER, M.M.	Ensign
BEACHAM, S.R.	Lt.	FREEMAN, D.C.	Lt(jg)	LANDRETH,W.L.	Lt(jg)
BELL, T.R.	Lt.	GILBERT, C.W.	Lt(jg)	MALONE, D.T.	Ensign
BITZEGAIO, H.J.	Lt(jg	GILE, C.D.	Lt.	MARCH, H.A.	Lt.
BLACKBURN, J.T.	Lt. Cdr	GUTENKUNST, D.H.	Lt(jg)	MAY, E.	Lt(jg)
BOWERS, G.F.	Lt(jg)	HEDRICK,R.R.	Lt. Cdr	MEEK, W.P.	Ensign
BURRISS, H.M.	Lt(jg)	HILL, R.H.	Ensign	MILLER, J.	Lt(jg)
CHASNOFF, J.M.	Lt(jg)	HOGAN, R.R.	Ensign	MIMS, R.	Lt(jg)
COOKE, L.D.	Lt.	INNIS, D.A.	Lt.	POPP, W.P.	Ensign
CORDRAY, P.	Lt(jg)	JACKSON, R.H.	Lt(jg)	SCHANUEL, M.	Lt(jg)
CUNNINGHAM, D.G.	Lt(jg)	JAGGER, F.A.	Ensign	SCHUB, W.J.	Lt.
DAVENPORT, M.W.	Lt.	KELLEY, L.M.	Ensign	SMITH, C.L.	Lt(jg
DUNN, C.H.	Ensign	KEPFORD, I.C.	Ensign	SMITH, J.M.	Ensign
ELLSWORTH, J.O.	Ensign	KILLEFER, T.	Lt(jg)	STREIG, F.J.	Ensign
FARLEY, J.W.	Lt(jg)	KROPF, T.F.	Ensign	TRAVERS, J.R.	Ensign
				WHARTON, W.C. Jr.	Ensign

HALL, G.F.	Ensign	Assistant Operations Officer
HENNING, B.D.	Lt(jg)	Operations and Air Combat Information Officer
HERRMANN, L.F.	Lt.	Flight Surgeon

FIGHTING SQUADRON SEVENTEEN
ALPHABETICAL LIST BY RATE OF SQUADRON ENLISTED PERSONNEL
(71 total) AS OF 31 DECEMBER 1943

ACMM	EDMISTEN, L.R.	AMM3c	ACOM	ARM2c
	FLYNN, E.W.			
MURRAY, B.(n)	GILL, H.M.	CRAIG,J.A.	FURZE, G.F.	ENGLER, E.C.
	GLOVER, D.E.	DUKE, G.C.		ENGLER, H.E.
AMMIc	GREEN, D.C.	EMANUEL,A.J.	AOMIc	
	GROCHOWSKI, N.R.	FISHER, T.B.		PR1c
BRETZ, K.G.	GROGAN, J.J.	GAFFORD, J.H.	BARAK, L.T.	
FEHR, L.F.	HARE, J.J.	GARDNER, G.C.	CANTRELL, G.G.	NEIL, J.L.
GOBER, E.W.	HOMEWOOD, E.A.	GARDNER, W.	McDONOUGH, G.J.	
GOYETTE, C.H. Jr.	HYDER, B.H.	GOLDBERG, M.		Y3c
MAUHAR, G. (n)	JAMISON, W.A.	HAMILTON, R.A.	AOM2c	
MORFELD, E.R.	LAMPE, G.H.	HOWARD, H.J.		MEETEER, H.U.
ODEM, F.R.	LANDRY, M.R.	JORDAN, L.W.	DINEEN, J.T.	
PITTS, T.S.	LeCLAIRE, T.	McLEAN, E.R.	OLAES, R.J.	S2c
POLITE, F.	McCABE,T.A.	ORMAN, J.E.	RANKIN, D.M.	
SARNECKI, J.A.	McLAUGHLIN, D.D.	SLETTERLINK, D.G.		BASKIN, C.R.
TAYLOR,R.E.	PARKER, W.L.	WHITLEY, R.N.	AM2c	HOYLE, B.C.
WHITE, M.A.B.	RASMUSSEN, B.			SHORE, M.E.
	SIMONEAUX, N.F.		JACOBS, E.W.	TURNER, J.R.
AMM2c	WESTPHAL, E.C.			WERT, E.M.
	WHITE, L.E.		AEM1c	
BRANDENBURG, F.M.	WOOD, A.K.			
COX, B.L.	YAGER, W.		KERN, C.J.	

FIGHTING SQUADRON SEVENTEEN
ALPHABETICAL ROSTER OF SQUADRON OFFICERS
AS OF 31 JANUARY 1944

TOTAL 47
PILOTS (44)

BEACHAM, S.R.	Lt.	FITZGERALD, L.A.	Ensign	MARCH, H.A.	Lt.
BEELER, E.E.	Ensign	FREEMAN, D.C.	Lt(jg)	MAY, E.	Lt(jg)
BITZEGAIO, H.J.	Lt(jg)	GILBERT, C.W.	Lt(jg)	McQUEEN, D.R.	Ensign
BLACKBURN, J.T.	Lt. Cdr	GILE, C.D.	Lt.	McQUISTON	Lt.
BOWERS, G.F.	Lt(jg)	HEDRICK,R.R.	Lt. Cdr	MEEK, W.P.	Ensign
CHENOWETH, O.I.	Lt.	HILL, R.H.	Ensign	MILLER, J.	Lt(jg)
COLE, M.W.	Ensign	INNIS, D.A.	Lt.	MIMS, R.	Lt(jg)
CORDRAY, P.	Lt(jg)	JACKSON, R.H.	Lt(jg)	PETERSON, E.C.	Lt(jg)
CUNNINGHAM, D.G.	Lt(jg)	JAGGER, F.A.	Ensign	POPP, W.P.	Ensign
DAVENPORT, M.W.	Lt.	KELLER, G.M.	Ensign	RICHARDSON, H.B.	Ensign
DIVENNEY, P.E.	Ensign	KEPFORD, I.C.	Lt(jg)	SCHANUEL, M.	Lt(jg)
DIXON, J.C.	Ensign	KILLEFER, T.	Lt(jg)	SCHUB, W.J.	Lt.
DUNN, C.H.	Ensign	KURLANDER, M.M.	Ensign	SMITH, J.M.	Ensign
ELLSWORTH, J.O.	Ensign	LANDRETH,W.L.	Lt(jg)	STREIG, F.J.	Lt(jg)
		MALONE, D.T.	Ensign	WHARTON, W.C. Jr.	Ensign

HENNING, B.D.	Lt(jg)	Operations and Air Combat Information Officer
HERRMANN, L.F.	Lt.	Flight Surgeon
MILLS, R.L.	Lt(jg)	Squadron Duty Officer

FIGHTING SQUADRON SEVENTEEN
ALPHABETICAL LIST BY RATE
OF
SQUADRON ENLISTED PERSONNEL

(92 total) as of 31 January, 1944

ACMM	FLYNN, E.W.	AMM3c	AOM1c	PR1c
	GILL, H.M.			
MAUHAR, G.	GLOVER, D.E.	ANDRIOLA, R.A.	BARAK, L.T.	NEIL, J.L.
MURRAY, B.	GROCHOWSKI, N.R.	CRAIG, J.A	CANTRELL, G.G.	
	GROGAN, J.J.	DUKE, G.C.	FOUTTY, C.R.	Y2c
AMM1c	HARE, J.J.	EMANUEL, A.J.	McDONOUGH, G.J.	
	HOMEWOOD, E.A.	GAFFORD, J.H.		MEETEER, H.U.
BRETZ, K.G.	HYDER, B.H.	GARDNER, G.C.	AOM2c	
FEHR, L.F.	JAMISON, W.A.	GARDNER, W.		S1c
GOBER, E.W.	JONES, C.N.	GOLDBERG, M.	DINEEN, J.T.	HAWKINS, E.O.
GOYETTE, C.H.	KAGEL, P.R.	HAMILTON, R.A.	OLAES, R.J.	HUCK, J.C.
GREEN, D.C.	LAMBERT, K.W.	HOWARD, H.J.	RANKIN, D.M.	KING, R.N.
LAMPE, G.H.	LANDRY, M.R.	JORDAN, L.W.		LERCH, R.C.
MORFELD, E.R.	LeCLAIRE, T.	KMIEC, E.M	AM2c	MESA, R.
ODEM, F.R.	MACIEL, M.R.	McLEAN, E.R.		
PITTS, T.S.	McCABE, T.A.	MOORE, E.L.R	JACOBS,E.W.	
POLITE, F.	McLAUGHLIN, D.D.	MAPARSTEK, H.		S2c
SARNECKI, J.A.	MOMIROV, G.	OLSEN, L.R.	AEM1c	
TAYLOR, R.E.	MOODY, R.J.	ORMAN, J.E.		BASKIN, C.R.
WHITE, M.A.P.	MORAN, C.P.	SLETTERINK, D.G.	KERN, C.J.	HOYLE, B.C.
	PARKER, W.L.	TEMANSON, M.L.		SHORE, M.E.
AMM2c	RASMUSSEN, B.	URCIUOLI, G.S.	ARM1c	TURNER, J.R.
	SIMONEAUX, N.F.	VORE, W.E.		
BRANDENBURG, F.M.	WESTPHAL, E.C.	WERT, E.M.	ENGLER, E.O.	
COX, B.L.	WHITE, L.E.	WHITLEY, R.N.	ENGLER, H.E.	
EDMISTEN, L.R.	WOOD, A.K.			
FISHER, T.B.	YAGER, W.	ACOM		
		FURZE, G.F.		

FIGHTING SQUADRON SEVENTEEN
ALPHABETICAL ROSTER OF SQUADRON OFFICERS
AS OF 29 FEBRUARY 1944

TOTAL 44
PILOTS (40)

BEACHAM, S.R.	Lt.	FITZGERALD, L.A.	Ensign	LANDRETH, W.L.	Lt(jg)
BITZEGAIO, H.J.	Lt(jg)	FREEMAN, D.C.	Lt(jg)	MARCH, H.A.	Lt.
BLACKBURN, J.T.	Lt. Cdr	GILBERT, C.W.	Lt(jg)	MATTHEWS, H.	Ensign
BOWERS, G.F.	Lt(jg)	GILE, C.D.	Lt.	MAY, E.	Lt(jg)
CHENOWETH, O.I.	Lt.	HEDRICK, R.R.	Lt. Cdr	McQUEEN, D.R.	Ensign
COLE, M.W.	Ensign	HILL, R.H.	Ensign	MEEK, W.P.	Ensign
CORDRAY, P.	Lt(jg)	INNIS, D.A.	Lt.	MIMS, R.	Lt(jg)
CUNNINGHAM, D.G.	Lt(jg)	JACKSON, R.H.	Lt(jg)	POPP, W.P.	Ensign
DAVENPORT, M.W.	Lt.	JAGGER, F.A.	Ensign	RICHARDSON, H.B.	Ensign
DITEMAN, J.E.	Ensign	KELLER, G.M.	Ensign	SCHANUEL, M.	Lt(jg)
DIXON, J.C.	Ensign	KEPFORD, I.C.	Lt(jg)	SCHUB, W.J.	Lt.
EINAR, R.M.	Ensign	KILLEFER, T.	Lt(jg)	SMITH, J.M.	Ensign
ELLSWORTH, J.O.	Ensign	KURLANDER, M.M.	Ensign	STREIG, F.J.	Lt(jg)
				WHARTON, W.C. Jr.	Ensign

HENNING, B.D.	Lt(jg)	Operations and Air Combat Information Officer
HERRMANN, L.F.	Lt.	Flight Surgeon
KINCAID, L.R.	Ensign	Assistant Gunnery Officer
MILLS, R.L.	Lt(jg)	Squadron Duty Officer

FIGHTING SQUADRON SEVENTEEN
ALPHABETICAL LIST BY RATE
OF
SQUADRON ENLISTED PERSONNEL

(94 total) as of 29 February, 1944

ACMM	AMM3c	AMM3c (cont.)	ACOM	ARM1c
MAUHAR, G.	DUKE, G.C.	ANDRIOLA, R.A.	FURZE, G.F.	ENGLER, E.O.
MURRAY, B.	EDMISTEN, L.R.	CRAIG, J.A.		ENGLER, H.E.
WHITE, M.A.B.	FISHER, T.B.	EMANUEL, A.J.	**AOM1c**	
	FLYNN, E.W.	GAFFORD, J.H.		**PR1c**
AMM1c	GILL, H.M.	GARDNER, G.C.	BARAK, L.T.	
BRETZ, K.G.	GLOVER, D.E.	GARDNER, W.	CANTRELL, G.G.	NEIL, J.L.
FEHR, L.F.	GROGAN, J.J.	GOLDBERG, M.	FOUTTY, C.R.	
GOBER, E.W.	HARE, J.J.	HAMILTON, R.A.	McDONOUGH, G.J.	**PhM2c**
GOYETTE, C.H.	HYDER, B.H.	HOWARD, H.J.		
GREEN, D.C.	JAMISON, W.A.	HOYLE, B.C.	**AOM2c**	MILLER, E.E.
GROCHOWSKI, N.R.	JONES, C.N.	JORDAN, L.W.		
	KAGEL, P.R.	KMIEC, E.M.	DINEEN, J.T.	**Y2c**
HOMEWOOD, E.A.	LAMBERT, K.W.	McLEAN, E.R.	OLAES, R.J.	
LAMPE, G.H.	LANDRY, M.R.	MOORE, E.L.R.	RANKIN, D.M.	MEETEER, H.U.
MORFELD, E.R.	LeCLAIRE, T.	NAPARSTEK, H.		**S1c**
ODEM, F.R.	MACIEL, M.R.	OLSEN, L.R.	**AM1c**	
PITTS, T.S.	McCABE, T.A.	ORMAN, J.E.		HAWKINS, E.O.
POLITE, F.	McLAUGHLIN, D.D.	SHORE, M.E.	JACOBS, E.W.	HUCK, J.C.
SARNECKI, J.A.	MOMIROV, G.	TEMANSON, M.L.		KING, R.N.
TAYLOR, R.E.	MOODY, R.J.	URCIUOLI, G.S.	**AEM1c**	LERCH, R.C.
WESTPHAL, E.C.	MORAN, C.P.	VORE, W.E.		MESA, R.
YAGER, W.	PARKER, W.L.	WERT, E.M.	KERN, C.J.	
	RASMUSSEN, B.	WHITLEY, R.N.		**S2c**
AMM2c	SIMONEAUX, N.F.		**AEM2c**	
	SLETTERINK, D.G.			BASKIN, C.R.
BRANDENBURG, F.M.	WHITE, L.E.		CADEN, L.T.	TURNER, J.R.
COX, B.L.	WOOD, A.K.			

FIGHTING SQUADRON SEVENTEEN
ALPHABETICAL ROSTER OF SQUADRON OFFICERS
AS OF 31 MARCH, 1944

TOTAL 41
PILOTS (40)

BEACHAM, S.R.	Lt.	FITZGERALD, L.A.	Ensign	LANDRETH,W.L.	Lt(jg)
BITZEGAIO, H.J.	Lt(jg)	FREEMAN, D.C.	Lt(jg)	MARCH, H.A.	Lt.
BLACKBURN, J.T.	Lt. Cdr	GILBERT, C.W.	Lt(jg)	MATTHEWS, H.	Ensign
BOWERS, G.F.	Lt(jg)	GILE, C.D.	Lt.	MAY, E.	Lt(jg)
CHENOWETH, O.I.	Lt.	HEDRICK,R.R.	Lt. Cdr	McQUEEN, D.R.	Ensign
COLE, M.W.	Ensign	HILL, R.H.	Lt(jg)	MEEK, W.P.	Ensign
CORDRAY, P.	Lt(jg)	INNIS, D.A.	Lt.	MIMS, R.	Lt(jg)
CUNNINGHAM, D.G.	Lt(jg)	JACKSON, R.H.	Lt(jg)	POPP, W.P.	Ensign
DAVENPORT, M.W.	Lt.	JAGGER, F.A.	Lt(jg)	RICHARDSON, H.B.	Ensign
DITEMAN, J.E.	Ensign	KELLER, G.M.	Ensign	SCHANUEL, M.	Lt(jg)
DIXON, J.C.	Ensign	KEPFORD, I.C.	Lt(jg)	SCHUB, W.J.	Lt.
EINAR, R.M.	Ensign	KILLEFER, T.	Lt(jg)	SMITH, J.M.	Ensign
ELLSWORTH, J.O.	Lt(jg)	KURLANDER, M.M.	Lt(jg)	STREIG, F.J.	Lt(jg)
				WHARTON, W.C. Jr.	Lt(jg)

HENNING, B.D.   Lt.   Operations and Air Combat Information Officer

FIGHTING SQUADRON SEVENTEEN
ALPHABETICAL LIST BY RATE
of
SQUADRON ENLISTED PERSONNEL

(63 total) as of 31 March, 1944

ACMM	AMM2c	AMM3c	AOM2c
MAUHAR, G.	BRANDENBURG, F.M.	BASKIN, C.R.	DINEEN, J.T.
ODEM, F.R.	DUKE, G.C.	CRAIG, J.A.	OLAES, R.J.
McLEAN, E.R.	EMANUEL, A.J.	GAFFORD, J.H.	RANKIN, D.M.
AMM1c	FISHER, T.B.	HAMILTON, R.A.	
	FLYNN, E.W.	HOYLE, B.C.	A.AM1c
	GILL, H.M.	SHORE, M.E.	
BRETZ, K.G.	GROGAN, J.J.	TURNER, J.R.	JACOBS, E.W.
COX, B.L.	HARE, J.J.	WERT, E.M.	
EDMISTEN, L.R.	HYDER, B.H.		AEM1c
FEHR, L.F.	JAMISON, W.	ACOM	
GLOVER, D.E.	JORDAN, L.W.		KERN, C.J.
GOBER, E.W.	LANDRY, M.R.	FURZE, G.F.	
GOYETTE, C.H.	McCABE, T.A.		ARM1c
GREEN, D.C.	McLAUGHLIN, D.D.	AOM1c	
	WHITE, M.A.B.		
GROCHOWSKI, N.R.	PARKER, W.L.		ENGLER, E.O.
HOMEWOOD, E.A.	RASMUSSEN, B.	BARAK, L.T.	
LAMPE, G.H.	SIMONEAUX, N.F.	CANTRELL, G.G.	PR1c
MORFELD, E.R.	SLETTERINK, D.G.	FOUTTY, C.R.	
PITTS, T.S.	WOOD, A.K.	McDONOUGH, G.J.	NEIL, J.L.
POLITE, F.			
SARNECKI, J.A.			Y2c
TAYLOR, R.E.			
WESTPHAL, E.C.			MEETEER, H.U.
WHITE, L.E.			
YAGER,W.			

Appendix F:
VF-17 Exhibits
in Navy Museums

WASHINGTON NAVY YARD

At the Naval Historical Center on display are Ike Kepford's medals, log book and memorial.

A Corsair painted in the markings of Tom Blackburn hangs suspended from the roof of the Navy Yard museum. This was delivered in 1985.

Jack Chasnoff donated his goggles and there is an exhibit to which Mel Kurlander donated several items.

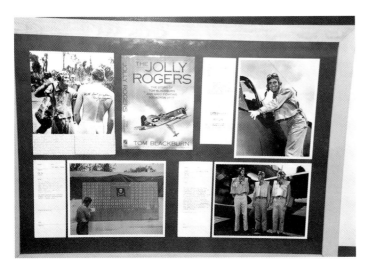

This airport which was formerly N.A.A.S. Manteo has a small museum about the airport. VF-17 were stationed here for training in the early part of 1943. There is an exhibit dedicated to VF-17 and a memorial dedicated to Ray Beacham who flew with VF-17 and was born and raised in the area. His medals and log book are on display. A model of a Corsair in his markings is suspended from the roof of the museum.

SMITHSONIAN NATIONAL AIR AND SPACE MUSEUM

In this museum they have on display the famous picture of Andy Jagger as part of their Sea-Air gallery exhibit.

NATIONAL MUSEUM OF NAVAL AVIATION N.A.S. PENSACOLA

VF-17 has an entry in the National Flight log (electronic archives).

The famous picture of Andy Jagger is on display at this museum.

RHODE ISLAND

The famous picture of Andy Jagger is displayed at this museum.

DARE COUNTY REGIONAL AIRPORT
(see left and next page)

Glossary

A/A: Anti-aircraft fire
A/C: Aircraft
ACORN: Aircraft Overhaul Repair Navy (overseas repair unit)
AK: Supply ship
AP: Armor piercing
ASW: Anti-submarine warfare
ATA 233A/ACA: Transmit/receive radios installed in Corsairs
Atabrine: Bright yellow pill to prevent malaria
AWOL: Absent without leave

B: Battleship
B-24: Consolidated Liberator 4 engine bomber
B-25: North American Mitchell medium bomber
Bail out: Jump out of aircraft
Betty: Japanese twin engine bomber
Birdcage: Early model F4U-1 Corsair
Bomber One: Main landing strip on Espiritu Santo
Bogies: Fighter direction code-unknown aircraft
Boondockers: Heavy shoes
Boresighted: Enemy in perfect firing position
Break: Signal to an airborne comrade to make an instantaneous turn in the direction indicated with the intention of avoiding being shot at
Bunker Hill: Essex class carrier CV-17

CAG: Carrier Air Group
CASU: Carrier Air Service Unit
Catwalk: Walkway providing shelter and fore and aft access, just below flight deck level
Chandelle: Steep high speed climbing turn
Charger: Small converted carrier CVE-29
Church key: Beer can opener
C.I.C.: Commander in Chief
CL: Light cruiser
Cocker Base: Fighter Direction Officer for Empress Augusta Bay
C.O.: Commanding Officer
COMAIRPAC: Commander Air Force Pacific Fleet
COMAIRSEPAC: Commander Air Force South East Pacific Fleet
COMAIRSOLS: Commander Air Forces Solomon Islands
COMAIRSOPAC: Commander Air Forces Southern Pacific
COMFAIRSOUTH: Commander Fleet Air South
COMFAIRWESTCOAST: Commander Fleet Air West Coast
COMFIGHTRON: Commander Fighting Squadron
COMTASKFORCE: Commander Task Force
CPO Club: Chief Petty Officer's Club
CV: Large aircraft carrier
CVE: Small escort carrier
CVL: Light carrier

Dane Base: Fighter direction station
DC-3: Transport plane
DD: Destroyer
Deflection Shot: The angle of a shot in gunnery measured between the line of sight to the target and the line of sight to the aiming point
Dogfight: An aerial battle between opposing fighter aircraft-aerial combat

E-Base: Elimination base
Ens.: Ensign

F2A: Brewster Buffalo, early monoplane fighter
F2F, F3F: Grumman biplane fighters
F4F: Grumman Wildcat
F4U: Vought Corsair
F6F: Grumman Hellcat
FDO: Fighter Direction Officer
Firewall: Maximum throttle
Flak: Anti-aircraft fire
Flathat: Low level flying
Full bore: Maximum engine power

G's: Force of gravity
GP bombs: General purpose explosive
Grab ass: Dogfighting
Grey out: Pass out
Groundloop: Loss of lateral control on the ground resulting in the plane making a sudden turn or change of direction. From this a wheel or gear strut may break and the plane could suffer considerable damage

Hack: Officers punishment
Hamp: Japanese fighter
High blower: Engine supercharger setting used at high altitudes
High side run: Steep diving attack pattern from side
Hop: Mission

IFF: Identification Friend or Foe (radar)
IJAAF: Imperial Japanese Army Air Force
Independence: CVL-22 light carrier
Island: Superstructure incorporating bridge, masts, etc, above the flight deck of a carrier

Jeep: carrier CVE

Kate: Japanese torpedo bomber

LCI: Landing Craft Infantry
LCT: Landing Craft Tank
Lead: The action of aiming ahead of a moving target. Refer to deflection shot
Lion Base: Cruiser Task Force
Listrus Bag: Canvas-like bag for drinking water
LSO: Landing Signal Officer
LST: Landing Ship Tank
Lufbury Circle: Horizontal ring of fighters for mutual defense
Lt.: Lieutenant
Lt(jg): Lieutenant junior grade
Lt. Cdr: Lieutenant Commander

M2S: Stearman training plane
MAG: Marine Air Group
MIA: Missing in action
MILS: Gunnery term of angular measurement
MG's: Machine guns

NAB Hospital: Naval Air Base Hospital
NAAS: Naval Auxiliary Air Station
NAS: Naval Air Station
NATS: Naval Air Transport Service

O'clock: The position of another plane sighted in the air as called out by its o'clock position from the observer. 12 o'clock straight ahead
Oleo: Shock absorbers
OS2U: Navy observation plane
Overhead: Steep diving run from above target

P-38: Lockheed Lightning twin engine fighter
P-40: Curtiss Tomahawk single engine fighter
P-47: Republic Thunderbolt single engine fighter
P-51: North American Mustang single engine fighter
Pancake: Land
PA System: Personal Address System
PBY: Consolidated Catalina twin engine seaplane
Plank Owners: Member of ship or squadron compliment from date of unit's commissioning
Pollywog: A seaman who has not crossed the equator
Pour on the coal: Full throttle
Princeton: CVL-23 light carrier
PT boats: Motor torpedo boats
PV-1: U.S. twin-engine patrol bomber

R & R: Rest and Recreation
Revetment: Embankment for protection from shells, bombs, etc. usually horseshoe shaped

Saratoga: CV-3
SB2C-1: Curtiss Helldiver divebomber
SBD: Douglas Dauntless divebomber
SCAT: Southern Cross Air Transport (army air force transport service South Pacific)
Scuttlebutt: Rumors
Shakedown: First operations of a new ship
Shellback: A seaman who has crossed the equator
Skip bombing: Low level bombing, bomb skips into target from water

SNJ: North American advanced trainer
Split-S: Violent half roll to an inverted position

Tail end Charlie: Last plane in a formation
TBF: Grumman Avenger torpedo plane
Tojo: Japanese radial engine fighter
Tony: Japanese in-line engine fighter
Tracer: A bullet containing a pyrotechnic mixture to make the flight of the bullet visible

Val: Japanese divebomber
VB: Bomber - aircraft type and squadron designators
VF: Fighter - aircraft type and squadron designators
VT: Torpedo - aircraft type and squadron designators
VP: Patrol - aircraft type and squadron designators

Washing Machine Charlie: Jap night bomber over solomons
Windmill: Propeller rotating on dead engine

Zeke (Zero): Principal Japanese fighter

ENLISTED PERSONNEL RATES

ACMM	Aviation Chief Machinist Mate
AMM1c	Aviation Machinist Mate First Class
AMM2c	Aviation Machinist Mate Second Class
AMM3c	Aviation Machinist Mate Third Class
ACOM	Aviation Chief Ordnance Man
AOM1c	Aviation Ordnance Man First Class
AOM2c	Aviation Ordnance Man Second Class
AM1c	Aviation Metalsmith First Class
AEM1c	Aviation Electrician Mate First Class
AEM2c	Aviation Electrician Mate Second Class
ARM1c	Aviation Radio Man First Class
PR1c	Parachute Rigger First Class
PR2c	Parachute Rigger Second Class
PhM2c	Pharmacist Mate Second Class
Y2c	Yeoman Second Class
S1c	Seaman First Class
S2c	Seaman Second Class

Bibliography

Blackburn, Tom. *The Jolly Rogers.* New York: Orion, 1989.

Foster, Col. Frank, and Lawrence Borts. *U.S. Military Medals 1939 to 1994.* Fountain Inn, S.C.: M.O.A. Press, 1994.

Olynyk, Frank J. *U.S.N. Credits for the Destruction of Enemy Aircraft in Air-to-Air Combat in World War II.* Aurora, OH: Frank J. Olynyk, 1982.

Tillman, Barrett. *Corsair: The F4U in World War Two and Korea.* Annapolis: U.S. Naval Institute Press, 1979.

DOCUMENTS

VF-17 Action Reports and Combat Statistics.

VF-17 War Diary

RECOMMENDED READING

Abrams, Richard. *F4U Corsair at War.* New York: Scribners, 1981.

Green, William. *Famous Fighters of the Second World War.* New York: Doubleday, 1962.

Guyton, Boone. *Whistling Death.* Atglen, PA. Schiffer, 1994.

Johnson, Frederick A. and Watanabe, Rikyu. *F4U Corsair.* New York: Crown, 1983.

Maloney, Edward T. and Feist, Uwe. *Chance Vought Corsair.* Fallbrook, CA: Aero.

Musciano, Walter A. *Corsair Aces The Bent-Wing Bird Over The Pacific.* New York: Arco.

Styling, Mark. *Corsair Aces of World War Two.* London: Osprey, 1995.

Veronico, Nicholas A. and Campbell, John M. and Donna. *F4U Corsair.* Osceola, WI: 1994.

VIDEOS

"Fighting Seventeen, The Jolly Rogers." Kenwood Productions, Minneapolis, 1990.

"VF-17 Remembered." RDR Video Productions. Northbrook, Illinois, 1984.

"World War Two Pacific Heroes." U.S. News Video, 1991.

"VF-17 at Oshkosh 1994." RAD Productions, Beverly Hills, 1995.

Dare County Regional Airport "Then and Now". Cable AD. Kill Devil Hills, N.C.

Every attempt has been made to obtain permission to include information, photographs, etc. into this book.

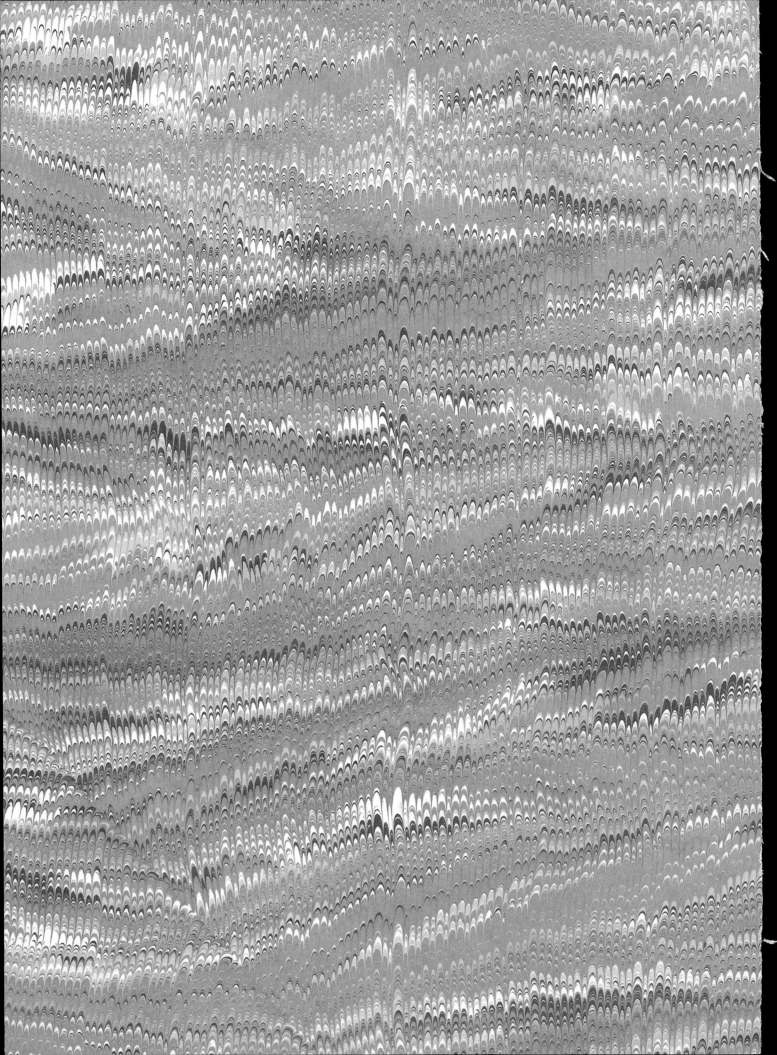